The Civil War
in North Carolina

Volume 1 : The Piedmont

The Civil War in North Carolina

Soldiers' and Civilians' Letters and Diaries, 1861–1865

VOLUME I : THE PIEDMONT

Edited by CHRISTOPHER M. WATFORD

McFarland & Company, Inc., Publishers
Jefferson, North Carolina, and London

Library of Congress Cataloguing-in-Publication Data

The Civil War in North Carolina :
soldiers' and civilians' letters and diaries, 1861–1865.
Volume I: The Piedmont / edited by Christopher M. Watford
p.   cm.
Includes bibliographical references and index.

ISBN 0-7864-1377-8 (illustrated case binding : 50# alkaline paper) ∞

1. North Carolina—History—Civil War, 1861–1865—Personal narratives.
2. North Carolina—History—Civil War, 1861–1865—Social aspects.
3. United States—History—Civil War, 1861–1865—Personal narratives.
4. United States—History—Civil War, 1861–1865—Social aspects.
5. Soldiers—North Carolina—Correspondence.
6. Soldiers—North Carolina—Diaries.   7. American letters—North Carolina.
8. American diaries—North Carolina.   I. Watford, Christopher M., 1978–

E464 .C484 2003   973.7'82'0922756—dc21   2002152909

British Library cataloguing data are available

Cover photograph: Volunteer Andrew Rinck,
one of three brothers in the Eleventh Regiment
(Courtesy of Mary R. Harbinson and the Rink/Rinck Family).

Manufactured in the United States of America

*McFarland & Company, Inc., Publishers
Box 611, Jefferson, North Carolina 28640
www.mcfarlandpub.com*

Contents

Acknowledgments   vii

Preface   ix

Introduction   1

1861   5

1862   33

1863   91

1864   143

1865   191

Appendix 1: Statistics on the Distribution of Documents   205

Appendix 2: Lt. Ashbel Fraley's "Purposes for Brigade Drill"
and "Maxims of War"   207

Appendix 3: Anatomy of a Typical Soldier Letter   209

Appendix 4: "A Prayer from Those in Distress"   211

Notes   213

Bibliography   229

Index   233

Acknowledgments

This book owes its existence to those state agencies, private and public institutions, and individuals who have conserved, protected, and preserved these documents for posterity so that their words may be heard again. While researching, compiling, and editing this work, I have come across many interesting and helpful people who provided support and encouragement not only for the project, but for me as well.

I owe special thanks to Mr. Eric Hall of Salisbury, North Carolina, who shared openly his knowledge on collections concerning the 4th North Carolina and soldiers from Iredell and Davie County. Thanks are also due to Mr. Jackson Marshall, North Carolina Museum of History, who introduced me to several collections and helped guide my research in its early stages.

For their contributions of privately held letters, I would like to thank Mrs. Agnes Cloninger of Boise, Idaho; Mr. Richard Conrad of Thomasville; Mrs. Geneva Ennis of Newton; Mr. Bob Fruches of Clemmons; Mrs. Mary Harbinson of Richland, Washington; Mr. Junius Hill of Lexington; and Mrs. Rachel Philpott of Lexington.

I also extend my thanks to Mrs. Laura C. Brown and the staff of the Southern Historical Collection at the University of North Carolina at Chapel Hill; J. Stephen Catlett and the Greensboro Historical Museum; the Catawba County Historical Association, Newton; Catharine Hoffman and Pam Daniel of the Davidson County Historical Museum; Dr. Nola R. Knouse of the Moravian Music Foundation in Winston-Salem; Mr. Steve Massengill and all the staff at the North Carolina Division of Archives and History, with special thanks to the search room staff; Thomas Perkins and Linda McCurdy at the Duke University Archives and Special Collections Department; Mrs. Jeanette Wilson and the Davidson County Public Library; the staffs at the High Point and Rowan County public libraries; The United States Army Military History Institute at Carlisle, Pennsylvania; and the staff at the National Archives and Library of Congress.

My thanks are also extended to those who have given me insight and have assisted in locating private collections: Mickey Black of Salisbury; Derick Hartshon of Newton; Mr. David Hunter; Mr. L. Phillip Leonard of Washington, D.C.; Mr. John Pagano of Maryland; and Mr. Glenn Summit of Newton.

My sincere appreciation goes out to my friends who have encouraged me and spurred me on, not just on the project, but in life: Mr. Lucas R. Clawson of Boone, a great friend at all times; Mr. Mark Bradley; Mr. Keith Alexander; Mr. Derrick Bowers of Southmont; Mr. Richard L. Conrad of Thomasville; Mr. Sim Delapp of Lexington, who taught me about the *noblesse oblige*; Mr. Mike and Mrs. Danita Gordon of Thomasville; Mr. Larry Jones of Cary; Mr. William G. Osborne II of New Mexico; Mrs. Katy Roenker of Greensboro; Mr. Lee Sherrill of Durham; Mr. James Thompson of Blowing Rock; Mr. and Mrs. Matthew D. Watford of Thomasville; Mr. Bob Williams; and the members of the Davidson and N.C. Civil War Roundtables.

Preface

This work is the first of a series of volumes collecting letters and diary entries that document the Civil War experience through the eyes of soldiers and civilians of the Old North State. Such a series has the potential purpose to answer many questions: What were the common experiences of the North Carolina soldiers? What problems were faced on the homefront? How were revolts in the state dealt with? How did the average citizen view the war and the government? How did a soldier use his writing? What do letters tell us about the state's ability to supply its forces? These are but a few of the issues that may be illuminated by such a compilation.

However, the true gift this project gave to me, and what I hope it gives to the readers, is the gift of emotion. When reviewing the compilation for the first time in its draft form I had a sense of being thrust into a universe that seemed familiar, yet alien; a universe in which men from one region were scattered over a continent. I was able to share their experiences, pleasant, unpleasant, and horrible. In these letters, I see excitement and ambition to tackle whatever lies ahead. I see childlike fascination in men who see the ocean and sailing ships for the first time. I see the effects of love and courtship from a Granville County private and a general from Rockingham County. I see sarcasm and dry humor. From some letters I can feel the sun on my face, the dust of a column marching forward into Maryland, the waters of the Rappahannock; I can see the masts of tall ships off Fort Macon, and hear brass bands playing Christmas music. I gain a sense of triumph marching through the small hamlets and large towns of Pennsylvania. I feel reverence for a soldier's commitment to God. I gain humility through their sorrows, their deprivations, and their defeats. I feel respect for their duty and their sacrifices. But most importantly, I gain wisdom—not from some great mind of academia, but from those who experienced the events of the war firsthand.

My previous work in Civil War history has focused largely on North Carolina genealogical and military records (*The Civil War Roster of Davidson County, North Carolina*, 2001) and other data. I always felt, however, that I also had a calling to explore the Civil War experience in primary sources—to read, to imagine, to appreciate, to understand. This book and its companion volumes are my response to that calling. I hope they call to you as well.

Christopher M. Watford
Thomasville, N.C., 2002

Introduction

Countless works have been written about the American Civil War. Most of those works focus on the causes, battles, generals, and great statesmen of the conflict, often neglecting the everyday citizen and soldier. Some recent authors have made more of an attempt to explore local history, culture, economics, and society in relation to the American Civil War, but even these have failed to build on what should be the cornerstone of historical study: the relationships between people in the face of time, economics, and social patterns. History is more than the positions of regiments or the posturing of grandiose diplomats; it is about the men and women who lived it.

Fortunately for those wishing to truly explore, evaluate, and document the American Civil War, there exists an enormous body of primary sources. These journals, letters, and other literary links to the everyday life of the Civil War soldier and civilian provide the background for scholarly research into the social, economic, political, and military history of the United States. Recently, researchers have shown a greater desire to understand and document the life of the individual soldier, putting aside the large historiographies in favor of

letters collections, focused unit histories, and museum exhibits and research centers devoted to furthering the understanding of the soldier and the world in which he lived.

In much of the United States it has long been a tradition to depict the South as an uneducated, backward place with only a handful of intellectuals. Perhaps this relates back to the "Lost Cause." Following the same logic used to create the "Cause," the South, it is argued, not only lost the war because of God's will: the South was just not smart enough. Many reasons exist to take exception to this stereotype. First, every economy depends on communication; the South was no exception. The professional occupations demanded literate workers, and even farmers had to keep records of crops, receipts, and credit extended to them. Second, reading and writing were methods of entertainment and information. The letters contained herein demonstrate this concept perfectly. These letters often inquire about relatives, friends, gossip, and the weather, along with proving information on business and current events. Third, religion played a major part in educating the South; many southerners learned to read by studying their Bibles. Furthermore, North Carolina's common schools had been valuable in shaping the Piedmont since 1848. While mandatory attendance laws did not develop until the 1880s, the majority of students were exposed to a public education of some kind from 1848 onward. In addition, soldiers learned to read and write in service from other soldiers who were literate. In fact, James A. Graham talks of the 27th Regiment's Brass Band putting on benefit concerts to raise money to purchase schoolbooks for the unit.

Literacy surveys utilizing the 1860 Census for Davidson (Northern District), Gaston (Woodlawn), and Stokes (Danbury) counties reveal that of the population over the age of eighteen, only 29 percent were unable to read or write. Numerous colleges, academies, and common schools invested in readers and other literary instructional texts. In fact, the most popular book among students and the Southern aristocracy was Victor Hugo's *Les Misérables*. The reader and student should keep in mind that literacy has different definitions over the course of time. While no typical citizen could be expected to quote Homer, Shakespeare, or the majority of contemporary writers, the typical citizen did possess the ability to communicate in a written fashion.

For a soldier in the forces of North Carolina, a letter from home was a welcome sight. It brought news of home, information about crop prices, encouraging words, an escape from the war for a few minutes, a break in the monotony and boredom, and hope. For one soldier in the 4th Regiment, letters came from the hand of a very special lady, but one letter came from some jokesters in his regiment. A soldier named John Strikeleather, of Iredell County, described the incident in his manuscript of postwar reminiscences:

Bob L. like many others had a correspondent back in Iredell, whose letters he greatly prized; her letters were always signed, "Libbie." No relation stronger than that of friendship existed between them. But, at times, Bob saw in Libbie's letters, expressions, that led him to hope that at no distant day the relation between them might be a stronger and dearer one. Such a letter had a very enlivening effect upon Bob; he would take a regular chicken fit, lie down, roll over, kick up his heels, and in various ways give expression to his feelings of joy, much to the amusement of his comrades; and finally the appearance of Libbie's signature alone at the bottom of a page was sufficient to produce one of the paroxysms of joy just described even before the letter was read. After a time Andy K. and myself messmates of Bob concluded that we would see if we could not cure him of his "fits." Fixing up a letter, dating it back, counterfeiting Libbie's handwriting and getting it into Bob's hands was more easily accomplished than might be expected. The contents of the letter were very respectful, but Bob was made to understand that friendship between them was the border beyond which he must not presume to go. As soon as the letter was handed him, before reading it seeing Libbie's signature at the close, he took one of his chicken fits; but alas! the reading of but a few lines of the missive showed him that in this instance at least he had counted without his host. Bob was artless in his ways and before he read the letter half through he turned to his friends, several of whom were near by, and with a woebegone countenance said "Boys, I thought that I had two strings to my bow but now I am not sure I have even one." In a short while he told Andy K. in all seriousness that he felt like hanging himself. Many such remarks fell from his lips before he retired to rest that night. Of course he had the sympathy of his comrades. He turned to

Andy K. and myself a short time after the letter was read and said, "Boys I want you to help me send her a Hell jolter." That night a little after dark he absented himself from camp for nearly two hours ... the evening passed with sadness to Bob. After all had retired to their bunks I broke the facts to him gently as I could, expecting an angry outbreak on his part. For a moment he was silent, but there was too much joy in his breast that it was all a joke [Strikeleather reminiscences, unpublished, courtesy Iredell County Public Library].

Many of the letters featured in this volume come from larger collections. For example, the six featured letters of Alfred M. Scales are selected from a body of nearly eighty letters. This should not be surprising when one considers how many letters could be written during the course of four years. If a solider wrote one letter or diary entry every day, he would produce approximately 1,460 pieces; if each soldier wrote at that pace, the letters from soldiers alone could possibly total 182,500,000 pieces. This, of course, is just educated multiplication, but it demonstrates the gargantuan scope of the body of information that exists for the state of North Carolina.

The Piedmont region of North Carolina, for the purposes of this book, consists of twenty-nine counties: Alamance, Alexander, Anson, Cabarrus, Caswell, Catawba, Chatham, Cleveland, Davidson, Davie, Forsyth, Gaston, Granville, Guilford, Iredell, Lincoln, Mecklenburg, Montgomery, Moore, Orange, Person, Randolph, Richmond, Rockingham, Stanly, Stokes, Union, and Yadkin. Over eighty men and women, soldiers and civilians, from diverse backgrounds, recorded the events in writing. Their words record their struggles to understand their roles, their lives, the events in which they found themselves playing a part.

1861

"This eaving I hav som liasure and will write you a letter to let you know where and how I am. I now about one mile the other side of garysburg in a butiful grove. I got here yesterday eaving and hav jest finsht cleaning and rising up our tents."

—Private Harrison Hanes, "Davie Sweepstakes,"
Company G, 4th Regiment North Carolina State
Troops, Garysburg, North Carolina, June 20, 1861.

"I take the presant opertunity of riting you a few lines to let you now where I am. I am at Moorehead sity on the sound inside the Fort. The sand nearly nee deep."

—Private John A. Jackson, "Moore Independents,"
Company H, 26th Regiment North Carolina
Troops, Morehead City, North Carolina,
September 3, 1861.

"I had remembered your promise and for weeks looked forward to its fulfillment until I had almost ceased to hope that you had even so much as remembered it."

—Colonel Alfred M. Scales, Rockingham County,
13th Regiment North Carolina Troops, Smithfield,
Virginia, December 23, 1861.

1. May 8, 1861

Corporal James A. Graham, "The Orange Guards," Fort Macon, N.C., letter to his mother, Source: The James A. Graham Papers 1861–1864, Southern Historical Collection, Wilson Library, University of North Carolina at Chapel Hill.

James Augustus Graham was born at Hillsboro, N.C. on July 7, 1841. He was the son of William A. Graham, one of the most influential Whig politicians in North Carolina and American history. James was a student at the University of North Carolina before he volunteered for service at age twenty on April 20, 1861. Corporal Graham served as part of the "Orange Guards," a volunteer company which was posted at Fort Macon during the early stages of the war. In fact, the date of the

James A. Graham of Orange County, depicted as a captain in Clarke's *Regiments*. (Courtesy of the N.C. Division of Archives and History.)

following letter pre-dates North Carolina's official entry into the Confederate States. The letter mentions Graham's preference in shirts, expertise at two kinds of drill, a "false alarm," and concern over his two dogs who he feels are wrongly accused of attacking sheep.

Fort Macon
May 8th, 1861

DEAR MOTHER

I received the box which you sent me by Mr. Strayhorn and am very much obliged for it, also for the books, for I never missed my books as much in my life as I have since I have been here. I have a good deal of leisure time and was bored a great deal by not having anything to do or to read. My shirts fit very well. I would like the collars made just the size of the larger one (it is ½ inch the largest) and the wristbands made shorter; not more than 1 inch wide. I have been drilling in Artillery for the last two or three days and like it, though it is harder work than Infantry drill. You wished to know whether Willie and I would both need a mattrass.* One will do for us both and you can either send it or let him bring it when he comes.

He had better bring a pair of blankets also and that is all that he will need as he and I will sleep together. Some ladies came over from Morehead City the other day and brought us a Southern Confederacy flag. We hoisted it and fired a salute of 9 guns. Some of the boys were down on the beach and when they heard the guns fire ran for the fort thinking that we were attacked, but soon found that they were mistaken and were laughed at a great deal for being so easily frightened. Our company numbers 65 men and can get as many more as we want. Tell Willie[1] that he can join if he comes down. I hope that you will not let Carlo & Alto be killed for I am certain that they did not kill anybody's sheep and I would not part with them for anything.

Tell Sarah Scott that her brother is well and that he received the things that she sent him. Tell her he says she must write to him as soon as she can. I must close as the drum has beat for drill. Give my love to sister Berrie and tell her that she must write to me. Johnny joins me in love to all. Write soon.

Your affectionate Son,
James A. Graham

*Mattras as spelled in original document

2. May 15, 1861

Jonathan Worth, Asheboro, Randolph County, N.C., letter to Daniel G. Worth, Wilmington, New Hanover County, N.C. Source: Hamilton, Dr. J. G., ed., *The Correspondence of Jonathan Worth*, Volume One, Raleigh: Edwards & Broughton, 1909.[2]

This is the first of several entries from Jonathan Worth, a member of the state legislature from Asheboro, N.C. The Worth family was one of the more prominent families in Randolph County. Daniel G. was one of Jonathan's younger brothers and was employed as an attorney in Wilmington, N.C. This letter also features a foreshadowing of incidents regarding the war, which secession opponent and Whig leader Johnathan Worth would see come to reality.

To D. G. Worth
Asheboro, May 15, 1861
I have been forced by surrounding facts to take sides, or rather front, with my section. I regard a prudent peace, even accompanied with contemplated secession of the State, and her union with the Confederacy, as preferable to a civil war on a gigantic scale; but I do not have a particle of confidence in the wisdom or the patriotism of the new rulers to whom we submit. I leave the flag of the Union and the flag of Washington because I am subjected and forced to submit to my master—democracy, detesting it with more and more intensity as I become better acquainted with its objects.

The masses, already deluded with the notion that Slavery is the cause, when in fact, it is now only the pretext with the leaders of both sections, will proclaim freedom and arm them against us.* I think the South is committing political suicide, but my lot is cast with the South and being unable to manage the ship, I intend to face the breakers manfully and go down with my companions. These are my calm conclusions.

What are your plans? Will you stay in Wilmington, or return to the back country and make corn till the war is over?

J. Worth

*While Lincoln's Emancipation Proclamation only freed slaves in the states which were in rebellion on January 1, 1863, it also paved the way for over 110,000 former slaves to take up arms against the Confederacy.

3. May 21, 1861

Captain Robert T. Wall, "Anson Guards," letter to John Hoke, North Carolina Adjutant General's Office. Source: Military Collection, Box 36, Folder 2, North Carolina Division of Archives and History.

Like many volunteer companies, the Anson Guards traveled to Raleigh and waited for the official declaration of secession. Equipping and managing this huge number of volunteers rested on the Adjutant-General's Department. In this letter, written only a day after North Carolina's secession, Captain Wall petitions Mr. Hoke for an issue of supplies. The Anson guards were assigned as company "C" 4th N.C. Volunteers on May 4, 1861.

Camp at Weldon, N C
May 21st 1861
John Hoke Adjt-General North Carolina
 Army
Sir

 I wish to call your attention to the condition of the company under my command in regard to certain necessary articles of equipment. My company is now provided with as handsome & substantial uniforms as any company either in or out of the state & if we had Knapsacks–shoes, & 20 blankets would be prepared for a campaign of one year duration.

 I desire therefore to call attention to the question whether it would not be better in an economical point of view to furnish us with these articles [which] should be attached to some regiment intended for immediate service rather than to give the preference to ununiformed, undrilled companies from Home?

 In enumerating the company's articles I neglected to mention arms and Tents. I hope sir that my command will no longer be neglected at headquarters. We have uniformed ourselves & also borne our own expense during the time we have been in service with the exception of sixty blankets & 12 days rations furnished us since we have been here. If this display of devotion to the good old state of which we are citizens and my command is to be entirely overlooked then I doubt not that you will agree with me in concluding that we had better return to our homes.

 I am sir, your obt servant
 R. T. Wall, Cap "Anson Guards"[3]

4. June 3, 1861

Private Louis Leon, "The Charlotte Greys," Company C, 1st North Carolina Volunteers, diary entry. Source: Leon, Louis, *Diary of a Tar Heel Confederate Soldier*, 1913.

Louis Leon was born in 1842 and worked in the city of Charlotte as a clerk in a dry goods store. One thing that set Leon apart from many of his comrades was the fact that Leon was a member of Charlotte's Jewish community. In his diary, however, there is no mention of Leon or several of his other Jewish comrades receiving harsh or discriminatory treatment while in service. Private Lewis began his military career when he volunteered for service on April 20, 1861, in the "Charlotte Greys," which later became company "C," 1st Regiment North Carolina Volunteers (Six Months).[4] The series of diary entries featured in this book begin with Leon and his company posted on the "peninsula," the area of land in southeastern Virginia which lies between the York and James Rivers.

June 3 (1861)—We marched fifteen miles and halted at Bethel Church, and again commenced making breastworks. Our rations did not suit us. We wanted a change of diet, but there were strict orders from Col. D. H. Hill that we should not go out foraging.* Well, Bill Stone, Alie Todd, and myself put on our knapsacks and went to the creek to wash our clothes, but when we got there we forgot to wash. We took a good long walk away from the camp and saw several goats. We ran one down, held it so it could not squeal, then killed it, cut it in small pieces, put it in our knapsacks, returned to the creek, and from there to camp where we shared it with the boys. It tasted good. Our comrade Ernheart did not fare so well. He went to a place where he knew he could get some honey. He got it all right, but he got the bees, also. His face and hands were a sight when he got the beehive to camp.

*Foraging, or the collection of food and other materials from the surrounding areas, though restricted by Col. Hill, in this case was a popular way for soldiers to supplement their rations.

5. June 10, 1861

Private Louis Leon, "The Charlotte Greys," Company C, 1st North Carolina Volunteers, diary entry. Source: Leon, Louis, *Diary of a Tar Heel Confederate Soldier*, 1913.

The following entry describes one of the first land battles of the war which was fought at Bethel, Virginia on June 10, 1861. The 1st North Carolina Volunteers under then Colonel D. H. Hill played a key role in the victory there.

June 10 (1861)—At three o'clock this morning the long roll woke us up. We fell in line, marched about five miles, then counter-marched, as the Yankees were advancing on us. We got to our breastworks a short time before the Yankees came and firing commenced. We gave them a good reception with shot and shell. The fight lasted about four hours. Our company was behind the works that held the line where the major of the Yankee regiment, Winthrop,[5] was killed. After he fell our company was ordered to the church, but was soon sent back to its former position. This is the first land battle of the war, and we certainly gave them a good beating, but we lost one of our regiment, Henry Wyatt,[6] who was killed while gallantly doing a volunteer duty. Seven of our men were wounded. The Yankees must have lost at least two hundred men in killed and wounded. It was their boast that they could whip us with corn-stalks, but to their sorrow they found out that we could do some fighting too. After the fight some of the boys and myself went over to the battlefield, and we saw several of the Yankee dead—the first I had ever seen, and it made me shudder. I am now in a school where sights like this should not worry me long. Our commander in this fight was Col. Bankhead Magruder. The Yankee commander was Gen. B. F.

Butler.* From now on I will never again grumble about digging breastworks. If it had not been for them many of us would not be here now. We returned the same night to Yorktown, full of glory.

*Colonel, later General John Bankhead Magruder (CS) and Brig. General, later Major General Benjamin F. Butler (US)

6. June 17, 1861

Sergeant James A. Graham, "The Orange Guards," Fort Macon, N.C., letter to his mother. Source: The James A. Graham Papers 1861–1864, Southern Historical Collection, Wilson Library, University of North Carolina at Chapel Hill.

On May 8, 1861, James A. Graham was promoted to sergeant. By June 17, 1861, the "Orange Guards" had still not been assigned to state service. Mr. Graham's second featured correspondence deals with the garrison life at Fort Macon. Officers often spent their leisure time in reading as Graham does here. Also interesting is the daily schedule Graham describes, which features three-hour shifts of drill per day, except on Sunday.

Fort Macon
June 17th 1861
DEAR MOTHER

I received your very welcome letter last Friday. It came Thursday night, but as I was on guard I did not get it till Friday morning. I would have been very glad to have been at home on the 8th, but could not get off. I hope to be at home, the last of this week or the first of next as almost all of our men have had furloughs and I reckon my time will come next, but it will depend on circumstances. I was on guard last Thursday (13) and, therefore, could not observe the day as I would have wished.

We had no drill but had preaching twice viz! at 6 in the morning and at

5 in the evening. I read the chapters; on Sunday; that you recommended. You wished to know how we spend our time. We have to get up at a quarter past 5 in the morning and have our beds made up and rolled up by 6, at 6½ we have to drill for an hour and then get breakfast. We then have nothing to do till 10, when we have to drill again for an hour. Drill again at 5 in the evening. Dress Parade at 6 and then Supper. Answer to Roll call again at 9 o'clock and have all lights out by 10. Between times we very often have some work to do. When I am not drilling I am generally sleeping, reading or studying military tactics. On Sunday we have no drills and generally have preaching once and sometimes twice. I spend the day generally in reading Spurgeon's Sermons or the Bible or sleeping. The salt air makes me feel sleepy nearly all the time. I keep a regular journal every day.

You wished to know who composed my mess. They are Stephen and Sam Dickson, Tom Whitted, George Lynch, Charley Parks, Haughton from Pittsboro and myself.* There were several more but they have either received commissions or gone home. I suppose that you have heard before this how well the 1st Regiment, under Col. Hill, did at Newport News Va.[7] There don't seem to be much chance of our ever having a fight down here, though we are well prepared for the enemy.

Your Affectionate Son
James A. Graham

*Messmates, all members of the "Orange Guard."

7. June 20, 1861

Private Harrison H. Hanes, "The Davie Sweepstakes," Company G, 4th Regiment N.C. State Troops, letter to Nancy Williams, Davie County, N.C. Source: Harrison H. Hanes Papers, Special Collections, Perkins Library, Duke University.

Harrison H. Hanes worked as a laborer on the farm of Enos James. Hanes volunteered for service at age 20 on June 15, 1861, and was assigned to Company G, "The Davie Sweepstakes" of the 4th Regiment North Carolina State Troops.[8] Private Hanes talks about his arrival in Garysburg, Northampton County, a camp of Instruction for newly enlisted North Carolina soldiers.

June 20, 1861

Dear Nancy

This eaving I hav som liasure and will write you a letter to let you know where and how I am. I now about one mile the other side of garysburg in a butiful grove. I got here yesterday eaving and hav jest finsht cleaning and rising up our tents. I think I can get a long splendid for we will stay here a good smart while. I think we are in a butifil grove about like Smithgrove. Nancy I haven't herd from you yet and I would be the gladest sort to here from you so I want you to write to me with out fail. You may hav writen me a leter but I haven't received if yet so I want you to writ me one as soon as you get this an write when you seen any of uncle Enos folkes and how they are I have wrote to them an got no aswer yet write when you saw John last and how and where he was. Nancy I am a many a mile from you but my heart and love and affection—is and will be with you as long as I liv that you may always depend upon. I still feel that I will get to see you before long. I think that the capten will giv us a furlow to go hom to see our folkes for all captens do and I think that ours will do the same for us but if he dos not the probaility is that I can any how after the 4 of July for it is thought congress will setle the mater but if they fail to [do] this thing it will be don by the bulet cirtin unless the north will let the south a lone.

They have been one more battle fought at Bethle Church in virginia but the southerns whip them and never lost but one man and the north 150.[9] This is the fact. I know nothing a bout the war only there many are men here a bout four thousand 4000. Nancy you must not forget to write to me as soon as you get this leter and when you write you must get Nath to take it to the Post offce and get the post master to back it to H.H. Hanes in the care of capten Wm Kelly[10] garyburge halyfax county N.C. Tell Nathan to ask the post master what county garysburg is in and get him to mail it to me in the care of capten Wm Kelly.

So I will bring my leter to a close for I hay not room to write any more for this is on the back of—my leter. You must write as soon as you get this leter. I will write again the first good chance. Yours affectonately until death.

Harrison Hanes to Miss Nancy Williams

do not put off writeing to me for I do want to her from you cirtin an sure.

8. June 23, 1861

Captain Alfred Belo, "Forsyth Rifles," letter to Carrie Fries, Salem, Forsyth County, N.C. Source: Shaffner papers, Private Manuscripts Collection, North Carolina Division of Archives and History.

Captain Alfred Horatio Belo was the son of wealthy Salem merchant Edward Belo, whose personal property was estimated at over $120,000 in 1860. Belo worked as a clerk for his father prior to volunteering for service on May 22, 1861, being elected as Captain in a company, the Forsyth Rifles, which would later serve as Company D of the 21st North Carolina Troops (11th N.C. Volunteers).[11]

Camp Hill
Near Danville, Va.
June 23rd /61

Dear Carrie,

According to promise I will now endeavor to fulfill, the very pleasant task by penning a few lines to you. On last Sunday evening at just this time we were on our way to Camp Magazine for the last time before our departure. It is unnecessary to allude to what transpired on the following morning at present. We arrived in Kernersville about twelve o'clock & partook of a splendid dinner, which had been hurriedly prepared by several of the citizens, After dinner we moved on to Bruces Cross Roads where we met Scales' company from Stokes Co. on its way to Raleigh.

We pitched our tents about ¼ mile from Scales. After seeing everything properly arranged for the night, Capt. Wharton[12] and myself drove over to Hillsdale so that we might reach Danville easily the next day.

The next morning we drove to Mr. R. P. Richardson's, where we overtook Len Leach's Company stopping for dinner. Capt. W.& myself remained here for some time during which in company with Dr. Douthit. We enjoyed ourselves very finely in the company of several ladies, among them Miss Sallie Richardson, formerly a pupil of yours. After each receiving a beautiful bouquet Capt. W. and myself drove to Reidsville & took dinner. After dinner drove to Danville.

The next morning we rose early and took a long walk before breakfast in search of suitable camping ground. After breakfast several of the principal citizens called on us & went with us to the Mayor, who received us very kindly and extended the hospitalities of Danville to us. From here we took an omnibus & drove around town, & finally selected a place about 1¼ miles from town as the most suitable for our camp. We have

Belo later in the war and in command of the 55th N.C. Troops, from Clark's *Regiments*. (Courtesy of the N.C. Division of Archives and History.)

very fine water, ample space for drill grounds, but the tents are on rather hilly ground. This is the best place, taking everything into consideration, that could be found in the vicinity. Gentlemen who have been to Manassas Junction, Richmond, etc. say our camp is the most pleasantly situated of any they have seen. About 12 o'clock we drove out and met our companies, marched them into town where we were formally welcomed to Danville in several speeches, after which we marched out here, took dinner, & then pitched our tents.

All along the road from Salem to Danville our reception was one of the most cordial kind, ladies waving their handkerchiefs, giving us their most pleasant smiles of encouragement, as

well as numerous beautiful bouquets. Gentlemen offering to do anything in their power that would contribute to the comfort of our men. We receive invitations nearly everyday to take tea or to come for dinner, but, we must respectfully decline, as we did not come here for enjoyment, but to work & prepare ourselves as early as possible to march, meet, & drive back the foul invaders of our soil.

Yesterday evening a barbecue was given for our benefit, within a few hundred yards of our camp, which all companies attended. It was well gotten up & everything passed off pleasantly. Speeches were made by several of the Captains now here, Hon. John Kerr & Mr. Bryant. Today I attended divine service at the Episcopal Church & heard a good sound sermon. There are four churches here viz, Episcopal, Baptist, Methodist & Presbyterian.

We have named our camp "Camp Hill" after Col. Hill of the 1st Regiment N. C. Volunteers. I have written this hurriedly, there is a good deal of noise in camp and it is difficult to keep ones thoughts collected in this hubbub. If I have omitted any items of news or any importance I suppose you will see it in the next Sentinel. Give my kindest regards to all the family and friends,

Write soon to your Cousin,
Alf[13]

9. June 27, 1861

Captain Lewis H. Webb, "The Pee Dee Guards," Company D, 23rd Regiment N.C. Troops, diary entry. Source: Diary of L. H. Webb, Lewis Webb Collection, Southern Historical Collection, Wilson Library, University of North Carolina at Chapel Hill.

On May 30, 1861, a company of volunteers was formed in Rockingham, Richmond County, and elected Captain

Image of the Forsyth Rifles at Danville, Virginia, just days after Belo's letter (June-July 1861). Belo is standing beside the gentleman in the top hat.

Lewis Henry Webb as their commanding officer. Webb, a 33 year old businessman, accepted this position and became the unit's first Captain.[14] This entry speaks of parting scenes in Richmond County when the company prepared for its departure on June 27, 1861. Such scenes were repeated countless times across the state and the nation.

Thursday the 27th day of June 1861
The Company was assembled in front of Temperance Hall in Rockingham*—the wagons which were to

convey us and baggage to the Rail Road were being loaded with the latter. We formed a hollow square and heard a few eloquent & stirring remarks by Col. Jno. W. Cameron & then with heavy hearts, marched to the Church where we had impressive religious exercises, by the Rev. Mr. Tillet. Several members of the Company joined the Chruch.

After the services were concluded came the farewells and such scenes I never witnessed before. Men shed tears who were all unused to the "melting mood." Mothers were clinging round the necks of sons. Fathers silently, with bedimed eyes wrung their hands and bade them go and serve their country. Sisters, wives, all were weeping around departing dear ones, and my own heart almost overcome by the scene while I wept bitter tears. Oh! These partings, these separations from loved ones, how they wring the hearts of the stoutest and most cynical. How many eyes do they cause to shed burning tears, and how many times do they render the abode of sadness and desolation?

Passing along the Aisle of the Church bidding sad adieus to kind friends, I suddenly encountered near the door one whom I had missed and who I feared I would not see. She was standing apart from the crowd, and as I went along gave me her hand, and while tears flowed freely, pressed my hand. Oh its memory shall linger in my heart as long as it throbs with life, a green spot in the desert of my existence.

Our partings over, and with sad hearts, we left and after a toilsome and weary day about sun down reached the head of the Rail Road and soon after embarked for Laurinburg which place we reached about dark and after supper at our Mess Chests, retired to our quarters in the Academy.

*Along with Rockingham, Laurinburg was another major town in Richmond County. Laurinburg is now the county seat of Scotland County, North Carolina.

10. June 30, 1861

Private John C. Turner, Company C, 4th Regiment N.C. State Troops, letter to friend, Miss Emily, Statesville, Iredell County, N.C. Source: Emma Cain Collection, Special Collections, Perkins Library, Duke University, Durham, North Carolina.

Iredell County native John C. Turner volunteered for service at age 23 on June 7, 1861. This letter is written from one of the many "Camps of Instruction" in the vicinity of Garysburg, Northampton County, North Carolina.[15] Private Turner describes his conditions and some encouraging events which the soldiers met along the way and comments on the one "drawback" to Garysburg.

Weldon Halifax NC Camp Anderson Northhampton Co June the 30th 1861
Miss Emily
You I expect will be somewhat surprised at the reception of these lines that I am about writing, and if you are surprised I hope you will not be offended. I wished to hear from all of you and this is the only means at present that will enable me to hear from you. I am now at Garysburg enjoying myself splendid. I met up with a great many of my old friends and acquaintances at this place, which afforded me a great deal of pleasure. I think we are in a healthy place, though there are at this time a few cases of sickness, but none serious. I left, I suppose, quite unexpectedly, to all of that neighborhood, and also of my own neighborhood but, I did so because I felt it to be my duty and I trust there were none who were displeased at my so doing. It was with sorrow and regret that I left my business, but I felt that I was doing not much good, and duty

The "Iredell Blues" Volunteer Militia Company outside Stockton Hall in Statesville; these men would later make up the core of Company A, 4th Regiment N.C. State Troops, and have members in three other companies. (Courtesy of the N.C. Division of Archives and History.)

seemed to say "go fight for your country."

Ghaston & Richmond are in the enjoyment of good health. Richmond received a letter a few days since which gave an account of the marriage of his sweetheart and it so mortified and distressed him that he cried. That is what Ghaston says. I expect we will leave here before long. The Regiment only likes two companies being made out, and when it is made out, we will leave either for Missouri or for Memphis Tennesse. I would like to stay here splendid were it not for one thing and that is there are no ladies here. I have not seen but one

since I have been here and she looked like she had been raised up in a cellar or some other filthy place. But I tell you we saw some noble hearted creatures. They would come flocking round the cars throwing in their beautiful bouquets waving their handkerchiefs. When such beautiful ladies are on our side we cannot be, the Great God of Battles will protect us. We are here our live exposed, we are liable to die and very liable to be slain by the low down trash of the earth. I trust that the good Being *will* fill their minds with something better than to attempt the subjugation of us innocent people. There is no doubt,

but we will have to fight, but I think we can soon thrash them and then come home. Companies pass here everyday going on to the seat of war. About five hundred passed on yesterday. I wish you to answer this as soon as possible and give me all the news. Though we are distantly separated, yet I will always remember you, for indeed as a lady and as a pupil you conducted yourself in such a way as is surpassed by none. Jack Anderson is here lying on his back singing. I must now close asking you if you write, write as soon as you get this and give me all the news particularly all the news from the cherry orchard. I hope you will condescend to answer this. So no more until I hear from you.
Truly you friend
J.C. Turner[16]

11. July 13, 1861

Private John A. Long, "The Alamance Regulators," Company E, 13th Regiment N.C. Troops, letter to his father, John Long, Graham, Alamance County, N.C. Source: Long Family Papers , Southern Historical Collection, Wilson Library, University of North Carolina at Chapel Hill.

John Long was the son of John and Letitia Long of Graham, North Carolina. John worked as a farm laborer before he volunteered for service in Alamance County on May 8, 1861. Two months later, John and his regiment, then known as the 3rd N.C. Volunteers, were reported under the command of John C. Pemberton in the Suffolk area.[17]

Head Quarters Camp Ruffin
July the 13, 1861
Dear Father
It is my duty to write you a few lines to let you know where I am and how my health. I am well and enjoying my self very well and I hope when you

John Wood of Rowan County rose from captain of Company to Lieutenant of the 4th North Carolina. (Courtesy of the N.C. Division of Archives and History.)

receave these few lines they will find you enjoying the same good health.

I just left Suffolk on the fourth of July and came to the old town on the James River* and we staid there three days and we left there and came down the river two miles and put up oure tents and I think we will stay here some length of time. I have nothing more to write at presant time. So I will close my letter with none.
Yours truly,
John A. Long

*Old English settlement of Jamestown

12. July 15, 1861

Private William M. Adams, Company C, 4th Regiment N.C. State Troops, letter to his mother, Statesville, Iredell County, N.C. Source: William Adams Papers, Special Collections, Perkins Library, Duke University.

William Adams was the son of moderately wealthy Iredell County parents when he volunteered for service in Statesville at age 23 on June 7, 1861. William describes how he is adjusting to army life. He tells of Sunday activities in the regiment and records his observations on the size and scope of the force of the 4th Regiment North Carolina State Troops.

July the 15 1861

Dear Mother

I received your box this morning. I was glad to get it. Every thing saved except the cucumbers. They wer not fit to eat. The pies are as good as they were when they started. When you send any to me don't send potatoes nor cucumbers. I don't care about potatoes. We have potatoes.

Tell Eugenia I recieved your letter to day. I was glad to here from home. I thought it a long time cince I heard from home. I have not been home sick cince I been here except last Saturday. I was not well that day except that I have well and enjoying myself tinily. I like the boys fare and the place very well. Very shady the water is very good. Nothing to brag on. The wells are about 15 feet deep. Ma if you ever send me any more put a piece of flannel to rub my gun.

I have not seen a lady cince I been here that I ever seen before and they sand hill gals and I tell you they don't look like Iredell girls somethng take a dozen here. Yesterday it was Sunday. They were taking a Sunday walk. They had a sho a piece. We had preaching here yesterday by the rev Mr Clause & after dinner we had nother alicourse by the rev Mr Wood. He is here yet is goind to leave to morrow. He told me that he would like to go with us. He say

that he is home here. He was very glad to see me. Tell pa that here is more men here than he ever saw. There is two regiments & half. There is 11 companys in our regiment. Our company is near the largest of any of them. I suppose in all there is 2500 men in the two regiments. Mr Wood[18] gives our company the praise of keeping the least fuss in the regiment. There 5 or 6 Company expecting leave this week for Va. We are not going this week. We have not got our uniform yet. There was a man here last Sunday as a week taking our measures. Sunday is no more than Monday here. We go out on dress parade every evening at 6 o'clock. Sunday not except. We drill battalion drill now every day.

Pa I am much oblige to you for my knife. Would rather had a pistol. If you can get me one and send to me I will send you money to pay as soon I get it. I got some of my money. If you get me a pistol get me belt made. I must have a belt anyhow. If you can send me one by some person that you know. I must have it. I can't cary my knife Pa. I want you to write to me and tell how you are getting along with the farm. Tell May & Eugea & Jane & O.C. & Ma also tell cousin Julia thus to write too. Give them all my love and the rest the neibours. Tell the negros I am well.

Direct your letter to Garysburg N.C. in care of Capt J.B. Andrews 4th regiment Camp Hill. Your son

W. A. Adams[19]

there is a train leaving now for Va from the other regiment. 8 cars full they are going to leave right of. They run the longest train of cars down I ever saw. 18 box cars the road is strait the largest engine you ever did see.

13. July 31, 1861

J. F. S., Alamance Militia, Camp Mason, Graham, Alamance County, letter to Carrie, Alamance County, North Carolina. Source: Civil War Collection, Davidson County Historical Museum.

The following letter was written by an unknown militiaman from Alamance County whose unit was dispatched to deal with some sort of uprising in Davidson County, N.C. In the letter blame is placed on the "executive officers" of the county; however, the identity of the person J.F. S.* seeks to admonish for this demonstration of disloyalty remains unknown.

Camp Mason, Graham, N.C.
July the 31st 1861

My dear Miss Carrie;

In a letter to your mother last Sunday I mentioned I had received orders to hold myself in readiness to proceed at a moments notice, with a detachment from this regiment to any given point then unknown to me.

On the following evening (Monday) we were ordered off to the expected scene of some action, the incidents of which expedition may prove interesting. It appears some of the good citizens of our adjoining county Davidson have not forgotten their once great love for the Union of all the States, and have taken to especial devotion to that prince of baboons-Abe Lincoln. They have endeavored to resist the laws of the state, and even permitted themselves to proceed in their rebellious course until the sheriff had to call out for assistance.

It was for this purpose we were detached; to aid the strong arm of the law to "suppress this rebellion" and had been led to anticipate a lively time, in that we had been told there existed a band 75 strong, well armed and sustained by the public opinion of the entire neighborhood. Our detachment numbered 160 men, commanded by Lieut. Col. Haywood, assisted by several inferior officers. We were quietly placed from the cars about two miles this side of Lexington, in one of the darkest of

nights, and on the side of the most rugged hill that could have possibly been found in the whole neighborhood. We finally managed to pitch some tents under which portion of the men found shelter, while others occupied a house nearby, and some even slept in the open air.† There we were to wait orders from Col. Haywood who had gone to Lexington to receive instructions from Judge Saunders, then in town. He returned after due time, informing us the difficulty to be settled. The ringleaders had that day been secured, and were safely lodged in the county jail. The whole transaction was a miserable farce, brought about by the cowardice of the executive county officer.[20]

J. F. S.

*J. F. S. was apparently a soldier in the Alamance Militia before it was re-organized in November 1861.

†The exact campsite of the militia is still unknown; however, the original path of the North Carolina Railroad went to the south of Lexington when it opened in 1855.

14. August 11, 1861

Private James W. Gibson, "Catawba Guards," Company F, 23rd Regiment N.C. State Troops, letter to parents, Catawba County, North Carolina. Source: Catawba County Historical Association, Mrs. Addie Cloninger, and the Gibson Family.

Private James W. Gibson was born in 1833 in Iredell County's Shiloh township. In 1856, this Iredell County farmer married Laura Stephenson. Sadly, the marriage would last less than a year with Laura's death on March 21, 1857. By 1860, James had taken up residence in neighboring Catawba County where he worked as a farmer and a blacksmith before volunteering for service in the "Catawba Guards" on June 7, 1861. Two months later, Private Gibson found himself writing home from the Manassas garrison in Northern Virginia.[21]

Manassas Junction Aug 11 1861

Dear Parents

I seat myself I'm in as good health as ever had in my life. We have a hard life to live and I would advise every boddy to do what they can. We are here and intend to stay till our time is out is and longer if we are before our all twelve months is out. But we are all in good plight for the Yankees but a few.

We have the {illegible} in our company but we have a wonderful side of wet weather her here we are greatly exposed at this time our tents are very bad they leak badly we are getting new ones and then I think we will fair better than we are now. I saw Joseph F about two weeks ago he is well they are fixed up just right. The last two or three months has been the longest 3 months has been the longest time that ever I put in since I have been upon ground but we live very well so far we have had plenty to eat yet but I have not had a apple or a peach since I left old North Carolina but if I ever live to get back to old North Carolina I mean to have some apples when I get back.

If there ever is any in the country but it is uncertain when we get to. We may get home soon and then it may be a long time before we get to the old north state we will go back a free people when we do so. We come here to be free or die if old Abe Lincoln sits his foot in our soil we will have to fight or die. We are at Manassas Junction now but it is very uncertain how long we stay we are to be redy to march in fifteen minutes notice but we have herd such word as that for some time we are always glad to hear from you but I have not got a scratch of a letter since I come. If you dont write to me I shall skip the business for a while. Joseph F. Gibson[22] was over and took dinner with me today. I went to see him a few days ago. This is the 18th day of August, Sunday, he has just left and will now write you a few lines to let you know that we are all well at present and hoping when these few lines come to hand they will find you enjoying the blessings come from heaven above we are both in the best kind of health at present Joseph is about one and a half or two miles from us we expect to leave here next Tuesday or Wednesday.

James William Gibson.

15. August 25, 1861

Private John A. Long, "The Alamance Regulators," Company E, 13th Regiment N.C. Troops, dual letter to his parents, John and Letitia, and his brother, Benjamin, Graham, Alamance County, N.C. Source: Long Family Papers , Southern Historical Collection, Wilson Library, University of North Carolina at Chapel Hill.

The following letter was written on the same sheet of paper and was sent to John's parents and his older brother, Benjamin, who would later volunteer for service. Within the next year, John would participate in the Peninsula and Seven Days campaigns and follow his unit's standard into Maryland. John was killed in action at South Mountain, Maryland, on September 15, 1862.[23]

Smithfield, V A
Camp Ruffin
Aug'25' 1861

Dear Father and Mother

I seat my self to rit to you to let you know now that I am well at this time and hoping When these few lines comes to hand May find you all well. I have nothin of Eney importance to rit you at this time. Dear father and mother I will say to you we ar still at this place and I don't know how long we will stay hear. I will say something a Bout hour fair. We hav a plenty to Eat and we been eatin Eney thing we want.

So we doo fair verry well. If wee never fair now evers than we hav sents

wee left home. We will git a long verry
well. I will say something Moore. We
hav a good Kind of Musick in hour
Regiment.[24] So nothin more at presant.
You rit to Mee as soon as you git this.
Your son and yours untell Death.

John A. Long

Smithfield Va August 25th 1861
Dear Brother

I seat My Self to rit few lines to let
you know that I am well at this tim
hopen when thes few lines comes to
hand May find you well. I hav nothen
of Eney importance to rit to you at this
tim I just thought I wold sit and write
to you at this tim to let you know I hav
not for got you. I hav not got nothen to
rit. I must Come to a close so nothen
Moore at presant. Write to Ma as soon
as you git this.

Yours untell Death
John A. Long to Benjamin Long

16. September 3, 1861

Private John A. Jackson, "The Moore
Independents," Company H, 26th Regi-
ment N.C. Troops, letter to brother-in-law,
Richard A. Cole, Moore County, N.C.
Source: Richard A. Cole Papers, Private
Manuscripts Collection, North Carolina
Division of Archives and History.

Private John A. Jackson, a 32 year old
Moore County farmer, volunteered for service on June 18, 1861. John served as a
member of the "Moore Independents"
which was later mustered into the 26th
Regiment N.C. Troops.[25] His description
of ships on the docks at Morehead City
is very interesting as he takes note of
their arrival and attempts to find out
what is on them. Given that he was from
Moore County, it is almost certain that
this assignment at Morehead City was the
first time John saw such sea-going vessels
and enjoyed a variety of seafood in his
life.

Moorehead sity Sept 3rd 61
Mr. R. A. Cole
Dear Brother

I take the presant opertunity of riting
you a few lines to let you now where I
am. I am at Moorehead sity on the
sound inside the Fort. The sand nearly
nee deep. I can see the ships sailing on
the ocean and there is an English ship
landed at this place now loaded with
salt. There is another ship here. I dont
now what it is tho. I was at it Yesterday
and saw them loading Rosin and I asked
one of the sailors where it was bound
and they said only the captain new that
so I said no more.

There is a large ship lying off the
coast in sight. I saw it yesterday. Some
say it is a yankey and others say an
English man of war and for my part I
dont now which but one thing. Some
seamed very uneasy and some did not
pay much attention to it. Some of our
boys was over at the Fort yesterday and
they said the men over at the Fort told
them it was a Lincolnite so they are
expecting an attack or that they will try
to land at some other point if they can
take advantage they are certain to do so.
I do not now how long we will stay at
this place. There is some talk of moving
to an island neare Fort Macon but it is
uncertain.

We can get as many fish heare as we
want fresh or pickeld. I can go round
the edge of the sound and see the fish
sport and our boys go and fish and some
times they have right good luck. They
can go in the sound and get clams and
oyesters as many as they want and take
morning and evening baths. It wont do
to go in any time in the heat of the day
and morning is the hot part of the day.
The most of our company is tolerable
good health at present. One or two sick
heare. We left our sick at camp carolina
something about 20 or 25 but none
considerd it dangerous. I heard from
them this morning. Martin McKinon he

staid with them the night before last and said they were doing very well. I understand from Lieutenant Dowd[26] since I commenced riting that it is certain that we will be stationed on an island some 3 or 4 miles away from Fort Macon. I do not now what direction. They say it will be a pleasant place. So I must come to a close by saying I am well at presant hoping these few lines may come to hand and find you all the same and mother and her family. So no more.

J. A. Jackson

Direct your letter to moorehead city in care of Capt W. Martin

17. September 9, 1861

Miss Carrie Fries, Teacher, Salem, Forsyth County, N.C., letter to Dr. John F. Shaffner, Surgeon, 11th North Carolina Volunteers. Source: Shaffner papers, Private Manuscripts Collection, North Carolina Division of Archives and History.

Caroline Fries (b. 1840) was the daughter of Salem Wool manufacturer Francis Fries. She was employed as a teacher at the Salem Female Academy at the outbreak of the war. She kept up a regular correspondence with Alfred Belo and John F. Shaffner.[27] In the letter to her friend Dr. John Shaffner, she talks about the residents of Salem, expresses concern over John, and tells about individuals such as Charlie Bahnson and Henry Meinung.

Salem, N. C., Sept. 9th, 1861.
Dr. J.F. Shaffner.
Dear friend;

Having heard through other letters how many were sick and looking to you for help, I was fearful your time would be much occupied that we need not look for a letter for some time, I was consequently all the more rejoiced to receive your nice long one of the lst inst. I was sorry to hear that you have so little help from the Assistant from Richmond. I hope by this time Dr. Tanner[28] is with you, Let me make one request, Do take some care of yourself, because even if Manaseas* etc. have no terrors for you, still there is such a thing as your breaking down possible. I have just read the above to mother, and she says I shall tell you it is good advise. I did not intend to be presumptuous to advise, but merely wished to remind you that your constitution is not of iron & may give way under constant anxiety & care. I hope Mr. Willie Pfohl has entirely recovered. He no doubt was rejoiced to see you. Mr. Barrow wrote me that you were tenting with them. I saw Charley Bahnson[29] at a distance this morning. Capt. Wheeler was talking with him, perhaps he was trying to get a new member for his company. Mr. Meinung[30] is quite sick today. I guess you have heard all about him from home, Addie Chitty came home with her brother & old Mr. Blum. She is said to be in the last stages of consumption. I was introduced to Mr. Blum—as an Indianian,—this morning, but he objected, as he says all persons from the north and west are looked upon as abolitionists here, and that he never gave aid or comfort to any Black Republican.

Today Mollie went to school with a "Confederate apron" on. I wish you could see her wear it. It is made of very bright colors, the three bars form the apron and the body is made of blue with twelve yellow stars in a circle. When we commenced making it, I thought it would look gaudy and out of place but since it is finished it really makes a very pretty and neat appearance. Father admires it exceedingly. He wanted her to wear it to church yesterday, but she was afraid she would disturb the congregation. She is making quite a show of her devotion to the Southern cause, but it is not all show, for she works for the soldiers in every spare moment she has. We are all knitting and soon as she finishes one thing she has another on the needles.

Mrs. Nutt from Haw River has been spending several days with us. She is a fine lady and I enjoyed her visit very much. The task however which I had intended should be completed by this time is not finished, and I must work all the harder this week to make up for lost time. My share for the volunteers must be ready before the cold weather. This whole morning was spent in walking over the Academy grounds, Museums &, and this evening I have such a headache from it that I shall not be able to do much, but tomorrow I will begin again in good earnest. Dont forget to let us know what is most needed to make the sick more comfortable.

There is a cruse of measles in the Academy.† One of the girls traveled with some soldiers who had them and took them. Emma has never had them, but father says she shall not stay from school for fear of taking them. He thinks it is really criminal to keep children from them when small, and subject them to the suffering we are daily hearing of by their having them in after life. His health is about as it was when you last saw him. The rest of the family are well. Give my best respects to Alf, Mr. Jamas, Mr.Barrow, and Mr. W. J. Pfohl.§ With many wishes for your continued health and safe return,

I remain
Yours truly,
C.L. Fries.

*As spelled in original letter

†Salem Female Academy remains in operation today in Winston-Salem as Salem College. The College remains for women only.

§Previously noted, all members of the 11th NC Volunteers with Shaffner.

18. September 23, 1861

Captain Lewis H. Webb, "The Pee Dee Guards," Company D, 23rd Regiment N.C. Troops, Diary Entry. Source: Diary of L. H. Webb, Lewis Webb Collection, Southern Historical Collection, Wilson Library, University of North Carolina at Chapel Hill.

As Captain, Webb faced a great deal of criticism while enforcing military discipline. Part of the discontent Webb speaks of in this letter comes from the Captain's decision to march offenders around at the bayonet-point as punishment for stealing from an orchard. Captain Webb resigned shortly after this entry due to "great dissatisfaction which had developed within the company."[31] Also interesting is the personal turmoil between Webb and Covington. Webb was very well bred and financially prominent, and between the two a severe clash of egos had been going on for months.

Monday, Sept. 23d 1861.
Up at reveille and drilled the Company an hour, of which there was not a Lieutenant present, all asleep, and continued so until after the drill. I received information that poor Thomas died last night about 11 o'clock.[32] This morning a large portion of the Company went over and buried him.

Heard today a remark made by Lieutenant Covington[33] that "it was a damned shame that the best blood of Richmond County should be punished by a damned Yankee" alluding to the punishment inflicted at Fairfax Station which is laid upon me still.* I think myself but rather that they should do a thing which rendered punishment necessary, and as to my being a "damned Yankee" why, I can easily prove that Lt. Covington said before leaving home that he would not go to the war unless I went, and as Captain too.

One more report too—showing how bitter some of the men are in their enmity towards me—instigated by that same rebellious and disobedient spirit of the conduct of my Lieutenants has endangered and fostered vis "that I had caused the death of Thomas by incarcerating him in the Guardhouse some time since when he was sick & keeping him there."

Now the circumstances were these. Thomas was found drunk & noisy by Col. Hoke and by him sent to the Guardhouse, of which I knew nothing at all until six hours after he was released. So much for that, but 'tis only in keeping with the baseness to which the men who for their own selfish ends, will resort to break down my influence and authority.

'Tis laughable too, to hear such men as Ben Covington talking about best blood. I won't boast of my descent, but I'll venture that I can show a longer genealogy and less mixed blood than either Lt. C or the men of whose "pure" and noble blood he prates so loudly. All he can do is show a large purse to sustain his brags.

*In reference to the punishment of the men for raiding a civilian's orchard. For more information see the citation in footnote 31.

19. October 5, 1861

M. Melchor, Assistant Commissary of Substinence, 20th Regiment N.C. Troops, letter to Mr. Allison, Mr. Silmer, and Mr. Williford, Pioner Mills, Cabarrus County, N.C. Source: J. E. Smoot Collection, Private Manuscripts Collection, North Carolina Division of Archives and History.

John R. Hagler served as a private in company B, 20th North Carolina Troops. John contracted "brain fever" while in service and died "at home on or about June 15, 1862."[34] While her husband was incapacitated with his illness and unable to

provide for the family at all, Caroline sought assistance for her family.

> Pioneer Mills, N.C.
> Cabarrus County
> Oct the 5th 1861
> Mssrs Allison, Silmar, & Williford Gentlemen,
>   Mrs. Caroline, wife of John Hagler,[35] whom you have made an allowance of 2 of a family thinks you ought to allow for her youngest child which is 8 months old. She says the allowance of 2 of a family will not support her. If you think proper, send me an order for one more of a family.
>   Respectfully yours
>   M. Melchor, Ast. Commissary

20. October 9, 1861

Private Julius J. C. Loftin, Company F, 7th Regiment N.C. State Troops, Carolina City, Carteret County, letter to his uncle, William H. Badgett, JP, Jackson Hill, Davidson County, Source: Badgett Collection, Davidson County Historical Museum.

Carolina City was the name of a large camp of Confederate forces defending the eastern part of the state. The location of the camp was in present-day Carteret County, near Morehead City, N.C. Here Loftin expresses anger over desertions from this place at such a crucial stage in the war to his uncle and Davidson County justice of the peace, William H. Badgett. Also of particular concern for Private Loftin was the rapid spread of disease through the camps at Carolina City, a major problem for all of the North Carolina units posted at that location.

> Carolina Sity, Cateret County, N.C.
> October the 9th, 1861
> Dear Uncle,
>   I now take the present opportunity of droping you a few lines to let you know

I am getting along. I am not very well at present. I have got the mumps and have to stay in the Hospitle until I get well. I think I will be well in 2 or 3 days. I hope that these few lines will find you and family all well. I havent anything of much information to wright at this time. I can say that I am veary well satisfied I can in form you that the davidson boys are sick but I dont think any of them are very dangeros. We are in a sickly place is veary bad and if we stay here we are in more danger of dying of sickness then if we spent four years in a battle. Some of the boys started home this morning from sum of the other companys and thay are a going to go from our company before long. I want to know what those cowardly boys are a doing back. Tell Samuel that I think if G. P. Johnson[36] will volunteer thay will giv him a cap that will do better than a hat. I must bring my letter to a close by saying I want you to wright soon and fail not.

J. C. Loftin to W.H. Badgett

21. October 23, 1861

Private Edmund Monroe Shoe, "The Cabarrus Phalynx," Company H, 8th Regiment N.C. State Troops, letter to his sweetheart, Esther Barrier, Cabarrus County, N.C. Source: N. A. Barrier Papers (373), Special Collections, Perkins Library, Duke University.

Private Edmund Shoe volunteered for service on August 5, 1861, at the age of 29.[37] In October 1861, the 8th Regiment N.C. State Troops was stationed on Roanoke Island, North Carolina, in an effort to strengthen defenses along the coast. In the following letter, Private Shoe writes to his "one true love," Esther Barrier, sister to M. A. Barrier. Apparently there has been some confusion about writing another woman, which Shoe dismissed. Also of interest is Shoe's attitude toward the war and duty.

Rhoanok island N C
Oct the 23 1861

My dear and well beloved friend

I have seated myself once More to let you know that I am well and hopeing that these few lines may find you in the same like blessings of god. I was glad to hear that you received five of my letters. I have received two of your letters and they gave me great satisfaction to hear from you.

My dear you had stated to me that you did not want me to Write any More to that girl. I answered that I want as long as you write to me but when ever you stop writing I will write to who I please. The reason that I wrote them few lines to her, I was a writing one for her brother and then I put in few lines. You had stated in your last letter that I should hurry and come back home and then you would tell all about that which for me to forget about it and to know it, I want not have wrote back to find [ill] whether it is so or not. I want you to give me the true statement whether it is so or not. In your last letter you had said that you would keep my likeness and I want you to do so.

My dear you had stated in your letter that you had been at preaching and there was a great many folks there but no boys but I would like to know where all the boys was that we left at home. You had stated that you did not talk to no boys since I was gone and that you do not intend two. You had stated to me that you had been at church to day but did not see me there. I should to like to been there.

My dear if it could be so it tis, we was a Many a mile apart, it near about breaks my heart to study and think back of the sweet hours that we have enjoyed together that I have to be here now to fight for our homes and firesides for freedoms cause we must fight. We trust that it may not ever come to any warlike test. We want our southern home secured in peaceful rest but if the blood of those we love in freedoms cause must flow with fervent trust in god above we bid them onward go and cheer them on there way. When wounded sore they lay for freedom must die and the by there side we must be when we are all called away and ask to see us home to Meet a smiling Savour there.

A few more lines to you my dear I hope and trust that I will see you again. Oh dear it looked shameful for us to leave you all and leave so many sweets there without a single beau. I know you liked to see leave but would not urge us to go but what are we girls to do when they are all gone away? We told them we could spare them here before they had to go. But bless there hearts we warrent aware that we would miss them so, we miss them in many ways. The greatest thing we miss is for seeing us about we will be contented if they cannot see us for though we are apart there is no reason why we may not open heart to heart, no more at the presant time. But write soon and not fail.

When this comes to hand remember me.

Edmund M. Shoe To
Esther Barrier my true love

22. October 25, 1861

Captain William B. "Dart" Clement, "The Carolina Rangers, Company B, 10th Virginia Cavalry Regiment, letter, to Mattie K. Martin, Mocksville, N.C. Source: W. B. Clement Papers, Private Manuscripts Collection, North Carolina Division of Archives and History.

This is the first of three letters from William "Dart" Clement, a cavalry officer from Davie County, North Carolina. William was born on February 3, 1835, to Jesse A. and Melinda Clement. Prior to volunteering for service, "Dart" resided in Davie County and was studying law. The Carolina Rangers cavalry company was organized from men from Davie, Davidson, and Rowan counties. After a brief assignment to the Wise Legion, the unit was assigned to the 10th Virginia cavalry regiment. Mattie Martin is the object of the Captain's love, and he has to balance his duties as a company commander with the desire to visit the one he loves. This letter was written on the same day the cavalry company enlisted at Liberty Church, Davie County.[38]

Camp Liberty Oct 25 1861

Your very kind favor was received by mail a few moments ago and eagerly read. You must not take me too seriously to task for not calling to see you last evening, and believe me, when I told you none could have felt more deeply the cruel necessity of passing by than your humble adorer. But my duty made it necessary for me to return. I have no one in camp who has any knowledge of how it should be controlled. I was very sorry to learn that you had given way to tears on account of my departure. Mattie, did you not promise me that you would not have the "blues" when I went away if you could help it. It makes me sorry very sorry to hear that your eyes have been dimmed by tears. But as I think of it, another feeling rises, something like pride, to think those tears were had for one as I.

Will you forgive me Mattie if I tell you that a feeling of happiness comes over me when I think that there is some one in this wide, wide world who cares enough for me to shed a tear on my account. But Mattie dear, please dont do that any more. You know that I love you better much better than I do anyone else and let me be absent or present, I am as true to you as the "needle is to the hole." So, please do not be sad any more. I hope there will be a chance before I leave the county of spending a few more moments in your society, and then who knows. But the war may be ended before long—and I permitted to return safe and sound—then we will be happy. Whenever you feel like having the "blues" just think of this and if you love me it will drive them away.

You said if I were to feel as much sorrow about leaving as you did, I could not go. Mattie, do not think I do not sorrow at the thought of parting with you, for I assure you I feel it more than any can imagine. But a sense of duty drives me on. I believe that we will not come out conquerors unless we turn out and meet the invaders man to man. Believing as I did and to not go and the worst was to happen, I would never feel right afterwards, but if I go and do my duty, I will feel that the blame does not rest upon me if we are defeated. I am sorry to leave you my dear one and feel as if all the happiness in the world is leaving me, but I can not act otherwise, and when you think of it I know you will agree with me.

You ask me how I like camp life, you know I am rather partial to that way of living—having been used to it for several years. But this is a little bit more laborious looking after fifty or sixty men, than attending the one. I have to see to the weighing of food for man and beast three times each day, besides attending to every thing else around the camp, seeing that every thing goes on right.

I accept your congratulations upon me elevation and feel more thankful for them as they come from you. From any other source I would not care for them. Although I could have held the position without any elections I did not want it unless my men wanted me to have it, and I am happy to say that I received a unanimous vote of the company. You asked me when we will be ready to receive visitors and always ready to see you dear Mattie, but will not be ready to receive visitors until next week as most of my men are away now. I can not tell you what time I will be in Mocksville. All of the officers are away this week and I will not have an opportunity of leaving any evening until after night, and not then if my men knew where I was going. So you see if I come at all, it must be late, so late that I can not come to call. If you should hear the signal you may know where I am if it is dark and the moon is shining. Charles* is waiting, and I hear the sound of my men stirring in camps. So I must close and look after them. Goodbye Dearest and please write soon.

> Yours
> "Dart"

Captain Clement's horse.

23. October 30, 1861

Private William Lillycross, "The Rowan Rifle Guards," Company K, 4th Regiment N.C. State Troops, request for transfer, to Captain F. Y. McNeely. Source: F. M. Y. McNeely Collection, Private Manuscripts Collection, North Carolina Division of Archives and History.

The following is a letter requesting a transfer from Private Lillycross, 4th N.C. Troops to the "Rowan Artillery" where his father-in-law is serving. It is not uncommon for officers, especially at this stage in the war, to entertain such requests.

> Camp Near Manassas, Va
> October 30th 1861

To Capt. M. Y. McNeely
Company K 4 Reg
C. S. Troops
Sir

I respectfully request that I be transferred to the Light Battery "D" N. C. S. Troops. My reason for applying for the transfer is that my fatherinlaw is serving in that Battery

and the Captain[39] commanding it is willing to accept me.
It would be a great satisfaction to me to be with, I
always desired to be in the
same company under him.
My fatherinlaw and I inlisted
under the impression that
his company belonged to the
4th Reg but on my arrival at
Manassas I found it was
detached therefore, I hope
my request will be granted.
I am Sir very respectfully
    Your Obedient servant
    Wm Lillycross
    Private Co. K 4th Reg
    N.C. State Troops

24. November 20, 1861

Musician T. Pinkney Gil-
lespie, 4th Regiment N.C.
State Troops Band, letter to
W. T. M. Phifer and wife, Ire-
dell County. Source: United
States Military History Institute,
Carlisle Barracks, Carlisle, Penn-
sylvania.

Thomas Pinkney Gillespie
had been a member of the 4th
North Carolina State Troops
Regimental band since September 15, 1861. This Rowan county
native volunteered for service on
June 19, 1861, and was even promoted to corporal on August 26,
1861, before accepting a position as
regimental musician and was transferred
out of company "B." Musician Gillespie
shared his talent with the regiment until he
was paroled at Appomattox Court House,
Virginia, on April 9, 1865.[40] Gillespie's
letter from the garrison at Manassas
speaks of his weight gain, a survivor and
exchanged prisoner of the 6th N.C. reporting on the battle of First Manassas, and the

William Saunders in the pre-war uniform of the
"Rowan Artillery," a volunteer artillery company
from Salisbury, N.C., which later became Company D, 10th N.C. State Troops, c. 1860. (North
Carolina Collection, University of North Carolina at Chapel Hill.)

improvement of the 4th Regiment's disposition.

    Camp Pickens
    Manassas Junction Va
    Nov the 20th 61
W.T.M. Phifer & Wife
Dear Brother and Sister,
    As I failed to send you a letter by
Hyde I now seat myself to drop you a
few lines which will inform you that I

Colonel Charles C. Fisher, a prominent resident of Salisbury and commander of the 6th N.C. State Troops. He was killed while leading his regiment at First Manassas. (Courtesy of the N.C. Division of Archives and History.)

am enjoying the greatest of health. I can't tell you how much I way. I haven't been waid for some time but I tell you I am just busting all the buttons off my cloths. I can't hardly keep them soed on as fast as they come off. You may say I don't put them on good but I tell you I do I am a first rate hand at this business. I can proove that by Lizzie. She knows I am a good hand with a needle an thread before I got a stiff finger. Well you can tell Mary that the wescut* she sent me would not meet on me with the strap buckeld. I had to loose it and let it goe, and my pants when I got them at Camp Hill I could draw then up smartly by the strap but now I have to let it goe loose. Well I think I have said enough to sattesfy you that I am a gallpuster

you may think I am joking but it the case.

Well Thos that Battle hasn't come off yet but still expecting it evry day. We still keepe fetching them in every few days. Since Hyde left there there has bin thirty two past the Junction going to Rich, they were caught in a corn field steeling corn. Since that there has bin seventy odd taken and some sixty or seventy odd horses and I don't remember how many wagons. There was 7 prisoners an forty two horses landed today. I can't tell when the rest will come. Well Thos I am going to undertake to tell you something about one of our prisoners that was taken in the Manassas Battle[41] of the 21—but I don't know wheather I can give you much sattasfacfion about it or not. If I could see you face to face I think I could but I fear I will fail by pen and ink. Well he was relieced on Perroll† this day was a week ago and arrived at our camp tonight. He belonged to Col. Fishers Regt§ he sais he was the only one that was taken from that Regt and there was but 25 taken that he saw in the hole Battle. He said he was tending to a wounded man and his Regt. retreated an he did not know anything about it and the first thing he new there was about 600 Zoaves in twenty steps of him and told him if he mooved they would shoot him down. He said when they took him they told him they loved to hang him. He said there was two took him by the arm and one behind him with his gun and wood stick him every once and a while with his bayonet. He said they fled him hand and foot for two days and nites and keep him in a stable. Then they took to washington City. When they got there they mobed them. They took all his money from him took his pocket knife took his pocket handkerchief and cut all the buttons of his coat that I saw with my own eyes they ware every one of. He said the Gov alowed them crackers an water to eat but he said he got plenty. He said he had plenty of friends there. The ladies made up $900 to feed them and was very kind to them. Some of them would curse them but he said he had plenty of friends. He said the ladies sent their best respects to the Southern boys. He said 2000 men could have taken the city at that time. He said lots of them never stoped till they got to N.Y. and what staid was looking for us for two or three days after the rite. He said he never saw as bad scatterd set in his life, they kept coming in for a week after the Battle. They were so bad scatterd they advertised in the city where they could find their corn and Regt. He said they never have acknowledged of being whiped yet, except the 21 they say we rather got them there, but they say we over powered them at Leesburg and they retreated. He said about a week after the Leesburg Battle they took out 25 men at washington out of the Potomac that washed down there. He said they had it in the papers there that N.C. had gone back into the union an that they were taken the oath of legion at Haters as fast as they could. He said they don this in order to keep there men in good spirits and make them go on. Well Thos I believe I will stop this subject. I have forgotten his name but there was 57 left when he did and he said there was but 29 left there. He said they sent all that they got in N.C. to N.Y. He is now on the hunt of his Regt. an levs to go home in a few days. Since writing the former part of this letter I heard that there was another train of Yankeess arrived at the Junction. I did not learn how many. They will leave in the morning for Richmond. The health of the Regt is improoving, Fuller is well. I hope these few lines may find you well. So nothing more but remains your absent brother as ever

T. P. Gillespie

P.S. Give my best respects to all and a large portion to your selves.

*Waistcoat

†"Released on Parole"

§6th Regiment North Carolina State Troops

25. December 23, 1861

Colonel Alfred M. Scales, 13th N.C. Troops, Pender's Brigade, letter to Kate Henderson, Reidsville, Rockingham County, N.C. Source: A. M. Scales Collection, Box 1 (Correspondence), Private Manuscripts Collection, North Carolina Division of Archives and History.

Alfred Scales (b. Nov. 26, 1827) was born into a family which was already established among North Carolina's political elite. It was no surprise then that his chosen profession would be the law. He was admitted to the bar after studying at the University of North Carolina and under the tutelage of Judge William H. Battle. By the year of his admission to the bar, 1852, Scales was appointed Solicitor of Rockingham County. Scales served as a member of the N.C. House of Commons (1852, 1856–57), and was later elected as a Representative to the 35th United States Congress (Mar. 4, 1857–Mar. 3, 1859). Upon his return from service as a congressman, Scales remained very active in the Democratic Party and favored the election of John C. Breckinridge in 1860. With the outbreak of the war, Scales volunteered on April 30, 1861, and raised a company of men from Rockingham County known as the "Rockingham Guards." Scales was elected captain of a company which would become Company H, 13th North Carolina Troops (3rd N.C. Volunteers). After serving as a company commander, Captain Scales was promoted to the rank of colonel and was given command of the regiment on October 12, 1861.[42]

Camp Ruffin
Near Smithfield, Va
Dec. 23rd 1861

Cousin Kate[43]

How shall I excuse myself for not long in this acknowledging the receipt of so beautiful a gift?

The time that has elapsed since its reception would argue to one less grevious than yourself that it was received with indifference, laid aside & soon forgotten. If such a suggestion even occurred to you I pray that you will at once dismiss it, for it would greatly misrepresent me & the facts in the case. I had remembered your promise and for weeks looked forward to its fulfillment until I had almost ceased to hope that you had even so much as remembered it. But it did come and was to me a most agreeable and pleasant surprise. I felt widely rewarded for the patience exercised in waiting.

The Slipper was examined and reexamined. My watch was placed in it and it seemed to have been made expressly for the watch and was carefully placed among my valuables to be taken out again and exhibited to my particular friends as evidence of your taste and skill. But the war came & was the reason for my long silence. I was then in the act of raising a company & was engaged night and day. When it was completed I was ordered off and started after great effort in ten days. Since that time you can well imagine my situation and will excuse my neglect.

And now Kate let me thank you sincerely for such a token of friendship. Our acquaintance though short was to me a most pleasurable one and I hope I am not presumptuous when I say that I shall cherish the gifts as evidence of the said feeling of my "little friend." No patriot should require a greater stimulus in this war than the love of country & the knowledge that that country was invaded but in the thickest of the fight I

Alfred M. Scales, a Rockingham County native and national politician, depicted during his term of service as regimental commander of the 13th N.C. Troops. (Courtesy of the N.C. Division of Archives and History.)

should need more I would be imitating the days of chivalry, take the slipper as my "Talisman throw it in the midst of the enemy & calling upon heaven, my Country and "Little Friend" cut my way through the ranks to regain it, or die in the attempt." And if successful I should feel richly rewarded by the bright smile from my Little Friend & to be dubbed by her "her Knight of the Slipper."

But cousin Kate I came back to inquire why it was that you style yourself my "little friend?" Was it to check any asperations which even a short apreciation with you would be seen to impossible by delicately reminding me of the dispartiy in our ages. In this way of the pen it was kind & I know you meant to be kind, for it would be crushing out in its first buddings a hope which if indulged might afterwards cost many a sorrowed moment. If this is to be so I want to thank you for the kindness and the delicacy with which it was administered. May I ask cousin Kate to answer this & explain the little friend. Give my regards to your mother and father and tell her about my continued esteem & high regard for my "Little Friend"

Respectfully & Sincerely
Your Friend
A.M. Scales

1862

"I think that we can hold our position here against any force that the enemy can bring against us, as we have an admirable position & are all ready. I can give you no idea when the general attack will take place. It may be this evening, tomorrow or at any moment as both parties are apparently ready & we have nothing to do but pitch in."

—Captain Charles C. Blacknall, "Granville Rifles,"
Company G, 23rd North Carolina Troops,
Yorktown, Virginia, April 22, 1862.

"I could not tell you how the times are here. If I ware to they only are hard and distresing so far as I can see."

—Private George W. Eddinger, Company B,
48th North Carolina Troops, Petersburg, Virginia,
August 15, 1862.

"Deare companion God has been Mercifull to me in Giving me health & protecting me in the hour of battle for which I am truly thankfull. Let us trust in him as he has Life & Death in his hands. May he give us Grace to Beare us up under our sore trials."

—Captain William G. Morris, "The Gaston Blues,"
Company H, 37th North Carolina Troops,
Frederick, Maryland, September 8, 1862.

26. January 1, 1862

Hon. Jonathan Worth, Asheboro, N.C., letter to Captain Leigh Andrews, Asheboro, N.C. Source: Hamilton, *The Correspondence of Jonathan Worth*, 1909.

The following is an invitation to dinner from state legislator Jonathan Worth to a volunteer company under Capt. Leigh Andrews of Randolph County. Worth's kindness was extended to all men of the company. Such invitations were usually reserved only for officers and upper-class citizens.

Dear Sir:

I would like to give you and the officers and men under your command,

James A. Breedlove of Granville County served in Blacknall's company as a sergeant from July 1, 1861 to August 15, 1862. Breedlove would eventually rise to the rank of Captain. (Courtesy of the N.C. Division of Archives and History.)

before you leave in the Military Service of your Country, some demonstration of my appreciation of your patriotism, and designed to invite you all to tea at my house tomorrow evening at 7½ o'clock—but I have just learned that you propose to leave tomorrow. I therefore invite you and your officers to dine with me tomorrow. If you intend to leave tomorrow I will have the dinner ready at as early an hour as possible. If you decide not to leave tomorrow as I would prefer, as I presume it would be most agreeable to you and your men, that you all come over and take a parting supper with me.

J. Worth

27. January 10, 1862

Captain C. C. Blacknall, "Granville Rifles," Company G, 23rd Regiment N.C. Troops, letter to wife, Virginia Blacknall, Granville County, N.C. Source: Oscar Blacknall Collection, Private Manuscripts Collection, North Carolina Division of Archives and History.

Captain Charles Christopher Blacknall lived as one of Granville County's most respected merchants. Mr. Blacknall and his wife, Virginia, also known as Jinny, lived a comfortable life in Henderson with their son Oscar. On June 11, 1861, he volunteered at the age of 30 and was elected captain of the "Granville Rifles," also known as Company G of the 23rd North Carolina Troops (13th N.C. Volunteers). This letters collection was kept by Blacknall's son, Oscar, and the entire collection of over sixty letters in available in the Oscar Blacknall Papers cited above.[1]

Head Quarters
23rd N. C. Regt. Jany 10/62

Dear Jinnie

I have just returned from picket and found Dock at camp and received from him your letter together with a full description of current events in our neighborhood told in his best style. I was highly delighted to hear such a good account of you and the family that all are getting on so well and that the family and friends are all in good health and doing so well, notwithstanding the war. I cannot express to you how much pleased I would be to pay a visit to you all. You are entirely mistaken when you think that I could get off home if I was as anxious to go as you are to see me. I assure you that I have used every honorable effort to get a furlough—and I will try no other and in every instance have been disappointed. I have known several officers to send up applications stating that their wives and children were on their death beds and in one instance that the wife of an officer was thought to be deranged or nearly so on account of the death of her last child & the absence of her husband, and all of these applications with these strong inducements for granting them were refused promptly and positively. But notwithstanding all of these discouraging circumstances, I have strong hopes of getting a furlough very soon as Col. Hoke[2] has consented to use his best efforts for me as I have been so prompt & unremitting in the discharge of my various and heavy duties.

We had a very severe spell of weather while on picket, snow and rain yesterday incessantly, we returned to camp today over the worst roads I ever saw, the mud was almost impassable, but we

Major Charles Christopher Blacknall of Granville County. (Courtesy of the N.C. Division of Archives and History.)

had to wade through it. I was in command of the battalion consisting of Five companies and had a very tiresome and disagreeable march. Soon after getting to camp, Col. Hoke sent for me and stated that he wished for me to take command of the pioneers—200 men— and superintend the building of our new winter quarters on the other side of Bull Run. So after being on constant duty for five days I will have to leave camp early tomorrow morning and will be overwhelmed with business for some length of time, at least until upwards of one hundred cabins are completed and ready to move in. I cannot tell with any certainty when I can be at home, but promise to see you as soon as possible which I hope wont be long. Give my love to all the family & friends,

                    Very truly & affectionately
                    C.C. Blacknall

The box sent by Dock has not yet arrived but I hope it is not lost.

28. January 24, 1862

Private John A. Jackson, "Moore Independents," Company H, 26th Regiment N.C. Troops, letter to brother-in-law, Richard A. Cole, Moore County, N.C. Source: Richard A. Cole Papers. Private Manuscripts Collection. North Carolina Division of Archives and History.

Private John A. Jackson has been in service now for six months and has still not seen combat. He seems annoyed by the repeated flight of New Bern's citizens. In this letter he discusses an attempted desertion, the presence of the Union fleet, the unfair way that furloughs have been granted to some and not others, and an attempted "defection."

                    January the 24th 1862
                    Carolina City Camp Vance
Mr. R. A. Cole and M. A. M. Cole

Dear brother and sister and family I received your letter this morning and you may be shure that it done me a greateal of good to hear from you and family and that you was well and the neighbors also. I am well at presant and the rest of the company is in very good health. A few are just geting over the mumps they are what I call in good health. I hope these few lines will come

safe to hand and find you and family all the same.

I have no newse of intrest to rite you only we have been expecting to be caried to Newbern. It was reported that there was thirty or forty vesels in side the bar at Hateras and bound for newbern and the people down hear are very uneasy and it is reported that a great many have left newbern and gone west. Everytime they expect this place or newbern attacted they leave and when the excitement is over they come back and wait for the next time.

It is reported that there was a man taken up at morehead that was tring to make his way to the lincoln fleet and that capt Pender[3] who was a capt of an artillery company and resigned some time since was also tring to do the same. They stoped the vesel and would not let her leave the port. Her Capt is suspected of something not right I do not know what they will do with him and if he is guilty it dont make much difference. They dont let him go without he gives some good evidence of his loyalty to the confederacy or wont try to convey off traitors and rascals.

I must come to a close as I have nothing to rite that is worth while. I was very glad to hear from James Martin and that he was well again. I was very uneasy a while about him. I should like to have been there to a went around with him. I think we could have had some fun but I dont expect to come home til my time is out but I am lucky then we will see about whether we go home or not. They wont grant furlows to any person now and still they want us to Volunteer for 2 years more but I dont think they will get many out of this regiment until the second relief comes on.* Especialy as long as they are so clever to grant furlows. There is several of us that has never been home yet and some that has went two or three times and when we ask anything about going home we can get no satisfaction or some short answer so I dont expect to come home til I get free. I should like to know Edward grahams Post office so that I could rite to him and hear the Va newse. So no more at present. You must excuse bad riting and mistakes. I remain your Brother

John A. Jackson to R. A. Cole & M. A. M. Cole

Richard do you think that Tom is going to make any money at his still or not. I feare it is a bad operation.

*Original volunteers signed on for twelve months, and at this time in the war they could re-enlist for the war. After the fall of New Bern and the Spring campaigns on the peninsula, all those who re-enlisted did so for the duration of the war.

William F. Kelly commanded Company G, 4th N.C. State Troops, until resigning on February 3, 1863. From Clark's *Regiments*. (Courtesy of the N.C. Division of Archives and History.)

29. February 2, 1862

Private Harrison H. Hanes, "Davie Sweepstakes," Company G, 4th Regiment N.C. State Troops, letter to Nancy Williams, Davie County, N.C. Source: Harrison H. Hanes Papers, Perkins Library, Duke University

This is the last of two letters from Harrison Hanes. Private Hanes was wounded in action at Seven Pines, Virginia, on May 31, 1862. Private Hanes was sent home to recuperate from his wound and was able to furnish a substitute, L. B. King, in 1863. Hanes lived in the Farmington township of Davie County until his death in 1923. He was the father of several children, including Sallie, Pat, John, May, Bulah, and Nancy Hanes.[4]

Manassas Va February 1 st 1862
Nancy
I received your leter yesterd and was glad to hear that you was well. Your letter found me enyoin good health. I am sory that I haven't any thing new or interestin to write. I will write something a bout the weather. It is very rough and has been for sore time and it seems like it will continue so, for it is raining and sleating and some snow occasionaly and the mud is from shoo top to knee deep. I hav been cooking this week and will be through to marrow night. You can tel the girls that they had better wait for me becous I can bee a great advantage to in the cooking line and also in sewing for I have a great deal of it to do but I get others to do my washing but I recon I'll take to doing that my self for it is getin so high, it is ten cents a garmet. Tel ms salley litle did I think of her getin married untel I had been gon twelve months but if that is her notion of court I have no obgections but I realy do think that she could go get a beter looking man than the one she is a goin to get. I know that she could if she had uv waited untel the

war was over. Tel her that I am much a blige to her for asking me to the wedin but I am sory that I can't com but I think that I will bee at one you mentioned. Tel Buley that I think maby I will bee at her wedin if she isent in too big a hurry. Tel her to not get mared untel the war is over for fear they coms a draft and they take her old man. Tel her that is my advise to all the young girls. The reason I do this is becos I am a fraid they will all get maried before I get back and I bee left a lone with out a wife. Tel marts John that he ma go to see margret but he musent say any thing to Elizabeth unless he talkes for me. Tel M. Ellis girls that I fear they will all bee married befor we get home for I understand that the maylors are flying a round and I think they suit very well. A few lines to Jimey and that is this that if a man falls down in the mud here he is a goner unless he gets help amediately. Tel him that I would like to see him and tel him all a bout the state of virginia an manassas but I recon Bill Taylor told him a nough to keepe him from wanten to com to see us. Give him my love and respects. I will close by saying to you to content your self a few more years and the war will bee over and then we will all com home. I hope this to. From

H. H. Hanes to Nancy Williams

30. February 19, 1862

Private Robert O. Linster, Company C, 4th Regiment N.C. State Troops, letter to father, E. U. Linster, Iredell County, N.C. Source: Special Collections, Perkins Library, Duke University, Durham, North Carolina.

Private Linster writes his father about what has been happening during the war. He speaks about some of the major generals of the early war eastern theatre including Gen. Longstreet while assigned as a provost marshal on detached duty. He also speaks about "Sam Fraly," the unit's first sergeant, taking over as a lieutenant. The letter is not complete. It has been edited to remove illegible passages.

Manass Junction
Feb 19/62

dear Father

Your letter came to hand to day. I have nothing of importance to write to day only the surender of Fort Donnelerson* with Gen Hindneman. I was on the Battlefield last week and also at Centeraville. I was sent by Maj Boyle to Gen Hays Head Quarters on some important Business. I saw Gen Stewart and Longstreet. I did not see Gen Johnson. I was at his Head Quarters. I was at the 1st North Carolina Caveraly, 9 of them was tacon prissioners. They were from Capt Ruffins Company, 2 of them were from New Bern. Fred Johnas and Bill Lune Noah Ford was out on Pickett so I did not see him.

I was sent to Warrinton Va last week to look after some deserters. Warrinton is in fawkin† County 50 miles from Manassas. Col McRays family is there. There is some talk of our Regiment going back to North Carolina but I don't think we will get back soon any how. I will not go with the Regiment as I am on detach Service. We herd here there was a there was a draft in.... I wish it would bring out some of them fellows there. We are very nice fixed here 4 of us in one Cabin and plenty to eat. Our Bread is Baked at the Bakins so we cook nothing but rice Beef and mak coffee. We have plenty of Coffee and Sugar now and Molass some times. We are a gong to draw our pay. The 25 of this month which is 25 cent extra evry day and 75 cents evry 3 day. That is the day we go on the Road.

I rec a letter the other day from Uncle fred. He said nothing about joyning the Army. Liet Ellison from Co. A gon to the 7 Regiment to be ther Quarter master. Sam Fraly taken his place as Lieutenant. So I have bee told. I have not been to the Regiment in 3 weeks. Col Young has gon Home on furlough. I saw him on the Cars and told him good by. He is a fine man. I want you to make me a Calico coat for this summer. They don't get dirty nor don't half to be wash so much. There is no hopes of a Fight here this Winter and if there is one I will not be in it unless they whip us which they never will No More

Your Son
R.O. Linster[5]

*Fort Donelson in northwestern Tennessee

†Warrenton, Faqueir County, Virginia

31. March 7, 1862

Third Lieutenant James A. Graham, Company G, 27th Regiment N. C. Troops, Fort Lane, N.C., letter to his father, William A. Graham, Orange County, N.C. Source: The James A. Graham Papers 1861–1864, Southern Historical Collection, University of North Carolina at Chapel Hill.

The Orange Guards were mustered into state service on June 22, 1861, and were assigned to the 27th Regiment as Company G. Graham was promoted to first sergeant on July 19, 1861, and was elected to the post of third lieutenant in August of 1861. Lieutenant James Graham was apparently being considered for the position of regimental adjutant of the regiment. From the way he sounds, it appears that he is weighing the options of other service or retaining his position once it is incorporated as a regiment of North Carolina Troops. Graham also talks about an early March snowstorm, not an unusual event (the heaviest snows in North Carolina have typically come within the first two weeks of March). The unit is currently with tentage at this stage in the war, since garrison duty provided the rationale for a static camp.

Fort Lane
March 7th 1862
MY DEAR FATHER

I received your very welcome letter last night. I am not yet fully determined as to what course I shall pursue about my adjutant's office*, but think that I will return to my company in a week or two. I would rather be with my old company than any company I know of; for it is the best drilled company I ever saw and one of the best companies I ever saw in every particular.

I will not go into the ranks again for if I am not re-elected to my present office I am not compelled to go into the ranks, but can quit and go to work recruiting on my own part. If I am re-elected and a better place offers afterwards I can take it then, but I think it would be rather the better plan to make sure of what I have. I must re-enlist again, for I could not stay at home contented and not bear my part while the war lasts. I will write again in a few days and let you know what I have determined really to do. Even if I should keep my place as Adjutant I will not want a horse as our present enlistment will be out in two or three months at the farthest and I may not be Adjutant in the next Regiment that we are put in.

We had a snow storm this morning for about three or four hours, but about mid-day the sun came out and the snow is already gone, though it is still pretty cold. Our men are living in tents, but seem to like this place better than Fort Macon. As it is so near warm weather I think that they will not build winter Quarters; for we do not know where we may be sent to as soon as the spring opens. I think it very likely that we will stay here until our time is out. I can very easily sell my saddle to Maj. Gilmer or Lt. Col. Singletary for what it cost me.

There is nothing new. Love to all. Write soon to

Your affectionate Son
James A. Graham

P. S. Our men were paid off yesterday. I will send you $300 of mine by the first chance. Please tell Mr Parks to make me a pair of heavy shoes like those he made for me last August. Tell him to make them inch longer than he did the others. I want them made as soon as possible for I am beginning to need them.

The position of regimental adjutant carried with it the rank of first lieutenant.

32. March 15, 1862

Third Lieutenant James A. Graham, Company G, 27th Regiment N. C. Troops, Kinston, N.C., letter to his mother, Orange County, N.C. Source: The James A. Graham Papers 1861–1864, Southern Historical Collection, University of North Carolina at Chapel Hill.

The fall of New Bern was Lt. Graham's baptism of fire, as it was for nearly all of the North Carolina units present at the engagement. North Carolina forces occupied the Fort Thompson line outside of New Bern, North Carolina. The defenders of New Bern numbered about four thousand and were composed of Clark's Militia Battalion, three batteries of artillery, the 2nd NC Cavalry, and six regiments of infantry. The left rested on the railroad track while the right extended beyond the brick kiln. When the Yankees advanced on the position the 14th the Confederate forces took position along Fort Thompson from left to right as follows: 27th North Carolina, 37th North Carolina, 7th North Carolina, 35th North

Carolina, Clark's Militia Battalion, 26th North Carolina, 2nd NC Cavalry (two companies), with the 33rd North Carolina held in reserve.[6]

Kinston
March 15th 1862
MY DEAR MOTHER

I wrote to you this morning to let you know that I was safe. I have since heard that Willie is also safe, but have not seen him. A gentleman told me just now that he knew him to be safe. Time will determine. I hope he is safe but have my doubts about it. I do not think he is killed, but he may be a prisoner. He was on the right where the hardest fighting was but I understand he was not engaged in it at all.

The enemy, 24,000 strong, came upon us about half past 7 o'clock yesterday morning. We numbered about 6,000 and were behind our entrenchments about 5 miles below Newbern. The strongest part of the attack was made upon our right. Our Regiment was upon the extreme left and was not much engaged but the shell fell thick and fast around us, bursting above us and all around us. It was terrible, but our men stood it nobly. There was but one man killed and three or four wounded in our regiment. About 10 o'clock the enemy turned our right flank and we were ordered to retreat and such a mess I never saw. I endeavored to get our men together, but every man was looking out for himself; we retreated to Newberne, but the enemy got there in their gun boats almost as soon as we did on land. We saw that we could not hold it and therefore set the town on fire and retreated to this place. I retreated with the regiment for four or five miles when the alarm was given that the enemy were upon us. We then scattered through the woods and every man took care of himself. I waded through several creeks and ditches about waist deep and at last came up with some of our cavalry and rode behind them to this place. We afterwards found out that this was a false alarm. All of the men in our company have come in except four or five. I suppose they will come in during the day unless they are prisoners, for none of our men were killed when I left them. Capt. Brem's Artillery was cut almost all to pieces, I understand, and their guns taken. We had 16 pieces of artillery and lost nearly everyone of them. We lost under 50 men killed, among them Lt. Col. Hoke 33rd Reg't and between 50 and 100 wounded. The loss of the enemy was 500 or 600. We took one or two prisoners. I do not know how many prisoners they took. I lost every thing I had except my uniform that I have got on and my overcoat. I do not know whether Aleck* escaped or not as I left him at our camp when we went to the entrenchments and I have not seen or heard of him since except that he came over to New-berne soon yesterday morning. I got here about 12 o'clock last night and went up to Uncle John's and got a pretty good night's rest. I did not sleep more than one hour and a half in the 48 hours before that and was wet to the skin nearly all the time. I have got along pretty well but am so tired and broken down now that I can hardly stand. I wish you would send me two shirts (check) two pair of drawers and two or three pair of socks for I have not had on any clean clothes in a week and am as dirty as a hog and have no clothes to change. I would write more but am so tired and broken down that I can hardly stand. I will write again perhaps tomorrow. Love to all. I hope to see you again some of these days.

Your affectionate Son
James A. Graham

*The identity of "Aleck" is unknown. It is believed that he is a friend of James's from Orange County who is serving in one of the other units present at the battle.

33. March 20, 1862

Captain Julius A. Robbins, Assistant Quartermaster, 15th Regiment N.C. Troops, letter to cousin Anna, Randolph County, N.C. Source: Julius A. Robbins Papers, Southern Historical Collection, University of North Carolina at Chapel Hill.

Joe Johnston's Army was holding and fortifying positions on the Peninsula formed by the York and James rivers. The last action fought was at Bethel Church on July 10, 1861. Despite long periods of boredom, business was going to pick up for the defenders of the Peninsula in the spring and summer of 1862. The naval battle to which Robbins is referring is the first cruise of the C. S. S. Virginia (Merrimac) on March 8, 1862. Particularly interesting is the manner in which the soldiers make sleeping quarters out of what could be carried on their backs. In addition, Captain Robbins talks about getting his "sick servant from camp" which may suggest that black body servants of officers stayed in a common camp with enlisted men.

Army of the Peninsula
March 20' 1862

Dear Cousin Anna

Your very welcome letter was received some months ago and ought to have been answered long before, and indeed, I have commenced writing you two or three lines but something has always prevented me from finishing. Even so, I have nothing of special interest to tell you: we have now been in the service nearly twelve months but have never been in any general engagement. We were very near the recent naval battle in Hampton Roads but were not where we could see the fight. We however, could hear all the guns and I heard very distinctly the explosion when the Congress blew up.[7]

It is said that Napoleon maintained always that Providence was on the side of the heaviest artillery but I am inclined to believe that Providence is on the side of our boat. Most of the troops on the Peninsula are now down at Bethel four miles below here and twenty miles from Yorktown. Our regiment went down yesterday morning without any tents. I rode down there and back today and it would amuse you to see the arrangements the soldiers were making to sleep; the weather was wet and cold. They took a common blanket and they put it over a little pole set up on forks two feet high and they made a little ridge just enough to creep under and roll themselves in another blanket. The arrangement looked to me like a poor one but they were able to keep tolerable dry in this way and the rest will too.

I have had a very sick servant here. I got permission from Col. Winston to come up to camp and I had him comfortably by my fire in my cabin here at winter quarters. Otherwise I would be down at Bethel roughing it with the rest of them.

I would be very happy to receive another letter from you. The only real enjoyment a soldier has is when he receives a long letter from some "loved one at home." Yours very truly

Julius A. Robbins

34. April 4, 1862

Hon. Jonathan Worth, Asheboro, Randolph County, letter to Allen M. Tomlinson, Society of Friends, Deep River Friends Meeting. *Source: Hamilton, The Correspondence of Jonathan Worth, 1909.*

In this letter state congressman Jonathan Worth is addressing the concerns of the Quakers in his constituency of Guilford and Randolph counties. The Society of Friends was the proper name for the religious sect known as the Quakers. As part of the Quaker doctrine, no member could kill or fight in any military conflict. This universal pacifism was well known and

caused major conflicts during not only the Civil War but also during the American Revolution when conscription was instituted to force Quakers into service against their will. Mr. Worth was in support of the Quakers and arranged a deal with his brother Milton* who ran the N.C. saltworks in Wilmington: If male Quakers worked at the saltworks, they would be considered exempt from conscription. However, Mr. Tomlinson considered this contributing to the moral evils of war and threatened to censure or even expel any Quakers who took advantage of this most generous offer. As a whole, North Carolina seemed sympathetic to the Quaker commitment to pacifism. Large concentrations of Quakers can still be found in Alamance, Guilford, and Randolph counties.

April 4, 1862

Dear Sir,

I felt extreme solitude to relieve such of your Society as were drafted, and from Morehead City and Wilmington earnestly pressed it upon the Govr. To allow such as would labor at the Salt Works or to send a substitute as a laborer, at a liberal rate of wages, to be excused from military service. He cheerfully assented to it. It never occurred to me that you would have any scruples about adopting this plan of relief. I am greatly disappointed and mortified at your decision. The well-intending efforts of brother Milton and myself instead of relieving you, I have no doubt will result greatly to your prejudice. As the lawmaking power would not relieve you entirely, we conceived we had fallen on a plan which would gladly and thankfully be adopted.

I understand it is intended to seize and send to the hospitals as nurses such of the Quakers as decline to comply, and I fear you will lose sympathy which many of the best men in the State have felt for you.

I sincerely hope you will reconsider your decision—at least so far as to allow such members to accept the proposed alternative without censure of the Society.

J. Worth

John Milton Worth was one of Jonathan's younger brothers who was employed as an attorney in Wilmington, N.C., and was appointed head of one of the salt works in the Wilmington area. A historical marker at one of these locations can be viewed along US 421 in New Hanover County.

35. April 22, 1862

Private Augustus A. Clewell, "The Forsyth Greys," Company E, 21st Regiment N.C. Troops, letter to his parents, Salem, Forsyth County, N.C. Source: Clewell Letters, Private Manuscripts Collection, North Carolina Division of Archives and History.

Augustus A. "Gus" Clewell was born in 1843 to Salem mechanic David Clewell and his wife, Dorothy Clewell. Clewell's older sister, Margaret, was a schoolteacher in the Salem area. He had three younger siblings, Anna, Edward, and Johnny. In the following letter, Private Clewell is describing action along the Rappahannock River during his tenth month in service. Prior to 21st North Carolina's participation in the valley campaign of 1862, the 21st had not been engaged in any major actions.[8]

Gordonsville, April 22nd 1862
Dear Parents,*

It is with pleasure that I again have the opportunity of writing to you to let you know that I am well and hope that you are the same. We left the Rhappa-

Another member of the 21st Regiment, Calvin H. Waters of Guilford County's Company M. Ambrotype taken c. March-April 1862. (Courtesy of the Greensboro Historical Museum—1983.201.2.)

hannock River last Friday and came to this place. On last Thursday we went on picket down to the river and there was a post on top of a hill about 400 yards from the river that I with 4 others occupied where we could see across the river for a long distance. Nothing could be seen until Friday evening when we heard the report of a cannon and in a moment or two we seen a bomb-shell burst down the river about half a mile where our reserve was at. The shell was well aimed as it burnt an area of 40 feet in and around a crowd of persons among them Captain Wharton[9] and others of our company. At that our guns opened on them and there was a fierce cannonading for about an hour. I could see the flank of every cannon that fired on both sides but none of the shells or balls came near me, but our batteries silenced them.

Where we'll go and when we will leave here I don't know for the last three days we had very bad weather. We get a plenty to eat and have tents again. In fact we are doing tolerable well. It is my opinion that we will have a chance at the yankees here before long and I don't care how soon.

There is no news of importance as I know of. The next opportunity you have I want you to send me a pair of drawers, a pair of pants, and socks. I am in no hurry of them thought but I'll need them before long. I'll let you know what we get at present. We get plenty of bacon, flour, and crackers when we are marching, sugar and salt and other little things like rice & etc. Give my love to all the children and Mag and Ann and all. So, be sure and write soon. I remain

Your affectionate son
A. A. Clewell

David and Dorothy Clewell

36. April 22, 1862

Captain C. C. Blacknall, "The Granville Rifles," Company G, 23rd Regiment N.C. Troops, letter to brother-in-law, George W. Kitrell, Granville County, N.C. Source: Oscar Blacknall Collection, Private Manuscripts Collection, North Carolina Division of Archives and History.

While Clewell records action around Gordonsville, over one hundred fifteen miles away, Captain Blacknall and the "Granville Rifles" have been assigned to the Army of the Peninsula and are entrenched near Yorktown, Virginia. Blacknall provides the reader with a great description of the Confederate battle line as it was prior to McClellan's advance. He

mentions the three prominent commanders under Johnston: Longstreet, D. H. Hill, and John B. Magruder. The action being described on the right was the battle of Lee's Mill, Virginia, on April 16, 1862.

In the Trenches near Winns Mill
Yorktown April 22nd 1862
Bro George

I have received your favor of a recent date & was much pleased to hear from home as letters are now quite rare & news from that portion of the country almost unattainable. This leaves me in good health, not withstanding the severe exposure through which we have recently passed. We were for three weeks without tents, blankets or cooking utensils and out in the worst weather that we have had through the winter, our only articles of furniture being an axe which we made fires and cut the bark of trees to make our trays ovens etc. But we are yet alive & well though many of my recruits have given away under the hardships, none however being seriously sick.

In the hurry & confusion of writing I can give you but little of interest in regard to military matters on the Peninsula. Suffice it to say we have a splendid army here under command of our best Genl. Our line of battle extends from Yorktown on York River to the James River across the Peninsula, a distance of 8 miles. The right wing is commanded Genl. Magruder, the center by Genl Longstreet & the left by Genl Hill, the whole being under Genl Johnston. The force is estimated to be 65000. I should think it will approximate that figure as we have brought the army of the Potomac with slight exception here and have concentrated many troops from other points. Our whole line is well protected with earthworks or rifle pits with redoubts for cannon at regular intervals. We have splendid siege guns mounted at Yorktown (to resist the gun boats, which lie Just below) and have quantities of artillery and mounted guns on the whole line. The enemy occupies our whole front in large forces being in full view. Their camps artillery and in fact all of their preparations are now in sight. Our pickets are but three hundred yards from theirs—all in the same field and just in front of us in full view. We have been lying in the trenches for five days. The enemy has kept up a furious cannonade on our whole line all the time, frequently firing all night on us. None of my company are yet hurt but we had a narrow escape a day or two since as a shell bursted in the company, the fragments flying in every direction. I had quite a lively & little affair with enemy's picket a few days ago while out posting our pickets—they fired on me in splendid style—the balls trimming around on every side but they had the gentility & kindness not to injure me for which I am obliged to them. We have had several severe fights with them since we arrived, our regiment not participating as the attacks were just to our right. They made four assaults on our entrenchments, with the intention of cutting our line & getting in our rear, in all of which they were repulsed with heavy loss. The 15 N. C. Regt acted very gallantly in one of these affairs, Col. Mckinny[10] being killed the other attacks were made in the night. The fighting was furious & desperate, they charged over our trenches & we encountered them in a hand to hand fight killing and wounding nearly the whole of the assailants. These men are selected for this purpose and fighting most desperately. Our Regiment has done no fighting yet excepting with the pickets (they fire constantly) but we have been compelled to take the enemys fire from their batteries & gun boats for five days. I have become quite adept at bowing as I very politely come down when a shell bursts over me, which being so frequent I have become extremely polite. But we have become used to it and our boys only laugh & cheer as they whistle and burst harmlessly over our heads. I think that we can hold our position here against any force that the enemy can bring against us, as we have an admirable position & are all ready. I can give you no idea when the general attack will take place. It may be this evening, tomorrow or at any moment as both parties are apparently ready & we have nothing to do but pitch in. I think the enemy are endeavoring to weary us out & exhaust our men by a constant cannoande & shelling and then charge our works with the bayonet while they attempt to take Yorktown with the gunboats. Our troops are in good spirits and bid defiance to the bayonets which now gleam before us.

No more, I will write again in a few days. Remember me very kindly to sister and Mrs. Taylor (if with you) also to Sallie & other friends. Dock is well but somewhat sick.

Very hastily and lovingly yours
C. C. Blacknall

37. April 30, 1862

Private James W. Gibson, "Catawba Guards," Company F, 23rd Regiment N.C. State Troops, letter to his sister, Catawba County, North Carolina. Source: Catawba County Historical Association. Transcriptions courtesy of Mrs. Addie Cloninger.

The Catawba Guards were a week away from completing their eleventh month in state service, yet they had not seen actual combat. The regiment was posted under the command of Gen. Joseph Johnston and helped form the Yorktown garrison occupying a line between the York and James rivers. The ranks of the company have swelled to over one hundred men, and Private Gibson is wondering if there will be more or at least a new set of officers when the election is held. While Blacknall, above, is satisfied and only briefly alludes to hardships suffered by soldiers at Yorktown, Gibson, a private in Company F, gives details about how the sea breeze helps to make things difficult for the enlisted men.

april 30 1862

Dear sister

I received you very kind letter which gave me much satisfaction to hear that you are all well your letter found me well and J. F. Gibson is here he is not very well but is not bedfast he is on dutie all the time there is many of us that have not been as well since we left Manassas as we were than, that was a very healthie country as we were most fixed to stay there when we had to leave and so we are not at Yorktown and have been expecting a battle every day till now we rather expect to evacuate this place in a few days.

That is the supposition we cant tell how it will be yet there are immense forces here both of yankees and our people but it is very doubtful when we leave. I think we will fall back toward Richmond some twelve miles from this point. We have been looking for a battle for some time ever since we came here but now we are rather in a leavening way for a few days and I suppose we will leave if we can get away. They have every advantage over us and we will try to get a place where we can have a fair chance at them. I suppose that we will have to stay here till the fray is settled and I intend to try and do the best I can for myself and others.

We will have a Bully* Company after while, we will have to have one hundred and twenty five men for a Company. I expect we will have a new set of officers altogether it is very uncertain who they will be but I know we will have a great many new officers. But I will not tell you who they will be yet for I cant tell

till after the election and then I will report to yous and let yous know who our officers will be. I wish I had herd that Hugh S. Gibson was going to volunteer, I should have said to him that he come out here as me and J. F. Gibson ware both out here but he is under a good Captain† and he is a great deal nearer home than we are and probably further out of danger than us.

We are in a place said to be very sickly place it is a very changeable place one hour very hot and then very cold. It is right on the sea coast and when ever the tide flows it is very cold and chilly it is said to be a great place for chills and fever but I hope we will get away from here before long and get to a better place we have been nearly all over this side of the southern and I think they will send us to the other side before long, if we get off from this without a fight we will be lucky, that is one thing certain.

I tell you that if we ever do fight here they will whip us just as certain as this world stands. But I think we will fall back from this place. You said the boys are all gone but Adolphs. Where is William? Tell him and Dolphus[11] to stay at home till they are obliged to come for when they leave their they leave home. But if they are old enough they will be obliged to come and if they have to come I should like to have them to come to me or Joseph F. one. But it may be that they will be as well off some place else as here give my respect to all. please write soon and give me all the news your brother sincerely till death separates

J. W. Gibson

*Bully: a expression meaning great, outstanding

†Joseph F.'s captain was named Andrews and was from Iredell County, North Carolina.

38. April 30, 1862

Private William P. Cline, "The Catawba Braves," Company K, 46th Regiment

N.C. Troops, letter to his wife, Mary C. Cline, Newton, Catawba County, N.C. Source: William P. Cline Papers, Southern Historical Collection, University of North Carolina at Chapel Hill.

William Pinkney Cline was born to Paul and Selina Cline of Catawba County, N.C., in 1837. William P. Cline married his wife, Mary, prior to March 13, 1862, when he volunteered for service in the "Catawba Braves," leaving his beloved wife at home.[12] This is an example of what is referred to in the introduction as a "typical soldier letter," a letter without a lot of description. It involves a request for clothing or personal items and is written in a very impersonal tone.

NC Wake Co. April 30, 1862
My dear wife,
I take my pen in my hand to let you now that I am well and I hope when thes few lines come to hand may find you all well. I wont you to go to newton and get my napsack and keep it. They is one blanket and one shurt and one pare of slips. It has a good bed blankit. It has rain here all day. It is hard on us When it rains. I wish to be at home. When it rains it is clear we can do prime. I wont you to tell mey how you are gitin along. I recen that…. I have not got nothen more to rite at present. I will send you a likeness as soon as I can git to go to Raly.* It is cold rain here. I have not got nothen more to rite you. When dis you see remember mey. Rite to mey soon
W. P. Cline to Mary C. Cline
NC Camp mangum
In the care of Capt. Bost
46 rigmen N. C. V.

*Raly: Raleigh

39. May 5, 1862

Private Bartlett Yancey Malone, "The Caswell Boys," Company H, 6th Regiment N.C. State Troops, diary entry. Source: Diary of Bartlett Y. Malone, property of the Wilkinson Family. Microfilm copy available in the Southern Historical Collection, Wilson Library, University of North Carolina at Chapel Hill.[13]

Bartlett Yancey Malone was a twenty-three-year-old Caswell County farmer when he volunteered to serve in the Confederate Army. We join Malone's Company of the 6th North Carolina State Troops as it is defending the peninsula against the advance of Major General George B. McClellan (USA). The Confederates hold a position between Yorktown and the old colonial capital of Williamsburg. Like William Cline above, Malone, a tobacco farmer, also practices phonetic spelling in his writing. Note: Bartlett's diaries are written for days at a time instead of a continuous day-by-day account. For the purpose of this chronological arrangement the date will be established as the last date mentioned in the entry.

The 2 day of May was a beautyful one And we had orders to leave Yorktown. And soon in the morning the wagons was loded and everything sent off but our knapsacks and about 12 o'clock the Artillery was all plast in a line of battle acrost the field and about dark we was all marched out behind it and Colonel Pender* told ous that they expected a large fight the next day and we lade that in the field all night with our guns by our side. And next morning we marched out in the woods And we stade that untell about 2 o'clock in the night And then we was rousted up and marched about a half a mile and then for sume cause we was stopt and sent back. And then about daybreak we started again and taken the same road back that we come down And about 12 oclock we got to Williamsburg and we onley went about 4 miles furher tell we stopt to stay all night And about 4 oclock in the eavning the Yankee Calvry overtaken ours clost to Williamsburg and we had a little brush but our men whipt thirs and we onley lost one kild and 3 or 4 wounded and we kild 9 of thirs and wounded sevrl and taken 10 horses. And the 5 day was a very raney one indeed and we was rousted up about 2 oclock in the night and marched all day threw the mud and water at night we arived in about 2 miles of West Point.

Colonel William Dorsey Pender, commanding officer, 6th Regiment North Carolina State Troops.

40. May 11, 1862

Private Julius J. C. Loftin, Company F, 7th Regiment North Carolina State Troops, letter to uncle, William H. Badgett, JP, Jackson Hill, Davidson County, N.C. Source: Badgett Collection, Davidson County Historical Museum.

This is a second letter from Julius Loftin of the 7th Regiment N.C. State Troops. This letter describes the disposition of the unit as of May 11, 1862. The Valley Army under Jackson had achieved some of the greatest victories in American military history. The 7th NC, while going into action at New Bern, N.C., in March 1862, had arrived too late to participate in some of Jackson's victories, which resulted in the captured men being sent through Gordonsville.

Gordensville Va
May the 11th 1862
Dear Uncle,

I am one time more blessed with the opportunity of writing to you to answer a few words that I receved from you while we was at Kinston. I was glad to here from you but was very sorry to hear that you was not well. I am well this time and I hope that these few lines will find you all well this time. We are now in Va stationed at Gordensville 76 miles northwest of Richmon. We left Kinston last Sunday the 4th and landed here the 6th. We are in a very healthy country

where we will git fighting to do a plenty, we came here for the purposes of Reinforsing Gen. Jackson—he is over in the mountains some 30 or 40 miles from here. He has about 25,000 men with him and there is several thousand around this plase.[14]

We are about 60 miles from Manasses and about 10 miles from the 5th Reg. There is many a thousand soldiers in old Va the Yankees are a trying to come through here & take Richmond. Gen. Jackson sends in prisoners every day or two. They brought in 24 yankees and I believe if we git a fair chance we will whip the yankees worse than they ever bin yet. I wont to know how times is back their you can tell uncle Samuel that Lieut. Williamson wont say any thing a bout my question that he wanted me to ask him but it is so or it he would a said that is was not. So I will close. Answer soon,

J. C. Loftin
Direct your letters Gordensville Va
7th Regt. N. C. S. T.
in care of Cap. Turner

41. May 18, 1862

First Sergeant Ashbel S. Fraley, Company A, 4th Regiment North Carolina State Troops, diary entry. Source: Typescript, A. S. Fraley Diary, Fraley Collection, Rowan County Public Library.

This is the first diary entry from First or Orderly Sergeant (later Lieutenant) Ashbel Fraley. Mr. Fraley was blessed with an ability to write and a very dry sense of humor. Fraley, a Rowan County native, was born in 1834 and resided in Rowan County prior to volunteering for service in Iredell County, N.C., on April 20, 1861.[15] In his diary entries he expresses a dislike for field officers and generals, a common thought among the men. He is very sarcastic and is not an admirer of Major General Daniel Harvey Hill.

May 18 Leave camp and travel 3 or 4 miles in a very circuitous route. Cant see that we advance any way. Stop occasionally & always in the broiling hot sun when shade equally convenient. Our commanders are very humane men. Especially the Col.* Who when he sees a poor fatigued & fainting soldier running to the well, gasping for a drop of water, orders him back in the most severe and harsh language and he makes us step into the middle of a mudhole & fill our shoes with mud when we could step over.

Will not permit us to go into a house or yard to buy something to eat when we are starving, & other regiments have the coveted privilege. Never stop to rest tho fatigued men & sick, are falling by the roadside completely exhausted.1 guard is in the rear with instructions to arrest such men & compel them to keep up. Guard the branches and keep us from bathing and washing our clothes even if we had time. In short, guard everything, & do to keep the soldiers from resting & keeping comfortable. Encamp again 2 or 3 miles from Richmond close to a little grave yard. "Some mute inglorious Milton here may rest, Some Cromwell guiltless of his country's blood." Preparations seem to indicate staying a day or two. A warm day. Sunday! a day of sacred rest, But not here. Having marched this morning as if ten thousand devils were at our heels I fain would rest.

5 P.M. Orders to be ready to go on picket duty. Start at dusk Go Six miles south east. Co A 4 N.C. & Co B 49 Va detailed for the night. Go 1½ miles further & post pickets.

*Colonel George B. Anderson, 4th Regiment N.C. State Troops.

42. May 18, 1862

Private James W. R. Cameron, Company F, 7th Regiment N.C. State Troops,

letter to brother-in-law, William H. Badgett, JP, Jackson Hill, Davidson County. Source: Badgett Collection, Davidson County Historical Museum

Private James W. R. Cameron (1837–1862) was from one of the more prominent families in Davidson County. He volunteered for service at Salisbury, Rowan County, and was assigned to Company F, 7th Regiment. James was killed in action during the battle of Malvern Hill, Virginia, on July 1, 1862.[16] In this letter written only forty-three days prior to his death, Private Cameron reports his current medical condition and talks about the whereabouts of his unit's supplies. He also discusses things that he has heard about, such as a Union invasion into North Carolina, perhaps targeting the Weldon Railroad. His observations of Jackson are particularly humorous, but are consistent with how a man from a wealthy family would have view the shrewd and eccentric "Stonewall" Jackson.

Gordon's ville, Va
May the 18th 1862
Mr. W. H. Badgett

Dear brotherinlaw I one more time take my pen in hand to drop a word to you to in form you that I am not so well at this time and taken the measles in the march to Stanton though had them vary little though. I am not well yet and often having measles some ten days and then taken the Diarea and flux so I am not stout by any means though I feel a great deal better for the last too days. I am left here with the sick the Brigade are gone to join Ewell or Jackson the left this place on the 15th on a march in that direction. We learned today that they have had orders to come back, so we hardly know where they are at. The wagons of the Brigade are on the way to this place from Kinston.* We left Kinston on the 4th inst we came the rail road, the wagons came the dirt road. Franklin Newsom, L. G. Sills, are with the wagons as a guard from our company. The last news we had of them they was in Richmond be on the few days so we will leave here in a few days and the Brigade will be back in a few days. There was 220 sick left in camp besides what was at the hospital that is in the 7th Regiment.

Stonewall Jackson is playing on the yankees to some extent he sends in some prisoners here every few days at one time he sent 25 at another time 7 and at another time 14. They sent them to Richmond today Capt Turner and Calvin Reid went to help carry the first lot of 25 they said they was paroled and sent off them and 835 more with them making 860 of the invaders. They are all stout fellows one of them that was sent off was wounded in the face in two places. We learn that the Yankees are making their ways to Peters Burge and it is thought that they intend to try to git in posession of the rail road junction of Weldon. If they succeed it will cut off all Rail road shipping from N.C. though our forces will give them fitts. I think we will have some of the bloodiest fighting up in here that has ever yet been don. Jackson and Ewell intend to march into Mayerland but President Davis is aposed to it. The troops are all gon from Manases in organge county I believe there has been several fights in Va latly though I know you have heard of them all times and again so I deam it necessary to tell them to you again. Also you have heard of the evacuation of Norfolk. The people of Richmond are some what fearful of the times now. However they fear that the next thing will be Richmond.

President Davis says that they will have to wad blood needeep before they git it. I wish I new what the opinon of the people back there and what they are doing. I learn that the Malitia are ordering out that is from 18 to 35. I sapose that if they are called for it will

show the spunk of many a fellow I can see them flinching and doging and trying to hire men that are forsd by age to substitute now it seams though I may be mistaken.

We will have hard times after we join Jackson. He is marching studdy from place to place he carries no tents dident last winter. They say they takes the weather as it comes like the Beast of the forest with one blanket. His headquarters is by the side of a tree or in some fence corner.† It is a hard road to travil to go a soldiering though the closer we stick to it the better we will come out. I am as well satisfied as I expected to be though I do not like our Lieutant Colonel Haywood.[17] I think he will cause the Death of hundreds of men in the Regt by drilling them to Death. He is a sot Drunkard I sopose he takes his quart per day and he drills them harder than he ever did. They say some 20 fell out in the Regt the last day they drilled before they left with one capt and several lieuts. I sopose that there is not one in the Regt that likes him.

I will close by asking you to write soon and give me all of the particulars in that vicinity. I hope that these few lines may reach there place of destination and find you all well.

Yours until Death
James W. R. Cameron

*This is a perfect illustration of some problems with logistics being unable to keep pace with troop movements. The wagons with supplies and tentage for the 7th N.C. State Troops were still at Kinston, N.C. By a modern map that distance is approximately 228 miles from Richmond via Raleigh; to make it to Gordonsville, the entire trip would be about 300 miles.

†All of these are popular descriptions of Gen. Jackson whose "headquarters were always in the saddle." Jackson was also known for pushing his men beyond extremes, as was the case in his "foot cavalry."

43. May 22, 1862

First Sergeant Ashbel S. Fraley, Company A, 4th Regiment N.C. State Troops, diary entry. Source: Typescript, A. S. Fraley Diary, Fraley Collection, Rowan County Public Library.

The following are Fraley's thoughts on the utility and true purposes of brigade drill as recorded in his diary, with a very stout criticism of General Hill's orders of increased discipline. Once again, Fraley's sarcasm is very evident. Such criticism is found in many Civil War letters, but not in letters from later wars due to the levels of censorship that were imposed.

> 22 Brigade drill. Regular humbug! Intolerable nuisance. Its general uses.
>
> (1) To keep the men from enjoying a little rest, which they so much need:
> (2) To take out the sick men that the surgeon always refuses to excuse from duty (tho' they are scarcely able to walk) that our Cols & Gen's may have the gratification of seeing them faint & fall in the broiling sun.
> (3) To make the men careless in drill that the officers may have the pleasure of speaking to them as to negroes.
> (4) To exasperate the men beyond the endurance of patience, that they may curse & swear so the devil will reap the greater harvest in eternity.
> (5) That the Gen. and his aides may show their uniform suits; and tho' they know it not, their ignorance
>
> "0 was some power the gift to gi' us, To see oursel' as others see us; It was from many a blunder free us, And foolish notion."

This day will also ever be memorable on account of Gen. Hill's humane order to shoot southern men for losing their guns and accoutrements, and buck them for straggling. Thus they treat the southern army.

44. May 23, 1862

Private Joseph F. Gibson, Company C, 4th Regiment N.C. State Troops, letter to parents, Iredell County, North Carolina. Source: Catawba County Historical Association. Transcription courtesy of Mrs. Addie Cloninger.

Joseph Gibson, an Iredell County farmer, volunteered at age 24 on June 7, 1861, one day after James W. Gibson volunteered in Catawba County. Joseph was a member of the 4th North Carolina and was greatly fatigued and sick when he was writing this letter. Conspicuous in this letter are the privations and difficulty the regiment has in retreating up the Peninsula. The 4th Regiment, after leaving Manassas, had already been forced to march without their baggage, and to make things worse, a warehouse established for North Carolina troops serving on the Peninsula was destroyed in the campaign.[18]

Camp Near Richmond
23 May 1862
Mr. John A. Gibson, Dear Brother,
I this morning have the pleasure of writing you a few lyns to inform you that I am still in the land of the living. I have not hird from you for some time I havent received a letter from home for two months I wood have written to you some time ago but I lost my nap sack on the march and I had no paper to write on. We had a very heavy march we marched about 60 miles we marched from Yorktown to Richmond or near Richmond we are within two miles of town. The yankees followed us for ten or twelve miles tho they ar some 76 miles from this place we all came thro safe and supposed youse have hird that I was taken prisoner in the march but that was false. I was sick when we left Yorktown I went in before with the waggons and got lost from them for five or six days. I had taken the wrong road

and went on ahead of the waggons. Nat Raymir got a letter and he told me that he hird that I was taken prisoner. I dont now who it was that sent such nuse as that home.

I saw James W. Gibson the other day he was well at that time there Regiment is Camped close here they are now on pickett guard now I believe we came off our pickett guard day before yesterday. I met them going out for three days then there will by some other regiment. We have to go ten miles on pickett. This is marching back and forwards I cant tell how long this will last I hope it may not last long I hope. How soon peace may be made and we may all get home. This marching thro the mud there is no fun in it certain and sure. We havent any tents now our blankets is all the shelter now. I lost all of my close and was not able to carry my napsack and it was put in the waggon and the roads was so muddy that they had to throw the napsacks out. John A. I want you to write to me as soon as you can and let me know where Hugh S. Gibson is and where Will is I have been looking for a letter from home for some time I have wrote two letters home since I received any you will please write soon I remain the same your Brother Joseph F. Gibson.

Direct as before only to Richmond VA.

(PS) I must write a few lyns to father and mother Dear Father and Mother I will endever to try to write a few lyns to youse to let youse now that I am still on southern soil I can inform you that my helth is tolerable good at this time tho I have ween unwell for some time I hope this may find youse all in good helth I suppose youse that the yankees had taken me tho that is not the case yet I must draw to a close as my paper is out, youse must write soon to Richmond I remain the same your son Joseph F. Gibson.

45. June 3, 1862

Captain Lewis H. Webb, Company D, 12th Virginia Artillery Battalion, Diary Entry. Source: Diary of L. H. Webb, Lewis Webb Collection, Southern Historical Collection, University of North Carolina at Chapel Hill.

Since January, Webb had been serving as commander of a battery of artillery. Though in a Virginia Battalion, Webb's battery was composed of North Carolinians, and he seemed much happier to be in that unit. In this entry Webb travels into Richmond, inquires about his old command's performance during battle, and meets a friend for a meal in Richmond's Spotswood Hotel.

Tuesday, June 3d 1862.

This morning after breakfast I obtained a pass, & accompanied by my servant boy (John Russell), I went down into the City, to transact some business preliminary to drawing bounty for my men. When I arrived there I found it impossible to transact the business for which I went by reason of the excited & hurried state of affairs incident to the recent battles.

While walking up Main Street I met the brother of one of the Pee Dee Guards who told me in answer to my questioning him that Stephen Webb[19] had been wounded slightly in the thigh in the late battle. He could not tell me of any other casualties in the Company. I continued my walk and soon after ran into Col. Christie, who told me that Ben Ledbetter[20] had been wounded, but distinguished himself by his gallant bearing. Christie gave me no other information about the Pee Dee Guards, either not knowing, or not wanting to tell me. He had been hurt by the killing of his horse under him & was on the eve of starting home. I did not think his injuries justified in the slightest degree his leaving the army now, and his regiment without a single field officer & only two captains out of ten fit for duty. I have no doubt that the regiment did well—as when have North Carolinians done otherwise.

A little further up the street I met Berry H. Knight from Columbia, S. C. with the hospital stores & wounded & sick soldiers from S. C. I made an appointment to meet him at the Spotswood House, to dine, and as he was in a hurry went to do some shopping & look around the streets for other acquaintances. At ½ past 1 o'clock to the Spotswood & was joined soon after by Knight and in an hour sat down to dinner.

As an incident of the times I will state that though the Spotswood is a No. 1 Hotel, yet the fare was exceedingly meagre and on the Bill of Fare occurred this sentence: "The proprietors have furnished their table with the best that the market affords but it is impossible to procure more than the commonest food and then only in limited quantities."

After dinner I returned to camp around 4 p.m. Learning after my return that Stephen Webb who was wounded was in one of the hospitals in the City, I borrowed a horse and riding down sought for him in several, but failed to find him. He has probably gone home as his wound was slight.

How shall I attempt to describe the hospitals? I can scarcely attempt it, and yet I cannot pass by it unnoticed. Suffice, that never before had I realized the horrors of war. I saw probably 250 wounded & sick men and one poor fellow dying. In one room I saw three noble looking young men who had each lost a leg. I was forceable struck with their patient, quiet, and almost cheerful countenances. Not a groan reached my ears, not a wrinkled brow indicated the agony some of them must have felt. But words cannot convey the feelings that filled my heart when I saw the noble heroism of the ladies of Richmond. At nearly every couch stood one, who with all the gentleness and care which a mother or sister could exercise, ministered to the sufferers. May God bless them.

Afterward I returned to camp & after supper early to bed, very much weary and sorrowful.

46. June 13, 1862

Private Augustus A. Clewell, Company B, 1st Bttn, N.C. Sharpshooters, letter to his parents, Salem, Forsyth County, N.C. Source: Clewell Letters, Private Manuscripts Collection, North Carolina Division of Archives and History.

Clewell and the other men of Company E, 21st Regiment N.C. Troops, were assigned as B Company 1st Battalion NC Sharpshooters (9th NC Battalion) on April 26th, 1862, but remained part of the 21st Regiment until officially detached as a battalion and an independent unit following the battle of Winchester on May 25, 1862.[21]

June 13th 1862
Dear Parents:

It is with great pleasure that I again have the opportunity of writing you a few lines to let you know that I am well and hope that you are the same. It has been a long time since I have written or received a letter, and I doubt very much whether this will reach you. I have been in some close places since you heard from me last but so far I have escaped unhurt. At Winchester on the 25th of May we had a severe fight, but it did not last long. Our Regt had a part of only fighting three Yankee Regts, and out of about 300 about 100 were killed and wounded then for the first time I seen my comrades fall around me. Lt. Colonel Pepper[22] was shot through both hips. On Sunday the 1st day of June, we marched out to Strasburg expecting another large fight, but there was only a little skirmishing and at night we commenced falling back until we reached this side of Harrisonburg. We do not know where the Yankees are now but we know they are not far off.

We are not very far from Staunton at present but I don't know where we'll be tomorrow this time. I believe that General Jackson is one of the keenest generals in the south and I know that he is the most successful one, but he is terrible hard on his men. He very often marches them day and night but he always accomplishes his aim. I think that I shall come home on the last day of next month according to the Conscript Act, I being under 18.

I must bring my letter to a close. Don't be uneasy about me if you don't hear from me for we seldom have a chance to write. Direct your letter to Staunton to the 7 Brigade.* Give my best to Mag and all the children and tell them that I should like to hear from them. I remain your affectionate son
A. Clewell

*This a rare time when a brigade is mentioned in directions for addressing letters to soldiers in the field in the absence of a regiment or battalion designation.

47. July 2, 1862

Second Lieutenant Ashbel S. Fraley, Company A, 4th Regiment N.C. State Troops, diary entry. Source: Typescript, A. S. Fraley Diary, Fraley Collection, Rowan County Public Library.

On June 22, 1862, Sergeant Fraley was appointed to Second Lieutenant of Company A. After the bloody Seven Days battles, the 4th N.C. State Troops were assigned the task of searching the battlefield for discarded gear and gathering it for future use. Here, despite his normal disregard for his regimental officers, Fraley

is touched by a simple show of respect, and promises no more bad feelings toward his commanders in the Fourth.

July 2
4th and 5th* continue gathering up army supplies. Find great quantities scattered everywhere. Rains furiously. After finishing our labours we proceed towards Richmond and pass the battlefield of Seven Pines. Were marching right in front. When opposite the graves of those of our regiment who fell there the Col. gave the command, "On the right by file into line—March." I was inwardly cursing him for his awkwardness in placing the markers, when the evolution was completed, at the same time unable to conjecture what he was going to do. But my unpleasant feelings toward him were suddenly stopped and changed to the warmest and most solemn affection, by a very unexpected and solemn scene. We were then fronting to the grave of the killed from our regiment on the 31st of May, 74 all buried together.[23] The Col commanded, "Present arms." Then taking off his hat he said, "Fellow soldiers, there is no more fitting place to render thanks to Almighty God that we have been spared to avenge their deaths, than by the graves of those who fell by our sides fighting so gallantly for their country's rights. Let each one silently within his own heart return thanks to God that we have been permitted to live, to again see the last solemn resting place of our companions and friends."

A solemn pause ensued. The Col. like the remainder of the regiment was not a religious man, but it made the scene more affecting. "Shoulder arms" & "Left face" was commanded and we proceeded towards Richmond. Went into camp 2 miles from the City.

*Refers to North Carolina Regiments, the 4th and 5th N.C. State Troops, not to be confused with dates though they are coincidentally close to the date of the diary entry.

48. July 24, 1862

Private George A. Williams, "Cedar Fork Rangers," Company G, 7th Regiment N.C. State Troops, letter to his wife Nancy Williams, Chatam County, N.C. Source: Williams-Womble Papers, Private Manuscripts Collection, N.C. Division of Archives and History.

George A. Williams was born in 1830 in Chatam County, N.C., in a region which could be modern Durham or Wake County. On July 28, 1861, George volunteered for service in Wake County as part of the "Cedar Fork Rangers," a unit which would later be designated as company "G" of the 7th Regiment North Carolina State Troops. By July 24, 1862, the 7th Regiment belonged to a brigade under Lawrence O'Brien Branch, under the division of A. P. Hill, Jackson's Corps. [24]

Captain Reuben E. Wilson, of Yadkin County, commanded Company A of the 1st Battalion N.C. Sharpshooters at Winchester, Virginia, on May 25, 1862. (Courtesy of the Greensboro Historical Museum—1974.90.17.)

Camp near Richmond
July the 24th 1862

Dear Wife I take the pleasur of writing you a few lines this eavning to in form you that I am well now and have bin since I left Ncarolina. I have bin able to kepe up and help to cook tho I cant do any other duty. I can hop that these few limes will come to hand and find you and the family enjoying the best of health. I have nothing of importance to write. Times is quite heer at this time tho I donte now how long the will remain so untill pease is mad. Som is of the opinin that the most of the fighting is don as to my on parte I cant say tho I am in hopsital is far I am tiard of the war & I want to be home with you all and am in hopes of so.

I can in form you that this is the forth letter that I sent to you and have never receive but one from you. If you haint got enough money for the postage I will send you some then you can write me until you stop.

Dear Wife I want you to send me som soape and tobaco. Tobaco is wirth one dollar and soape 2 dollars {illegible sentence*} We have quite a desir if anything at all and whiskey is too much. I want you to tell Mr. Plesent that I am in hopes that I will get home in time a nuff to help him drink som of his cider and Brandy. So I will close nothing more and by

Private Cline's "capten," and commander of "The Catawba Braves," Company K, 46th Regiment N.C. Troops. (Courtesy of the N.C. Division of Archives and History.)

remaining your affectionate Husband untill death.

G. A. Williams

It is possible that perhaps George wanted to operate a side business, selling those items of demand to fellow soldiers.

49. July 25, 1862

Private William P. Cline, "Catawba Braves," Company K, 46th Regiment N.C. Troops, letter to his wife, Mary C. Cline, Newton, Catawba County, N.C. Source: William P. Cline Papers, Southern Historical Collection, University of North Carolina at Chapel Hill.

The 46th Regiment was posted at Camp Lee outside of Petersburg, Virginia. This letter is written after the closing of the Seven Days battles around Richmond (June 25–July 1, 1862). This is the second letter where private Cline is sending clothing and material home. William is rather offended by the price of certain goods such as "Uneons" (onions) and "Molases." He also includes a very personal post-script.

> Peters birg, state of Va
> July the 25 1862
>
> Dear Wife
>
> I take the plesur to anser your kind letter that you rote the 20 of July. I reseved it last night which gives me much plesur to hear that you was all well and fond me in good helth and I hope when these few lines come to hand may find you all in good helth. I hant got nothen now to rite at dis time. I sent my black coat and one shurt to newton and I wont you to go and git it for it has been in the box all summer. I want you to make me to culard shirts as sune as you can and I want a good warme blankit dis fall.
>
> I was glad to heare that P & R Cline was giting beter and all the boys was giting beter. Our fare is not very good and stuff is hi and we can not buy it. Lited pipe is twenty-five sents. Apels is 50 sents a dozen. Chickens is a dollar an fifty sents. Potato is $3 a bushel. Uneons is five sents a pease. You may gess that there is der eaten. Molases is five dollars a galen. I will send you five stamps in dis leter. That is all that I have got at dis time but I can git more for we are close to tone. I was in tone the uther day and I can state to you that it is a tone dat wood make too tones* like newton. I have saw lots sense I have left home. I cood tell you lots if I cood see you but I still hope that the time is comen that we will meet a gane and if we dont meet in dis world I hope that we will meet in Heaven whear part no more. If Cane Huit (?) is gone or not tell him to stay as long as he can. I got a

leter from Calvin Cline and he dont like it a redey but he dont now nothen yet. He is rite at home. I wood now talk a bout sumpthen yo sed taht wood like to see me come home but I dont now when I will git to come. I wood be as glad to see you as you wood me and I wood like to see you all. So I must come to a close. When dis you see remember me. A meny miles a part we will be I will reamin your efecten husban ontel deth so rite as soon as dis come to hand.

Peters birg, Va Camp Lee
In care of Capten Bost the
46th Regiment NC Troop
W. P. Cline to Mary Cline
[On side of bottom margin:] I would like to sleep with you one night more

*tones: towns

50. July 31, 1862

First Lieutenant Ashbel S. Fraley, Company A, 4th Regiment N.C. State Troops, diary entry. Source: Typescript, A. S. Fraley Diary, Fraley Collection, Rowan County Public Library.

Election day was often a holiday in nineteenth century America, and especially in the South. Nearly the entire county would descend on the seat to cast ballots, hear speeches from the candidates, take in a wide variety of spirits, and meet with old friends. In this entry, Fraley shows that voting rights were extended to soldiers in the army.[25]

Thursday—Election day for N. C. Soldiers, one week in advance of the time in the State. But ah! How sadly different from the elections in the "olden time." No little one-horse, two-horse, and three-horse wagons with white covers and hind gates off. No boisterous crowds and merry carousals of freemen met together to exercise a glorious and Heaven born privilege. No cavorting and praiseworthy ripshoning

around. No candid, earnest, patriotic, and incontrovertable arguments of the pugilist so wholesomely and gently administered by the fist or a bosom friend. In short, none of that pleasant and popular recreation commonly called—fist & scull fighting.

None!—But yet we had an election Voted for Governor Sheriff Senate & Commons. Candidates for Gov. Col. Wm Johnston & Col ZB Vance. Voted for Johnston with this platform on the ticket, "My unremitting prosecution of the war," the war to the last extremety; complete independence; eternal separation from the north; no abridgement of Southern territory; no alteration of Southern boundaries; no compromise with enemies, traitors, or todes." "Jeff Davis, Our Army and the South."

Eternal success to that ticket. May its voters be as numerous as the stars that deck the azure hue of Heaven.

My friend Wm F Wasson received 31 votes for Shff of Iredell, LQ. Sharpe 16 for the senate, W.P. Caldwell 32 for the commons J Young Esq 30 Thos A Allison 13 & T.N. Ramsey 2. Rainy day. Polls closed with out excitement.

51. August 5, 1862

Private John C. Pickler, "The Stanly Rebels," Company I, 52nd Regiment N.C. Troops, letter to his father. Source: Joe Pickler, New London, N.C., typed copy of featured letter in *Stanly County Genealogical Journal* in author's possession.

John Calhoun Pickler of Stanly County, N.C., enlisted as a private at age 21 on March 25, 1862. He served in Company I, "The Stanly Rebels" of the 52nd Regiment N.C. Troops. John was reported present until captured at Gettysburg, Pennsylvania, during the Pickett-Pettigrew assault on July 3, 1863. He was confined at Fort Delaware, Delaware National Prison, until October 23, 1863, when he died of "dysentery chronic."[26] During the month of August 1862 the Union Army of the Potomac was still present on the Peninsula despite its defeat during the Seven Days Campaign. Sharp skirmishes occurred between both armies during this time. Few Confederates in the area were aware that a Union army under Major General John Pope had advanced out of Northern Virginia and had engaged Stonewall Jackson's II Corps at Cedar Mountain, Virginia.

August 5 day 1862

It is with plesure that I take my pen in hand to Drop you a flew lines to let you no that I am well at this time and I hope this flew Lines may find you all well and harty. Dear father I have no muse of Import to Rite tho I will give you the Best I have at this time there are some sharp skirmishes about here on James River for we can here the cannons Evry fiew Day tho the yankeys wont come out to fight us yet I think that they Dred us tho & Dont care if they Do stay away for If they came out we will have to fight them and I Dont think that there is much fun in fighting for someone must Be killed If we fight and we cant tell who It will Be till it is tride for I wish this war would End for I am tired of camp.

Father I wood Be glad for you to come out to see me if you have the chance you can come with McCorcle[27] when he comes back you wood see more than you can Ever see in old Stanly I want to no if Palmer have paid you for them cows and if Auston have paid for them hogs I want to no how you are giting a Long with your taming lether I want to no if you got all your newgrounds in and if you got all your grass and wheat and oats cut I thought of you about harvest and wished to Be there to help you cut I want you to read this to all the children I want to no if Dock ever says Enything about me so I must clos by saying I Remain your

trew son J.C. PICKLER to Mr. R.G.D. Pickler

52. August 6, 1862

Second Lieutenant Ashbel S. Fraley, Company A, 4th Regiment N.C. State Troops, diary entry. Source: Typescript, A. S. Fraley Diary, Fraley Collection, Rowan County Public Library.

The life of a soldier is filled with orders to move. The soldier never knows quite what to make of the overall situation from questionable orders, and of having to fight the elements to obey them. Fraley compares the climate in Virginia to that of "the most scorching plains of the Sahara desert."

6—Having been notified last night; had reveille at 4 A.M. and marched 2 or 3 hours after. Went by where the balance of the brigade were throwing up breastworks. They joined us. Waited there for orders till it was good & hot, and then proceeded down the Charles City road. It was mid-day and we marched constantly; The climate seemed hotter than the most scorching plains of the Sahara desert. Therefore it was not a surprise to see occasionally a poor fellow lying by the side of the road gasping for breath; some of them never to rise again. Stopped in the evening 3 or 4 miles from Malvern Hill, and made every seeming preparation for an attack. I thought we were in for it again. And my faith was made stronger by seeing Gen. Lee, present.

Cos. A, C, F & K were detailed as skirmishers to act in concert with a corresponding number of the 2nd N.C. the whole to be under the command of Col Tew. A & C were held in reserve F & K deployed. We awaited orders to advance, and remained waiting all night and next day till 10 O'clock when we received orders to join the Brigade.

53. August 9, 1862

Private Hartwell S. Pool, "The Stanly Marksmen," Company H, 14th Regiment N.C. Troops, letter to his father, Rev. John Pool, Montgomery County, N.C. Source: Lassiter, Mable, *Pattern of Timeless Moments: A History of Montgomery County, North Carolina*, 310–311, nd.

H. S. Pool was a Montgomery County farmer and father of three when he was conscripted into service in Company H, 14th Regiment N.C. Troops, on July 16, 1862. Hartwell was reported present until he died in Charles Town, West Virginia, on November 9, 1862.[28] This letter was written two months prior to his death. Hartwell was a preacher's son. When he reached the army, what he found was a completely different world. The Confederate Army was known for its religious leaders, and for the fervor of the men toward spiritual callings; however, Hartwell does not see this during this period of service. He is surprisingly honest about his weakness and his uncertainty about the future.

> Richmond, Va. Aust. 9, 1862
> Dear father I take the opertunity of dropping you a few lines to inform you that I am well at this time and hop theas few lines may find you all agoing for the blessing of life. I got to richmond on the 7th of this instant I could not get of from this terible by no way that I could apply by no means. I have seen agreat deal sens I left hom. There is a heap of curis things in this world it loks lik the people in run away in wikness there is some few Christian hearted men in camp i think there is some good singing and praying in camp. I am within two miles of the battlefield at the seven pines the pickets run the Yankes backed to ther gunboats on Wednesday be low Petersburg They expect a battle there. I can't tell you whear I am station yet I can't tell you what I hav seen we have no Shelter but the shelter of the allmity's covring* I thank the that things is as well with me that it is. I have ben her trying to pray for grace and peace you must try to pray fer me when it gos well with you for I nead more grace to sustain me in this army for I can't tell you when I will get to come back hom in this life I want you to do the best you can with my horses if you can sell my fily do so if you think best if the old man Robin don't want it too cheep till I com back if it is thy will to bless me with so favorable blessing sell them three beefes when you can and keep the hids† I haven't got long to exspress what I hav felt and seen. Yours respectful

> Hartwell S. Pool

*Without any covering or sleeping gear

†Hids: Hides; Hartwell wants his father to sell his beef cattle and keep the hides

54. August 12, 1862

Second Lieutenant Ashbel S. Fraley, Company A, 4th Regiment N.C. State Troops, diary entry. Source: Typescript, A. S. Fraley Diary, Fraley Collection, Rowan County Public Library.

The following is an excerpt from Fraley's "Maxims of War" and is a treat for all Civil War scholars and enthusiasts. Fraley composed these maxims out of his normally dry sense of humor. The list would eventually include six statements of profound military truth. The entire list is reproduced in Appendix 2.

> 12 Aug march at any time. What now! Perhaps another Malvern Hill pleasure trip. However I am about as well prepared to write out my "maxims of war' (so admirably adhered to by our army) as I will ever be.
> 1. When you take a strong position from the enemy, leave it, and let them have it again, that you may have the fun of taking it a second time.

William M. Eddinger, George's brother and a fellow soldier in Company B, 48th North Carolina Troops, c. 1863. (Courtesy of Mr. Richard L. Conrad, Thomasville, N.C.)

2. When you are going to attack the enemy be certain to march your army 25 or 30 miles immediately preceding, so as to have your men well fatigued. Backward movements must be resorted to when you are nearer the enemy than the above named distance.

3. In the winter season, when the weather is severely cold & rainy; roads muddy, & nights dark and Cloudy, be certain to always march after night. In the summer when it is hot and sultry; especially in the month of August "when the dog Star rages" commence your march at 9 O'clock in the morning and push on without stopping till night.

Moonshiny nights make the reasons for the above maxim the stronger.

The above maxims have been deduced from actual experience, and will be continued at some future day. See the proclamation of the secretary of War of the U.S calling for 600,000 men to subjugate the south. But this does not appal us. The Liberties of the South are registered in Heaven.

I have read her destiny in the faces of her soldiers, upon their country's warfields, in the dreadful hour of battle.

55. August 16, 1862

Private George W. Eddinger, Company B, 48th Regiment N.C. Troops, letter to his wife, Mary Ann Clodfelter Eddinger, near Thomasville, Davidson County, N.C. Source: Private Collection of R. L. Conrad, Thomasville, N.C.

George Washington Eddinger (1836–1862) was the son of John and Crissila Kennedy Eddinger. George worked as a farmer, and in 1861 he married Mary Ann Clodfelter. George volunteered for service on March 8, 1862. From his time enlisting in service, it is apparent that a soldier's life is not for him. By the time of this letter, his communications bear hallmarks of depression, though he clings to his religious faith. John and Crissila Eddinger had five sons enter the war: David (Co. C, 70th NC), George, John R., Phillip, and William M. (Company B, 48th NC). Of this number, only William would survive the war. John died of typhoid fever in Richmond's Chimbarazoo Hospital, while both George and Phillip died within the county at the Thomasville Smallpox Hospital in 1862. George was wounded at Sharpsburg and was finally sent home. However, he contracted smallpox, and his life ended on December 27, 1862.[29]

Petersburg
August the 16th 1862
Dear companion I rec'd your kind letter the 15th of the present month

which found me well and I was glad to
hear that you was all well. I could not
tell you how the times are here. If I
ware to they only are hard and distresing so far as I can see. You spoke
something about sending my type back.
I will do so if I can for I just want to see
it one more time, it would I think, grat-
ify me very much. You spoke of wanting
to see me. I know that you are no more
anxous than I am to see you. I cannot
express to you how bad I want to see
you all. It does seem like it would be the
greatest satisfaction in the world to me
to be at home with you all once more
where I could tell you my troubles and
trials living the life I am now living. I
do not mean to grumble there is a
supremer being than any of us and I
wish to submit to his will who has
promised us if we do put our trust in
him we shall come out conqerors in the
end and I also want you to put your
trust in that good being, and if I never
return again he has promised good to all
of them that trust in him. A father to
the fatherless and a husband to the
widow. You can tell Mr. Osbornes[30]
mother he is in our camp with the rest
of the boys and has been very sick for
some time but is now on the mind it is
thought. You pay over to Polly for that
weaving she don for you and tell Polly
I have not forgotten them all yet. I will
bring my letter to a close by saying
write soon.

> Your affectionate husband
> until death
> George W. Eddinger[31]
> Co. B, 48th Regt of N.C.T.,
> Com. By R. C. Hill, col.

56. August 20, 1862

Second Lieutenant Ashbel S. Fraley,
Company A, 4th Regiment N.C. State
Troops, diary entry. Source: Typescript, A.
S. Fraley Diary, Fraley Collection, Rowan
County Public Library.

Aroused at daybreak. Travel till near
11 O'clock and stop at a beautiful little
Village on the Fredricksburg R.R. called
Ashland. This seems to have been a
place of pleasure and fashionable resort.
Rest here in the shady grove till about
4 O'clock when we proceed onward.
March very hard till after night. Nearly
every one was al. most exhausted with
fatigue. We laid the flattering unction to
our souls, that we again would get to
rest till morning. But alas! we hoped in
vain! We had hardly fallen to sleep
when the order came round to get the
men under arms immediately. I know it
was an impious wish. I could not help
it. For once I wished for power to
control the destinies of earth—that I
might reverse our cruel—cruel fate. It
was distressing to a sympathizing heart,
to hear the lamentations of the poor
wearied soldier, recited in simple but
feeling language of their hard lot. What
they had a moment before so vainly
hoped to enjoy. What they now more
needed than all else besides. What it was
almost death to be deprived of now. In
short, the greatest blessing that earth has
in store to give, Quiet Rest, was now
torn away by a cruel (perhaps) necessity
of war. I thought so then—and think so
now; that nothing short of immediate
danger or a surprise—overwhelming
slaughter & defeat could justify that
movement. We marched toward
Hanover Junction—passing it and going
5 or 6 miles. It was impossible for the
men to hold out. The result was, we left
the Brigade broken down, scattered
along the road. A few of us reached the
residence or a Mr. Anderson on the
Central R. R. and slept on arms until
morning.

57. August 25, 1862

Laura E. Myers, Germanton, Stokes
County, N.C., letter to her husband, First
Sergeant Adderson C. Myers, "McCullough's

Avengers," Company D, 52nd Regiment N.C. Troops. Source: A. C. Myers Papers (3653), Special Collections, Perkins Library, Duke University, Durham, N.C.

Laura and Adderson Myers were the parents of two children and made a home in Stokes County, North Carolina. Adderson worked as a farmer prior to volunteering for service on March 19, 1862. He was promoted to first sergeant on May 28, 1862.[32] Laura's letter describes the situation at home as far as agricultural sales, and also gives an interesting account of Dr. Bitting's illness.

Germanton
August 25th 1862

My dearest husband,

I received a letter by William Matthews & is the last I have received. I have not got one for some time before that. You said you were sick which I was sorry to hear. I am afraid you are not able to write. How are you are you any better or worse. I want to know if you get no better try and come home. Write if you can and if not get some friend to write it for you. I am so afraid you will be ordered away from there. We are all well and getting along very well.

I have sold your tobacco for twenty dollars per hundred to J. A. Bitting.[33] He will come after it tomorrow. He sent after it once before but it was too dry to move and it is now a wet spell. I wrote to him to come after it. I am looking for the thrashing machine this week and then I will write to you how much wheat we will make not much I think. I don't think I think the corn crops will be tolerable. I think you had do well let your father know about the land and what you will do if you come home next spring. I don't think this war will end some time yet . I have got out of all patience in waiting for it. Oh my dear husband, I do want to see you!

Do you remember the last time I wrote to you about Dr. Bitting[34] going over the mountain. He has never been here to stay since he went over to the spring last week to stay and they sent after his folks last Tuesday to come after him. They say it took ten men to get him in the waggon he came through here about 12 oclock Saturday. They said he kept turning his head about. He had not a particle of sense the night they took him home. He tried to jump out of the window. He has dropsy and is swollen very much so much so he cannot bend down. You have seen him the last time.

My dear husband I would be so glad to see you. It seems to me it has been a year or two since you left. If there is any way or chance I will try and send you some socks and something to eat. I do not believe Mr. Vaughn is going at all. They say the 21st Reg is lousy. They are full of body lice. Do try to keep them off yourself. You will have to be very carefull to keep clear of them. Little Matthew says tell Papa to come home. Write often to your ever true and devoted wife,

Laura E. Myers

58. September 2, 1862

Second Lieutenant Ashbel S. Fraley, Company A, 4th Regiment N.C. State Troops, diary entry. Source: Typescript, A. S. Fraley Diary, Fraley Collection, Rowan County Public Library.

After the victory at Second Manassas, the Confederate army was on the move. Anderson's North Carolina Brigade did not participate in the battle as they began to arrive the first of September, but they did view the chaos and the aftermath. Once again, Fraley expresses his opinion about General Hill.

Rained on us last night. Nothing for breakfast this morning. A hungry soldier thinks of good things to eat at home, and then wishes to be there. Clear—cold

and windy. March a mile and draw
1 day 5 rations of flour & 4 oz of fresh
beef to a man, and are allowed I hour
to cook it. Hour expires—rations not
half cooked, but have to go—eat it raw.
Pass over the battle field of Saturday.
Great number of Yankees are scattered
over the woods and along the road,
stiff swollen and black in death. Their
loss must have been fearful. Leave the
Warrenton & Alexandria turnpike and
travel across the country in the direction
of Leesburg till we strike the Leesburg
& Alexandria turnpike and travel
towards Alexandria till we are with in
7 miles of Fairfax C.H. Nearly the
whole Brigade break down & fall out by
the roadside. March till about 9
O'clock. I suppose Gen. Hill could not
hold out to ride any further, and so he
had to stop. Had it not been for this the
Lord only knows when we would have
stopped.

59. September 3, 1862

Private John W. Armsworthy, "The
Western Rangers," Company H, 54th
Regiment N.C. Troops, letter to his wife,
Edna Armsworthy. Source: Private Col-
lection, Mr. Bob Furches, Clemmons,
N.C.

John Wesley Armsworthy was 32 years
old when the war intruded upon his life.
This Yadkin County farmer lived in the
Forbush township with his wife, Edna, and
their three children, Levi (7), Ella (4), and
Mat (1). Armsworthy enlisted on April 17,
1862.[35] Some of his first duties included
cooking for the officers' mess. In this first
selection, Armsworthy talks about the aftermath of the battle of Second Manassas and
the humorous incident where the coat of
the Union commander was captured. At
the time of this letter, the 54th and 57th
North Carolina Regiments were in Virginia; however, they had not yet been
placed in a brigade.

Camp Stokes Va. Sept. 3rd 1862
Dear Wife

I seat myself to write you a few lines
to let you know where & how I am. We
are stationed five miles north of Richmon on the Gordonville Road, very
pretty here & good water. I am well &
well sadisfied & I hope when these few
lines come to hand may find you & all
the family & friends enjoying the same
blessing. I have seen a great many things
since I left home & I can say I am well
sadisfied with this country. We are not
as close to the Yankees here as we was at
Kinston but I expect we will go on to
Jackson. He is giving the Yankees fits.
He has got old Generel Poop[36] coat &
flag in the capital at Richmon but they
did not get him. Jackson sent a good
many prisaers to Richmon a few days
ago & they expect a big battle at Man-
asees if the Yankees dont run. There is a
great many trope going on. The Georgia
Cavelry past here today. They looks like
they would make them get furder. I
today that the Yankees was leaving
washington Citty & Jackson was in sight
of the Citty. We have had a very good
time since I have been in camp. I wrote
you a few lines the other day for I did
not know how we going & before I
could finish it the male started so I made
it short. I have seen some of Capt.
Speers company that was taken
prisner.[37] They say they was in New
York. They say they had to work hard
while they was there. Jack Melton is in
the hospital sick. I did not see any of
them that I was aquainted with but
some of our company was. Tell Isace
Logan that Soloman Phillips is in this
Regt. & is well, he is Drummer. I have
got acquanted with a great many persons
since I have been here. I think I have
got some good friends here so I think
I far just as well here as any company
I could have got in. Tell Isace Logan
I want him to write to me soon & I
want you to tell all my folks I would be

William Steele was a private in Company A, 33rd N.C. Troops, until he died of disease at home in Iredell County on May 10, 1862. He was attended by Dr. John Shaffner. (Courtesy of the N.C. Division of Archives and History.)

glad to here from them all If M.B. Chafin comes to Richmond on any business I want him to come to the camp. I dont want any more clothes except a Wesctoat if the pants come. I must bring my letter to close. Write soon. Direct your letters Richmon 54th Regt. Company H in care of Capt Cockram.

Your Husband untill Death
J. W. Armsworthy

60. September 7, 1862

Dr. John F. Shaffner, Surgeon, 33rd Regiment N.C. State Troops, letter to Carrie Fries, Salem, Forysth County, N.C.

Source: Shaffner Papers, Private Manuscripts Collection, North Carolina Division of Archives and History.

Dr. Shaffner's medical career in the Confederate service was varied. The doctor started out as an assistant surgeon in the 11th N.C. Volunteers from June until November 1862, when he functioned very briefly as an assistant surgeon in the 29th North Carolina Troops. On March 5, 1862, Shaffner was promoted to surgeon and was transferred to the 33rd North Carolina Troops. Shaffner won the respect of the 33rd for exposing himself to the enemy's fire in order to administer aid to wounded on the battlefield. He was captured in such an action on May 5, 1862, at Hanover Court House, but was exchanged shortly after. [38] At the battle of Second Manassas, Dr. Shaffner saw the action of the battle first hand as surgeon for Branch's Brigade.

Frederick City,
September 7th 1862

My dear Friend,

Once more I am permitted an opportunity of sending you a letter. We have been from any mailable location so long, that no chance of sending occurred until now. By my heading you will perceive that we are at last in My Maryland. The events of the past three weeks would require much time to describe. I cannot do so fully, but will endeavor briefly. When last I wrote it was to Miss Mollie, this day three weeks ago, from Rapidan River, near Orange, C. H. We remained there a few days, 'then started in pursuit of the enemy. We reached Rapphannook River but found the enemy across, and his batteries commanded every available ford, we moved rapidly higher up, but with vigilance he followed us. A few days were thus lost to us. The following Sunday witnessed a severe Artillery duel across the river, our Brigade supported several batteries. We had a few men killed and wounded. Monday morning at four we started on a rapid march and by ten at night had accomplished more than 28 miles. No one knew whither we were going, but all knew that Jackson was aiming a bold blow in some direction. Four o'clock Tuesday morning we were again on the tramp, and had not proceeded far before we reached Salem, a town on the Manassas Gap Road. Here I first had an idea of our proposed destination. With Broad Run station, through Thoroughfare gap, Hay Market, Gainesville, and by night the head of our column had possession of Manassas Junction. Here after a short engagement, we captured immense stores, consisting of provisions and equipments, also some 6 or 8 pieces of Artillery. We had had nothing to eat for 24 hours, and here we found abundance including many delicacies. Our men suplied themselves with all they could carry, all captured wagons were loaded, and the remainder was then burned. Our Brigade got about $25,000 worth of Medicines—I got two horses. Wednesday night we marched upon and took Centerville. There we rested until noon, when we commenced our march backward. Jackson had about 20,000 men—the enemy in large force under Pope, lay between us and Longstreet to intercept us. McClellan with an immense army was marching upon us from Washington.—About four o'clock Thursday evening the battle opened, and raged furiously until about 10 o'clock. All was quiet for the night. Neither side had gained any advantage.

Friday all day the battle raged, yet

Major Pfohl, an officer in the 21st North Carolina and a personal friend of Shaffner. Pfohl survived the campaigns of 1862. (Image from Clark's *Regiments.* Courtesy of the N.C. Division of Archives and History.)

still against tremendous odds, we held our own. Longstreet should have arrived Friday morning but where was he? Would he come in time? Could we hold out until then? These painful questions occurred to me hundreds of times. Late Friday evening the distant "boom-boom" of cannon was heard upon our right.—We all understood it.—A Joyous shout rose from our lines—"Longstreet has come," "Longstreet has come," was the universal exclamation of delight. He had indeed arrived with 30,000 fresh troops. Soundly we slept that night. All must be well on the morrow.—By early dawn the fight was renewed—& before sunset we remained victors on the field of Manassas, rendered famous a second time. The confused and routed masses of the enemy were rapidly falling back upon Washington. Many prisoners were taken, thousands of small arms, a number of cannon and many other stores. His dead and wounded literally covered the ground. Sunday we employed in burying the dead, caring for the wounded.—I had plenty to do, being the Brigade Surgeon.

Monday evening we had another fight near Farifax C. H., which resulted again in our favor. Our loss in this series of engagements will not exceed 5,000. The enemy admit 15,000.

In the 21st, Col. Fulton was killed, Major Graves painfully, but not mortally wounded, Lts. Jackson & Owens killed, Capt. Hadly & Lt. Miller wounded in hands. Sergt. Shepperd wounded. Sergt. Copeland, Donell Wright, Old town Gus Butner killed—none other that I have learned. Sam is unhurt also Capts Pfohl and Miller. Col. Hoke is wounded in hand, our two remaining Captains also wounded. We lost quite severely, being engaged in every fight.* General Pender was slightly wounded, but is now with his Brigade. General Ewell lost a leg, and is reported in Critical condition. General Trimble wounded.

On Friday we crossed the Potomac into Maryland & yesterday occupied this city, which has a population of some 12,000. The people are mostly glad to see us & hail us as deliverers. We have certainly made a tour of conquest, the most remarkable in history. Our troops are enthusiastic & under Lee and Jackson invincible. Will not our enemy now make peace? Must we again & Jackson demonstrate our invincibility? Time will show. I sent the receipt for pills to your mother, but fearing they may not have reached you, I will give it again extemporaneously. Perhaps the two differ slightly but their effect will be the same: Blue Mass—60 grains, Calomel—30 grains, Rhubarb—20 grains. Make it into 30 pills of which one to two make a dose.

Please give my kindest regards to your parents and Miss Mollie. Also to the others of the family. I would write more but time presses. We know not our destination, but think its onward. Address letters to Gordonsville. Let me enjoin upon all to take good care of yourselves & remain well. Surely our prospects are bright enough now to give joy to every heart. If I could communicate with loved ones at home more frequently than our opportunities allow, I would be better pleased. I am quite well. Write early as convenient, and believe me as ever

Yours most truly
J. F. Shaffner

*All officers in the 21st North Carolina Troops

61. September 8, 1862

Captain William G. Morris, 37th Regiment N.C. Troops, letter to his family, Dallas, Gaston County, N.C. Source: Mr. Charles Daniel Wilson, Dallas, N.C., and the letters of William G. Morris, William G. Morris Collection, Southern Historical Collection, Wilson Library, University of North Carolina at Chapel Hill.

William Groves Morris worked as a carpenter lived with his wife, Louisa Costner, and their children, Margaret, Mary, Charles, Catharine, and Sarah, in the Dallas township of Gaston County, North Carolina. Morris volunteered for service in Company H and was elected as second lieutenant. Upon Rankin's promotion to major, Morris was promoted to captain of the Company on March 20, 1862. Only four months later, Morris was promoted to major in July of 1862. In the following letter, Morris describes the invasion of Maryland as a member of A. P. Hill's Division, discussing casualties at Manassas, the Maryland Confederate volunteers, the bounty of coffee and sugar, and the importance of the campaign. What makes the letters from

Morris even more interesting is that unlike most field officers, he is not a planter, a professional soldier, lawyer, or even a politician, but a middle-class carpenter, an occupation which was scarce among the officer class of the Confederate Army.[39]

Fredrick City, Maryland
Sept 8th 1862
Dear Companion & Famely

I am well for which I am thankful to God & I hope when these lines reaches you they may find you all well as can be expected. I have Droped several Lines to you in the Last 10 Days but for fears that they may not reach you I will Drop a Short letter this morning as I Know you are very anxious to hear from me & I fear you may fret yourself too much about my safety. If I could fool satisfied that you children could reconcile your Selves to what might befall me I could be better satisfied as I think that I am in Discharge of as high a Duty as I could be intrusted with. As far as I an concerned I am willing to Leave the Result of my fate in the hands of God. I could be very happy to see you & our Sweet Little Children & I trust & prey that the time is not far Distant when I will be permitted to sit Down together by the fireside as in Days past & gon.

Since we Left Richmond I have been in Several fights—victorious in every one, Driving the enemy before us from Orrange courthouse Va 18 miles north of Gordonsville to this Point, a Distance of some 150 miles. To be shure we had some hard times. I have been in 3 or 4 hard fights at & Neare Manasses, Loosing some of my best men. I had Jas H Fits killed on friday the 20th of August, Allso Robt S. McGinnas, Wm Ford & Nathan Reynolds wounded. On the lst of Sept we had a fight neare fairfax courthouse. I was struck with a shell which knocked me Down but did Not hurt much. My Loss at this place was Alfred Rhyne Killed, Jacob Costner &

George Beem wounded. Beem had his Leg cut off above his knee. Costner was Struck with a minie Ball in the left side of his neck, passing through his neck and came out below his Right nipple. I am feafrull that Costner & Beem will not Recover. I talked with Jacob next morning before I left. He was perfectly Resigned. I have not hurd from then since.[40]

Deare companion God has been Mercifull to me in Giving me health & protecting me in the hour of battle for which I am truly thankfull. Let us trust in him as he has Life & Death in his hands. May he give us Grace to Beare us up under our sore trials. If you think best you may hire Bill for 2 or 5 months more as you best Judge. I cannot say how Long we will stay at this place as Jackson keeps his plans to himself & sometimes starts to march One Direction & turns around & Goes a differant Direction. I Guess he has the yankeys rather by the horns. I suppose they have Left Baltimore.

The Citizens heare are fighting among themselves. 600 Marylandors came to our flag since we came to this Place. This is a Delightful country. We find many Friends heare. Everything is Cheep, Coffee 55 ct pr lb, shugar 11 ct, Milk & Butter to Give to soldiers. We have a bad chance to Guet out to Guet such things.

Deare famely I suppose you would be truley Glad to see me come home but Let us beare a Little Longer. This is an important crices. Now is the pinch, we have the Enemy Terabley Frightened. Thousands of them will never fight us as well as they have done after being Defeated so often. We have fought them every time with a Less number than they had but they Never Drove our men 1 inch but was Repulsed themselves & Driven miles, being terabley Disorganised. Several of the Prisoners told me that there Men would not half of them fight us. I would like to Give you a full history of all our fights but I have but little time to wright. You may Believe allmost anything you see in the Papers about our fights because they Cannot make it much worse than it really is on the Enemy, they are Badly whiped.

Your Husband,
W. G. Morris

62. September 11, 1862

Second Lieutenant Ashbel S. Fraley, Company A, 4th Regiment N.C. State Troops, diary entry. Source: Typescript, A. S. Fraley Diary, Fraley Collection, Rowan County Public Library.

Confederate authorities believed that an expedition into Maryland would rally the citizenry in support of the South; however, this proved not to be the case. Particularly interesting in this entry is the way Fraley describes the looks and attitudes of the Maryland citizens he comes in contact with.

(Thursday) Leave camp early. Pass through Frederick City—a place of 10,000 inhabitants. Some little Southern feeling shown—but very little. Tried to create some enthusiasm with our Reg. Band but succeeded badly. Took the pike, round to Hagerstown road passed through a little village called Fairview and over the Cockaton Mountains. We next came to another village called Middletown from its situation between the Cockaton Mountains & the Blue Ridge. Here the people seemed Union to the core. All ages & sexes looked as if they had been practicing ugly sour & unpleasant looks for months—perhaps since the war commenced—and this morning reached a state of perfection, incredable and surprising. I saw some old fellows looking as grim & terrible as Satan on his

dreaded throne, surrounded by all the regal splendors of sulphuric majesty, when he had just heard that a great revival was going at a big camp meeting. Reached the Blue Ridge and took up camp for the night. After eating supper and attending to all my duties in camp, I had made my bed (consisting of an oil cloth & Blanket) and tired as I was I anticipated a sweet night's rest. But again that *hated* order came to 'fall in to move the Reg. at once" We hurriedly packed our knapsacks, and moved up the side of a steep mountain near by so as to give us an advantageous position, if we should be attacked—when we slept on our arms—and slept in spite of rain till morning.

63. September 22, 1862

Private John W. Armsworthy, "The Western Rangers," Company H, 54th Regiment N.C. Troops, letter to his wife, Edna Armsworthy. Source: Private Collection, Mr. Bob Furches, Clemmons, N.C.

Three weeks since Armsworthy's last letter, the 54th Regiment was still unassigned and stationed at Richmond, Virginia. John has just received a pay ration and is anxious to settle his debts back home. The end of the letter asks the question: "Did Howard kill Foster?"

Sept 22nd 1862 Richmon Va
Dear wife I Rec. yours of the 13th just yesterday & was happy to here that you and the children was all well. Your letter found me well & this leaves me the same. I was sorry to here that Aunt Edney was unwell. I have Received three letters from you & one from father is all since I left home. You stated you had sent four letters. I have Rec. Three, you have got all I have writen. We arrived here last evening. I do not know what is the name of the Camp. It is about 2 & half miles form Richmon on the road

from Richmon to Drurah* Bluff. I do
not know how long we will stay here. I
dont expect many days. We may haft to
go to Williamsburg. They have been
fiting there & have cut our forces bad or
that is the Ruiner.† In camp I have been
looking for a letter from uncle Mathew
but have not seen it. I want him to
write. You said you got the money I
sent you but did not state the amount.
I want you to pay Isom Bayty that note
I owe him. I have got my wages from
the time I volinteered up to the first of
July wich made $26.76 there 2 months
wages that will be Drawn in a few days
that will $22.00 & when I draw that I
send you some more if I have a good
chance.§ I want all my debts paid if you
think you wont need the money. If
there is any thing sold at Mats sale that
you want buy it let it Bring what it will.
I would be glad to be there. I could tell
you more in one hour than I could
write in a day. I want you to write to
me how the corn crop is & what Uncle
thinks you better do to fatten more hogs
than will do you or to sell them. I want
you to be sirtan to prepar anuf for you
& the children for twelve months if you
think you wont have corn anuf engage it
soon. I dont write this because I think
uncle Mathew will do all he can, it is
because I want to know what arrangements is made. I wrote to father the
other day to tell uncle Mathew to do as
he thought best with the colt if Loggans
will not take him for his Fred. You can
direct your letters as before & they will
come if we move from here soon.

I will write as soon as we get
stationed. I guess there is more
confusion there than is here. They are
very calm here, if they were called on to
fire, I think we would do it quite chirful
or they talk that way. I must bring my
letter to close. I dont know of any thing
more that would interest you & dont
that what I have wrote will for is so
scattered but you must excuse me for

I have a bad chance this morning. Write
soon & often give me all the news. You
did not say whether Howard kild Foster
or not. I suppose he did if he shot the
boddy so no more at present but
Remain Your

Husband untill Death
J. W. Armsworthy to
E. J. Armsworthy

*Drewery's Bluff
†Rumor
§Equates to a pay ration of eleven dollars a month

64. September 21, 1862

T. M. Shoffner, Jamestown, N.C., let-
ter to Gov. Z. B. Vance, Raleigh, N.C.
Source: A. L. S. Governor's Papers (Vance),
North Carolina Division of Archives and
History.[41]

Alamance County native T. M. Shoffner was exempt from service while working
at the Jamestown Arms factory in Guilford
County, N.C. Shoffner, nervous about
his exemption status, requests some kind
of assurance that if he returns home he
will not be conscripted into Confederate
service.

Jamestown N. C.
September 21st 1862
Venerable Sir I desir to lay my former &
present course befor you hopeing you
will be so kind as to answer me and tell
me what I may depend on in regard to
the subject which I shal hear address you
upon. Sir I am a native citizen of the
county of Alamace & early last spring at
the request of Mr. Jils Meaban[42] one of
the representatives of our county I toke
stepes to rais a companey for sirvis &c
was joined in that efort by Mr. G. M.
Albright[43] & had elisted men to the
amount required to give me a commi-
sheon but not a sufficient number for
a ful company when I was sent for by
Messrs Mendenhall Jones & Gardner to
worke for them in thear gun mansfac-

toring esstablishnent near Jamstown N. C.[44] I then had to give up my companey & Mr. Albright who assisted me in raising it becum the captain of the companey he is now in the armey & I have bin imployed by Messrs Meridenhall Jones & Gardner from that time on. It is sum distance from my place of imployrnent to my residence in the county of Alamance though I make it a rule to go home to my famely once a month & have never yet been malested on my way to or from home

But thear has bin men arrested on thear way to home & to this place & tooke to the army & put in sirvis, this has all occured since the inroleing of the conscrips.

I would have had no objection to going in the armey if I could have went last Spring when I had the chance of being capten of a companey but after having maid up a companey I would be very reluctan to have to go now as a privet when I had the chance of a more honorable persition which I would have held had. it not have bin that I was put on another Duty

Now Sir as thear seams to be no bounds to the Milatary arthoroty I wish to know wheather or not I may Expect your protection if I should be arrested when on my way home & back to this place. The time that I loose is but very little as this establishment is near the N. C. railroad and I can go the most of the way by railroad.

And the arthoretys of the confederat stats has saw fit to exemp men from Military service who were imployed in manufactoring fire arms for the goverment. I thearefore would prefur to remain at my present vocation.

T. M. Shoffner

65. September 26, 1862

Calvin H. Wiley, Greensboro, Guilford County, N.C., letter to Gov. Z. B. Vance, Raleigh, N.C. Source: A. L. S. Governor's Papers (Vance), North Carolina Division of Archives and History.

Calvin Wiley (1819–1887)[45] was the State Superintendent of Schools in 1862. Prior to holding this position he graduated from the University of North Carolina in 1840 and worked as a newpaper editor in Oxford, N.C., and a novelist. In 1850 he returned to Guilford County, where he sought election to the legislature with educational improvement as his primary goal. This letter shows the complicated nature of the educational system as it existed along with the state's war effort.

Greensboro, N.C.
Septr 26th 1862

It is my duty to inform you that the annual meeting of the State Educational Association will be held in Linclonton on Tuesday the 14 of October, Commencing at 7 o'clock, P. M.—By reference to the Acts of Assembly, Session of 1860–61. Chap. 20 you will see that the Association is incorporated, with a small annual appropriation to enhance its utility—& that to prevent abuses of its privileges certain safeguards are thrown around it, & among other provisions, its annual meetings are to be made known—Sept. 5th fifteen days in advance to the President & Directors of the Literary Fund Permit me to say that all the provisions of the Act were proposed by myself, & that having solely in view the permanent good of the State, I desired to make the State Educational Association an efficient agency to that end; & while adding to its means & powers for that purpose, to guard zealously against their perversion—Allow me, also, to add, that nothing would afford me greater pleasure than a careful personal examination, on the part of the Chief executive Magistrate of the State, & of the Members of the Legislature, of the various means & appliances adopted by the Superintendent of Comn-Schools to harmonize, combine & advance all the educational interests of North-Carolina—. The first annual meeting of its character, after the acceptance of its charter in 1861, is to be held in the midst of one of the most terrible wars of modern times; but as the struggle, on the part of our people, is for the most sacred rights of civilized man, no statesman can fail to see the infinite importance of developing those moral elements which constitute the true greatness & happiness of nations—

Unless the present generation be morally great it is in danger of being overcome by the physical forces which it is creating, on a vast scale, for its defence and if the successors of the present race are ignorant & vicious how long will they enjoy the liberty won for them by priceless sacrifices of life, hardship & treasure? Besides: the War forced on the Confederate States of America by a proud & pharisaical enemy is one which boldly inpugns before the whole Christian world, the civilization of our country. We are charged, before the Bar of Nations, with being an inferior people—necessarily inferior from a social system which, it is falsely alleged, is inimical to the development of moral power. We are appealed to by every consideration which can influence our pride, our patriotism & our manhood to vindicate our character by diligent & ceaseless care in nourishing all the sources of inner national life, by keeping alive or rendering more & more efficient all the moral agencies of Society, & refusing to sacrifice for any illusive exigency of the moment the rights of freemen. If we will do this, building always on the Divine Law, & properly seeking Divine protection, we never can be conquered by an external power—for physical force can never overcome moral power which is in its nature eternal in duration & infinite in resources—External power may wound—it is the failing of inner life that causes death—these are very plain truths—yet in the confusion & weakness of the times many are in danger of being carried away by those old plausible errors which assume that the interests of freedom require its own destruction for the present. Your Excellency, called in the Providence of God, by an overwhelming popular vote, to preside over the destinies of a State most distinguished of all the Confederate sisters for promising elements of moral strength, cannot fail to see what an immensity of good may now be accomplished by the blessing of Heaven, by encouraging words from your high position—your fellow-citizens universally confide in your wisdom & honesty, & will respect your opinions; & while you are thus placed, behold the best interests now trembling in the balance in this glorious land of our birth; Other States boast of their materials resources, their great staples from a teeming soil, & of their commercial advantages: Nature, apparently more harsh, but really more generous to N. Carolina, locked up her material interests & gave the key to science. We could not be rich until we were morally great—discovering this great truth a few years ago, every hill & valley, every mountain top & bog & swamp was lighted up with the cheerful radiance of a vast system of schools, & guided by these the iron tracks of commerce, & agricultural & mining enterprize were pervading the state—Most of all, in these Schools was, under God, created & enlarged that love for N. Carolina, that respect for her character, & that enthusiasm at the mention of her name which have made her sons the heroes of this war in every great battle from Bethel to the hills of Maryland.

You cannot contemplate, without emotion, the possible drying up of the chief earthly source of so much good in the past & of such inestimable promise in the future to a State clear to you & to me as the place of our birth & the repository of the bones of our fathers—dear from the varied & beautiful scenery with which God has diversified its face, & the benignant climate in which he has placed it—dear from the memory of past generations of free, modest & kindly men—dear to us on account of the sneers & slanders of its enemies, & for the battles we have fought in defence of its honor—

Please excuse the feeling with which I write & the length of a letter much longer than I intended when I began it—As I wrote I became impressed with a deep sense of the importance of the position which you now occupy—& ever feeling my own responsibility to God & to future generations I felt that I could not discharge my conscience by saying less than I have—No one can estimate the responsibilities of those now occupying influential positions in the Confederate States; & as the interests of education in N. Carolina have been partly committed to my care I am ever fearful that I shall not act up to the dignity & the wants of this great crisis—I do not pretend to think that I can enlighten you as to your duties.

My great concern is to use the position God has given me to maintain the right—You know as well as I do that every state always contains an element opposed to its true greatness: an element that would, on various plausibles pretexts, repress the elevation of the masses to preserve, in fact, a perpetual ascendancy for itself—This class will now be busy among us; & the people, led off from the real issue, by suggestions of necessity, may permit a deadly blow to be stuck at this future welfare before they know it—

Entertaining no doubt of your sentiments—Knowing that you understand the real dangers of the times, & that you belong to that class who would

rather see equals in a free intelligent & prosperous population, than hold hereditery rule over a poor, ignorant & vicious people, I can freely call on you to utter, from your high place, sympathetic words of encouragement to the great cause of education in this State. We cannot expect you to attend the coming meeting of our association—but may we not count on your sympathy & cooperation in our Counsels for the good of dear old North-Carolina?[46]

66. September 26, 1862

Second Lieutenant Ashbel S. Fraley, Company A, 4th Regiment N.C. State Troops, diary entry. Source: Typescript, A. S. Fraley Diary, Fraley Collection, Rowan County Public Library.

Since the 14th of September, Lieutenant Fraley had been ill. He traveled with the army in field hospitals and in wagons reserved for the sick and wounded. On September 26, 1862, the Confederate wounded were removed from Shepherdstown, West Virginia, and transported south. Lt. Fraley died of typhoid fever at Methodist Hospital in Staunton, Virginia, on October 14, 1862. His body was returned and buried in Unity Church Yard in Rowan County, North Carolina.[47]

As to the sick I hardly know what to say about them. Those that were least sick generally made most fuss. So with the wounded too. Some would lie down and groan like a dying horse for half the night because they could not get a cup of coffee. Others could put any possum in Christendon to the blush on grinning. As we grew better the ladies attention diminished, and we were left to bread & beef and beef-soup. All of the worst kind. We were attended by a citizen physician—Dr Lagle—from the country. We also had a hospital steward and ward master. Neither of which were medical men. The former was a clever man—the latter a perfect jackass. During my sickness here there was some heavy hard fighting done by the two armies in Maryland & Va.—but I have not been able to gather many particulars. Ours is now again in Va. higher up the Potomac. I have been surrounded for several days by the enemy. 200 cavalry have possession of Shepherdstown. They have not molested any of the sick in the Hospital. However to day our pickets have taken possession of the town for the purpose of trying to get some of the sick & wounded to Winchester. Late in the evening I was very much surprised by the unexpected appearance of my brother Dr. J.R. Fraley of the 4th Reg. who has come to try to get me away, with a train of ambulances. We started after night & traveled 7 or 8 miles—a safe distance— in side of our own pickets—and encamped for the night in the road.

67. September 27, 1862

John Thompson, Thompsonville, Rockingham County, N.C., letter to Gov. Z. B. Vance. Source: A. L. S. Governor's Papers (Vance), North Carolina Division of Archvies and History.

With so many men gone to conscription, abuses in exemptions were very common. Here Mr. Thompson (1799–1881) makes the governor aware of several he knows of in an adjoining county. Thompsonville was in the corner of Rockingham County and had easy access to Caswell, Alamance, and Guilford counties. In the opinion of Johnston, who edited a volume of the Vance Papers, the situations Thompson describes seem to fit Alamance County better than either of the other two.

Thompsonville N. C.
Sep 27 / 62
I have lately returned from a trip in an adjoining County and have been informed of so many cases of men trying to avoid doing their duty to our common country under cover of the exemption Law—this as well as what I know in my own county has induced me to write you a few lines on this subject, not that I would presume to dictate to you, but believing that you cannot know the conduct of men in different Localities unless you were informed on the subject. I take the liberty to address you on this subject hoping that there might be some way to bring all such men to a sense of their duty and their interest in the great struggle now going on for the procurement of the Liberties of our oppressed and outraged people. I know some several men who are pretending to make Salt Petre for the Government and are claiming exemption from military duty on that account, and the whole company of six men dont make 12 lbs a month I know several men who are also claiming the same on account of age Some claim to be under 18 and some over 35 so as not to be subject to the conscript act and no measures have been instituted to correct these abuses I know also several Post Master who should be in the Army stout able bodied healthy men who are glorying in their exemption whose places could be as well or better filled by men too old for service. I know also several men who are pretending to carry on Government shops—Making shoes and guns of various other things who are no workman and have given large premiums to get employment to save them from the Army. "There is a Screw loose in the government Waggon some where" and it ought to be examined we want Patriotic men in office who will know their duty and perform it fearlessly and who are not Partizans or Speculators

There is the most Heartless speculation going on in the prime necessaries of life, in Leather shoes, in cotton Yarn and Domestic cloth, and many other articles, which the Poor are compelled to have or suffer, and it is high time our authorities had taken some action to regulate these things, this is, if not a military necessity at least a civil one and one of deep interest to many of our People.

I Hope that you will excuse me for these suggestions and would father say that you will find me always ready to aid in correcting any abuse of law or privilege when called upon so far as I have authority or may receive instructions to do so.

J. Thompson

68. September 29, 1862

John P. Nissen, Esq., Manufacturer, Waughtown, Forsyth County, N.C., letter to Gov. Z. B. Vance, Raleigh, N.C. Source: A. L. S. Governor's Papers (Vance), North Carolina Division of Archives and History.

John P. Nissen was a member of the House of Commons from Forsyth County in 1862 and had run on the Vance Ticket. While as a member of the 1860 convention, he was seen as a "Union man." Nissen, who held a government contract, wanted to put all doubts aside and refute the claims of W. J. Yates, editor of the *Charlotte Western Democrat*, that he was a vile traitor and could not be trusted. Here Nissen requests the name of the author of an offensive letter; however, Vance knew nothing about the letter and was encouraged by Nissen's tenacity.

Waughtown N. C. Sep 29. 1862
Recently I learned that some insidious sneaking, Scoundrel had written a letter to Gov. Clark assailing me in a most false & slanderous manner impeaching my loyalty as a southern man and insisting that I should forthwith be deprived of the government Contract which myself & Son have to furnish wagons etc, for the Army. On hearing of this I at once went to Raleigh to see your Excellency & get the name of the writer but finding you absent from the city, I called on Genl Martin who handed me a copy of the letter without any name which he had received from the Governor dated August the 11 hence he was unable to furnish me with the authors name. I pronounced the charges contained in it of disloyalty to the South as a wicked and malicious falsehood in every Shape, Shade & manner & I desire to get the authors name, I have no doubt it was one of the miserable lying dogs who were assailing me while a candidate last summer and whom I denounced all over the county of Forsythe as unprincipaled & lying Scoundrels. In which I was sustained by a majority of upwards of five hundred of my fellow citizens, Some one of these miserable whipped dogs, smarting under the castigation which I gave them & the triumphant manner in which I have been Sustained, by as inteligent & as patriotic a people as the South contains, now secretly injuring my private business, & for this purpose writes this false & lying letter to Gov Clark.

I feel it due to my character and to my constituents whom he assails in assailing me, to respect fully ask of you the kindness to furnish me with the writers name & a copy of the letter, which I presume is on file in your office.

John P. Nissen
Nissen Wagonworks,
Waughtown

69. September 29, 1862

Third Lieutenant James A. Graham, "The Orange Guard," Company G, 27th Regiment N. C. Troops, Winchester, Virginia, letter to his father, William A. Graham, Orange County, N.C. Source: The James A. Graham Papers 1861–1864,

Southern Historical Collection, University of North Carolina at Chapel Hill.

The battle of Sharpsburg was a watershed in North Carolina military history. Lt. Graham's regiment, along with the 48th North Carolina, the 46th North Carolina, and the 3rd Arkansas, was assigned to the command of Gen. Van H. Manning. At the time Graham wrote his father with this account of the battle, Confederate forces had abandoned their Maryland incursion and had fallen back to the safety of Northern Virginia.

Camp Near Winchester, Va.
September 29th 1862
MY DEAR FATHER

I received your very welcome letter of 14th inst, two days ago enclosing the letter to Gen. Jackson, which I will hand to him if we are camped anywhere within reach of him again. We were within about a mile of his camp all last week near Martinsburg, but we were moved down here two days ago and I do not know where his corps is camped now. Speaking of my getting a higher position I think that our Colonel stands a very good chance for promotion to a Brig. Gen'ship, as there are several vacancies now, and I feel pretty certain that I will be on his staff if he is promoted.

Our Reg't has been on the march ever since we left Rapidan (Sept lst) with the exception of four or five days last week when we were camped near Martinsburg Va. We went from Rapidan via Culpepper C. H. Warrenton Manassas & Leesburg to Frederick City, Md. then recrossing the Potomac we came to Harper's Ferry and were there when it surrendered. We left there the day after its capture and crossing the Potomac again at Shepherdstown proceeded to Sharpsburg Md and were engaged in the battle there on the 17th. Our Reg't went into the fight with 299 men and 26 officers, were engaged for 7

hours and lost 187 men & 16 officers killed & wounded. Our men behaved very well and we were very highly complimented by every Gen. on the field.

Our Col. (Cooke) commanded our Right and the 3d Ark. Reg't and Gen. Lee said that a charge that our two Reg'ts made changed the fortunes of the day. During the hottest part of the fight the enemy brought up two pieces of artillery to within 250 or 300 yards of us, Col. Cooke ordered our Company and three other Cos on the left to fire upon them and before they could get their pieces into action we had killed every horse hitched to them and about half the men. Our two Reg'ts were then ordered to charge. This we did with a yell and the enemy opposed to us (34th N. Y. & 125th Pa Reg'ts) ran like sheep.[48] We pursued them for nearly half a mile when seeing that we were not supported by other forces and our ammunition giving out we were ordered to fall back to our original position. This we did in good order and maintaining our position there during the remainder of the day.

If we had only been supported by the rest of our troops we would have carried the day before us for we broke their lines completely. We lay on the battlefield all that night and the next day and the next night were ordered to fall back to this side of the river. The enemy no doubt will claim a great victory there, but they did not get it, for they were driven back both on the right and left and we held our own in the centre or rather drove them back a little.

Lt. Jas. Y. Whitted[49] was wounded and taken prisoner when we fell back from our charge and I was in command of our Co. during the rest of the fight as Lt. Dickson was sick and Capt. Webb in Raleigh. I have heard since that Lt. Whitted's leg has been amputated, but do not know whether it is so or not. Our Co went into the fight with 29

Lt. Richard H. Battle, Jr., resigned his commission in the "Anson Regulators" on September 2, 1862, to serve as a personal secretary to Governor Vance, helping with the governor's correspondence. (Courtesy of the N.C. Division of Archives and History.)

men and lost 23, but several of our wounded have since returned to duty—as they were only slightly wounded and a good many of our sick having gotten welt and come in we now number 45.[50]

Among the officers killed in our Regt was Capt. Wm Adams a son of Mr Peter Adams of Greensboro. Gen. L. O'B Branch and Col. Tew were also killed. The Yankee papers admit a loss of 13 Gens. killed & wounded. I have seen no official account of the loss on either side but feel certain from what I saw of the battlefield that the enemy's loss far exceeded ours. I escaped without a single scratch. The balls seemed to hit all around me as thick as hail, but fortunately they missed me.

Please get a pair of my old bootlegs at home and have Parks to foot them for me, for I will need boots this winter if we stay in this part of the country. Tell him to make them ? size smaller than the last pr of shoes he made for me last June or July. Please send them to me as soon as he can fix them or by the first person coming up this way. We have had two or three pretty heavy frosts during the last week and the nights are quite cool, but it is still right warm in the middle of the day.

Cap. Webb caught up with us about four days ago and brought me a letter from Mother. Tell Mother that I will write to her in a few days. Ask Mother please to have me some yarn socks knit, for they will be better than cotton socks in this part of the country. I will write as often as I can. Love to all. Your affectionate son,

James A. Graham

70. October 10, 1862

Gov. Zebulon Vance, letter to Francis & Henry Fries,[51] Fries Woolen Mill & Salem Manufacturing Company, Salem, Forsyth County, North Carolina. Source: Vance Letter Book, North Carolina Division of Archives and History.

In a fashion which mirrors modern times, military contractors had a reputation for slow production, not living up to their contracts, and price gouging. In this letter from the governor, the two Fries firms are blasted for such behavior as Vance displays the fashionable temper for which he was famous in his time as a United States congressman.

Executive Dept. of N. C.
Raleigh Oct. 10th /62

I have seen with regret and mortification your note to Captain Garrett, AQM, in which you say you cannot comply with the provisions of the Exemption Law requiring manufacturers to furnish goods at 75 per cent profit over the cost of production and therefore declining to sell the State any more cloth for supplying the wants of our brave soldiers in the field. It is melancholy in every sense. If the Standard of patriotism was no higher in the great mass of the people, we might treat with the enemy tomorrow and consent to be slaves at once & forever. Poor men, with large & often helpless families, go forth to bleed & suffer at $11 per month, supporting their wives & children God knows how, with flour at $20, shoes & cotton goods at fabulous prices and yet men who stay at home in protected ease to reap a harvest of wealth, which might be truly called a harvest of blood, from the necessities of the Country, cannot afford to take 75 per cent above cost for the garments in which his protectors stand guard & do battle for his liberties? What per cent, gentlemen, do you suppose the soldier is reaping, with a half starving family, a shattered constitution, ragged & bare-footed, sleeping on the bare earth or languishing with gaping wounds or raging fever in loathesome hospitals? If he can incur personal and pecuniary ruin for his country's sake, cant you afford to eat good food, sleep in a warm bed every night on 75 per cent clear profit for the country's good also? Alas, Alas, that such a state of things should exist in North Carolina I will not pursue the subject.

Suffice it to say that without the assistance of the manufacturers the State cannot clothe the troops & they must brave the severities of the coming winter naked. When men of intelligence and public spirit take such a position, we may expect suffering & ruin to overwhelm our country. There is only one remedy to arrest the evil which threatens us: and that is for the civil authorities to permit the military to put forth its strong arm & take what it

wants. The Confederate authorities have desired my permission to seize the Mills of N. C. and work them for the benefit of the Army: should it be formally asked of me again I shall withdraw my objections & permit them to do as they wish, unless they will make reasonable contracts with the State.

I should state as a matter of justice that you have been quite as liberal & perhaps more so with the State, as any others, but no amount of company can render extortion justifiable or Respectable.

Governor Z. B. Vance

71. October 14, 1862

Lettie Long, Graham, Alamance County, letter to Benjamin P. Long, Company I, 57th Regiment N.C. Troops. Source: Long Family Papers, Southern Historical Collection, University of North Carolina at Chapel Hill.

Letitia or "Lettie" Long of Graham, North Carolina, had already lost one son, John, to the war. Her other son in service was Benjamin, a soldier in the 57th North Carolina. Her letter talks about her husband's visit to the company, discusses different ailments and health, and encourages Benjamin to remain strong in his faith.

October 14 1862
My Vary Deare Son,
I thout it proper to rite you a few lines to let you heare from us and how we get along while youre father was with you all we wer vary lonsom and unplesant. Father and them had a safe Journy and returned home and Monday eavening at 2 oclock was worn down and not vary well but is better to day since his ride. They got to richmon just before the hard rain came and to raleigh and stade there all knight and had vary good luck in coming home and we are all thankfull to see them and heare you

was all well. Youre father wishes to be remembered to all of the Alamance Boys that are there that he talked with when there. He dos talk of them a grate deal.

I have had a trying time of troble and am in vary muche at this time trobled with rumatism that you are not acquainted with but the cloudy wether is mity aganst old people. There has bin a long dry spell and I fear to tis rite before a wett time and that will be mitty aganst the corn. Tell Mason Tarply[52] he came home safe and has not forgotten him and tell him that he did not say but he may come to see you all agane if he likes as he loves you all my deare son. Be a good boy and like neare yure duty and do not be led off by the wicked on and bad company that is in camp for tis a hard place to live a christian. But pray and do not neglect it for the sake of your Mother that gives you good advice and obey it and pray for me that the lord may help me to bare my trobles and for John and for all those of my family has left me and gon never to return to me agane heare on earth.

I do feel like I will not stay heare mutch longer as I do feel like I will not stay long for I feel mitty sick and frail and it may be that if you have the luck to git home I may be dead and gone home to meet my deare Sones that gone home before and I think I will soon meate them and I want you to be a good boy and be shure to meate me in heaven. We shold still recite and pray for full redemption and should confidently wate.

Your mother,
Lettie B. Long

72. November 6, 1862

Private Archibald Curlee, Company I, 53rd Regiment N.C. Troops, letter to Gov. Vance, Raleigh, N.C. Source: A. L. S. Governor's Papers (Vance), North Carolina Division of Archvies and History.

Private Curlee volunteered for service in Union County on March 20, 1862. Curlee was reported present until sent home on a sick furlough in August 1862. Reviewing his present condition, Curlee offers his services as a shoemaker.

Saturday Evening
November 6th 1862
i comence this note not noing i Shall be able to Speak my minde up on the Subject or not, as i am writing to One i never have seen you will be informed that i am in Bad health and has bin ever Since April last i Volenteered and went of to the army an Come home in August just a live i've not seen nary well day since i have bin in the army So i write these lines to you as we truley hope there is sompthing i Can do that i Cold live out of the army for i assure you i Cant live there long i Can put up as good Shoes an Boots as any man, So i have folerd the trade Before i went off Some, ge So if you Can or will Git me out of the army and let me go to making Shoes i Should do good deal more good and be of more Benefit to the Confederacy So Mr Gorvnor if you Can Say or do any thing to my Case i Shall more than thank you a thousand times although you may give me a Short answer or nun, i am young and green about the law in these Criticle times, i want you to write to me an let me no whither Such Cold be dun or, no will inclose 10 cts male your Letter pleuse write to me as Soon as this you recd

Direct your Letter Olive Branch N. C.
A. Curlee[53]

73. November 7, 1862

Mrs. M. B. Moore, Pine Hall, Stokes County, N.C., letter to Gov. Z. B. Vance, Raleigh. Source: A. L. S. Governor's Papers (Vance), North Carolina Division of Archives and History.

In the early stages of Vance's governorship, North Carolina found herself in need of adequate goods to supply her units in Confederate service. In fact it was suggested that civilians help to provide for the soldiers at the front. Mrs. Moore here points out an abundance of supplies in several Piedmont counties. Within the next six months, Vance established an efficient contract system, and began to set up a state-owned blockade running enterprise, which ensured that North Carolinians would be some of the finest equipped soldiers in the field.

Pine Hall, Stokes, N. C.
Nov. 7th 1862

This cold and wintry day reminds me of the destitution of our soldiers; and I hope you will deem it too much trespas upon your time and patience, if I drop you a line upon this subject.

We are told our brave boys are suffering for clothing; and more especially for blankets. We are told that it is the duty of southern women to supply these things. The government cannot supply them, because it can not make them. Woman must do the work: the State is willing to pay for it. I wish to inform you that there are a great many blankets yet in N. C. While many have spared the last one, others have more packed away from a dozen to fifty, good blankets. Most of these persons are Quakers some of Union sentiment. The former, you are well aware, are opposed to war in all its forms; and consequently will neither give nor sell articles for the army. I have good reasons to believe that if you were to press these things, many of them would really thank you, for the opportunity of assisting their county, with out violating the rules of their order. Thus much good would be affected by such a step; and public opinion, generally, would approve it. Those who have strained the last nerve preparing for the comfort of our dear brave soldiers; take it hardly to see so

many others holding up those necessaries (to the soldiers) which they could so easily spare.

I am not disposed to dictate to your Excellency; but should you think proper take measures for securing these things, I will simply state, where you may find them in abundance. In the counties of Randolph or Guilford, you will find blankets most abundant. In Montgomery, Davidson, Forsythe Stokes Rockingham &c you will find some. I am not so well acquainted in the other counties; but have reason to believe that there is an abundant supply, if they are only collected.

For further information on this subject, I refer you to J. Worth? member of the State Legislature and Rev. S. Branson* Raleigh N. C.

Pardon the liberty of an unpretending woman in addressing one in your position.

M. B. Moore

*Methodist minister in New Bern, N.C., who was forced out of his home and had fled to Raleigh.

74. November 10, 1862

Henry W. Ayer, state agent on contracts, Bethania, Forsyth County, N.C., report to Gov. Z. B. Vance, Raleigh, N.C. Source: A. L. S. Governor's Papers (Vance) North Carolina Division of Archives and History.

The following report by Agent Ayer gives crucial insight into the way the state and individuals contracted war-related labor and materials production. This report lists all of the state contracted manufacturers in the Forsyth County area and their progress in producing the contracted goods. It also informs the governor on those who are delinquent.

Bethania Forsythe County
Nov. 10th. 1862

I have been busily engaged since my last communication to you, but have not a great deal to show for it. Those iron works I alluded to in my letter from Salem have been visited and have an outward appearance of honesty, but there are some rumors afloat against them, which I could not trace up as true. The one owned by Stephen Hobson is situated in Yadkin County, he has at present 50 employees, detailed to him from Forsythe, Iredell, Davidson and Yadkin Counties by the Cols. of the Regts to which they respectively belong. In addition to these he has 17 others, who have not been enrolled, being between the ages of 18 & 45 now, but were under 18 & over 35 at the last enrollment. He has no state or Govt. contract, further than a sub Contract, from Jno. P. & J. J. Nisson of Waughtown, who have a Govt. Contract for wagons and horse shoes, which sub Contracts Hobson agrees to furnish 3000 lbs of iron every two weeks—He now runs two fires and one forge—is interested in 3 other new forges now being erected, and wishes to have some 38 hands more in addition to the 50 he now has detailed, Thinks he will be able then to furnish 1000 lbs iron pr day The opinion of some of his neighbors is that he is erecting the new forges for the purpose of screening some of his friends from the army, as he is a Quaker, but my own opinion is he is doing it for the dollars and cents he can make by it, as he employs these conscripts for $10, pr month He has a foundry also—and has been engaged in the manufacture of Iron with one forge for the last 20 years—You can make your own calculations whether the amt. which he now produces to the Govt. (3000 lbs. in two weeks with 50 hands) is a paying business or not, and whether it will pay to raise the number of operatives to 88 for the sake of 1000 lbs, pr day—Jesse Wooten near him has one forge completed and at work, & two others on the way—will be in operation in a few weeks—15 conscript hands—a sub contract with Nisson—and furnishes 15000 lbs, every two weeks—at least that is his contract. Neither he or Hobson however quite reach the stipulated amt, Wooten has been at the business some eight years—and has as he says only the same number of hands that he always had— some of them are new however, oweing to the fact, that a part of his men went to the service in the early part of the war I would not have visited either of these establishments, had I not heard that they were frauds upon the Govt. Hobson has been heard to say "That he would ease the conscience of as many of the neighbors as he could, from fighting in the war. Both of these establishments are in the bounds of the 75 N C M. Col. Cowles

I visited also the Shoe Shop of Mess Kerner & Gentry at Kernersville, Forsythe Co. find the working 13 hands—12 whites, 1 Blk. 11 Conscripts, Contract with State, for 1000 prs pegged and sewed shoes. Stipulation pr month 200 prs. Date of Contract 23 of May, Average pr day to the hand 1½ prs. was another contract just made with Q. M. Sloan for which he has not yet gotten the papers from Mr Sloan—Enclosed find if you please, the report of Mesr Fries & Fries, Salem, for woolen goods—and Mesr Hine & Co—for Leather, The report from the Cotton factory of Gray & Wilson, Salem has not been made out yet owing to the absence of Mr Gray—It will reach me at Greensboro—and will be for in my next. I am authorized and requested by Chief Justice Pearson,* to lay before your Excellency the following facts, There is a man in Yadkin county near Mount Nebo—75 Regt, N. C. M. named Elkanah Willard, who openly defied the law, first, By rescueing his brother who is a conscript (he himself is not) from a guard who had him in custody by a display of arms and open force. Secondly, by putting Capt Flemming† of that district and the men accompanying him at defiance, in such a way that they were obliged to shoot him down or rush upon him armed as he was at the iminent danger of their lives The Capt says he could have shot him down or at the risk of his life have attempted to arrest him but as he was a man of most desperate character and has 5 other brothers as bad as himself, the better plan he thought was to let him alone—It is the opinion of the well affected neighbors in order to avoid bloodshed that the best policy would be to send an officer with 12 or 15 armed men—to arrest him, supposing that this display of force would let them see their resistance was hopeless and that they would surrender without opposition Whereas it tampered with and not put down at the start it may result in some dreadful evil. The effect of armed men in the neighborhood, would be wholesome in many ways, as there is some disaffection in that part of the County. This man Willard has said he would rather join the Federal Army than ours—The above statement are facts, vouched for by Judge Pearson. Any thing else coming to my knowledge will be promptly reported to your Excellency.

H.W. Ayer
Bethania

*Chief Justice Richmond M. Pearson of the North Carolina Supreme Court.

†Captain Flemming of Yadkin County served under Col. Cowles, 75th NC Militia.

75. November 13, 1862

N. A. Waller, Reads, Granville County, N.C., letter to Gov. Z. B. Vance, Raleigh, N.C. Source: A. L. S. Governor's Papers (Vance), North Carolina Division of Archives and History.

By 1862, debt, inflation, and speculation had brought the southern and North Carolina economy to a critical point. The Confederacy refused to make its paper currency issues legal tender. Waller raises an interesting question: If all you have is Confederate money, then what is to be done with a man who refuses to take Confederate notes in payment of a debt?

State of N C Granville County
November the 13th day 1862
I send you a few lines to ask of you what ought to be done with a man who refuses to take Confederate notes in payment of Debt. What corse the Law wood have with him and if I cant do any thing with him I want you to urge it on the presant Legislator to do somthing that will compel such person to take Confederate notes in payment of Debt I am owing amah som money and he refuses to take Confederate money[54] inpayment of what I ow him and said that I could not git my not without the Goal & Silver but that he did not demant of me I have bin to to the man I ow and have offered him both intrust and principal in the presence of three respectible witness and he refuses to tak it from me and give me up my note I think you ought to prees such men in to servis or cose them to loose the Debt for I consider such men and enemy to our country for if we had enough such men our Country would be ruined for the credit of the southern Confederacey would be ruined If you have the time I would like to have your vuse on the matter and urge it on the Legislator to do somthing with such men for they are and ingury to our country my adress is Knap of Reads Granville County

76. November 15, 1862

Colonel Alfred M. Scales, 13th N.C. Troops, Pender's Brigade, letter to Kate, Reidsville, Rockingham County, N.C.

Source: A. M. Scales Collection, Box 1 (Correspondence), Private Manuscripts Collection, North Carolina Division of Archives and History.

Colonel Scales' Regiment was posted south of Winchester after the retreat from Sharpsburg. Alfred and Kate were evidently very much in love and intended to be married. Kate was from a prominent family, the Hendersons, who were very accomplished in the law. The scene of the fire at the opening of the letter is very interesting and demonstrates Scales' attention to detail. Also described in this letter is an undisclosed battle between Scales' command and an unknown Union unit.

Camp Near Winchester
Nov. 15th 1862

My Dear Cousin Kate

I am seated today on the leaves in the open air before a huge log fire which seems to take pleasure in throwing its smoke towards me wherever I may chose to be. The weather is clear cold & windy. At one time my eyes are filled with smoke and I can almost suffocate at another gust of wind comes whistling and frolicking by & behold a cloud of white ashes gather and fall upon me in the ink and all over the paper. I am too far from the fire to make much benefit from it. My feet are freezing in my boots. My hands are benumbed with cold so that I can scarcely guide my pen & yet notwithstanding all this I persevere & write and somehow take absolute pleasure in doing so.

My heart beats warmly, my mind for the moment is far from here. I bid adieu to the war and all its horrors and defiance to the weather with all its severity that I am writing to own my Dear Kate. She has agreed to give up home & mother & kindred and pledged herself to be mine by faith and all sacredness of a compact requested in Heaven. Then pardon me & still permit me the expression, "My Dear Kate" for

I love to write it and feel that it is my province to cherish through life & should you have sorrows, "mine is the hand to dry your tears and to comfort still."

How I shall discharge this sacred trust the future will alone develop, but it is a work of love and heaven will aid me in its performance. Since my return to the army my attention has been much engaged yet no day has passed that I have not often thought of you and the relation we bear to each other. I am filled with melancholy feelings as I contemplate the difficulties and dangers which may get mixed up to prevent our union is not forever. The war with all it horrors & its bloody front will sometimes come over me like the fall of a never ending night & for a season shuts out all the bright moments of happiness and makes the world cold and dreary.

Then again, I look with faith to the end & suffice in the prospect of a day of not far a day where it will be a day of peace when we will be brought together in the bonds that shall never know parting until life itself may leave. God grant that it may and that then will be no longer a necessity for such strictness in regard to furloughs. Of all this you shall be advised of in due time. In the meanwhile I would not have you look to any other day or think a promise broken.

I reached camp two weeks ago. My regiment had first left it was thought to meet the enemy. I galloped after it & came up upon them about two miles from camp. They received me with a shout long & loud & I was convinced that danger must be met along with my noble boys who had so often given me such unmistakeable evidence of their attachment. Gen. Pender left on a sick furlough and I was placed in command of the Brigade consisting on five Regiments.[55] A few days ago when I was sent out with the entire command, we had a brisk little skirmish with the enemy. It was ended by a flag of truce on their side asking permission to take off their wounded. The Yankees confess to a loss of 40 killed and wounded. Nobody was hurt on our side. At present we are in five miles of Winchester and all is quiet. The troops are in fine spirits though the poor fellows are without tents, badly clothed and badly shod such self sacrificing devotion deserves and will be rewarded. With the help of God we will drive the invaders from our soil. Present my kindest regards to your mother & all dear Effie & the baby for me again. Say to Effie I would very much like to hear from her. I shall find time in a few days to fulfill my promise to her. You must write in the reflection of this and write me a long letter. My address will be at Richmond; Col. AM Scales, Pender's Brigade, A. P. Hill's Divison and then direct to the care of W. L. Hill at Richmond who will forward to me wherever I may be. Farewell, may heaven be your guide & happiness here after be your patron.

Devotedly yours
M. Scales

Two of Scales' soldiers from Company B, Private Levi J. (left) and his brother, Lieutenant Henry Walker. (Courtesy of the N.C. Division of Archives and History.)

77. November 29, 1862

Jamina A. Thomas, Iredell County, N.C., letter to Gov. Z. B. Vance, Raleigh, N.C. Source: A.L.S. Governor's Papers (Vance), North Carolina Division of Archives and History.

Many of North Carolina's citizens were left destitute with their sons, brothers, and husbands gone off to war, reducing the workforce considerably. Here an old and nervous Jamina Thomas writes the governor to inform him of her situation, asking for relief. It is easy to understand Mrs. Thomas' plight through the simple language of a lady at her wits' end.

Nov The 29 1862
NC Iredell Co
Ser it is with and aking hart and tremelous hand I seat my self this

morning to inform you of my condition my only der son[56] volunteered and inlisted to fite for his country May the 2 1861 he rented my farm to Mr Shearer left my self and a sister in his car he dide last april I cold not get any person to tend my farm my dotters ar of delacate constnuuon my friends ar all in the army and the most of them ded my so en lar went with the recrutes in March and dide from the forteague of the battles around Richmon hour farms join he left 6 children his name was Edson he lost his life for his country my der son lives as far as I no I received a letter from him last weak he was in the valleys in Va ner strors Burge. Gen Lees army N C A Troops co H car of capt Osburn* he is serg in that co he is as Fin a soalder as ever lived he fort thru the battles around Richmon and in Mererland and agrate many more The God of battle has spared his life he is as tru a son as aMother ev er rased he oud 50 od dollars when he inlisted for which I was security for my land is now advertised for sale for That det he has bin Trying to pay that deat ever since he left it has Taken all he cold get for my serport and to alorate his own sufferings The cost and in Trust on that det now amounts to ninty dollars pleas bee so condersendin as to bar with my weak partision as nesesaty compels me to apply. I have made all exsersions during This awful war to do all I cold Towards cloathing the soalders tho it is hard to get much don at that the Specurlators will prove too hard for us as we have every thing to by and so little to by with som times I am all moast reddy to giv up the strugle as That is no ey to pitty or hand to suath her I li in a pore neighberhood Those That can asist the nedy will not do so tha all have exceuse some say I cold of cept my son from going other say thars wold not have gon if it had not bin for him. I had one side of bacon from the Goverment the

summer after my son left is all I have hade I am in my 72 yer my husban served 6 months in the last wor he has binded 10 yer and I was left my son had age anuf to take car of this awful war had oppresed me so I am roast to apply to you my condission is un none to my son I do not no What he wold do if he nu it pleas excuse bad speling and writing and help me if you pleas I canot see well I oald and nervus.

J. A. Thomas

Captain, later Colonel, Edwin Augustus Osborne, a Statesville attorney.

78. December 4, 1862

Private John W. Armsworthy, "The Western Rangers," Company H, 54th N.C. Troops, letter to his wife, Edna Armsworthy, Forbush, Yadkin County, N.C. Source: Private Collection, Mr. Bob Furches, Clemmons, N.C.

The 54th Regiment was assigned to the brigade under Evander M. Law, Hood's Division, Jackson's Corps. The two armies began to concentrate around the picturesque city of Fredericksburg. Here thousands of the "typical soldier" letters were written and sent to their destinations across the South. The following is a good example of a soldier's letter, asking about home, requesting items and an update on acquaintances, and discussing rations.

Camp near Fredricksburg
December 4th 1862
Dear wife I seat myself to drop you a few lines to let you know that I am well at present & hope these few lines will find you all enjoying the same blessing. I received your kind letter Dated the 23rd of November & I was glad to here that you was all well I am sorry to state that I have not got the box that you started to me. I would be glad to here whether you have heard from them or not. Lovel seams to hate it mity bad

William H. A. Speer of Yadkin County. In this letter Private Armsworthy spoke of Speer's promotion to major. (Courtesy of the N.C. Division of Archives and History.)

that he could not bring them. He said he had some boxes for himself and had to leave them. I dont want you to send me any clothing if you have the chance except a par of pants & one vest. I have got a par of gloves. I want some new suspenders that is all the clothing I want at present for I cant carry them for we may have to march for several days at a time. I would be glad if I could get something good to eat from home. If I could only be there. I would be glad if I could get a furlow to come home at Christmas but I fear there is no chance for there is lots of Yankees not far from us but it all quiet that is there is no fiting & I dont think there will be here. Jackson's Army is here. Capt Spear is now Major of the 28th Regment. I would be glad to see the 28th Reg. but the guard wont let anybody pass, they

are only about two miles from us. I am faring very well, we have a plenty to eat yet but it is not very good, it is Beef & crackers it is dry eating. I am still cooking for the capt. I get plenty to eat & that is good. I want you to write soon & give me all the news. You must excuse my short letter, I will do better next time. Tell father to write, this will do for you & him, as I thought very strange of his not helping bawl your corn. I send my best respects to Aunt Edney & Uncle Mathew and all the rest of mine & your folks, write soon.

> J. W. Armsworthy

79. December 7, 1862

Sergeant Jonas N. Bradshaw, "Rocky Face Rangers," Company G, 38th Regiment N.C. Troops, letter to his sister, Mrs. N. S. Bradshaw, Alexander County, N.C. Source: Jonas A. Bradshaw Papers (620), Special Collections, Perkins Library, Duke University, Durham, N.C.

Jonas Bradshaw was an Alexander County farmer living in the Pisgah area prior to volunteering for service on November 2, 1861. This twenty-six-year-old husband and father of a young girl, Mary, was mustered in as a sergeant.[57]

> Petersburge Va
> Dec the 7th 1862

Dear sister

It is with heart felt pleasure that I this morning atempt to write you in answer to your kind and affectionate lines that came to hand and found me well and I was glad to hear that you and youre little girl as it seems that you was in a heap of trouble. But you must learn that money is not worth while to draw after him fore he is out of this world of trouble. You ought to be glad that you have such a friend as he is in heaven. Nancy I would be glad to see you and Ladeama but I shall ever see any of my folks any more. I hear not thar is a vantageous times can tell.

Times is hard as usual. We have anuf of nothing hardley to eat and nothing to eat but hard worke to be done and heavy duty in abundents to do. Franklin is well and harty and sends you his Best respects. Nancy you must do the best you can. Nancy you must think hard of me for not paing for my letters. I hant got no stamps nore are they any in petersburge. What is the matter with Mary that she has quit writen to me. I will write a letter more often these times that will make some body shed tears. Norman is well. I will close writen. Write soon and give me all the news be shure and give me all the news. I remain your brother and friend.

Jonas A. Bradshaw

If I was there I could be a better friend to you Nancy.

80. December 15, 1862

Chaplain James W. Jones, 3rd Regiment Arkansas Volunteer Infantry, letter to his uncle, John Long, Alamance County, N.C. Source: Long Family Papers, Southern Historical Collection, University of North Carolina at Chapel Hill.

James W. Jones, a native of Alamance County, was assigned as Chaplain of the 3rd Arkansas Regiment. Though not a participant in the battle of Fredericksburg, he saw the results first hand. In this case, one of the deceased soldiers was his cousin, Private Benjamin Long of the 57th North Carolina Regiment, who was killed as part of General Law's Brigade. Private Long had been in service since July 4, 1862, and had completed twenty-two weeks as a soldier prior to being killed in action.[58]

Camp near Fredericksburg Va
Monday Decr. 15th 1862
Dear Uncle John,

It is my painful duty to write to you a few lines informing you of the Death of your son, cousin Benjamin N. Long. He was killed in a charge last Saturday evening near the Rail Road. I happened to find him yesterday evening (Sunday) just as they were going to bury him, so I got a board and cut his name on it, at this head and feet. He was shot in the head and killed immediately, so the poor fellow died I reckon without much pain. A young man named W. J. McRay[59] helped to bury him in a grave with seven other poor fellows by Lt. Hall. I held prayers over them.

I am acting Chaplain to my regiment, 3rd Arkansas, now and I don't have to fight, thank God. I heard the Artillery & musketry such as I never heard before. The Enemy was driven back finally with great slaughter. They commenced crossing Thursday morning and had a desperate fight opposite town, 3 or 4 miles above, that in the Rail Road on Saturday also. Gen. Cook was wounded in the head and drove the yankees back with great slaughter & killed a great many of our men too.

We are looking hourly for the fight to come off. They say the valley below town is black with the Yankees this morning. Oh! May the Lord save us, and put a stop to such cruel horrors. You may know that I was sorry for poor Ben, when I found him; but we can't help these horrors, and must try to be resigned to the will of God. I know it will almost kill poor aunt Letty. May God give us grace to sustain us in these troubles.

My love to all my family and to aunt Betty Mize and family. I don't know where Fred is. I heard Jim was dead.

Very truly your nephew
James W. Jones
Chaplain to 3rd Ark. Regt. Vols.

81. December 15, 1862

Elizabeth White Nims, Woodlawn, Gaston County, N.C., letter to Leonidas

S. White, Ft. Mill, York District, SC. Source: Nims-Rankin Papers, Southern Historical Collection, University of North Carolina at Chapel Hill.

Elizabeth Nims was married to Massachusetts native and factory owner Frederick Nims. The two lived in the Woodlawn Isle township of Gaston County where Frederick and his brother, Horace, operated a mill. Elizabeth would bear three children by 1861—Luther, Franklin, and Susan. The Nims family was of means, with $3000 in real estate and over $23,000 in personal property.[60] The addressee of the letter is perhaps a relative of Elizabeth's from South Carolina who is trying to avoid the war in numerous ways.

Woodlawn N. C.
Dec 15th 1862
My Dear Leon,

I was glad to hear from you again. You write a very good letter. There is no occasion to laugh at it and you need not fear my laughing at it. You must not talk about going off to live like Daniel Boone that is not a natural way to live for we naturally desire to mingle with our fellows and it is proper to do so. So go ahead and find your natural life but know that some have to go ahead of you and others come with you and others come behind you. It is not too late to learn to put your hands to do things, yet.

Wm Nims has received Pa's letter and has answered it. I had not received a letter from Sidney in some time. I suppose it is because I have not written as punctually as I ought to have to him. Mrs. Cooper will send her servants to Charleston this week and if they do not start too late in the week I will send this letter by them. Chub must come with you or John. I suppose Chub has made a visit recently to Jinny. It will be but fair for John to go next, but I shall like them both to come.

My children have bright expectations concerning Christmas and if you come through Charlotte you must buy me a dozen apples for them and I will pay you when you next come. Tell Sophy to send some eggs by you and I will pay her.

I don't know what to tell you about avoiding conscription. I was at the end of my row when I suggested going to the Arsenal. If Pa wanted you to have an education there are plenty of Academies besides the Hillsborough Military Institute. I don't know anything about the Machine Shop in Columbia, and if you fancy trying it I know of no objection to it.

I hope you are all well. You must get here the day before Christmas, and bring me those apples for the children, if you can get them, and the eggs if you can.

I am affectionately yours,
E. W. Nims
PS Bring the squirrel if you like with you, the boys will be delighted with it.

82. December 19, 1862

Sergeant George Richards, "Waxhaw-Jackson Guards," Company B, 26th Regiment N.C. Troops, letter to Gov. Z. B. Vance, Raleigh, N.C. Source: A. L. S. Governor's Papers (Vance), North Carolina Division of Archives and History.

Private Richards, a furloughed solider from "Waxhaw-Jackson Guards" Company B, 26th N.C. Troops,[61] writes Governor Vance, his former colonel, and wishes to report several abuses in the exemption system that he sees in Union County, North Carolina. None of the men named below were found in *Moore's Roster* or in *N.C. Troops 1861–1865*, but all were confirmed as residents of Union County, North Carolina, in the 1860 Census.

Monroe Union County N. C.
Decr 19 1862
After my respects to you, I would say that I have had a long & sevear spell of

sickness, allmost ever since our retreat from Malvern Hill, My recovery has allmost been a miracle. When I became convalescent & received a sick furlough to visit this place where my brothers & sisters live hoping that good nurseing & kind attention would restore my broken health & shattered constitution, and it is with pleasure I state, that my fondest hopes have been realized, & I hope soon to be able to join my Regt the gallant Old 26 N. C. that still look with fondness on you, their gallant leader.

To day I have witnessed a rich & extraordinary seen, To wit, The enrolment of conscripts from 18 to 40, and just here I wish to inform you of the many subterfuges adopted by some of those who are subject to the act. First & foremost I believe there is a collution between the Malitia Capt & some of his favorites, with whome the most flimsey excuse is suficient to pass them over ge lay them on the Shelf.

One man by name of John W. Rose, a man of some property about 35 or 36 years of age, who attempts to get out by buying an interest in a contemplated tannery, just started build a house for that purpose, or rather, to avoid going into service—No Mechanic himself but purely a Speculator in every sense of the word, ever since the war broke out.

The next is one Marshel Broadway a very stout able young man about 24 or 25 years old who bot out a little mail contract carried on horse-back once a week 10 or 12 miles, and he in his turn, hires another conscript one Moses Gordon very stout & able about 35 or 36 years of age to ride for him, so this little 10 mile mail, (formerly carried by a little boy) once a week deprives the service of 2 very stout able men,

The next is one John Shute a speculator about 36 or 37 who has Managed to get 2 or 3 neighbors to pretend to have him as an Overseer but realy attends to speculating & not to their

business, & one of those persons pretending to hire him is only 35 or 36 years of age, but he is a Post Master,— So this favorite slips the noose—

The next one is one John Holm, with a little sore on his leg that no one heard of before, got a certificate from a hired Physician of disability and he slips through also, The next, a pretended *"Doctor"* Henry Tribble who never obtained diploma or perhaps never heard a Medical lecture a man of Very limited education a near-quack, who has been trying to practice physic in a very obscure neighborhood no more than 3 or 4 years & he too runs through. There are 2 others John Irby & William Woolf what they feign, I have not heard, All the above, with one exception are in the little Town of Monroe Union County N C.—The name of the Capt of this Beat is Stanly Austin.[62] Perhaps there are many others who never came under my observation I saw enough however to disgust a member of the Old 26th NC

G. Richards

83. December 29, 1862

Major C. C. Blacknall, 23rd Regiment N.C. Troops, letter to mother, C. G. Blacknall, Granville County, N.C. Source: Oscar Blacknall Collection, Private Manuscripts Collection, North Carolina Division of Archives and History.

The following letter was written to Blacknall's mother in Granville County, N.C. Blacknall was wounded at Seven Pines on May 31, 1862. After being pinned down by his dying horse, Blacknall was grazed seven times by enemy fire. Three days later, Blacknall was promoted to major of the 23rd North Carolina.[63] What stands out in this letter is the amount of destruction left by the Federals when they abandoned Fredericksburg. It seems to have had a profound impact on many soldiers, including Major Blacknall.

Head Qts. 23 N. C. Regt
Near Fredericksburg Dec.2

Dear Ma

I have written home frequently since I reached the army several times to Jinny, at least once a week & have not received a line good, bad or indifferent from her and only know that you & my family are in the land of the living by a letter just received by Lieut Overton from brother George. I cannot account for so long a silence for surely I am not aware of having committed anything to put me outside of the pale o£ civilization. But presuming that the reason is owing to some irregularity of the mail & not to any inattention or neglect at home. I will attempt to write you a hasty letter hoping that you at least will answer & let me know how all are getting on about home. I have nothing of interest to write as I have already written all the particulars of the late Battle around Fredericksburg. I will however for want of better matter give you a few lines in regard to a visit to Fredericksburg, which I made on yesterday in company with some friends. I must state that Fredricksburg is a larger town or City than Raleigh, containing formerly I suppose about 6000.

You can form no idea nor can I describe its condition at present. Such a scene of destruction & desolation has scarcely ever been witnessed in any country. I rode through the principal streets & all was still as death, nothing meeting the eye but destruction & ruin on all sides. The inhabitants had fled precipitately on the commencement of the bombardment by the enemy, leaving all they possessed in the world at the mercy of the army. The cannonading was kept up for the greater part of two days from the opposite side of the River only a few hundred yards distant. The shot & shell rained upon the unhappy City with a rapidity & a fury which the world has never seen surpassed. They flew through all parts of the town striking houses, trees, & every possible object in every direction, knocking down chimneys, steeples, walls crashing through buildings of every kind bursting inside of rooms & tearing their contents into fragments & doing a deal of damage that surpasses anything that I ever imagined. One house alone that I examined had 132 cannon balls passing through it, each one tearing & crashing the timbers where it went. Many of the families that could not get out before had to retire to the cellars & witness this awful scene. Those who left have now returned many of them to look up their lost property and find their houses sacked, furniture all stolen or destroyed, provisions of all kinds consumed or taken away and nothing left of their Former estates but heaps of ruin. I do not know of a single house in the town that escaped this general destruction. I entered several splendid mansions & found the most costly furniture such as fine sofas, divans, bureaus, wardrobes, bedsteads, elegant mirrors, costly paintings (some worth hundred of dollars) all left at the mercy of the Yankees who occupied the houses as hospitals & what they were unable to carry away in their hasty retreat were so much mutilated as to be unfit for use. I assure you that the Yankees received full and complete punishment for this work of destruction & robbery. Just in the edge of town where they made such a terrible charge on our lines behind a stonewall, the work of death was awful beyond description. The like has never been witnessed I think on this continent. They pressed forward their men column after column and they were swept down with awful slaughter, the front men falling to make room for others who shared a similar fate. The ground was actually covered with the dead & even now the whole face of the earth is bloodier than any slaughter pen you ever saw. On a small lot after the fight ll60 dead yankees were counted and at the same time our loss was so light as to amount to nothing at all in comparison.[64]

During the fight our Regiment was posted on the right, some five miles below Fredericksburg where the fighting was exceedingly severe & where the enemy lost thousands in killed and wounded & our loss was very small. We lost but few in our Regiment & that from cannon shot. A Lieutenant near me had his head shot off by a canon ball & several balls passed very near me, but I came off unhurt. The canonading far exceeded anything I have ever heard before. But I have written all of these things before & imagine that they will afford you no interest.

We have been blessed with the finest weather I ever saw for this season of the year. Today reminds me of spring. I write out of doors without fire. I think of your planting garden peas, onions, potatoes etc. of which I hope you will have a good supply by next summer as I hope to be with you by that time, the war permitting. I write this with haste as we are about to go on picket on the River. We go within 100 yds of the enemies picket but as we are on very friendly terms I apprehend no harm from the nearness of our quarters.

I hope you are all getting on well. I learn that everything is still going up in price, in the way of provisions. You see my prediction is true in regard to the price of corn, rice, and pork.

You must tell Jinny that she must write, if she has not forgotten how. I sent her stationery enough, but have never seen any use she has put it to, so far as writing to me is concerned. Give my love to all the children, and remem-ber me to Bro George & family, Dock & bride & Sally, also Mr. & Mrs. Parrish. With many happy new years to you & my family I am, in great haste
Very truly and affectionately yours
C. C. Blacknall

84. December 31, 1862

Private Bartlett Yancey Malone, "The Caswell Boys," Company H, 6th Regiment N.C. State Troops, diary entry. Source: Diary of Bartlett Y. Malone, property of the Wilkinson Family. Microfilm copy available in the Southern Historical Collection, Wilson Library, University of North Carolina at Chapel Hill.

The year 1862 was eventful for Private Malone, with the 6th Regiment very active in the battles of Seven Days, Sharpsburg and Fredericksburg. The year ended with a night across the river from the Yanks. A normally jovial and trading relationship carried on by pickets was put to an end by Confederate officers who disapproved of such "fraternization" between pickets.

And the 31 day which was the last day of 1862 was cool and cloudy and our Regiment had muster inspection in the day and at nite our Company had to go on picket gard down the bank of the Rapahnok River whar we was in about a hundred Yards of the Yankees pickets. They was on one side of the river and we was on the other. We was in talken distence but our officer would not alow us to talk. They would com down on the bank and hollow at ous and say if we would bring the boat over that they would com over on our side and have a talk. So that was the last of our works for the year 1862.

1863

"Tell mother that she need not be weary about my washing as it is done up as neat as anyone could wish and if Mag hasn't made me any collars yet that she needn't for I can get me some more in my ration, but the shirt I want since there are none to be had here"

> —*Private Augustus A. Clewell, "The Forsyth Grays," Company B, 1st Battalion, North Carolina Sharpshooters, Raleigh, North Carolina, January 3, 1863.*

"I see some as it is for I am aware of some of the Difaculties where you are but you must bar it patiantly for I think you should be thankful for the favor uncle Mathew & aunt Edney Does for you"

> —*Private John Wesley Armsworthy, "The Western Rangers, Company H, 54th Regiment N.C. Troops, Fredericksburg, Virginia, March 13, 1863.*

"We had a fine time in Pen until the fight. We could get plenty of Milk, Butter, & Bread. The citizens seemed very kind and clever in some parts of the country some claimed to be good southern people and were opposed to the war."

> —*Private John W. Hundely, Company C, 21st Regiment N.C. Troops, Darksville, Virginia, July 19, 1863.*

"Then we was doubbelquicked down to the river (which was about 5 miles) and crost and framed a line of battel in our works and the yanks was playing on ous with thir Artillery & thir skirmishers a fyring into ous as we formed fyring was kept up then with the Skirmishers untell dark."

—Sergeant Bartlett Y. Malone, "The Caswell Boys," Company H, 6th Regiment N.C. State Troops, Rappahanock Station, Virginia, November 10, 1863.

85. January 3, 1863

Private Augustus A. Clewell, Company B, 1st Battalion NC Sharpshooters, letter to his sister, Anne Clewell, Salem, Forsyth County, N.C. Source: Clewell Letters, Private Manuscripts Collection, North Carolina Division of Archives and History.

Here Private Clewell has survived the fall and winter campaigns of 1862–1863 and chooses to send a couple of lines to his younger sister Anne back home in Salem. One thing that is striking is the tone and abrupt manner in which Clewell ends his letter.

                    Raleigh, Jan 3rd 1863
Dear Sister
    I was very glad to get a letter from you and was still more pleased to hear that Mother was almost well. I received a letter from Mag and Eddie and when I received it I did not know what to make of it. Before I saw the address I thought it was an order form the War Department. Tell mother that she need not be weary about my washing as it is done up as neat as anyone could wish and if Mag hasn't made me any collars yet that she needn't for I can get me some more in my ration, but the shirt I want since there are none to be had here. The other morning when I went to breakfast I happened to look on the register and never was more surprised when I saw Captain Wallace's name there. He told

me that he has been to Salem and brought some more girls with him. I am getting tired of writing, give my love to all and write soon
        I remain your affectionate brother,
                              Gus

86. January 4, 1863

Private Jacob H. Hanes, "The Davie Sweepstakes," Company G, 4th Regiment N.C. State Troops, letter to his sister, Catharine, Davie County, N.C. Source: The Catharine E. Hanes Collection, Southern Historical Collection, Wilson Library, University of North Carolina at Chapel Hill.

Jacob H. Hanes was born in 1840 to A. and Jane Hanes of Davie County, North Carolina. Jacob was a student prior to volunteering for service on June 14, 1861. He was assigned to the Provost Guard through August 1, 1863.[1] Hanes talks here about some type of social function to raise money for the citizens of the town, which had been ravaged by war and overzealous Yankee foragers. Perhaps this event was some type of musical show or dance.

                    Gordonsville Va
                    Jan 4th 1863
Dear Sister
    Your very kind letter was duly received and its contents well pondered. We have no news here of importance. I

believe our victory at is not all to gather as … as it was represented to us by the first report. We were all at hearing the fate of the Monitor which sank off cape Hattess. I carried some deserters to the Army last Saturday. I went within 4 miles of Fredricksburg to a little place call Hameltons Crossing. There I delivered my prisoners over to the Provost Marshal Capt Scott.

I left Gordonsville on Friday evening and got to Hanover Juction about 4 o'clock. The tranes not making connection there I had to lie over all night there being no accommodation there. We had to lie on the ground and the worst of all one of my prisoners escaped about midnight. I expected Major Boyle would give me a hauling over about it though he did not. One of our guard received a letter from Capt Chambers* stated that the pickets were firing at each other constantly and that he thought the prospect verry good for another engagement verry soon.

Capt Chambers once belonged to our guard. He was elected Capt of a company through the influence of his cousin. We have lost 4 of our guard quite lately by promotion and J.F. Fraley will probably leave us soon. The young Gentlemen and Ladies of the village are going to have a … Friday night for the purpose of making up money for the sufferers of Fredricksburg. There are about 6000 in all. I suppose who are thrown out and destitute of homes. We have hired a most excellent cook and are living tulerbly well. Mr Balentine one of clerks gave a New years supper. It was the nicest supper that I have set down to in many a long day. I will tell you what the supper was composed of Baked Turkey, chicken, chicken sailet, cellry, Real coffee, oysters, pickled and stewed, cakes & jelly and—other good things too numerous to mention. After we had got through with supper went to another

room where we amused ourselves for a while at cards and checks. In a short time the eggnog was handed round which was verry nice. It was then about 2 o'clock. After singing a few spiritual tunes the crowd dispersed. Dr Craig (Hill) of the post Surgeons and some of the wardmasters and the Guard went to the crowd the supper I recon must have cost Mr Balentine $100, which is right liberal for a soldier drawing $17.00 per month. No more at present. I very affectonately you loving Brother
                    J. H. Hanes
I would be verry much pleased to hear of you and George starting to school.

*Captain Henry A. Chambers: Captain Company C, 49th Regiment North Carolina Troops. Guard: In reference to Provost Guards.

87. January 22, 1863

Major William G. Morris, 37th Regiment N.C. Troops, letter to his wife, Dallas, Gaston County, N.C. Source: Mr. Charles Daniel Wilson, Dallas, N.C., and the letters of William G. Morris, William G. Morris Collection, Southern Historical Collection, Wilson Library, University of North Carolina at Chapel Hill.

Colonel Barbour and Major Morris were both wounded during the battle of Fredericksburg, Virginia, on December 13, 1862. Morris remained with the regiment after recovering from his wound in the right ear and took charge of the regiment in the absence of its colonel and lieutenant colonel.[2] It is interesting how Morris reports the morale and fighting spirit of the Federal forces across the river.

> Head Quarters Camp Gregg
> near Fredricksburge
> Jan 22nd 1863

Dear Fameley
I am well & hope these Lines may find you all well. I have Not Recd a letter from you Since the one Roberts

brought. The Enemy are making Some Demonstrations to cross the River but I think it is onley to Keep um from Going to NC to Reinforce General Smith. We was ready Last week to march but the order was countermanded. I think as Soon as it is certain that there will be a General Engagement in NC, we will Guet orders to march. It may be that the Enemy will attack here & at N C at the Same time, if So We may not be Sent to N C. I hardley think Burnsides Army will attack us hear unless they find that part of our forces are Gon. They are badly Demorilised. We was on Picket Duty a few Days ago. The Enemy on one bank of the river & we on the other about 200 yds wide. They are very Friendley & want to talk a Great Deel. They curce the war & Say there time will be out next May & will Go home peace or No peace

General James Lane, commanding a brigade consisting of the 7th, 18th, 28th, 33rd, and 37th North Carolina Regiments after the death of General Branch in September 1862. (North Carolina Collection, University of North Carolina at Chapel Hill.)

& if the Abolitionists want the Negroes set free they will have to do there own Fighting.

It has been Raining hear for 3 Days & tolerabley Cold. Some of our reinlisted men are Gon home on furlows but none granted Since the Enemy have made signs to cross the river. Lieut J C Moore made application for furlow a few Days ago but has not herd from it. I am looking for Col Barber to return in a few days. I expect to make application for Leave of abscence for 30 Days as Soon as he returns. General Lane Says he will do all he can to procure me a

furlow as soon as Barber guets back. Lieut Col Ashcraft is with us at Last. I think when Barber returns that him & Ashcraft[3] could Shurely manage the Regt for 30 Days without me as well as I Did when a capton withiout even company officers to assist me. They say they Dont want me to Leave During a prospect of a fight. I will say to you but to go no further that had it not been for Me our Regt would have been Disgraced. I have been told By officers from capton to General that I was looked upon as being the Onley field officer in our Regt that would do in time of a

fight. I Expect you to Keep this a Secret.
I am as high in office as I feel myself
cappable to fill. If I wished Glory of this
Kind Long Since I Could of had my
name in the Papers as having done won-
ders on the Battlefield but all the Glory
of this war that I Desire is our rights &
to be Permited to Return Safe to my
Deare Fameley to Enjoy the Blessings of
Peace Once Moore. I must Close. Do
not Neglect to wright. I will make a
Strong Effort to come home as soon as
Barber returns. Give my love to all.
Remember me in your Prayers. It is my
Constant Prayer to be spared to See you
& our Deare little Children.

> Your affectionate Husband
> W. G. Morris

88. January 23, 1863

Col. Jacob C. Barnhart, 84th NC
Militia, Pioneer Mills, Cabarrus County,
N.C., letter to Gov. Z. B. Vance, Raleigh,
N.C. Source: A. L. S. Governor's Papers
(Vance), North Carolina Division of
Archives and History.

The situation with deserters in central
North Carolina seemed to worsen every
week. The job of the militia was to arrest
and return those deserters to service. Col.
Barnhart of the Cabarrus County militia
was fooled by a couple of deserters and
believes them hidden by a sympathetic family. Vance disapproves of the militia's
breaking into homes, unless the officer
knows for a fact that the deserter lies
within a private residence.

> Headquarters 84th. Regmt N C M
> Pioneer Mills NC Jany 23rd./63
> Gov Z B Vance

Dear Sir
Some two months ago I ordered two
deserters from the Army to meet me, to
return to their Regmt The Capt of the
Co in which they resided reported that
they had gone to rejoin their Cos. But

never reported as I learned afterwards
The Captain today informs me that it is
Suspected that they are secreted in the
neighborhood & at their home and are
probably kept under lock & key to prevent any one from seeing them He
asked me whether he should break locks
& doors where he suspected them to be
secreted and could not get admittance
otherwise Not being able to answer the
question with certainty I told him I
would refer the matter to you for
instruction as I did not wish to get him
into any dificulty You will please answer
as early as practable and your orders will
be obliged

> Your Humble Servt.
> Jac. C. Bamhardt Col
> 84th. Regmt N C M

89. February 4, 1863

Private Louis Leon, Company B, 53rd
Regiment N.C. Troops, diary entry.
Source: Leon, Louis, *Diary of a Tar Heel
Confederate Soldier*, 1913.

On February 4, 1863, Private Leon
was a well-known member of Company B,
53rd N.C. Troops. Leon reenlisted into service and was assigned to this company.
Along with Leon there were several other
Jewish members of company B, including
Jacob Donau, Jonas Engel, Aaron Katz, and
Cpl. Henry Wertheim.[4] The 53rd N.C.
Troops (Daniel's Brigade) was assigned to
the Department of North Carolina and was
posted outside of Goldsboro, North Carolina.

February 4 (1863) — This morning at 4
o'clock we were waked up by the pleasant sound of the long roll. We were
ordered to get ready to march. It is very
cold, snow nine inches deep. We laid in
Goldsboro until noon expecting the cars
to take us away, but we were then told
we would have to march to Kinston. We
took up our line of march at 3 in the

evening and halted at dark. It is truly awful. The snow is very deep and as cold as thunder. We marched eight miles without resting. We then fixed our bed in the snow and stole fodder for a bed and rails* to make a fire. We took snow, put in our kettles, and made coffee. When I say coffee I mean Confederate coffee—parched corn—that is our coffee. Ate our corn bread and bacon and retired to our couches and slept as good if not better than Abe Lincoln.

*Fence Rails

90. February 6, 1863

Private John H. Leonard, Company H, 48th Regiment N.C. Troops, Military Hosptial, Lynchburg, VA, letter to his sister, Elizabeth Leonard, near Lexington, Davidson County. Source: Leonard Collection, Davidson County Public Library.

John H. Leonard opens his letter by stating that "Hear the people are all strange and awful wicked." This statement could be referring to local merchants who used economic hardship to radically increase prices when soldiers were passing through; it could also mean that Private Leonard simply does not understand local customs. John wants a furlough. He wants to come home and cites reasons why he should.

Febr, 6th 1863
Lynchburg, Va.

Dear wife I now sit my self to drop a few lines to in form you that ime some on the mend but haint satisfied. Hear the people are all strange and awful wicked an I can in form you that I cant hardly liv on what we have to eat. We get beef broth and bred for brekfust and turnip broth and bred and a few irish potatoes for diner and a small pece of beef for the sum of the day. The price of food is so high butter a dollar, milk 50 cents a quart, honey 50 cent per

pound, chickens 1.00 to four dollars, eggs 1.00 per dosen, onones 1.00 per quart, apple two dollars per dozen, sweet cider one doll per quart. That looks like kiling a man be fore his time.* I hate to spend my money for you all know that I never made away with more than our teer in the time that I was riting this letter. I would like to come home I hear they giv furlowes at this hospital and som others get dischargs sometime. If my old and aged mother was only hear I think she could maby get me home one more time I shant get able for duty in two or three month. My weight is not more than eighty pounds and before I was in hear my weight was 150 pounds.[5] I am very poor and if I must stay they tell me I will be giv duty hear at this place. I want you to write me and let me know what chance you think there is too send for {marked through} I hope and trust to god that these lines may find you all well and hearty. I prey to get home to your side till I get well. I put my trust in god to see you agan. Direct your letters to lynchburg, va to berdens hospital so I must close my few lines by asking you to write soon and often . I remain your husband,

John H. Leonard to Mrs.
Elizabeth Leonard

*John is reviewing the prices of certain goods sold by local merchants. The effects of inflation are evident upon the Confederate economy, especially in terms of the radical increase in prices.

91. February 8, 1863

Private James E. R. Yancey, "The Townsville Guard," Company B, 12th Regiment N.C. Troops, letter to cousin, Rosa Lupp, Van Hooks Station, Person County, N.C. Source: Louis P. Sherman Collection, Private Manuscripts Collection, North Carolina Division of Archives and History.

Yancey is about to rejoin his company

which is posted at Guinea Station, Virginia. He worked as a carpenter prior to volunteering for service on April 26, 1861. Yancey served in the "Townsville Guard," a unit from Granville County, N.C. He has some very fond words for his cousin and refers to a "question" which he needs answered. The description of family and friends showing off Yancey is very interesting and makes one wonder exactly how many times such a scene was repeated during the war.

Brownsville, N.C.
Feb 8th 1863
My Dearest Cousin Rosa

Your very kind and interesting letter of the 2th came to hand in due time and never was there a letter perused with more pleasure than yours by me. Although absent from the one I love in person yet my heart is with you dearest one. With fond remembrance does my mind wander over past which we have seen…. I hope a kind Providence has good in store for us but alas, I fear there is no happiness for me as before. It is in your power to make me happy or to make me miserable. I hope it is not in such a noble and gentle hand as I fancy. My dear cousin if I knew my such would be my fate my life would be a burden to me. I will continue to look on the bright side unless otherwise directed by you Cousin Rosa. You seem to deem it unwise to answer the question that I requested of you to answer in every instant. Shurly you have not thought of my fair heart of probably you have not made up your mind what you intend to do. Cousin Rosa if you have I appeal to you to give me some satisfaction do not trifle with my feelings any longer and if you are determining not to give me any satisfaction by letter you will please say no more in your reply. I want you to be right plain with me and allow me the same privalige.

Cousin Rosa I shal leave in the morning to rejoin my company. I can not feel satisfide at home when I see me country is needing me. I received a letter from father last night. He advised me to stay at home my capt has not sent for me yet but I feel it my duty to all I can for my country.* Mother seems to take on a great deal in fact the whole family hates to give me up. If you want to see red eyes come down this evening and you will see plenty of them. Cousin Rosa I will have to close at this time. My friends are coming in to see me. There are 6 young ladies in the house now looking for several men but I had much rather see you now than any body on the earth. I am in hopes this unhappy War with soon come to a close.

Cousin Rosa I hope you will pardon all you see amiss. I have nothing else of interest to write this evening My heart is too heavy and Sad for fear of not seeing you again. My love to all. Farewell my dear Rosa untill I hear from you again please write soon and may angels guard you. That is my prayer.

Your devoted cousin and friend J.
Yancey
To direct your next letter to
Guinnia Station, Va Co "B"
12 N.C. Troops
D. H. Hills Division Iverson Brigade

*Oddly, no record of a furlough for this soldier exists; nor does any discipline for being absent without leave.

92. February 24, 1863

First Lieutenant Thomas Branson, Company F, 46th Regiment N.C. Troops, letter to sister, Emily Branson, Randolph County, N.C. Source: Branson Family Papers, Private Manuscripts Collection, North Carolina Division of Archives and History.

A teacher and veteran of Sharpsburg and Fredericksburg, Thomas Branson had served with the 46th North Carolina since volunteering for service in Randolph County, N.C., on March 1, 1862. Nearly a year later, the brigade under Gen. John R. Cooke (15th, 27th, 46th and 48th North Carolina) was sent to strengthen the defenses along the South Carolina and Georgia coasts.[6]

> Camp of 46th N.C. Regt.
> Pocotaligo, South Carolina,
> Feb. 24th 1863.

My Dear Sister Emily,

Only a short letter today. My diary runs thus: Feb. 17th left Holly at 4 o'clock P.M. and arrived at Burgaw Station at 12 A.M. 18th Left Burgaw at 4 o'clock P.M. and arrived at Wilmington at dark, taking quarters at Camp Lamb. 19th remaining at Wilmington. 20th left Wilmington at 10 o'clock P.M. on W. and Manchester R. R. 21st Arrive at Florence, S.C. at 12 o'clock A.M. and left there at 10 o'clock P.M. on the Darlington and Charleston RR. 22nd Arrive at Charleston, S.C. about 9 o'clock A.M. and left there at 3 ? o'clock P.M. on the Charleston and Savannah and arrived at Pocotaligo S.C. about 12 o'clock at night in which place we went into camp.

This place is about half way between Charleston and Savannah and we (Cook's Brigade) are probably sent here to be convenient to run to either place in case of an attack, which is daily expected. At what place is not known. A great battle will perhaps occur at Charleston but our generals and most of the soldiers are confident of our success & that Charleston is called a second Sevastopol.* Her defenses being very formidable and led by the illustrious Beauregard we feel safe.

The furloughs are stopped at present just as I expected they would be before I got off. I shall go soon as I can. I have not received the detail for Charleston yet as I know you have written me to know what has happened to it. I wanted to stay at home but I have no chance now. I am well equipped with clothes and I believe I can save back some money here.

I hope the outlaws will trouble you no more, since the cavalry are in Randolph. Tell mother we are doing finely and are some firstrate boys. Tell Father we would be mighty glad if he could pay his boys a visit. It is not further than Richmond and he could come by Charlotte and Charleston, then on the Savannah RR. We are in one mile of the rail road. I will close. Write soon and direct as you did before only change to Pocotaligo, S.C.

> Affectionately,
> Tom

*Sevastopol: name of a Russian town which was fortified and a major objective of British forces during the Crimean War.

93. March 7, 1863

Major C. C. Blacknall, 23rd Regiment N.C. Troops, letter to wife, Virginia Blacknall, Granville County, N.C. Source: Oscar Blacknall Collection, Private Manuscripts Collection, North Carolina Division of Archives and History.

This letter deals with the subject of privation in camp as well as at the homefront. Blacknall also responds to a question about the war and the prospects for peace, appearing to have expectations for a long continued war, with the United States government passing conscription to fill the ranks of the Union Army.

> Head Qts. 23rd N. C. Regt
> Guinea Station March 7th/63.

Dear Jinny

I have just returned from picket on the Rappahannock where the regiment remained three days and found on reaching camp two letters from you and one from Bro George from Florida.

Your last letter directed by Mr. Overton being at hand. You enquired about the proper directions, there is no difficulty about that, all have been directed correctly, this (23rd N. C. Regt. Iversons Brigade Guinea Station Va.) in a plain hand & they will get here after awhile though the delay recently have been unaccountable.

We have no news at all in camp, as I have been down on the River for three days, I have been unable to hear anything of interest. I saw Alex today, he is looking very well & sends his love. Rufus was to see me on yesterday but as I was not in camp I did not see him.

Our health is now very good & we are getting on very well although I have been somewhat unwell recently, am now well & hearty. We have been living very hard lately but are doing better now. Have an abundance of sugar & get Confederate coffee from the Sutlers. Our supply of beef recently out off, so we have to live on bacon sides which we dont much relish. Bro George writes me that he has purchased a large lot of sugar so you must get as much as you need. You had better get at least 200 lbs. I would like for you to put up some preserves etc. If we have fruit & you may not get another opportunity in getting sugar. I will write to Bro Geo to let you have what you need. He has money of mine to pay for it. If you need other articles in the way of provisions, buy them by all means if possible regardless of price, as they will go up greatly from present prices.

You ask my opinion of the war & the prospects of peace. I can only answer that all human calculations have proved unreliable in regards to predictions concerning its terminating. I thought & so did all persons of intelligence with whom I conversed that the prospects of peace at an early day were very good one month ago, but the Yankees have taken fresh hold and have passed the conscription act which may prolong the war indefinitely. At any event will carry it through the approaching campaign. I have made up my mind to continue until Judgment Day if I live that long rather than give it up & shall bequeath to my children as my best legacy to carry it on through life. But I hope for the best while prepared for the worst. I have written frequently of late.

Very affectionately
C. C. Blacknall[7]
Mrs. V. Blacknall

Love to Ma & the children. Give the enclosed likeness to Charley, it is one that Col. Christie drew for me

94. March 13, 1863

Private John W. Armsworthy, "The Western Rangers," Company H, 54th Regiment N.C. Troops, letter to his wife, Edna Armsworthy, Forbush, Yadkin County, N.C. Source: Private Collection, Mr. Bob Furches, Clemmons, N.C.

Since John's last letter the 54th had received its baptism of fire at the battle of Fredericksburg, December 13, 1862. Both armies went into winter camp in the general area of Fredericksburg with the Rappahannock River as their border. Here John takes the available time to instruct his wife on domestic matters and voices his opinion on family matters.

Camp near Fredericksburg
March 12th 1863

Dear wife your kind letter dated 2 ist came to hand yesterday wich gave me great sadisfaction to here from you & to here you was all well. It found me well. This leaves me the same except bad cold. I am very sorry you tuck up the notion that I had quit writing to you as often I ought to. I write two letter to you to one to any body els. I know you have not Rec. all the letter I have started to you. I started one to father a few days ago with one in it to you. You wanted to know if they had been writing to me that caused me not to write oftener to you. They have not. They have wrote very favorable about you & the children. They allways seem to think you are doing well. I would not of thought they would of grumbled about the sheep after uncle Mathew being at as much trubble. Nither would I of thought they would not of done something for you in some way before this time but I expected they would think that, where you are you would have plenty so they got shut of any trubble for you & no you are not sufering. They are willing for some body els to have the trubble. I dont want you to let on, do the best you can. Dont do or say anything that would caus any fuss. You wanted to know if I give in last summer. I did though I am one tax behind to Sherif Long. I want you to see if it is paid & get the Receipt. So far as you hiring some boddy to come to bring me some things, I dont want you to do that for I had much raither do with what I get than for you to give part of what you have got for I would rather you would try to make prepeartions for you self in the future for I get annuf to live on here and so far as living by your self the way things have turned out I would of seen much more uneasneys. I see some as it is for I am aware of some of the Difaculties where you are but you must bar it patiantly for I think you should be thankful for the favor uncle Mathew & aunt Edney Does for you for I consider it a great favor there letting you have a cow to give you milk beside getting wood & doing your milking. I would be glad to know if uncle Mathew has worked my colt. If he has not I want him to. I would like to know if Chafin will have to come. They say here that Malitia Officers* will have to come. I want to know also if Loggins will have to come for if he comes there is no

chance for my land to be tended this year. I would like to come but I dont see much chance. There is some getting furlows from this company but is those that come out first & have never been home but if they dont stop the furlows my time will come after a while if I live. I would like to write to Logans & I think I shall in a few days. I want to know if he is making any preperations to tend my land. Dear Jinia I want you to write as soon as you get this and let me know how all the things is Doing. Be saving with your provisions for it will be a trying time nest year I fear for you to get any thing. Give my love to Gamma & family & uncle Mathew & aunt Edney for that is all I can do. I often think of there kindness. I must close by saying when this you see think of me though at a distance we be. Tell Branch Elley & Matthew to be good Children I will be at home some time I hope.

Your Dear
J. W. Armsworthy

*Under the rules of conscription, militia officers were exempt from service; however, rumors circulated that not even the militia could be exempt any more.

95. March 15, 1863

Major William G. Morris, 37th Regiment N.C. Troops, letter to his family, Dallas, Gaston County, N.C. Source: Mr. Charles Daniel Wilson, Dallas, N.C., and the letters of William G. Morris, William G. Morris Collection, Southern Historical Collection, Wilson Library, University of North Carolina at Chapel Hill.

In the following letter, Major Morris of Gaston County reports an experience on picket during the late winter of 1863. Several items of interest in his letter include an evaluation of Union morale, comments on the purchase prices of Negro slaves and land, remarks on the receipt of gift boxes, and advice to his children.

Hd Qts. Camp Gregg Va 37th N C
March 15th 1863

Dear Fameley

I am well and trust when these Lines
reaches you they May find you all well.
I have Just Returned with our Regt
from Piquet* Duty on the Rapahan-
nock. We found all quiet on the Piquet
Lines. There was four yankeys crossed
the River yesterday and came to us
declaring they was Done fightin for the
North. They say that Desertion is
becoming common among the yankeyes,
the Northern Papers Say that an average
of about 2 Regts are payed off at Washington every week. I suppose they are
Men that have Served out there time. I
have herd that our forces Expect to
attact New Burn N C Soon. I am of
Opinion that Jackson will attact Hooker
as soon as the Roads will Permit. I think
it is the better Plan than to wait for
them to attact us. I have Nothing of
intrest to wright you. I wrote to
Stephen a few days ago that he Might
buy a young Negro for Me if he Saw a
chance to Guet one 11 or 14 years old
for $1000 or 1500. Perhaps it would
be better to buy Land if there is an
opportunity. I think I could afford to
Give Willy Linebarger Two Thousand
Dollars for his Land if it could Not be
Bought for less. It would bee a Great
addition to the farm on which we Live
in case we Remain there. I think it
advisable for Me to buy Property of
some sort to the amount of about
$1000 or 1500 Dollars. I Gave Randle
$10 Dollars & told him to Do the
best he could, he said he would, he
told Me that Charley appeared to be
a Good man to work. I told him to
Give Charley a chance to Do what he
could.

I have Not herd from you since I was
at home. I am Looking for a Letter
Every day with anxiety. Tell Randle that
I could not See him at the Station when
I Got in the cars but after the train

Started I Saw him holding the horses
but could Not tell him Good buy. I Got
the letter & Scarf you sent by Sifford. I
think it a very Good One. I used it last
Night on Piquet & found it very comfortable to My Ears. I Satisfied that I
Sent My Box back as I Saw Several men
in Raleigh as I passed through with
Boxes for Our Regt & Just arrived yesterday with considerable of there
provisions Spoilt, but had some fine
apples of which I am cordially Invited
to partake. I wish you could be with Me
to Eat some of them. Lt Moore, Jonas
Linebarger, Fred Hoffman Emanuel
Cloninger, Miles Weathers & Morrison
and A. A. Morris are all well.[8] Give My
Love to your Mother & all the children.
Tell the Children I would rather they
would call there little Brother Lee than
Willy and I would prefer Bill to Willy.
Tell Eleanora & Mary that I consider
them old Enough to Know how to
Behave themselves at home & abroad,
Especially to love & Respect there
Grand Mother & you. I am happy to
believe that Our Deare Children are all
well Disposed & may Some Day Be an
ornament to Society. I trust they will
hold themselves above the conduct of
Some in the neighborhood. Tell Lully I
would bee Glad to See her Little red
cheaks & Kiss them. May God Guide &
protect us all.

Your affectionate Husband & Father
W. G. Morris

*Piquet: Picket duty

96. March 16, 1863

Private Louis Leon, Company B, 53rd
Regiment N.C. Troops, diary entry.
Source: Leon, Lewis, *Diary of a Tar Heel
Confederate Soldier*, 1913.

General Pettigrew's and Daniel's
brigades were advancing on New Bern and
encountered an enemy force at Deep Gully
on March 14. After a pitched four-hour

fight, the Federals fell back; however, the Union forces did not retreat far. Private Leon writes two days later of action following the battle.

> March 16 (1863)—A picket came in this morning and reported the enemy advancing. We were put in line of battle to receive them, and after marching one mile up the road to get to our brigade we were put at the extreme left of our line and made breastworks out of rotten logs. Stayed here one hour, when another picket came and reported them ten miles away. So we resumed our march for camp and got there at 7 o'clock—twenty-one miles today. Tom Notter, Aaron Katz,[9] and myself pressed into service a donkey and a cart with a negro, who took us to Kinston. Each of us drove at times, and I was fortunate enough to stall in a mudhole. We had to get out and lift the cart and donkey to dry ground again. Thus ends the march and fight at Deep Gully.

97. March 20, 1863

Sergeant William A. Adams, Company A, 4th Regiment N.C. State Troops, letter to sister. Source: McClelland Family Papers, Southern Historical Collection, Wilson Library, University of North Carolina at Chapel Hill, N.C.

William writes his sister in his second letter. Some points of interest include William asking for tape to construct his sergeant chevrons, giving the width of each "stripe" at a half inch wide. Also, William talks about the brigade's new commander, Stephen D. Ramseur of Lincolnton, North Carolina. Exactly why William does not want his father to read the letter is a mystery.

> Camp near Fred March 20th 1863
> My dear sister
> As I have nothing to do I thought I would write you a few lines to let you no that I am well with the exception of the cold. I no news to write of interest. We have some very cold weather at this time has been snowing for three days and is snowing and sleeting to day the ground is covered with snow at this time. I hope it will snow till August but hope it will not snow at home that long, but I wish it will snow here till that time. Mat tell Ma to send me some good thread and some black tape about, a half an inch wide to put on my coat for sergt stripes and some black thread to sew them on which it will take a yard and a half. You can put it in a letter and send it by some body that is coming. If you get this letter before Tom Stevenson leaves sent it by him. The other thread I mention any kind will do so it is strong enough to patch my pants and to sew on buttons &c. I have been appointed a sergt scince I came back to the regt. It is some better than a corpl.
>   As I have nothing more to write I will tell you how often we drill. Don't drill but three times a day. Once before breakfast and once before dinner and then regimental drill over dinner and then dress parade after all. Gen Ramseur is giving us the very devil on drilling. He is a good general but he is as tite as the very devil. He is a very nice man but I tell you can't hurt me by drilling me it is out of his power. If I can get enough of bread to eat. We are now drawing some new bacon now quarter of a pound a day that is big rations. I can eat mine at one time and draw more sugar than we no what to do with. I will close by asking you to write soon. Mat I what you to kiss sis and OC for me and also Gus. Kiss them a cupple a times for me. Tell Tump to send me a kiss in the next letter you write. Write soon to your brother. Wm Adams
>   don't you let Pa see this letter. I don't care for Ma seeing it.

98. March 21, 1863

Soldier's Wives, Salisbury, Rowan County, N.C., letter to Gov. Zebulon Vance, Raleigh. Source: *The Papers of Zebulon Vance*, North Carolina Division of Archives and History: Raleigh, 1996.

As governor, Vance inherited the problems of war from his predecessors. This letter was written on behalf of the wives of several soldiers. It attests to the hardships at home in regards to price gouging of food and seeks a definite solution from the governor. The lead writer of this letter appears to be Mrs. Mary C. Moore of Salisbury, who asks that the governor's response be returned to her.

Salisbury, N.C. March 21st./63
To His Excellency the Gov of the State of NC
Dear Sir—

Having from absolute necessity been forced into measures not at all pleasant to obtain something to eat by the cruel and unfeeling Speculators who have been gathering up at enormous prices, not only bread stuffs but every thing even down to eggs Chickens & Vegetables to carry out of our State for the purpose of Speculating upon them We feel it now our duty Honored and esteemed Gov to inform you truthfully of our proceedings and humbly pray to inform us whether or not we are justifyable in what we have done—and if not for Heavens Sake tell us how these evils are to be remedied.

We Sir are all Soldiers Wives or Mothers our Husbands & Sons are now separated from us by this cruel War not only to defend our humble homes but the homes & property of the rich man and at the same time that we are grieved at this separation yet we murmur not—. God bless them our hearts go with them and our prayers follow them for Heavens protection through all the trials and difficulties that may surround them, but

Sir we have to live and we must live while they are gone from us and that too without much or in many cases any assistance from them for how far will eleven dollars go in a family now when Meat is from 75 to $1oo pr pd flour $50 pr bll. wood from 4 to $5 pr load, meal 4 an 5 dollars pr bushel, eggs 50 to 6o cts pr doz chickens $7oo pr doz, Molasses $7oo pr gal rye 20 cts pr qt. & and, addition to that we are willing and do work early and late to keep off starvation which is now staring us in the face, but the government only allows us 50 cts a pr for lined pants and 75 cts for coats and there are few of us who can make over a dollar a day, and we have upon an average from three to five helpless children to support and still we complain not at Government prices if we can only get bread divided among us and meat at a reasonable price but Sir many of us work day after day without a morsel of meat to strengthen us for our Labors and often times we are without bread Now Sir how We ask you in the name of God are we to live.

Laboring under all these difficulties Sir we as we have told you in the commencement of this letter were from Stern necessity compelled to go in serch of food to sustain life and some forty or more respectable but poor women started out backed by many citizens to get food we took our little money with us and offered to pay Government prices for what we took but the Speculators refused us any thing or even admittance into their premises We then forced our way in and compelled them to give us something & we succeeded in obtaining twenty three blls of flour two sacks of salt about half a bll of molasses and twenty dollars in money, which was equally divided among us in the presence of our highly esteemed friend and Lawyer Blackmen, besides many other gentlemen of good and high standing in society. Now Sir this is all we done and necessity compelled us to do it and the reason we have addressed you Sir is that we understand that we have been reported to you as plunderers of the town disturbing the peace and quiet of the community, but Sir we have honestly told you the whole proceeding and we now pray your protection or a remedy for these evils—we as much as any one deplore the necessity of such proceeding and do humbly pray you in behalf of our helpless children to so fix the prices of bread and meat that we can by our own labor gain an honest portion of that which sustains life.

To whom else can we go but to you our highly esteemed and cherished Gov to redress these evils. You were the choice of our Husbands and Sons and we too look up to you Sir with perfect confidence as being able and willing to do something for us—we ask not charity we only ask for fair and reasonable prices for provisions and leather for Sir many of us have been shoeless this whole winter except the cloth shoes we can make for ourselves which are no protection even against the cold, in conclusion Sir we humbly beg you after carefully and prayerfully considering our letter to let us hear from you—you can address Mary C Moore Salisbury NC and that Heavens richest blessings and a long life may be your portion with your happy family is the earnest and heartfelt prayers of many

Soldiers Wives

99. April 4, 1863

Elizabeth Waggoner, letter to Sallie Hundely, Stokes County, N.C. Source: Hundely Family Papers, Southern Historical Collection, Wilson Library, University of North Carolina at Chapel Hill.

Since her husband's departure to the war, Sallie Hundely has made a marginal success of her household and her farm. Her

sister, Elizabeth Waggoner, takes this time to write her a few lines to express her desire to be with Sallie. The handwriting in the original is very poor quality, possibly because the writer is rushing to finish before the mailman arrives, or possibly because her writing deteriorated in her illness; she mentions both factors in the letter.

Dear Sister   April 4th 1863
Once more I seet my self to write you a few lines to let you know that I am as well as comen though never well but I senserly hope when this comes to hand it may find you enjoying good helth. Sallie, if I could see you I would be so glad but I see no chance to see you soon. Sallie I wish you could come and Stay with you. I bought some leather from William and I have more than I need so I will send it to you in this. Sallie I have not time to write much else as I am rushed the Maile will leave before I come to a close. Sallie you must write soon and often. If you can read this letter I have not been writing since my illness. The preacher is helping me as I am writing your letter please excuse any mistakes. You must give me all the news in your next letter. So I will close by saying I remain your Affectionate Sister, untill Death.

Elizabeth Waggoner to Sallie Hundely

100. April 5, 1863

Colonel Alfred M. Scales, 13th N.C. Troops, Pender's Brigade, letter to Kate, Reidsville, Rockingham County, N.C. Source: A. M. Scales Collection, Box 1 (Correspondence), Private Manuscripts Collection, North Carolina Division of Archives and History.

The following letter is excerpted due to illegibility and fading in the original. Alfred and Kate Henderson were married in January 1863, despite the aforementioned difficulties. With the relative peace and inaction at Camp Gregg, Scales could not foresee the violent campaigns of the upcoming spring and summer of 1863.[10]

Camp Gregg April 5th 1863

My dearest and ever true Wife,

I have received no letter since I wrote you in the 2nd inst. Your letter started on last Thursday night to have reached you before this & has given me much disappointment but I am afraid that the delay is to be attributed to the irregularity of the mail which must also be delivered to you for your failure to get mine. According to your last you had not rec'd but one from me and this is the fourth I have written you since that one. By this time you should have rec'd them all & I hope they will come safely to hand.

We are still at Camp Gregg prepared to march at any moment. Last night gave us another heavy snow fall and it is covering the earth this morning at a depth of five or six inches & it is still snowing. The air is very cold and this will delay our movement for several days to come. What I would not give to spend this time as I am lonely and dreary as it is in Camp without my beloved wife! To deny your request to visit me is to deprive myself of the greatest pleasure which could be afforded me but duty & affection alike forbids it. I am forced to stifle the impulses of the heart & listen to the stern dictates of the Army. If at any time I can get a furlough to visit Richmond I will notify you so that we can meet there. In the meantime we must make the best of our lot.

I have suffered a good deal since I came back in the torpedity of lines. I think there was a slight attack of Jaundice, but I am much better now and in a day or so I will be perfectly restored with my health. There has been a considerable improvement in my spirits &

though my darling Kate occupies the greater portions of my thoughts, I have learned to submit to our separation with a calm resignation and abiding hope that it can not last for too long.

Night before last I had a sweet dream it was the only time where I could almost feel my sweet Kate, if only in my dreams. We were together, your hand in mine & your head resting on my shoulder. I was too happy to think of where we were but its was enough to know that my dearest wife was by my side with her head pillowed on my bosom.

I look anxiously for you next letter on this evening and trust it may come. My best to your mother & kindest regards to all. Three shirts are plenty for me now & I could do with two more of them, so let me know when they are ready. Farewell, a fond farewell to my own dear wife. God bless you.

Your devoted Husband
AM Scales

101. April 14, 1863

Captain E. Fletcher Satterfield, Company H, 55th Regiment N.C. Troops, letter to father, Person County, N.C. Source: Satterfield-Merritt Family Papers, Southern Historical Collection, University of North Carolina at Chapel Hill.

Captain E. Fletcher Satterfield was born to Roxboro merchant George and his wife, Mary Satterfield. Fletcher was twenty-one years old when he volunteered and was commissioned as a second lieutenant in the "Roxboro Grays," a company of the 24th North Carolina, on May 5, 1861. Lieutenant Satterfield served with the company until he was defeated for reelection on March 17, 1862. Afterward, Satterfield was appointed as first lieutenant in Company H, 55th N.C. Troops, on October 19, 1862, and was assigned to that post until promoted to captain in March 1863.[11]

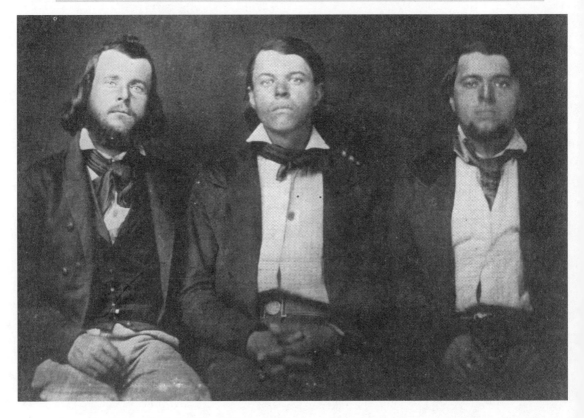

Captain Peter Mull (left) and Ezra Mull (center) of Catawba County served along with Satterfield in the 55th. Their other brother, William (right), fought in the 11th N.C. Troops. (Peter Mull Papers, Special Collections, Duke University Library. Reproduced by permission.)

This letter is written by Captain Fletcher during Longstreet's siege of Suffolk, Virginia.

Camp 3 miles from
Suffolk Apr. 14th

Dear Papa,

We are all now near Suffolk and I reckon we will have a battle we return but everything seems to indicate that the expedition is almost over for the first time since we left Camp on the 9th and have been gone three days today.

There has been considerable shelling ever since we arrived as far as I can learn. We have had only two or three wounded in the Brigade. Our regiment is in fine fighting order and will. I have no doubt it will do its full share. With respect to the forces on the other side I have not the remotest idea. Gen Longstreet is in command and that I think is a sufficient indicator that all will be well.

I have at last received my commission and now my full pay. I have no idea how long we will be posted down here. I will write when I get a chance to get a letter from the office, so don't be fooled by any idle rumors you may hear. I or Jordan[12] will telegraph to Hillsboro as soon as everything is situated. Send word to Uncle that we are both in fine spirits.

Yours with much love
E. F. Satterfield[13]

PS I would write more but the mail is about to leave.

Captain Satterfield in 1861. Satterfield would be killed in action during Pickett's Charge on July 3, 1863. (Satterfield-Merrit Family Papers, Southern Historical Collection, Wilson Library, University of North Carolina, Chapel Hill.)

102. April 16, 1863

Private Daniel W. Badgett, Company D, 62nd Battalion, Georgia Cavalry, Camp Birney, Pitt County, letter to brother, William H. Badgett, JP, Jackson Hill, Davidson County. Source: Badgett Collection, Davidson County Historical Museum.

Daniel was 18 when he moved to Camilla, Georgia, to work as a plantation manager in 1859. It was common for young men who were single to venture out and work as managers and overseers on plantations at this time. While serving as a manager in Georgia, this Davidson County native was caught up in the furor and enlisted in a Georgia unit.[14] This unit was a mix of two companies of cavalry from Georgia and four from North Carolina. The battalion's commander was from Wilmington, N.C. The battalion was apparently formed in late 1862 and was part of the garrison defending the eastern third of NC from further Federal incursion.

Camp Burney, Pitt Co., N.C.
April the 16th, 1863

Brother, I seat myself to drop you a few lines. My health is good and has been since I wrote to you before. There is nothing strange here that could write you about—times here are pretty exciting there has been more or less fighting at Washington everyday for the last 3 weeks. We are in camps 25 miles from Washington. Our picket posts in about the same. We can hear the artillery very plainly our guns have sunk two of their gun boats at Hill's Point five miles below Washington.* We hear various rumors here first that Gen. Hill is waiting for the women and the children to get out of the place and two that he is fortifying the place that he will be able to hold it when he should take it. Another is that he is going to starve them out and still another that he is only holding the Yankees off till he can get provisions from Washington and Hyde countys. I hope he will take the place. The Yankees I learn are getting very uneasy about Newbern, they are moving commissary and other governmental stores to Beaufort. I presume of Hill should take Washington then he will try Newbern. We have had a hard little fight today at our picket post a whole Yankee regiment attacked us across the River. We fought them till they brought up a gun boat to lean on us when we had to leave.[15] We got one man wounded—the ball entered the Jaws one inch from the mouth on the left side and was taken out on the top of the Right Shoulder. How it rapped around the neck without doing any more damage is more than I can see.

I believe every body in and out of the army have come to the conclusion that the war is likely to continue for an Indefinite period of time. All of the soldiers have given up hopes of the War closing. I have given up all hopes for Peace and I have given up all hopes for our country. Starvation will soon be at our doors. While in service the soldiers are acquiring habits that will be Ruinous to Society when the war is over. I cant say I am much worse than I arrived in service but I do know that I have done things I would have never thought of doing at home. I got a letter from J. C. Loftin the other day, he seems to be well. I wish you would inform me what a good house he bought in your section. Let me hear from you,

Yours truly,
D. W. Badgett

Here, Pvt. Badgett is describing combat with a gun boat. Gun boats were very common in eastern North Carolina and in the war. A gun boat (actually pioneered by Thomas Jefferson) was usually small, having only one or two pieces mounted on it. This small design helped it to navigate farther inland on rivers such as the Cape Fear, Tar, Roanoke, and Neuse.

103. April 28, 1863

Sergeant Bartlett Y. Malone, "The Caswell Boys," Company H, 6th Regiment N.C. Troops, diary entry, Source: Diary of Bartlett Y. Malone, property of the Wilkinson Family. Microfilm copy available in the Southern Historical Collection, Wilson Library, University of North Carolina at Chapel Hill.

Recently promoted to sergeant, Bartlett Malone had a habit of recording sermon notes in his diary, as did other Confederate soldiers. These notes would not be extensive, but they usually referred to the scripture on which the sermon was

based. The action being described in this entry is probably preliminary action to the battle of Chancellorsville, referring to a Union movement across the Rappahanock River.

And the Preacher taken part of the 16th chapter of Luke commencen at the 18 virse for the foundation of what remarks he made And in the eavning we had preachen in our Regiment from a preacher in the 18th Virginia Regiment. And his text was in Proverbs 18th chapter and the later clause of the 24th virse which reads thus: Thar is a friend that sticketh closter than a brother:

The morning of the 28 befour I got up I herd a horse come threw the camp in a full lope* and it was not meney minutes untell the man come back and sais Boys you had better get up we will have a fight hear to reckly and I comenced getlng up and befour I got my close on they comenced beating the long roal. And it was not but a minnet or too untill I herd the Adgertent hollow fall in with armes the Reg. Then was formed and marched to the Battel field the Yankies comenced crossing the river befour day and by day they had right smart force over the pickets.

*Gallop

104. May 3, 1863

Captain Columbus H. Dixon, "The King's Mountain Tigers," Company G, 49th Regiment N.C. Troops, letter to his wife, L. A. Dixon, Cleveland County, N.C. Source: C. H. Dixon Papers (1517), Special Collections, Perkins Library, Duke University, Durham, N.C. (Excerpted from original due to decay.)

Captain Dixon was born in Lincoln County but resided in Cleveland County prior to volunteering for service on March 18, 1862. He resided on a sizable farm with his wife and family. Dixon was elected to the post of first lieutenant upon his enlistment and would be promoted to captain in March 1863.[16] The 49th North Carolina (Ransom's Brigade) was posted in North Carolina just as other units were engaged in the battle of Chancellorsville. It is unknown why he asks his wife's response to be directed to him in care of Captain Petty's Company, especially since Dixon commands his own company.

> Camp Near Kinston N C
> May the 3rd 1863
>
> Kind and Affectionate Wife,
>
> I wrote you a few lines last evening. But as I have nothing to do on this Holly Sabbath evening for the first time this year. We have not had any inspection to see if our guns are clean. All we have to do all day is clean our guns. Our out-post fired the other night and had our Regiment out in a line of battle but it proved to be a falce alarm. Company G was the first company on the field and with their guns loaded and was ready for the infernal Murderous yankees.
>
> I have been reading all day and I have read through Revalations to day. But I am not all together pleasant to the Deity of Parents to their children which I do not believe. I will send for you before long. I am to send this letter by M. L. Connall. John Kanipe landed safe last night.
>
> If I don't get to come around this month I want you to get Sarah Rosalyne Baptised. I have not heard from our small pox men since last Tuesday. There is no more pox in the company. Give my respects to all. Write soon for I remain your true husband,
>
> C. H. Dixon
>
> Direct in care of Capt. Petty's Co.

105. May 9, 1863

Private John A. Jackson, "The Moore Independents," Company H, 26th Regiment N.C. Troops, letter to his sister, Martha Jackson, Moore County, N.C. Source: Richard A. Cole Papers. Private Manuscripts Collection, North Carolina Division of Archives and History.

By this time Private Jackson's regiment, the 26th North Carolina, along with Pettigrew's Brigade had been transferred to the Army of Northern Virginia after a considerable stay in eastern North Carolina. Private Jackson tells his sister about a stream of captured Federals passing the bridge his unit is guarding, bound for southern prisons.

> Hanover Court House Va
> May the 9th 1863
> On the Fedricksberg Road at the
> bridge on Northanna River
> 27 miles from Richmond
>
> Miss Martha R. Jackson
>
> Dear sister I rec'd your kind letter yesterday morning and it was a welcome visitor. You may depend I was more than glad to hear from you and all the rest of the family and Cole and family and the Neighbors generaly and that you were all well. I am well at presant and hope these few lines will soon come to hand and find you all the same. The company is in very good health at presant but very few sick in it. We have very near 100 men for duty at any rate we draw rations for 99 and they are all able for duty.
>
> I havnt much news to write you at this time only they say that General Lee has whipt the yankeys again at Fredricksberg and taken about then thousand prisoners and several peaces of artillery and drove them back across the rapahaoc with heavy loss. There is suposed to be some where about 40 thousand kild wounded and mising and our loss 10 thousand.[17] I saw yesterday 2000 prisoners pass the bridge that we are garding and some 1200 more this morning passed down the Railroad in about the ½ of mile of where we are

standing. Some of our boys saw them this morning. I did not see them I was off fishing when they passed this morning. I hear there is a great many behind yet. They say it was one of the hardest fought battles that has been fought since the war commenced. So I shal say no more about the battle for some body else can give a better description than I can and that will be put in the papers for every body to read.

I have no newse of importance more than what I have wrote that is worth spoiling paper with. You said Mother wanted to know how I was geting along in the army. Well just as I always have only I dont get but a ? pound bacon per day but I got shugar now in the place of meat ? of a pound per day. Times is hard here but if they dont get any worse I think I can stand it at least I intend to try it a while longer before I do like B. Stutts[18]. So I must close by saying write soon and direct your letters to Richmond Va. 26 Regt NC Co H in care of Capt J. D. McIver Pettigrews Brigade. Give my love to Mother and Brother and my respects to the rest of the family & all enquiring friends.

Your ever loving Brother
J. A. Jackson to M. R. Jackson

106. May 11, 1863

Private John A. Jackson, "The Moore Independents," Company H, 26th Regiment N.C. Troops, letter to his brother, S. T. Jackson, Moore County, N.C. Source: Richard A. Cole Papers, Private Manuscripts Collection, North Carolina Division of Archives and History.

This letter was written two days after Jackson's previous letter (above) but was mailed in the same envelope. One thing that stands out is his report of Jackson's death being caused by a bum shell striking him. All students of the war know that Jackson died of pneumonia while recover-

ing from having his left arm amputated. Also curious was the fact that Jackson bought shoes. Normally shoes were given to enlisted men as part of their clothing issue.

May the 11th 1863

S. T. Jackson
Dear Brother

I take the presant opertunity of droping you a few lines to let you know that I have not fogotten you. If you have me it seames that you dont intend to write to me any more or if you do I dont get you letters. I want to know what is the matter that you dont write or have I done any thing to keep you from writing. If so let me know what it is so no more on that subject at presant.

I am well at presant and hope these few lines will come safe to hand and find you and all the family well and Cole & family. I have no newse of much importance to write you only General Jackson departed this life yesterday. He rec'd a wound in the last battle at Fredrickberg in his left arm. Our own men done it but I heard today that is was a bumshell that struck him and that he never recovered from the shock.

It is a great loss to us and I fear that it will bother us to find a man to fill his place thought I hope we will and soon (god can give us a man to stand in his place) I hope it is for the better if it is gods will for us to gain our independance it is all right. I saw about 2000 yankey prisoners yesterday going to Richmond. There has went some 5000 by us to Richmond and a good many others so no more on that subject.

You need not send them shoes that I wrote to you for I have bought a pair since and dont need them at presant. So I must close for the presant by saying write soon and direct your letters to Richmond Va 26 Regt N.C. Troops Co H General Pettigrews Brigade. Give my love to mother and Martha and all the family and Cole and family. So no more at presant only I remain your loving Brother

J. A. Jackson[19]

107. May 14, 1863

Private Berry Kinney, "The Cleveland Guards," Company D, 14th Regiment N.C. Troops, Hamilton's Crossing, VA, letter to William H. Badgett, JP, Jackson Hill, Davidson County, N.C. Source: Badgett Collection, Davidson County Historical Museum.

Grenberry and Alfred Douglas Kinney were brothers who served in company D, 14th N.C. Troops. In this selection, Berry is describing the battle of Chancellorsville, Virginia, which was fought between Gen. Lee's Army of Northern Virginia (65, 000) and Joseph Hooker's Union army (110, 000) on May 1–3, 1863. The battle was known for the famous flanking march led by Stonewall Jackson, whose corps came out directly in the rear of Hooker's 11th Corps, routing them thoroughly, resulting in over 17, 000 Union casualties. The victory came dear to the Confederate side, however, with nearly 12,500 casualties and the loss of General Jackson.

May the 14th 1863
Hameltons Crossing
Sir, I seat myself this morning to in form you that I am tolerable well and truly hoping these few lines may find you all in good heatlh. The rest of the boys is tolerable well. Dobys boys complaining some of not being well. I and Smith got to his Reg the 6th day of this month went to the 7th and stayed a day. A. D. Kinney was slightly wounded in the brest not dangerously. So some of the company told me since I came hear and I am hopeful that he will get a furlogh on the account of his being hoarse so he can not talk if he does not get a

furlough he will soon come to camp. I like camp just as well as I expected and not very well at that we got Enough to east such as meat and bred 1 pint of flour and they say ? pound of meat and draws some sugar. That is as much as I can eat the way we have to cook. If I was at home I could eat it one meal so I let that suffice.

Everything is very high hear peas is $1.75 per quart, butter 4 dollar lbs soda $6 lbs. I am in better hopes of the army being supported than I was for if they have another such a fights as they had it will not take much to support the army. Them men back always boasting of our men getting so many arms they do get a lot and ours is killed from the breech of hundreds of those arms and they take a great many from the yankee. This is said to be the greatest and most compleat victory of the Confederacy and it want take many more such victorys to finish our army though they whipted old Joe and some 7,000 yankees came up and surrendered and they taken a good many of our men. So you in no doubt have heard more than I can tell you. The 7 regt was badly cut up and they said they had nothing but fun. You can guess at it there was 186 wounded and killed in the 14 regt. Some companys in the regt has not more 8 or 10 men left. They think they will never attempt to come over hear again but I cant tell what they will do. I heard some men say before I left home they would never attempt to cross hear. This time every body says old Joe made the best move that any of them has ever made. If he had been a little sooner, he would have surrounded the army. The men hear is powerful tired and some 6 leaves every night. Since I have been hear we drawed rations. Since I have been writing and I could eat it up if I had to work and not have half enough though I get plenty because no body can eat much such a doings as we have flys on our meat and never wash it. You can hear the sand crack and when our bread get could you can put it in your mouth clamp you teeth and bide it some half a dozen times before you can get off this is so as I have not been here long. I will say no moore. I should like to be on the Nooe Hill plowing my corn if it was convenent. Alfred Smith thinks it severe but he will get to liking it after a little. T. F. Tippett was hit by a spent ball not seriously. We had no difficulty in finding the Reg. Times is hard and will be no better till this war is over. You must tell the girls to work + make corn + save the harvest, I pitty them but I cant better their condition miself. I should love to get back we are so badly fixed here that I can not write to do any good. You must look over it a time or too. So I must close by asking you to write soon.

Yours Respectfully, B. R. Kinney

Direct your letters to Guinney Station, Va Co D, 14th NC Troop in care of Capt Weere, Ramseur's Brigade*

PS—WH Badgett

Sir if you get this letter I wrote one home a few days agoe and you may get yours and they may not. If you get this letter and anyone is hoping to hear from me tell them we can see Yankees tents every day. When I write again I hope I will have something else to write on but my hand and knee.

*Ramseur's Brigade was commanded by Stephen D. Ramseur of Lincolnton, N.C., and was composed of the 2nd, 4th, 14th, and 30th N.C. Troops.

108. May 20, 1863

Private Hughey Clodfelter, "The Carolina Rangers," Company B, 10th Virginia Cavalry Regiment, Culpeper, VA, letter to unknown friend, Davidson County, N.C. Source: Clodfelter Collection, Davidson County Public Library.

Hughey Clodfelter was like most young men of J. E. B. Stuart's Cavalry Division. He was eager, he loved the cavalry, and he was naive. Hugh was a student at Yadkin Institute before the war, and he volunteered for service in Davie County on October 29, 1861. This cavalry unit under W. B. Clement was placed in the 10th Regiment Virginia Cavalry, one of several North Carolina companies to serve in Virginia units.[20] In this letter Hugh writes back home about one of Stuart's reviews held at Brandy Station, Virginia. The imagery of cheering crowds, men and horses engaged in a choreographed mock battle, and the sounds of the entire gay affair are far from the reality of the war. These reviews boosted morale in the cavalry, but Stuart was nearly defeated when Federal cavalry launched a surprise attack during one of these celebrations.

Camp near Culpeper C. H. May 20, 1863
Dear Friend

I take the pleasure this evening to drop you a few lines to let you know that I am well at the present time. Hoping these few lines may find you and your family well and injoying selfs fine. I will inform you how we are getting along at this time. Our fare is tolable good at this time a plenty to eat and a plenty for our horses and not much duty to do hear. We drill one hour a day and that is just good exersize for us. I think that we will take a ride round in Pensylvania in a few days, fur I think that General Stuart is fixing fur it. His Division is all hear together now. There is about twenty thousand cavalry hear now. We had a general review hear the other day. They was about fifteen thousand men and horses on the field at one time. They was twelve pieces of artilry firing at once.

Also we had a sham battle. The cavalry made noble and gallant charges. They was about five or six hundred ladies out to see us on the review. It was a right smart to see. Mr. Leonard, I want you to give all the pretty girls mine and Wm Hedricks best love and respect. If we do take that saddle me and William Hedrick and McGuire will go if we never get back any more.[21] I rote you three letters that I don't think that you ever got them. I havent got a letter from any of my friends in a month or more, only what Joseph A. Hiatt brought me. I havent any news of any importance to rite at this time. I will try and do better the next time so no more at present.

> yours truly

Hughey Clodfelter rote by friend
  Wm Hedrick
Direct you leter to Richmond but in cear of cap W. B. Clement Co B 10th Va Cavalry, W. H. F. Lee Brigade tell my folks that I am well but is not satisfied out hear.

109. May 25, 1863

Private John W. Hundely, Company C, 21st Regiment N.C. Troops, letter to his wife, Sallie Hundely, Stokes County, N.C. Source: Hundely Family Papers, Southern Historical Collection, University of North Carolina at Chapel Hill.

John Hundley worked as a farmer prior to being conscripted into service on August 4, 1862, at the age of twenty-five. Hundley and his wife, Sallie, lived in the Danbury area of Stokes County. John was assigned to Company C, 21st North Carolina Troops. In the following letter, John writes about recent casualites suffered by the 21st NC at the Battle of Chancellorsville.

> May the 25th 1863
>   Camp near Fredricks burge, Va
> Dear Wife
>   I sete my self this evenin to drop you a few lines to in form you that I was well as coman and I dearely hope when

Private Hubbard Wilson of Rockingham County was among the seventy-eight casualities suffered by the 21st Regiment during the Battle of Chancellorsville. (Courtesy of the N.C. Division of Archives and History.)

thes few lines comes to hande they may finde you well and doin well.

I will in form you that I haf gote to my regemente and it was easy to finde my company and my mess her. They sayed they did not no or expect me back as they hade bin in a fite and have bin wounded and they taken prisoners and from me I wanted to no wether Jorge is dead. He got killed in this batel and William Faris is a prisoner and John Franses is wounded in the hede and Harry Franses is wounded in the leg and they are a grate deal more that is wounded and captured prisoners and has not been seen.[22]

Well now that I am her and must ask you to rite as soone as you get this and rite all the nuse in the country for it is im posable to get nuse from home some times. If you can rite often as I look forwart to hearin from you. Direct your leter in car of capten Sno in the 21 regemente nc troopes.

I must end my leter this time by sayin rite soon

John Hundely

110. May 28, 1863

Private John W. Armsworthy, "The Western Rangers," Company H, 54th Regiment N.C. Troops, letter to his wife, Edna Armsworthy, Forbush, Yadkin County, N.C. Source: Private Collection, Mr. Bob Furches, Clemmons, N.C.

Since John's last featured correspondence (see numer 94), the 54th along with Early's Divison had been involved in a second battle at Fredericksburg. While the Battle of Chancellorsville was raging only miles away, Early's force guarded Lee's extreme right flank against the Union forces under John Sedgewick. It was in this action that Private Armsworthy would be captured. By the 27th of the same month, Private Armsworthy and his comrades in the 54th Regiment were processed, transported, exchanged and reported present for duty. His treatment while in the hands of the enemy was fair, and he even remarks on the supply of the Union Army, saying, "They can continue this war for twenty years."

Camp near Fredericksburg Va.
May the 28 1863

Dear wife I seat myself to write you a short letter to let you know that I am still in the land of the living but am not very well though I feel better today than I have for the past two weeks though I have been up all the time. I am weak & trimly though I think I will come it

now. I have got back to the old camp. You have heard of the fight at Fredericksburg. I was in the fight for five days, that is in line of battle. We was not fighting all the time. We made a charge on the Yankees the 4th day of May, some of us charged so far we got taken prisoner. There was six of my company & one Lieutant. There was some from every company in the Regment. We was sent to Washington, staid there two nights, then on through Baltimore to Philadelphia. There we got on the stare Boat & went to Fort Delaware where we staid for 15 days. We was then sent to City Point in Va. where we was exchange. We then come to Petersburg, staid there two nights. We then come to Richmon staid there two nights. We come to the Regment yesterday. I found my company very small. There was but two killed on the field. There was several wounded & there has twenty run away since the fight. I expect to tuf it out a while longer. I dont think there is much fun in running away from here. I expect you know as much of the fight by the papers as I can tell you. I think it is sirtain we whiped the Yankees pretty bad. I recun you would like to know how the Yankees treated us prisoners. They was kind ennuf & give us plenty to eat for they have got it. They have got plenty of every thing & some of them say they can continue this war for twenty years before we shall have our independance then others say they are as tired of the war as we are. If I had been well I could enjoyed the trip very well but I was sick all the time & it was no sadisfaction to me. I feel thankfull to my God that my life was spared for we went through heavy fire like it was impossible for any of us to be missed but I come out unhurt.

This is the third letter I have written since I got back, I got yours dated the 17th of this month. I was glad to here you was all well Dont send Bran &

Elley to school every day, it
is too confirming. I hope
these few lines will find you
all well I must close for the
present by saying write soon.
Tell father I have not Rec.
any letter from him in two
months. I got a few lines
from Mathew. Write soon
give me all the news.

> Your Husband far
> from home
> J. W. Armsworthy

111. May 29, 1863

Brigadier General Stephen
D. Ramseur, Rodes' Division,
letter to sweetheart, Ellen
Richmond, Milton, Lincoln
County, N.C. Source: Paul W.
Schenk, Jr., and Dodson R.
Schenk, Jr., of Greensboro,
N.C., and extracts of corre-
spondence, S. D. Ramseur
Papers, Southern Historical
Collection, University of North
Carolina at Chapel Hill.

Stephen Dodson Ramseur
was just twenty-five years old
when he was appointed to command Anderson's old brigade.
The Lincolnton-born son of Jacob and
Lucy Ramseur had graduated from the
United States Military Academy in 1860
and had served as a lieutenant in the 4th
U.S. Artillery prior to volunteering for
state service. Ramseur served as a major of
artillery, commanded at Yorktown, and
was elected colonel of the 49th North Carolina, where he won fame during the Seven
Days battles and received a severe wound
at Malvern Hill. Ramseur returned to service in March of 1863 and led his brigade
valiantly at Chancellorsville, winning the
respect of Generals Rodes and Jackson,
and being mentioned by Lee as "among the

Stephen D. Ramseur, a Lincoln County native, led
his brigade to victory during the Battle of Chancellorsville. (North Carolina Collection, University of North Carolina at Chapel Hill.)

best in the Army ... and at Chancellorsville,
General Ramseur was among those whose
conduct was especially commended to my
notice by Lieutenant-General Jackson."[23]
One item of interest is the importance
which Ramseur places on the defense of
Vicksburg. This is one of only a couple of
instances where action in the western theatre is mentioned in a letter. This letter is
extracted from the original.

> H'dqtrs, Ramseur's Brigade
> May 29th '63

My Dearest Ellen
Today Gen'l Lee reviewed our Division. We made a splendid appearance,

but it was very sad to see the thinned ranks of our Veterans. So many now lie in their graves and so many more lie on beds of pain. We are awaiting "Fighting Joes" movements and are engaged in watching him closely.

Yesterday heavy clouds of dust indicated that the Yankees were moving towards the far creek; it may be with the ultimate intention of moving the mass of his forces to the Peninsula or to the south bank of the James River. We have had no intuition as yet of any movement on his part. No doubt Gen'l Lee will be ready to meet him at any point and with his Veteran army so often blessed by our father in Heaven, to drive him back with loss and disgrace.

We feel very anxious about Vicksburg. Though the news today was a more cheering prospect. Should Vicksburg fall, our God forbid, I believe the war will be prolonged about indefinitely. If we are victorious in Vicksburg our army there will be replaced. Bragg's army at Tullahoma can be greatly strengthend and Rosecrants' army can be driven through Kentucky.

I confess, as I see matters which I have already explained, I can see but little reason to hope for a "speedy" conclusion to the war.

S. D. Ramseur

112. June 5, 1863

Eliza Clodfelter, Davidson County, letter to her cousin, Mary Ann Eddinger, Davidson County. Source: Richard L. Conrad.

Mary Ann (Clodfelter) Eddinger was the widow of George W. Eddinger, whose letter was featured earlier in this work. This letter is very special, not only because it was correspondence sent between two lower middle class women, but because of the break from the war that it provides. This letter provides an inside look into domestic life and all of its issues.

June the 5th 1863
To Mary Ann Edinger

Dear Cousin with pleasure I embrace the present opportunity of writing you a few lines in order to let you hear from your old settlement. We are all well and I hope these lines may find you all enjoying the blessings of good health. We have got no thread for you or ourselves since you left. Hutson goes and gets thread and sells it out before he gets home. It is now ten dollars a bunch. Pappy went to see old Elic as you call him yesterday. He has sent two letters about your money and got no answer yet. He told him he sent the last one with Rans. Rans had a furlough for fourteen days he went back about two weeks ago. If old Elic gets a letter this time he will write and then you will get to come down. I heard that Pop and Rans was so mad about every thing that it done them no good to see him. Billy came home last week he is going to start back next Monday. I believe the old woman has got well they say she goes about every day. We don't hear anything they say about you, but we hear they say they intend to have part of Phillips estate yet.

Pappy went down to your house yesterday. He said he went to the door but no body opened it and he did not go in. He says your wheat looks sorry. The blossom is not yet on it so you may know it is not ready to cut. Your heifer grows fast an looks well. Trueboy stays at home all the time. I have now told you all that I know about your business. We have had dry weather and everything looks backward. I think if people would quit killing one another we might then look for better seasons. John Yokely is in the woods and they say Jake Wagner has got back and is with him.[24] We see runaways going along the road every few days. I don't care how soon they all get home. Ellen Nancy is in Richmond with John. He is badly wounded.

I suppose you have heard of the death of Barbara Sink. She was buried the third Sunday in April. Solomon Sinks wife lost one of her little boys with the sore throat and three of Israel Long's children and his wife all died with the same complaint.

Mary Ann you don't know how glad I would be to see you and Jinny coming up the road like you used to. Tell uncle Tice and his folks I want to see them. Tell Jinny if she will come she may have the hind leg of a chicken for her supper for I know she is just like old Crissie. Alpheus says tell Jinny he wishes he could see her in her shirt tail fighting with the shovel. Tell her she has to come and kiss me for rags. She kissed a negroe for rags* and never kissed me. Eda says tell you she is as well as common and has plenty of work to do and wants to see Jinny. I know whoever reads this is tired no not tired now but will be tired reading this bad writing so I must close. If you cant come before long write, and let us hear how you are all getting along.

Your Cousin, Elvira E. Clodfelter

*For rags: For nothing, free.

113. June 5, 1863

First Sergeant Jonas A. Bradshaw, "Rocky Face Rangers," Company G, 38th Regiment N.C. Troops, letter to his wife, Nancy Bradshaw, Alexander County, N.C. Source: Jonas A. Bradshaw Papers (620), Special Collections, Perkins Library, Duke University, Durham, N.C.

Sergeant Bradshaw of Alexander County (see number 79) was wounded in action at Chancellorsville, Virginia, on May 3, 1863. After a brief convalescence, Bradshaw was promoted to first sergeant and joined his company along the banks of the Rappahannock River.[25]

> Armey of the Rhappahanock Va
> June 5th 1863

Dear wife

It is agane that I imbrace the oppertunity of droping you a few lines to inform you of my helth. I am well and harty and I hope these few lines may find you well and all the rest of my friends well. I have no news worth relating onley we have orders to cook two days rashions. The troops are moving some ways but we cant tell where. I think thare is a chance for us to get into a rather big fite. It would not surprise me if we were not in a fite before you get these few lines and it should be my fate to fall dont let it greave you. I hope God will take cear of me and sheald me.

Dear loving wife pray for me and for my success that he may sheald me and give me Grace and strength that I may withstand all the trials and tribulations of this world and after all gone to that selestial sitty. Dear wife I oftentimes think of you and think how happy we were wance when little Mary was with us an know wars to disterb us but alass it pleased God to call little Mary into his armes and know I am in the armey and you are and our onley little Babe is left at home. I hope God will bless you and preserve your lives and after deth reseve you in heaven with little Mary and that we may all meet to part no more on that happy day.

Dear wife give my love to all of our famely that they know that I would be glad to see them and it does me so much good to hear from them. Tell Abner Bar that I send him my love and best respects to him. Tell uncle Billy Gaultney that I send him my love and best respects and if I should see him no more on erth I hope that we may meet in heaven. Tell C. F. Bradshaw and J. Query[26] that I want them to write to me and that I send them my love. Tell them to be good boyes. I will close at presant. Write to me soon and let me hear from you and I want you to write whether you have heard any thing from Samson Gaultney or not and Criss Barker. I would be glad to hear. Nancy I want you to draw every thing that is dew you from the state for you have as good a write to it as any boddy. So fare well hear is a dollar or two.

J. N. Bradshaw, ordley

114. June 9, 1863

Private Louis Leon, Company B, 53rd Regiment N.C. Troops, diary entry. Source: Leon, Louis, *Diary of a Tar Heel Confederate Soldier*, 1913.

With the campaign in eastern North Carolina over, the 53rd and the rest of Daniel's Brigade was ordered to rejoin the Army of Northern Virginia. The following entry discusses the battle of Brandy Station, Virginia, when Confederate Cavalry under J.E.B. Stuart was surprised by Federal troopers under Gen. Pleasanton. The resulting engagement on June 9 was the largest cavalry battle in the western hemisphere.

June 9 (1863)—We were ordered to Beverly Ford, to support Gen. Jeb Stuart, who is engaging the Yankees, and they are having a very hard cavalry fight. Got here in a round about way, and formed in a line of battle, with two lines of skirmishers in front. When we got to the Army of Northern Virginia we were told that each company must furnish one skirmisher out of every six men, and there was a call for volunteers for that service. So I left the colors and went as a skirmisher, whose duty it is in time of battle to go in front of the line and reconnoitre and engage the enemy until a general engagement, then we fall in line with the balance of the army. As

soon as the enemy saw that the cavalry were reinforced by infantry, they fell back. Quite a number of prisoners, and camped two miles from the battlefield. We marched twelve miles today.

115. June 11, 1863

Private Bartlett Yancey Malone, "The Caswell Boys," Company H, 6th Regiment N.C. State Troops, diary entry, Source: Diary of Bartlett Y. Malone, property of the Wilkinson Family. Microfilm copy available in the Southern Historical Collection, Wilson Library, University of North Carolina at Chapel Hill.

Bands contributed greatly to the improvement of morale among soldiers and civilians. The band of the 6th Regiment N.C. Troops featured sixteen musicians [27] who also served as functioning litter-bearers and performed a variety of other tasks. As Malone describes, the martial music of a brass band could stimulate morale and boost the spirits of the soldiers and civilians.

The 8th day we got to Culpeper and stopt to cook Rations. The 8 day we staid at Culpeper untell about 3 O'clock in the eavning and was then ordered down to Brandy Station about 4 miles from Culpeper whar the Calvry hat bin firing all day and we staid all nite and the next morning we found that the Yankees had all gon back on the other Side of the River and we marched back to Culpeper again and cooked another days rations and about 3 O'clock in the eavning we started again in the direction of Winchester and we got as far as Hasel Run [Hazel Run or Deep Run] by nite And the next morning which was the 11th we started about sun up and about 9 O'clock we got to a littel town cauld Woodwin and whilst we was a passen threw the 6th N. C. Brass Ban plaid the Bonnie Blew Flag. And about eleven

O'clock we got to a littel town cauld Sperysvill 5 miles from Woodwin And about 2 O'clock in the eavning we past threw Washington and ther we found a meney pritty and kind Ladies they had water all along the streets for the Soldiers to drink and we dident go but a few miles futher untell we stopt for the nite after going about 20 miles that day.

116. June 17, 1863

Second Lieutenant Leonidas L. Polk, "The Anson Regulators," Company I, 43rd N.C. Troops, letter to his wife, Wadesboro, Anson County, N.C. Source: L. L. Polk Papers, Southern Historical Collection, University of North Carolina at Chapel Hill.

Second Lieutenant Leonidas Polk of the "Anson Regulators." (Courtesy of the N.C. Division of Archives and History.)

Leonidas Lafayette Polk was born on April 24, 1837, to Andrew and Serena Autry Polk. At the age of eighteen, Polk began his own farm inheriting 353 acres of land and seven slaves. Also in 1855, Polk entered Davidson College in Mecklenburg County and completed a one-year degree as a "special student." Upon his return to Anson, he married Pamela Gaddy on September 23, 1857. With the start of the war, Polk volunteered as a member of the "Pee Dee Wildcats" and eventually rose to the rank of sergeant major of the 26th North Carolina Troops. Polk was later promoted to lieutenant and was transferred to "The Anson Regulators," Company I, 43rd North Carolina Troops.[28]

> Petersburg Va
> June 17th 1863
> My Own Dear Wife
> I have arrived here safely after a long, dirty, hot, & fatiguing ride. Since I left home until 3 o'clock this morning, I have been riding constantly resting only about 2 hours. As I anticipated, I will have to lie over a day to procure the Colonel's clothing. I have just been down to call upon Mrs. Page and family finding some of them sick. They are all very glad to see me. I am now in Charlie Reid's office who is busily engaged in the tedious undertaking of selling some Clothing to a tight fisted Lt who wants to "jew" him on government prices. Charlie is indeed a nice boy and I should be highly pleased if I were connected with him in the Dept. Capt. Reid of whom you heard me speak is also one of my favorites in Virginia. It is very seldom that we of the dispised old North State meet with that kindness and generous hospitality which had so conspicuously characterized my short connection with its gentleman and ladies.
> In the news items of this morning, nothing of interest occurred except a

dispatch from Gen. Lee stating that Gen. Early after an engagement with the enemy, succeeded in capturing Winchester, which place he now holds. He gives nothing of the particulars.

I see by the papers that Gen. Robertson's Brigade was not in the fight at Culpeper* though this is gained from Virginia papers & as his Brigade is comprised of North Carolinians, of course they could not say anything about it. No news from Vicksburg though a spirit of confidence seems to prevail. If it falls, in my humble opinion, it will be the death blow to our independence.

I am feeling as well as I could hope after my tedious ride and am recovered to some extent from my blue spell. I wish I could have felt more lively and bouyant while at home, but it is attributable to the depression which pervades the whole country. I shall start tomorrow at 5 am. If you write before I do again, which I hope you will, direct your letter to Richmond. I hear that our Regt has been transferred to Gen. Ramsuer's Brigade, but do not know that is true. Hoping to hear from you <u>soon</u> and <u>frequently</u>. I remain your devoted husband,

Leon

PS Kiss our Babies for me.[29]

*The brigade of Robertson (2nd, 3rd, 4th, 5th NC Cavalry Regiments) was not involved in the battle of Brandy Station (Culpeper) on June 9, 1863.

117. June 25, 1863

Private Louis Leon, Company B, 53rd Regiment N.C. Troops, Diary entry. Source: Leon, Louis, *Diary of a Tar Heel Confederate Soldier*, 1913.

After the battle of Brandy Station, the 53rd North Carolina joined the Army of Northern Virginia on the campaign into the north. This was the unit's first such incursion into enemy territory, and the majority of the men had no idea what this expedition might have in store.

June 25 (1863)—Marched on, passed through Leesburg, Canada, Hockinsville, and Centreville, all small villages. We got to Carlisle, Pa., at sundown. Marched 21 miles today. This city is certainly a beautiful place. It has 8,000 inhabitants, and we were treated very good by the ladies. They thought we would do as their soldiers do, burn every place we passed through, but when we told them of the strict orders of General Lee, they were rejoiced.* Our regiment was provost guard in the city, but were releaved by the 21st Georgia Regiment, and we went to camp at the U.S. Barracks. So far we have lived very good in the enemy's country. We stayed here until the 30th, when we took the Baltimore Pike road, crossed South Mountain at Holly Gap, passed through Papertown and Petersburg. We then left the Pike and took the Gettysburg Road—17 miles today. This has been a hard day for us, as we were the rear guard of the division, and it was very hot, close and very dusty, and a terrible job to keep the stragglers up.

*On crossing into the North, General Lee ordered that no foraging or destruction of private property would be conducted by any soldier in the army. If a soldier wanted something he had to buy it from a civilian.

118. June 28, 1863

Second Lieutenant Leonidas L. Polk, "The Anson Regulators," Company I, 43rd N.C. Troops, letter to his wife, Wadesboro, Anson County, N.C. Source: L. L. Polk Papers, Southern Historical Collection, University of North Carolina at Chapel Hill.

Lieutenant Polk's 43rd North Carolina (Daniel's Brigade, Rodes' Divison) had "carried the war" far into southern Pennsylvania for certain. Polk talks about the "festivities" in Carlisle, home of the United States Army Barracks, and he sees the civilians as friendly and advocating peace. Polk's reference to Pettigrew's Brigade goes back to his days as sergeant major of the 26th North Carolina and a company of Anson men in Company K of that same Regiment.

Carlisle Pa.
June 28th 1863

My own dear Wife,

You see that I am in Pensylvania with the army that has so long threatened to "carry the war into Africa." I caught up at Chambersburg the day before yesterday after a few days of the hardest marching I ever did, having walked 74 miles in 2½ days! I wrote you from Strasburg & hope you got the letter as it was a diary of my travels and troubles, observations, vexations etc. Our force crossed the Potomac and took all the towns, villages, and public property, then came straight through Maryland into this state. We have destroyed millions of dollars in public property and captured about 5,000 prisoners & are now encamped in and around the town of Carlisle. The Yankee forces fly at our approach without firing a gun, frequently. Gen. Hooker* is somewhere near Washington, or far in our rear, evidently outgeneralled one time again. We are within 18 miles of Harrisburg, the Capitol.

There was a force here yesterday but when they found our cavalry approaching, they that camped here left leaving everything and we are now occupying the barracks. They are splendid quarters and are comfortably furnished. We all have just as much ice, sugar, molasses, beef, bread, etc. etc. as we want. Our whole army is on this side of the Potomac. This campaign is pregnant with great events & how or when or where it will end, is with Gen Lee & our God. The people are almost frightened to death and render a servile complacency to allow acts which it is painful to a bold Southernor to behold.

I am well & doing very well. I would like to write you a long letter but I must close, just hoisted the National flag. Speeches are to be made by Gens Ewell, Rhodes, Daniel, Trimble. Anson Guards, Ellis Rifles, doing well. Sam Tillman is well, please let his family know. Billy May is well and all the boys are in fine spirits. Will write again soon as possible. Hope to hear from you soon, but it is doubtful as we are going further from home every day. I will write you again as soon as I get the chance to send it though. I have written 3 letters since I came from home.

We are all hopeful of good results from the campaign. The people are very kind & are all for peace now. All for McClellan for President. Kiss our little darlings for me, write soon and be sure to put Rhodes Division, Daniels Brigade. I remain, as now your ever devoted & affectionate

Leonidas

Gen Pettigrew is on behind, not far. We have captured about 6 or 8 thousand cattle, the finest I ever saw & I suppose 3 or 4 thousand of the very best Black Dutch horses. Nearly all our boys have new clothes, shoes, and hats. We buy Calico 50 cts, everything cheap. If I was to get back I will try to bring something to you. They allow us 50cts on the dollar for our money. The storekeepers are bound to take it. We hear nothing from Vicksburg. If it will only hold out!

General George G. Meade was officially in command of the Union Army of the Potomac at this time.

119. July 1, 1863

Private Louis Leon, Company B, 53rd Regiment N.C. Troops, diary entry. Source: Leon, Louis, *Diary of a Tar Heel Confederate Soldier*, 1913.

After passing through Maryland and southern Pennsylvania, the two armies would finally clash at Gettysburg. The

Iredell as depicted in Clark's Regiments. "Major Iredell of our regiment came to me and shook my hand and also complimented me for action in the fight." (Photograph courtesy of the N.C. Division of Archives and History.)

battle was begun when troops under Confederate General Heath encountered and engaged dismounted cavalry under Gen. John Buford. Rodes's Division came down from the northwest of the town and was confronted, not by cavalry, but by members of the Union 1st and 11th Infantry Corps.

July 1 (1863)—We left camp at 6 A.M. and passed through Heidelsburg and Middleton. At the latter place we heard fighting in the direction of Gettysburg. We were pushed forward after letting the wagon trains get in our rear. We got to Gettysburg at 2 P.M., 25 miles. We were drawn up in line of battle about one mile south of town, and a little to the left of the Lutheran Seminary. We then advanced to the enemy's line of battle in double quick time. We had not gotten more than 5 paces when Norman of our company fell dead by my side. Katz was going to pick him up. I stopped him, as it is strictly forbidden for anyone to help take the dead or wounded off the field except the ambulance corps. We then crossed over a rail fence, where our Lieutenant McMatthews and Lieutenant Alexander were both wounded.[30] That left us with a captain and one lieutenant. After this we got into battle in earnest, and lost in our company very heavily, both killed and wounded. This fight lasted four hours and a half, when at last we drove them clear out of town, and took at least 3,000 prisoners. They also lost very heavily in killed and wounded, which all fell into our hands. After the fight our company was ordered to Pick up all straggling Yankees in town, and bring them together to be brought to the rear as prisoners. One fellow I took up could not speak one word of English, and the first thing he asked me in German was "Will I get my pay in prison ?" After we had them all put up in a pen we went to our regiment and rested. Major Iredell of our regiment, came to me and shook my hand, and also complimented me for action in the fight. At dusk I was about going to hunt up my brother Morris, when he came to me. Thank God, we are still safe as yet. We laid all night among the dead Yankees, but they did not disturb our peaceful slumbers.

120. July 3, 1863

First Lieutenant James A. Graham, "The Orange Guards," Company G, 27th Regiment N. C. Troops, Richmond, Virginia, letter to his father, William A.

Graham, Orange County, N.C. Source: The James A. Graham Papers 1861–1864, Southern Historical Collection, University of North Carolina at Chapel Hill.

July 3, 1863, is a very famous day in the history of the American Civil War. Seldom mentioned in discussions of the summer campaigns of 1863 is the role played by the three brigades left to guard Richmond while the rest of the army was nearly 300 miles away in Gettysburg. Indeed, there was a Federal presence which threatened Richmond. The brigades of Cooke (15th, 27th, 46th, and 48th N.C. Troops) and Ransom (24th, 25th, 35th, and 49th N.C. Troops) were among the forces left to guard Richmond in case the Federal contingent on the peninsula wished to take advantage of the situation. Promoted in April 1863, James A. Graham reports the action around Richmond.

Camp Near Richmond, Va
July 3rd 1863
MY DEAR FATHER

We have just returned from a trip after the Yankees. Richmond for the past three or four days has been all astir with reports of the advance of the Yankees. Wednesday night it was ascertained that the enemy had advanced on the Williamsburg road to within 15 or 16 miles of the city. Some persons said they were 10,000 strong and some went even so far as to put them down at 40,000. Thursday morning our brigade, together with the rest of the troops around here, started to meet them. We advanced across the Chickahominy river; or rather creek, for it is a very small stream where we crossed it; and when we were some three or four miles beyond it the troops in advance came upon the Yankees who began to fall back after firing a few shots. After they once got started they did not stop except to fire a few rounds now and then. A portion of Ransom's

N. C. and Jenkins S. C. Brigades with some Artillery were the only troops engaged on our side. Our brigade was held rather in reserve. After following them till about 10 o'clock last night we started on our return to camp. We reached Camp this morning pretty tired and sleepy as we had slept only about 7 hours during the past two nights. I heard this morning that our cavalry had driven the enemy under cover of their gunboats at the White house on the Pamunkey river. Instead of finding the enemy from 10,000 to 40,000 strong, as was reported, we found only two Brigades who were out on a foraging expedition, at least so I heard this morning, and the "On to Richmond" turned out to be a mere nothing. Our loss as far as I have heard was only one killed and two or three wounded. I do not know what was the loss of the enemy. We took several prisoners and they seemed rather glad of being taken than otherwise.

I received your very welcome letter a day or two ago, in which you stated that you had written to me on the 13th ult. and sent me $50, also that you had written to me two or three times since. I went to the Post office and enquired but could find no letter there for me. I suppose it must have gotten lost somewhere on the way, for your last letter is the only one I have received from you since I was at home.

I received a letter from Mother this morning by Mr Hall. Also my boots and vest. The boots are a little large, but will do very well, the vest fits very well. Johnny and Robert are still camped near us. I saw Johnny yesterday. I do not think their Regiment was engaged in the skirmish yesterday.

Everything seems to be as quiet here now as though there had not been any Yankees near here lately, and but for the soreness of our feet we would hardly know that we had been marching at all.

In July 1863, the "Orange Guards" were without Private Lorenzo Bennett who died of disease in late 1862. (Courtesy of the N.C. Division of Archives and History.)

We have had rain almost every day for the past week or ten days but it seems to have cleared up again. The weather is very hot. Please send me the $50 I wrote for when you receive this as I am a little behind in the money line just now. Love to all. Write soon to

Your affectionate Son
James A. Graham

121. July 12, 1863

Amanda E. Murph, Lincoln County, N.C., letter to her husband, Daniel Washington Murph, "Washington Grays," Company K, 10th Regiment N.C. Troops (1st NC Artillery). Source: Daniel W. Murph Papers (3811), Special Collections, Perkins Library, Duke University, Durham, N.C.

Daniel W. Murph, a Lincoln County farmer, left his wife, Amanda, and his four children, Delila Ann, Sarah Jane, Mary, and Martha, when he enlisted into service in Lincolnton on March 12, 1863, for the war.[31] Amanda's letter updates Daniel on the happenings at home from a case of whooping cough to prices for crops and brief remarks about each of the children.

The State of N C Lin. Co.
July the 12 1863
Dear husband

It is through the kind protection of god that I am again permited to drop you a few lines in answer to your kind and affectionate letter which gave me a great satisfaction to hear from you. But I was greatly mortified when I heard of your affliction. I my self am well but the children all has the hooping cough lately and Ann is the worst off of any of them but they are not dangerous I hope. I hope that these few lines many find you in a better situation of health than you was.

When you wrote last you desired me to inform you how long it took between letters to come from there to me it is about 4 and 5 days. You wanted to know if any person was working any of Aunt Betseys grounds except my self. There is no person who works it except me. I get corn at $2 and a half a bushel, wheat $9 a bushel. Wheat is capital this year and is very splendid I tell you dear husband I long for the time to come when you shall return home to your business. I long for the time that this most cursed war should come to a speedy end. I wish to see you verry bad but it is my desire that you should not grieve after home nor me more than you can help. Rest contented and put your trust in god that you may get home.

You wanted me to save 5 bushels of wheat for meal. I am going to do so if I like. Corn looks just as fine and I can make some meal out of that and I may be able to make more meal out of corn next year but that depends on the hogs.

All looks as well as could be expected at for the time of year. The potatoes look splendid both the irish and the sweet.

[ill] is one of the sweetest children your ever saw in your life. She can talk some. Little Martha is the pretyest and in the crowd Ann is the smartest one. They are all well and are smart children. They obey me as they are the obedient children. Marys head is very sore outside it has not healed since you left here. So I shall close for this time. I want you to write to me as soon as you get this. Write soon

    I remain you affectionate wife
        E. Murph to D. W. Murph[32]

122. July 16, 1863

    Captain William B. "Dart" Clement, "The Carolina Rangers," Company B, 10th Virginia Cavalry Regiment, letter to Mattie K. Martin, Mocksville, N.C. Source: W. B. Clement Papers, Private Manuscripts Collection, North Carolina Division of Archives and History.

    Since the last letter from "Dart," his life has changed dramatically. On March 18, 1863, while at home on furlough, he married Ms. Mattie K. Martin. Since his return, W. H. F. Lee's cavalry brigade has seen some of its most intense fighting of the war at Brandy Station, the East Ridge, guarding the retreat from Pennsylvania. Clement also refers to the "no foraging order" issued by General Lee, as it was enforced in the cavalry and prevented him from going "shopping."

        Lee Town Jefferson County,
            Virginia
           July 16th 1863
My own darling Mattie

    Since I wrote to you last July 9th I have received three letters dated June 21st 28th & 31st, the last yesterday evening and you may rest assured darling. I read and re-read them with a great deal of pleasure. After my last letter from Williamsport we went to the front and was kept there skirmishing with the enemy several days until all the arrangements for crossing the river were complete. When on a very dark and very rainy night the whole army crossed safely to the Virginia side, the cavalry bringing up the rear and crossing the next morning after sunrise. Just as the last of us were crossing , the enemy dashed up to the bank on the other side and commenced firing upon us, but we turned and soon put them to flight. The right wing of the Army crossed several miles below town on a Pontoon Bridge. The balance had to ford. We are now stationed near Charles town watching the enemy who is in considerable force at Harpers Ferry in pursuit as they think of a disorganized and retreating foe—all of which they will find their mistake when they meet us.

    Since the 9th of last June our brigade has been engaged in twelve severe battles and skirmishing every day. It has done more than any other brigade of cavalry. The men are nearly all worn out with loss of sleep and heavy duty. We haven't more than four hundred men in the brigade left for duty out of four regiments where generally each regiment has more than that, but I hope we will get some rest soon. My horse is about broken down and I intend sending him home to you for a riding horse by first one passing. I captured a very pretty horse in Pennsylvania which I am riding. He is gentle, I wish he was at home for you to drive. He is more gentle and much prettier than Black Hawk, but if nothing happens you will see him someday.

    I was very sorry that I did not get into a single store in Pennsylvania. Genl Stewart was so particular and would not have any of them opened so nobody got anything except as few who broke open several which I would not do. I was so anxious to do some shopping for you, as well as to get a pair of boots for myself which I am needing very badly, but was disappointed.

I have thought about you very often darling in the last several weeks. I have been so situated that I could not write so often, and I know what you have been thinking, but dear darling wife do not get low spirited. This will not last always and we will be so happy when we meet again. I was very much astonished to hear of our new relatives. Why didn't you say our relatives instead of "your nephews" and tell Jane that Marshall will not be excused from military duty by the next board of Surgeons. I think that this is the first time ever such a thing happened in our family. Do you think it will be the last? Write often my own darling. I am thinking and dreaming of you all the time. Give my love to all. I will write again in a few days and I hope we will have time to write another letter. Good bye

Your Husband

123. July 19, 1863

Private John W. Hundley, Company C, 21st Regiment N.C. Troops, letter to his wife, Sallie Hundley, Stokes County, N.C. Source: Hundley Family Papers, Southern Historical Collection, University of North Carolina at Chapel Hill.

This next letter was evidently written for Private Hundley, somewhere in the vicinity of Martinsburg, Virginia. At the Battle of Gettysburg, Hundley was wounded in the hand on the first day of the battle. Here he reports the events of the campaign from a safe location across the Potomac.

Darksville Va
July 19th 1863

Dear Wife

As I have an opportunity I have concluded to write you a few lines. We are resting now a few days after one of the longest and hardest marches of the war. We have marched through Maryland into the center of Pensylvania and fought on of the bloodiest battles of the war. We crossed the Potomac the 22d June and was in Maryland & Pensylvania until the 14th July. We had a fine time in Pen until the fight. We could get plenty of Milk, Butter, & Bread. The citizens seemed very kind and clever in some parts of the country some claimed to be good southern people and were opposed to the war.

We passed through some nice towns and villages. We had a despirate battle at a town called Gettysburg. Our Regt lost a hundred and ten men killed wounded and missing. I was wounded slightly in the forth finger of the right hand. We captured five or six thousand prisoners and several pieces of Artilery. While the army was in Pen they captured two or three thousand Horses & Mules and about three hundred Waggons

We are camped at this place between Martinsburg and Winchester. The country about here looks like a desert. The fences are all burnt & the crops burnt out. I am a little unwell at this time. Write soon.

Yours etc.,
John Hundely[33]

124. July 21, 1863

Mary Jane Farris, visitor to Thomasville, letter to Mrs. Margaret Dalton, Little Yadkin Hotel, Stokes County, N.C. Source: John D. Phillips Papers, Private Manuscript Collection, North Carolina Division of Archives and History.

This letter is barely legible but provides the reader with a mystery and some interesting background on the time period. Illegible passages are here replaced with ellipsis points (...). Even without such interruptions, Farris's letter appears to jump randomly from topic to topic. Perhaps her desperation over the war, her relatives' wish to go off and fight, her husband's illness, and several other things might fuel such writing. The individual she is referring to is a mystery. It does seem like it could be her husband, Charles; however, no service record was found for Charles Farris. Apparently she was with her husband when he fell sick during the war and has traveled with him several places to help cure him of his disease. Among the places they have traveled are Salisbury, N.C., White Sulphur Springs, Virginia (noted for its healing waters), and Thomasville, N.C., which was the site of a smallpox hospital. It is unknown how long Mary stayed in Thomasville, but she apparently wants to go back to the Little Yadkin, a large plantation home in Stokes County owned by D. N. and Margaret Dalton.

> Thomasville, Davidson County,
> N.C. July 21 1863
> Dear Mrs. Dalton[34]
>
> Dear Madam,
>
> Will you receive these lines from one whom you have almost forgotten or if not forgotten perhaps your regard for she writes of these times have been long gone since evaporated. Indeed after such a long silence between you and myself. I feel somewhat inadequate and even ashamed to address you. I acknowledge the twelve months in Kinston. I will make any excuse and lines from you Pardon for the neglect that time but fully. I received your letter a little before preparing to start to Virginia. I postponed it until I got to Virginia but there was so much hear and trouble there that I continued to put it off until I was almost ashamed to commense. Please excuse me this time provided I do so no more. I wish that I could see you and tell you all. I have not been to Virginia since summer of 61. I could begin

to tell you my troubles since April 61. He was in the Army all last year but did not go at its commensement but it keeps me always excited and miserable knowing that he would go be a quartermaster of disrememberable regiment no so much Exposed I suppose as some but you may be sure. I rest very little all the time. I have been through this miserable, wicked, war since I saw you therefore you would hardly know me. I think that I look 10 years older than I did before the commensement of the War but they say not. He was sick at Richmond during his stay in the Army and looked of sending for you but he got better. Two of my cousins were with him all the time. He had a final discharge about the first of December and went to the office in Charlotte.... I do not know whether he will go in the Army again or not. I shall feel uneasy until this war ends. Luke wants to go in the Army. I can hardly hold him. He has always wanted to go and he would have gone if I had been willing. John is living at Salisbury only because there is nothing else for him to do. I do not want him to stay there I don't think Salisbury suits John. He don't look very well having just got a spell of measles which made him look very sick. He spent five weeks at the White Sulphur Springs which benefitted him very much, yet he still looks thin and pale. Well I must say something about myself. I am here at Thomasville. It is a right pleasant little place but I am getting tired of it. If you will board me Again I will come Board with you Again when the war is over which I hope will bee soon. When the war is over I want to go to Va only if I don't remain with you. I would like to go to Little Yadkin again and board with you a few months.... Lo[35] knows nothing about it but I can do as I like.... If this proposal will meet with your approval I will spend a few months with you again at

Little Yadkin. Be sure to write to me immediately Mrs. Dalton. If you please I would like to come see you as soon as possible.... I would like to see you and your little family I wonder how many you have. My best respect to Mr. Dalton. Please excuse any deficiency. Your Affectinately, M. J. Farris

Mary Jane Farris

125. August 4, 1863

Captain Lewis H. Webb, Company D, 12th Virginia Artillery Battalion, diary entry. Source: Diary of L. H. Webb, Lewis Webb Collection, Southern Historical Collection, University of North Carolina at Chapel Hill.

Many times during the Civil War, soldiers relied on civilians for transportation or provisions to help make their life a little easier. In this entry from Captain Webb, we see that the civilians of Averasboro do not intend to help this group of soldiers.

Aug. 4th (At Fayetteville)

I cannot describe in such a manner as I wish our trip from Barclay's to this place. From Barclay's we walked about five miles, when completely overcome with fatigue & heat I could travel no farther & stopped about 12 o'clock at the house of a Mr. Truelove, where we got dinner and I induced him to take us in his wagon to Averysboro—seven miles.

Arrived at Averysboro about 5 o'clock p.m. & then started to walk again inquiring at every house to see if I could hire a conveyance to Fayetteville but without success. I had a carpet bag with a change of clothes, a heavy sabre and pistol besides my overcoat to carry, and after walking until 8 p. m. I was completely "used up" & we laid down under a tree near the road & went to sleep. Nor did I wake till daylight when

I found we were just in front of a fine house, where doubtless we might have got a good bed and a good supper.

As soon as we awoke we "shook the dew drops glistening from our garments" and started again. Three miles walk brought us to the house of a Mr. McKethan where I stopped to see if I could get a wagon to take us to Fayetteville. The man seemed to be from his surroundings to be wealthy, but he not only declined to help us on our way but treat us very "cavilearly" indeed. His breakfast was announced while I was sitting in his presence and he got up and went to it without asking me in. Disgusted with the man's meanness, I went out in front of his gate in full view of his front door and though desperately hungry, broke my fast since dinner the day before, with one hard cracker and a piece of raw meat.

We stopped at every house, to rest, get cool water, and try to hire a horse and cart and was invariably told "about two miles farther on lived a gentlemen who would certainly let us have a conveyance to town." At least a half dozen "clever" men were just ahead a little piece, but it seems we could never catch him. Verily, I thought, we have fallen among a peculiar people, who could so carelessly look on upon our weary, sore feet and not help us.

126. August 6, 1863

Second Lieutenant Leonidas L. Polk, "The Anson Regulators," Company I, 43rd N.C. Troops, letter to his wife, Wadesboro, Anson County, N.C. Source: L. L. Polk Papers, Southern Historical Collection, University of North Carolina at Chapel Hill.

Following the Gettysburg campaign, Lieutenant Polk was sent to Petersburg to recuperate. In this letter, Polk talks about a furlough, the heat, and a visit from Governor Vance. Polk also talks about rules that Lincoln established for captured Confederates in regards to retaliation for any Confederate action against U.S. Colored Troops.

Petersburg, Va
August 6th 1863

My own dear Wife,

I have just taken a very pleasured bath & am seated at Charlie's desk with a sheet of Government paper to write you. I wrote you on Monday about 6 pages. I have but little time this day to write you as I must get if off in the next mail.

I am not altogether as well as when I wrote but am not sick. I am suffering with pains in my legs but hope it is nothing worse than Rheumatism. I also have the piles in a very bad form, caused no doubt by walking on crutches & the excessively warm weather. The thermometer has been at 100 several times in the last few days. I did not read Miss Mary's P.S. because she promised you to do all she could to try to get me a furlough. One of the officers boarding with me took sick and the Surgeon came to see him and Sure enough she and her Aunt, Ma, and Mrs. Reid turned loose on him and made him promise that he would do all he could for me, though I fear it will not amount to much. Still, do not be surprised to see me one of these days.

Gov. Vance went through here to Richmond yesterday & inquired for me. He will probably be back tonight if so, he will be able to have such an opportunity. If I am so fortunate as to get home on a furlough I will be sure to stay until I get well. Did you get your music? Miss Mary is very sick today.

There was a fight on the James this morning with Gun Boats, results not known. The Yankees are pressing us hard everywhere. Lee is falling back toward Richmond, and Meade is

pressing him. I imagine before 7 weeks that another great or the greatest battle will be fought again around the walls of that City. I look for the bloodiest battle of the war to come off on the blood-stained plains of the Chickahominy, before long. The authorities contemplate something of the Kind as they are calling on the farmer to carry in an abundant supply of provisions. Old Abe has issued an order saying that he will henceforth treat us just as we treat his Negroe prisoners. If we put them to work he will put a like number of our men to work for the same length of time. If we kill any of them, he will kill too.

So we go. Yankee papers say that N.C. is back in the Union and quote Holden as the authority. The militia of this place is ordered out & are on duty. I saw a man today who was taken with our sick in Penn. He brought me a full list of all of them, and I sent it to the Daily Progression in Raleigh & requested the Observer to copy it. Two more officers, Baker & Alexander dead from our Regt. I heard that F. E. Flake had a furlough and had went home![36]

I hope you are doing well. Tell Isaac to write to me. I would write to him but I would have to write the Same that I wrote you. Well, I have made this a lenghty letter after all and it is needless to say that I was in a hurry, you can tell that provided you can read it at all. I hope you will make out to understand it for I havent time to read it over. Kiss our babies sweetly for me. How much I wish to see you all.

Write as often as convenient
Your devoted &
affectionate husband
Leonidas

127. August 15, 1863

Brigadier General Stephen D. Ramseur, Rodes' Division, letter to sweetheart,

Ellen Richmond, Milton, Lincoln County, N.C. Source: Paul W. Schenk, Jr., and Dodson R. Schenk, Jr., of Greensboro, N.C., and extracts of correspondence, S. D. Ramseur Papers, Southern Historical Collection, University of North Carolina at Chapel Hill.

In the months following Gettysburg, Ramseur's Brigade continued to grow in experience and in numbers, as wounded men returned from the ranks, and as his brigade avoided circumstances which proved disastrous for Scales', Pettigrew's, and Iverson's brigades. Ramseur, like many North Carolina commanders and politicians, blames W. W. Holden for causing great turmoil among the men and contributing to desertion rates. The following is extracted from Ramseur's letter.

Camp near Orange C. H., Va
August 15th 1863
My Dearest Ellen,

I am having Division Drills on a small scale. According to what I believed prudent I have consolidated Iverson's (Old) Brigade into two Regiments under the command of Colonel Garrett. In addition, have also placed the 2nd and the 14th Regiment under Colonel William R. Cox and the 4th and the 30th Regiment under Colonel Bryan Grimes. Pretty girls on fine horses ride out every day to observe our drills and the drill hour is looked forward to with pleasure by the officers and men.

Our army is being increased quite rapidly. My Brigade is 150 stronger than when I went into Pennsylvania. The gain is caused by the return of my wounded heroes from Chancellorsville. I am sorry to say there are a good many deserters from our army. W. W. Holden is responsible, in great measure for the desertions among N. C. Troops.

The Yankees are daily sending off men to bring up their newly conscripted units. I think if Gen'l Lee attacks, as I

think and hope he will, it will be done before the 8th of September. If Gen'l Lee does not attack, I don't believe the Yankees will. With such inactivity, I hope to gain a furlough to get married, as previous events prohibited such a furlough. In any event, we will be married.

S. D. Ramseur

128. August 27, 1863

Lt. Colonel William G. Morris, 37th N.C. Troops, letter to his family, Dallas, Gaston County, N.C. Source: Mr. Charles Daniel Wilson, Dallas, N.C., and the letters of William G. Morris, William G. Morris Collection, Southern Historical Collection, University of North Carolina at Chapel Hill.

Morris was wounded in the right foot at Chancellorsville, Virginia, received a promotion to lieutenant colonel on May 29, led his command on the march into Pennsylvania, and was captured during Pickett's Charge on July 3, 1863. From there Morris was confined at Johnson's Island Prison in Ohio via Fort Delaware, Delaware. Morris comments on some of his officers from companies H and D who are prisoners with him. He seems to be doing fine in prison life.

Johnsons Island Near
Sanduskey Ohio
August 27th 1863
Dear Companion

I drop you a line to inform you that I am Still living & Enjoying Good health. I trust these lines May reach you & find you all well. The health of the prisenors at this place is very Good. Our Quarters are comfortable & rations very good. We are Not Kept in close confinement but have the priviledge of Several acres. There is One hundred & fifty officers from North Carolina at this place. Capt Alexander & Lieut Nolen & Lieut

Kindrick from Gastonia are prisenors at this place. Capt Johnston, Lieut Ramseur & Lieut Caldwell from Lincoln are allso here all in fine health.

You Should not be uneasy about Me as I am not suffering for anything, a friend Suplied me with what clothing I want for the presant. Confederate money is Worthless heare Except among ourselves but a friend from Tennesee Suplied us with some Federal money & I am living as well as I Could wish. We can buy any thing heare that we want to eat or weare. Though a prisenors life is One Not very desirable I am passing the time better than I expected. I cannot inform you as to the length of time I May be Kept prisenor but trust the time will be Short.

Give my love to the Children & Mother & all the fameley. I am looking, forward to the time when we May meet Once more. May God Give us a Speedy peace. Direct to W G Morris prisenor of war Johnsons Island Ohio Via City point Flag of Truce. Leave your Letter unsealed, put a confederate Stamp on the out side, a united States Stamp Enclosed.

Your Affectionate Husband & Father
W. G. Morris

129. September 1, 1863

Private Louis Leon, Company B, 53rd Regiment N.C. Troops, diary entry. Source: Leon, Louis, *Diary of a Tar Heel Confederate Soldier*, 1913.

After the defeat at Gettysburg, the Confederate army fell back into Virginia where it was still very active despite its losses. In the next entry, Leon talks about going on a special duty to hunt out and arrest deserters.

September 1 (1863)—Today we went on a general hunt in full force. We went into a house where we suspected there was a deserter. We hunted through all the outhouses, then went to the house, and the lady strongly denied there being any one there, but would not give us permission to look. We then searched the house, but found no one. I then proposed that we go in the loft. She objected again. But of course we were determined. It was pitch-dark in the loft. We called in, but no answer came. I then proposed, in a loud voice, so that if any one was there they could hear me, that we fix bayonets and stick around and satisfy ourselves that no one was there. Still no answer. I then got in the loft, took my gun and commenced sticking around. At last an answer came from the far corner that he would surrender. The way I got into the loft was, I being a little fellow, and Si Wolf[37] a tall man, they put me on his shoulder, and in that way I crawled in. We then left for camp, passed a church, and was in time to see a wedding. We drilled for the ladies, and had a good time.

130. September 13, 1863

Dr. John F. Shaffner, Surgeon, 4th Regiment N.C. State Troops, diary entry. Source: Shaffner Diary, Shaffner Papers, Private Manuscripts Collection, North Carolina Division of Archives and History.

Dr. Shaffner was transferred to the 4th N.C. Troops in August 1863 and was sorely missed by the members of the 33rd North Carolina. The doctor had recovered from jaundice and was using the railroad to return to service when he ran into a friend, Col. Ridson Tyler Bennett of the 14th North Carolina. Dr. Shaffner's progress was slowed due to the large body of troops moving southward on the trains. Later in the diary, Shaffner reports the movements of Jenkins' brigade, one of the brigades which traveled through North Carolina on its way to reinforce Bragg at the battle of Chickamauga, Georgia.

Colonel Risdon T. Bennett, a friend and fellow passenger of Dr. John Shaffner on September 13, 1863. (William A. Smith, *The Anson Guards*, 1903.)

13 September—Having spent twenty-eight days at home on sick "Leave of Absence," disease Jaundice, which proved to me one of the happiest periods of my life (though not entirely free from gloomy and sad reflections, particularly because of the recent death of my very dear and true friend, with whose family I am intimate, and the members of which are now sad with the burdens of their many afflictions) the time for my departure had arrived. By the kindness of one very dear to me, I was provided with a private conveyance to High Point for which place I left home and all its endearments at ½ past 7 oclock Sunday morning, Sept. 13, 1863. My friend, Mr. Ch. T. Pfohl, accompanied me in carriage. At High

Point we met with Mr. Henry Fries, who returned in the conveyance that brought me down. The train had been delayed the previous night, and soon after I reached the station it arrived about 12 hours behind schedule time. The detention was caused by the passage of Longstreets Corps of troops from Gen'l Lee's to Gen'l Bragg's army. Upon the train I found Colonel Bennet of the 14th Reg't N. C. Troops with whom I traveled as I came homeward, He was returning, recovered from a wound received at Gettysburg, Pa. He informed me that during his stay home he had married, and although he had received an extension of thirty days, he was returning to his command with the extension in his pocket!—A wonderful man! In consequence of the continued trains of troops passing Southward, our progress was slow, consequently we failed to make connection at Raleigh with the train for Gaston. We reached Raleigh about midnight, and having learned that a train for passengers would not leave before 10 o'clock A. M., the next day repaired to Exchange Hotel where we were provided with a good bed and excellent breakfast next morning.

131. September 16, 1863

Private Jacob H. Hanes, "The Davie Sweepstakes," Company G, 4th Regiment N.C. Troops, letter to his brother, Davie County, N.C. Source: The Catharine E. Hanes Collection, Southern Historical Collection, University of North Carolina at Chapel Hill.

Jacob arrrived back on active service from the Provost Guard on August 1, 1863. One of the most hideous spectacles a soldier can witness is the execution of his comrades. Here Hanes describes such a scene, which involved a certain amount of pomp and circumstance. Hanes was in favor of the execution and even says he wishes it had happened sooner to deter desertion from the very beginning. He refers to Unionist newspaper editor William Woods Holden and a raid conducted on his press by members of two Georgia units.

> Camp 4th N.C. Regt
> Near Rapid Ann River
> Sept 16th 1863

Dear Brother

I received your verry kind and interesting letter some days since. I should have answered it sooner. Though we have been moving occasionally ever since I received it. We have not much excitement in camp only accasionally we can hear the roaring of cannon. On day before yesterday there was a right smart little skirmish between the pickets. We lost some 10 or 15 killed and about twenty five or thirty wounded. Well Brother I witnessed one of the most horrible scenes about an hour ago that I ever beheld in all my life. What do you imagine it to have been. It was the execution of one of our fellow soldiers for desertion. The whole Division was ordered out to witness the sad fate. He was accompanied from his place of confinement to the stake by the Chaplin of the 14th Regt who he had employed as his spiritual counsel. The Band of the 4th Regt also formed a part of the procession, which added greatly to the solemnity of the scene by playing the Dead March. This man belonged to the 2nd N.C. Regt. A few days ago there were 10 shot out of the 3rd N.C. Regt. They were shot for desertion and murder.[38] Isen't it shameful how the N.C. Soldiers are acting. What a pity it is that an Official did not resort to shooting at the begining of the war. It is a deplorable necessity and will have to be enforced or desertion will ruin our army. I was verry much pleased to hear of the soldiers making a raid upon old

Holden's office. It undoubtedly would have been the primary step towards promoting the honor of N.C. had they have pitched old Holden into the streets and broke his neck instead of his press.[39] The Raleigh Standard has a bad effect upon the ignorant class of people who are not able to comprehend its design. It should not be allowed to be sent to the army. I was verry glad to hear that you and Pleas had acknowledged the worshiping of the Devine Spirit. I am sorry to say that the good Spirit has not manifested itself towards me yet. I hope that I may proffit form the good example set before me by my younger Brother. I was <u>glad</u> to hear that you were going to school at Clemmonsville.*

It is useless for me to urge upon you the value of time for I fell that you can fully appreciate and will undoubtedly improve it. We are getting plenty to eat (Beef and Bread) and as good as soldiers can expect. We are now encamped on the top of a mountain where we get the fresh air and can see for miles around. We have the best Brass band in service which tends greatly to us when we get low spirits. You are gong to school and will no doubt want your corespondents to use gramatical language and also to write a legible hand, for that—I offer a few faint apologies. You will almost— — two different hand writings in this letter. It is the result of changing pens. I have not had a letter from Spense since I left home. As it is getting late I will have to close. Nothing more at present. Only I remain your affectionate Brother

> J. H. Hanes

PS Always direct your letters to me as follows J. H. Hanes 4th NC Regt Ramsuer's Brigade Rodes Division Richmond Va

*Clemmonsville: Northernmost township in Davidson County in 1860. Land ceded to Forsyth County, N.C., in 1890s.

132. September 27, 1863

Private John Fuller Coghill, "The Granville Targeteers," Company E, 23rd Regiment N.C. Troops, letter to sister, Mildred Coghill, Granville County, N.C. Source: John Fuller Coghill Papers, Southern Historical Collection, University of North Carolina at Chapel Hill.

John F. Coghill volunteered for service in Granville County on February 20, 1862, and served with the Granville contingent. He was promoted to corporal in January of 1864. Coghill was last reported present in December 1864.[40] In his letter, John describes a series of movements and counter-movements conducted by the 23rd and its brigade during the month of September and notes that enemy pickets were very friendly when they were contacted.

> Camp 23rd Regt. N. C. Troops
> Sept. the 27 1863
>
> Dear Mil,
>
> I received your most welcome letter dated the 21, and I can assure you that its contents was rec'd with great delight. This leaves me well and hearty. I have no interesting news to write this morning as I know very little of what it going on for our Brigade is about ten miles from our army.
>
> I will try to give you the particular points of our travels since we left Orange CH. We left there and reached the Raccoon Ford or at least in two miles of it and took up camp. There we were expected to have a battle as the cannons were roaring like thunder, but the Yankees did not advance so we staid there until we was then ordered off to leave and go to Wortham's Ford. When we arrived at the Place, we formed in a line of battle and I was ordered to the front with the Sharp Shooters. That was on Friday and I staid there until Saturday night then I was relieved.
>
> The Division in very short time built very good breastworks on Sunday and we remained behind them until Monday when we were moved out and took up camp in or about two hundred yards of the breastworks. So we staid there until Wendsday and at night we received orders to come to this place and by the dawn of day the next morning our command was centered around this Chemanak Ford on the Rapidan River. Our Regt was sent out on Picket while the rest of the Brigade commenced to build breastworks. Our army has a fortified line from Orange CH to Fredericksburg.
>
> While we are on picket we would talk with the Yankees and would swap news papers and we would go down to the river to wash our face and hands. The Yankees would come and wash theirs on the other side about 20 yards so we were very friendly. It seemed like but if they was some of our soldiers, except it looked like they had fed on hogs for the last 40 days.
>
> I was glad to here that you all had such a good meeting at the Old School House. I would like to have been there but I cannot come and see you. But the time is not far distant when peace shall return and prevail through our land. So I must bring my letter to a close as I have not lines enough to write any more so I remain as
>
> Your affectionate Brother
> John Coghill

133. October 1, 1863

Private Richard Womble, "The Wake Rangers," Company G, 7th Regiment N.C. State Troops, letter to sister, Mary Williams, Chatam County, N.C. Source: Williams-Womble Papers, Private Manuscripts Collection, N.C. Division of Archives and History.

Private Richard Womble (listed as "Wamble" in *N.C. Troops*, vol. 4, pg. 482) volunteered for service in Wake County on

July 28, 1861. He was assigned to company G, 7th Regiment North Carolina State Troops, along with his brother-in-law, George A. Williams. Both men were farmers and were related through George's wife, Nancy, who was one of Richard's sisters. Womble would serve as a teamster for most of the war. He was reported present through October of 1864 and was paroled at Appomattox Court House, Virginia, on April 9, 1865.

> Camp near Orange Court House Va.
> Oct the 1th 1863
>
> Dear sister I seat my self to rite you a few lines in answer to your kind letter I got yesterday and let you no that I am well at this time hopeing these few lines will find you all in the best of health. Dear sister I can say to you sence I saw george we hav bin moving a bout. I don no where he is. I would be very glad if we could be to gether so you and my wife could both come to gether an we could see each others.
>
> You and Martha said you wanted to come befour it got cold wether. It is very cool here rite now for the season we had frost here last week. It is very cool here of nites. Dear Sister I want you to rite often and let me no all of the nuse in the country. So I will come to a close by saying I remain your dear brother until death. Riten by Francis M. Medlin[41] to Mary Williams

134. October 11, 1863

Private Thomas C. Riddle, Company D, 42nd Regiment N.C. Troops, letter to his wife, Sophia Riddle, Farmington Township, Davie County, N.C. Source: Courtesy Ann Ellis Sheek and as printed in the Davie Dossier.

Private Thomas Calvin Riddle of Davie County, North Carolina, was born on July 31, 1835, to William and Nancy

Captain Crawford of Davie County commanded Company D, 42nd North Carolina. (Courtesy of the N.C. Division of Archives and History.)

Ridge Riddle. Thomas was conscripted into service on September 28, 1863, and was placed into Company D, 42nd Regiment N.C. Troops. Thomas writes to his second wife, Sophia Butner Riddle. (His first wife, Susan Vogler Riddle, had died shortly prior to the war.) In the following letter, Thomas addresses activities of the 42nd N.C. Troops which performed garrison duty in eastern North Carolina during the first three years of the war. Riddle mentions that his unit has "plenty to eat," which is inconsistent with the common perception of the Confederate soldier. The reader must keep in mind that the supply trains could keep up with garrison troops more easily than with active campaigning troops, and also that Thomas Riddle's unit was stationed near the busiest seaport in the Confederacy and had access to all kinds of food to supplement their rations.

October 11, 1863
Wilmington, North Carolina
Dear Family,

We left Kingston [Kinston] last Friday about 10 o'clock mounted the cars and landed in Wilmington about 2 o'clock that night. We have marched out of town about two miles and took up camp. We don't think we will stay here many days. Some think we will go on to Bald Head Island about 40 miles below here. We may go to Charleston.

Wilmington is on the Cape Fear River. I saw one steam boat and I was on it and took a good look at the curious thing. I saw a great many flat bottom boats and skiffs and other new curiosities that I never saw before. As we were on our way to Wilmington, a young man was killed instantly dead. He was standing up on top of the car and was struck on the back part of his head in running under a bridge and it broke his skull. His name was Dean.[42]

I have enjoyed good health so far and I hope I will stand a camp life better than we all thought I would. We had the hardest march yesterday for the distance this Regiment has ever taken. The sand was shoe top deep. I don't know where we will go from here but I think we will go down to the seacoast. We are close to the Yankees. We might have to fight them shortly and we may never have to fight. One thing I know this Regiment wasn't the ones to starve. Don't be worried about me as I am well satisfied as any man in our company. We get plenty to eat or need and other things we have to buy.

I want you to write. I have got no letter yet from home. I must close. All the boys that came with me is in good health. I send you all my best love hoping you will not grieve after me.
Thomas C Riddle to his family

Direct your letter to Wilmington, N.C., Co. D, 42nd Reg. In care of Captain Crawford

135. October 30, 1863

Corporal Jacob H. Hanes, "The Davie Sweepstakes," Company G, 4th Regiment N.C. Troops, letter to his sister, Catharine, Davie County, N.C. Source: The Catharine E. Hanes Collection, Southern Historical Collection, University of North Carolina at Chapel Hill

Promoted to corporal on October 1, 1863, Jacob Hanes of the 4th N.C. Troops would not be involved in any major action until May of 1864. Besides a reference to the battle of Bristoe Station (October 13, 1863), Hanes is more concerned about his past youth, family and friends at home. Corporal Hanes served in his post in Company G until he was killed in action at Spotsylvania Court House, Virginia, on May 12, 1864.[43]

Camp 4th N.C. Regt
Oct 30th 1863
Dear Sister

I received your verry kind and affectionate letter some days since. I should have written you before but the thief of time overcame me. You must not forget to remember me to your roomate Miss Julia Martin. Tell her that she must not for a moment imagine that I had forgotten her although we have been prohibited from enjoying each others conversation as we did at the receptions at Jonesville. My mind often steals away from the horrors of war and retrace the foot prints of youth and pleasure. We used to think that Mr Van Eaton was very rigid in his discipline and he was to some extent though I only wish that I could realise another such a time. Tell Julia that she and Mr Gray have my best wishes at all times. I heard by letter from home that they were expecting cousin William March verry soon to spend his Furlough at Mothers. I would like so much if I could be there when he comes. Well Catherine we have had quite a toilsome march scince I wrote you last. I am sorry to say that it was a fruitless one acording to my opinion. I do not think we acomplished any think atal. We had several skirmishes with the enemy. The men would sometimes run short of rations and would have to eat rosted corn and acorns. They were so hungry it seems to me that there was nothingbut whatthey could eat some of it. We went within 4 milse of Manassas Junction. Genl's Cook and Kirkland's Brigades engaged the enemy near Bristoe Station and were repulsed with considerable loss. We are now in camp and the men have most all constructed comfortable quarters. Uncle Lewis come to see Bill and I the other day though he had but a short time to stay. William sends his love to you. As it is getting late I will have to close for the present. Give my respects to Miss Julia Nothing more at present. Only I remain your Affection-ate Brother

J. H. Hanes

136. November 10, 1863

Private Bartlett Yancey Malone, "The Caswell Boys," Company H, 6th Regiment N.C. State Troops, diary entry. Source: Diary of Bartlett Y. Malone, property of the Wilkinson Family. Microfilm copy avail-able in the Southern Historical Collection, Wilson Library, University of North Car-olina at Chapel Hill.

In the following entry, Private Malone describes the action at Rappahannock Sta-tion, Virginia, where a large contingent of North Carolinians were captured. Also, Malone reports on the way that Confeder-ate prisoners were processed and sent to the North for confinement, as well as a list

of all men from Company H who were cap-tured and with him at Point Lookout, Maryland.

The 7th about 2 o'clock in the eavning orders came to fail in with armes in a moment that the enemy was advancen. Then we was doubbelquicked down to the river (which was about 5 miles) and crost and framed a line of battel in our works and the yanks was playing on ous with thir Artillery & thir skirmishers a fyring into ous as we formed fyring was kept up then with the Skirmishers untell dark. And about dark the yanks charged on the Louisianna Bregaid which was dost to the Bridg and broke thir lines and got to the Bridge we was then cutoff and had to Surender: was then taken back to the rear and staid thir untell next morning The morning of the 8th we was marched back to Warrenton Junction and got on the cars and about day next morning we got to Washington we then staid in Washington untel 3 o'clock in the earning of the 8th then was marched down to the Warf and put on the Stemer John Brooks and got to Point Lookout about one O'clock on the eavning of the 10th day of Novem-ber 1863. The names of the men that was taken primer when I was belonging to Co. H. was Capt. Lea Lieut. Hill W. H. Bowldin N. W. Hester W. W. Mur-rie C. Rile H. Malone I. R. Aldridge L. T. Anderson A. I. Brincefield I. E. Cov-ington T. Y. Compton I. C. Chatham T. H. Evans G. R. Grimstead W. A. Hughs N. Hooper H. Kersey A. More W. D. Richmond F. Simpson R. Swift L. Sawers H. Roscoe A. Tucker John Walker W. S. Walker W. F. Wells I. Wren S. Hensley And Segt. A. P. Rudd

137. November 15, 1863

Private M. Benson Lassiter, "The Uwharrie Boys," Company H, 38th Regi-ment N.C. Troops, letter to cousin, Emily

Branson, Randolph County, N.C. Source: Branson Family Papers, Private Manuscripts Collection, North Carolina Division of Archives and History.

Benson Lassiter was born in the northern district of Randolph County in 1840. On November 4, 1861, Benson volunteered for service and was briefly promoted to corporal for four months in 1862. Private Lassiter was reported present until wounded at Chancellorsville, Virginia, on May 3, 1863, and was reported absent wounded through November of 1863, when he was assigned light duty as a hospital guard in Richmond, Virginia. The following letter was written during Benson's assignment as a hospital guard.

General Hospital No 24
Richmond, Va
November the 15th 1863

My Dear Cousin Emily

This morning finds me seated for the purpose of trying to write you. I have delayed in writing you much longer than I intended when I received your last letter though I think I should have written sooner, but I kept thinking that I would be returned to the army very soon, so I thought I would wait until I got to camp as you would know how to address me, so I hope you will pardon me for not writing sooner.

I have been very unwell for some time but I am some better than I was a week ago, though I am yet unable for duty, but I hope it will not be long until I can go back to camp. I am very anxious to see the boys and you know how bad I dread to stay in the Hospital. The fare at this place is anything but good, but I am not the one to complain. I should have gone to the Regiment, but when I got to this place yesterday they would not let me go any farther. In fact I was able to travel but then I did not like the idea of being left at the Hospital, but I guess that it was the best for

me to stop at the hospital. I think that I have improved very much since I came hear. I think I am clear of the chills & fever, but the Doctor says that is not all that ails me. If I thought that was all myself I would not feel as right good spirits.

There are several sick and wounded in this hospital. There is one case of small pox and several awful cases of inciphlus. The most of the wounded came in a week ago and they received their wounds at Kellys ford on the Rappahannock. It is reported that the Yanks captured two of our Brigades at that place. It is rumored that old Mead is advancing his whole force and that General Lee is falling back. If it is true for General Lee I think he is falling back to a better position. Mead had better mind how close he gets or General Lee will give him a good flogging.

Cousin Fletcher inquired about you and said that he would like very much to see you. I do not think that he is as full of deception as the balance of his peoples. Though there is not one bit about uncle Micajah if ever I loose confidence in him I do not know who I should put my confidence in. I would right Cousin Priss but I do not know where she is. If she is at home tell her to write. I will write to Cousin Salley in a short time. Now I hope you will not delay in writing me as I am so anxious to hear from you. It seems like a long time since I heard from you. Write soon.

As ever,
Benson[44]

138. November 16, 1863

Private Felix Miller, Company H, 48th Regiment N.C. Troops, near Orange Court House, VA, letter to his wife, Elizabeth, Davidson County, N.C. Source: Rachel Philpott, *Letters of Felix Miller*, typescript copy in author's possession.

Felix Miller (1824–1864) was born on October 24, 1824, to Nicholas and Eliza Livengood Miller. He worked as a farmer in the Northern District of Davidson County, and on June 30, 1844, he married Elizabeth Temple. Felix and Elizabeth would have nine children—Levi (1845), Christina (1850), Isaiah (1852), Amelia (1853), Sarah (1854), Ellen (1856), Delilah (1857), William (1858), and George W. (1861)—before Felix was conscripted into service in Wake County on October 14, 1863. Felix was reported present until he died of chronic diarrhea at Gordonsville, Virginia, on May 29, 1864.[45] In this letter, Felix, who is already in service, is trying to find ways to keep his son Levi out of the fray, or at least in the position where little harm can come to him. It is interesting to note that in a separate letter dated the next day, Felix mentions that the 48th NC had "no fifers," which seems curious, given that the fife and drum were present in infantry bands.

Camp near Orange Court
House, Va.
NOV the 16th 1863

Mrs Elizabeth Miller

My Dear Wife It is again I take the pleasure of writing you a few lines to inform you that I am as well as common and hopeing those few lines may reach the hands of you and find you and all well and doing well. Yours of the 8 reached me last night and I was glad to hear from you and that you was all well except Levi and I was glad to hear that he was geting along well. I hope he will be able to work again soon. I will now tell you something about the march we had when we came here from the Rappahannock in the first place on last Saterday night was a week ago after we had lay down to sleep we was called up to stack arms and cook up one days rashings and be ready to fall in at any time and we cooked up the Rashings as we was orderd to do and then we lay down again and about three hours before day that was sunday morning we was called up again to leav and we left it and we marched till after day and the yankees in hot persuit after us and about nine o clock we formed a line of battle and we remained in line of battle day expected they would attack us every minuit. I tell you I felt about as bad for while as I ever did in my life not to be sick but as luck would hav it they did not attack us at that place but they got around on our left wing and they fought all the afternoon and at night we started away from there and we everlastingly got away from there and we marched all night and it as cold as sixty and monday morning we lay down to rest awhile and then we started again and we got here on monday evening and it was a snowing very nice for a while and we got back across the Rappadan river but we hav been under marching orders for several days we hav to keep two days rashings* cooked up all the time ready to leav the very moment we are called on yesterday the orders came to tare down and leav rite off and we started and we went about a half a mile and the orders came to go back to our quarters and we came back but we are one stand ready to leav at any time we are called on I understood this morning that the yankees tried to cross the river yesterday and old whiped them back and so they did not need us and they sent us back to our quarters. I am glad to hear that you are done sewing wheat and glad to hear that the neaghbors are so kind as to help you. I was also glad that you borrowd mony and that you got some leather. I am also glad to hear that my baby was sasey. I am glad that your corn turned out as well as it did I am also glad to hear that you are getlng along as well as what you are If Levi has *to* come I want him to come here and bring a fife with him if he can get it. I tell you I could write a good deal more if I had time as soon as I can get the chance I will write to you again I want you to write and let me know how mutch wheat you sowed and give me all the news so when this you see remember me write soon a soldiers life is a hard life so I remain your kind husband until death Direct your letters as you did. Felix Miller

*Rations

139. December 3, 1863

Brigadier General Stephen D. Ramseur, Rodes' Division, letter to sweetheart, Ellen Richmond, Milton, Lincoln County, N.C. Source: Paul W. Schenk, Jr., and Dodson R. Schenk, Jr., of Greensboro, N.C., and extracts of correspondence, S. D. Ramseur Papers, Southern Historical Collection, University of North Carolina at Chapel Hill.

In October 1863, while at home on furlough, Stephen D. Ramseur married his sweetheart, Ellen Richmond, in Lincoln County, N.C. Their time together was brief, however, as duty called the general away to northern Virginia. The battle mentioned in the next letter is perhaps on during the Mine Run campaign of winter 1863. The following is an extract of Ramseur's letter.

At old Camp near Morton's Ford
December 3rd 1863
My own Darling Wife,
The Yankees came over to whip us. They have obviously retreated without carrying out their purpose. One of our Divisions under Major General Johnston in marching over to his position in the line of battle was attacked by an entire Corps and one division of another Corps of the enemy. These forces, after a sharp fight of over two hours were repulsed with very great loss.
Sunday, Monday, and Tuesday, we waited in line of battle for the enemy to

attack. Failing to come up to the mark as we expected. Tuesday night Gen'l Lee made his dispositions to attack the enemy, but when Wednesday morning's sun arose, lo the Yankees were retreating and crossing the river. They commenced retreating Tuesday night at dark and kept up their retreat through the night, with our skirmishers in hot pursuit.
This attempt on their part is the most cowardly of the war and its moral effect must be very damaging to the Yankee's spirit. Although they had 63,000 troops they were afraid to be attacked by Gen'l Lee's 30,000, when they came over to for that very purpose.
We are quiet for the present. How long it will remain so, I cannot say, but a few days will certainly determine the course of the winter's campaign. May God give us strength to overcome our enemies and to establish a permanent Government and with all controlling principle will be done and obedience to His Commandments.
S. D. Ramsuer

140. December 8, 1863

Private John W. Armsworthy, "The Western Rangers," Company H, 54th Regiment N.C. Troops, letter to his wife, Edna Armsworthy, Forbush, Yadkin County, N.C. Source: Private Collection, Mr. Bob Furches, Clemmons, N.C.

The Battle of Rappahannock Station (November 27, 1863) proved disastrous for the 54th N.C. Troops. They, along with the 57th North Carolina, rushed across the Rappahannock under the impression of light Federal resistance. Within a matter of minutes they were assailed by an entire corps. The swift, overwhelming attack left Armsworthy wounded and, like his regiment, captured and in the hands of the enemy. Armsworthy was sent to Federal hospitals in Washington, D.C., where he was treated. The following letter was written to let his wife know what happened and that he was all right. John was eventually transferred to another hospital (Lincoln), where he died on February 3, 1864, of "pyemia."

Dec 8 1863
Harewood Hospitle
Washington, D.C.

Dear Wife

It is with the greatest of Pleasure that I take this oppertunity of writing you a few lines to you to let you know that I am in Hosptile in Washington and I am getting along forstrate* and I also hope that I soon will be able to come home to my family. I got wounded at Rapperhanock Station but thank God it was not verry bad wound. I got wounded in the wright arm. It was a fleas wound and I think it is improving frostrate. Do not get uneasy abought me for I am well attended to hear. I have plenty to eat and all togeather I am well taken care of. That is since I have taken prisoner. I cannot think of nothing more at present so I will close my letter by sending my love to all and remaining your beloved husband.

J. W. Armsworthy

*frostrate: first rate

141. December 27, 1863

Second Lieutenant John F. Sink, Company A, 42nd Regiment N.C. Troops, Wilmington, New Hanover County, letter to uncle, Michael Sink, Lexington, Davidson County. Source: Davidson County Historical Museum.

The 42nd North Carolina was posted at Wilmington, North Carolina, on Christmas Day, 1863. Among those who kept the holiday in the officers' mess with a good eggnog social was Lieutenant John Franklin Sink. In the following letter, the last of 1863, Sink talks about his time at the eggnog with the officers (who get "prety

funey" under the influence), contemplates his time in service, and reports on his family members in service.

Camp 42nd Regt. NCT
December 27th 1863

Dear Uncle,

I this beautiful morning have the opportunity to take the pleasure of writing you a short letter to let you know I am still among the living + I hope these few lines may find you enjoying life. Uncle, I am well as could be expected. I have had a vary bad cold but it is some better now I hope these few lines may reach your family well. It is pleasant weather here. Uncle, this is the third Christmas that I have spent in he Service of our country & I am getting tired of it but complaining is no good. I hope I will live to see another Christmas pass but I want to get out of this troublesome war. This is three years since we commenst fighting and now there is no more prospect for peace than was at the commensment. I think the best law in the South that has ever been in the Confederate States is about to pass and that is to bring all the Rich men in the service. These men hire subs and shirk out in several ways. It is here it will bring in good men who need in fields for pervisions, but in order to get these skulks it will take good men. It will make our Army in NC twenty-five thousand.

Our Lt. Colonel gave a fine Eggnog that Christmas evening it was splendid. Some of the officers got prety funey. Our Colonel has resigned and I am sorry to hear that as he was a very fine man.

I will give you the news that I have heard. The enemy has shelled Charleston all day long and burned fifteen houses in the operation. I will give prices of things here—Flour 1.00 per lb., Chickens 3.00 per head, what a price. Brandy, $3 per drink, whiskey, $2 per drink.

If you have anyone inquiring about our company we now number 100. The boys are all well from our section of the county. Obe is well except Boiles, Uncle Gideon is well an is as fat as you please. He is heavier than he ever was. Daniel, Franklin, is well and hardy. I will bring my few lines to a close. Please give my love and best respects to my friends and excuse the same for yourself.

Obedient Nephew until deth,
Lt. John F. Sink[46]

Direct to Company A, 42nd Regt. N.C.T., Martine's Brigade, Wilmington, N.C.

1864

"You must take good care of the hogs and pigs. Dear wife, I will say to you that if you get that colt you must get some slabs hauled and weatherboard a stable. Maybe you can get Fry to do the work for you"

> —Private Andrew Rinck, Company I, 11th Regiment
> N.C. Troops, Orange Court House, Virginia,
> January 4, 1864.

"There are more men here than I ever saw at once. Our loss I think on our side is some between 3 & 4 hundred killed and wounded. I think the yankeys loss was about the same as ours."

> —Private M. A. Barrier, "The Cabarrus Phalynx,"
> Company H, 8th Regiment N.C. State Troops,
> Bermuda Hundred, Virginia, May 19, 1864.

"I am broke down my feet is all blisters and my legs is stiff and I hav suffered more than I ever did in my life I can tel I was in another hard fight the hardiest fight tha we ever had yet I com out safe again."

> —Private Jesse Hill, Company K, 21st Regiment
> N.C. Troops, New Market, Virginia, October 21,
> 1864.

"The 4th which was the Sabath I went to meating at the School house Mr. Morgan lectured on the Parable of the

Sower & in the eavning I was at the Same plase and Mr. Carol preached a good Surmon from the later clause of the 2 virse 7 chapter of Amos"

—Sergeant Bartlett Y. Malone, "The Caswell Boys," Company H, 6th Reigment N.C. Troops, Point Lookout Prison, Maryland, December 4, 1864.

142. January 4, 1864

Private Andrew Rinck, Company I, 11th Regiment N.C. Troops, letter to his wife, Rebecca Rinck, Catawba County, N.C. Source: Members of the Rinck/Rink Family: Sarah R. Wallace, Mary R. Harbinson, Edna R. Shufford, Bettie Mims, Brenda Witherspoon, Sarah M. Rink, and Mary Setzer Rink.

Andrew Rinck worked as a small farmer near the town of Newton, Catawba County, North Carolina. The Rinck family included Andrew, his wife Rebecca, and their children. With the outbreak of the war, thirty-eight-year-old Andrew chose to remain at home with his family. Three years later, Andrew enlisted into service at Camp Vance on October 17, 1863, and was assigned to Company I, 11th North Carolina, a unit where his two brothers, Noah and Daniel, were already serving.[1] This letter brings Rebecca up to date with where Andrew is and gives her advice on running the household finances. Also, Andrew asks for locks of hair from each of his children.

Camp near Orange
Courthouse, Va.
January the 4, 1864

Dear wife

I seat myself to let you know that I am tolerable well; only my feet and legs is swollen so I can't hardly get along. I hope these few lines will come safe to hand and find you all well and doing well. I received your kind and welcome letter New Year's Day which was dated Dec. the 25, and I was glad to hear that you was all well and doing well. You said in your letter that you was about to make a trade for a colt if I was willing. You do as you please about it. If you think you can make a good trade, go ahead and do the best you can. I will say to you if you buy the colt you must sell the old mare if you can; and if you can't, you'll have to keep it.

Dear wife, I would like to see you all again if I could but see no chance, anyways shortly. Frances Elnora. and Rebecka, James Esquire. Dear wife, I want you to send me a little bunch of each one of the children's hair. Put each one's hair in a bunch to itself.

Dear wife, I want you to put all the ground out in corn that you have got that you didn't sow in wheat, and I want you to plant a good patch of molasses cane. Dear wife, I want you to let me know whether your hogs is fat yet or not and how your corn holds out. You must take good care of the hogs and pigs. Dear wife, I will say to you that if you get that colt you must get some slabs hauled and weatherboard a stable. Maybe you can get Fry to do the work for you.

Dear wife, I can tell you that we have moved 3 miles east of Orange and put up winter quarters, and we are in them now. I would a wrote to you sooner, but we had everything tore up and building our houses that I did not have the chance to write any sooner. Dear wife, I

have a hack of plank at the sawmill yet.
I want you to get Jeffry Turner to haul
them sometime and you must be sure
and hack them up again. You can put
them to use. I want you to get Fry to fix
your porch for you if you can get him,
and I will send you money to pay for it.
I will get my bounty money shortly and
two months' wages. If you get the porch
fixed, you must get flat rocks to put
under the blocks and have the blocks
hewn on two sides and weatherboard
from the ground up.

Write soon. I remain your affectionate husband till death.

Andrew Rinck to Rebecca Rinck

143. January 24, 1864

Private John A. Smith, "The Bun-
combe Rangers," Company G, 9th
Regiment N.C. State Troops (1st NC Cavalry Regiment), letter to his sister, Cabarrus
County, N.C. Source: J. A. Smith Papers
(4891), Special Collections, Perkins Library, Duke University, Durham, N.C.

John Allen Smith volunteered for service in Cabarrus County on June 15, 1861.
As a member of a western North Carolina
company, the twenty-six-year-old "Mill
Hill" resident would go on to serve as a
faithful trooper in the 1st N.C. Cavalry
Regiment for two and a half years from the
date of this letter.[2] Smith is writing his sister, Mary C. Smith, about small numbers
of desertions. He passes along information
that the 4th NC Cavalry (Robertson's
Brigade) will be heading back into North
Carolina. Ladies are also on his mind, as
he knows that the girls back home "would
like to be squeazed a little."

Jan the 24 1864
Carolina Co. Va
Dear Sister,

I seat my self this evening to drop
you a few lines to let you no that I am
in the land of the living yet and in very

good health at this time and I hope that
these few lines may find you injoying
the like blessing and find the famely all
well. I hav no news of interest to write
more than there was some heavy cannon
nading yester day in the direction of
orange C. H. though I hav not heard
any thing from Co. A and one of Co. C
deserted last Monday night and I sopose
went to the yankeys.

They had took an express last night a
week ago and in thes fight brök* one
mans leg and struck another on the
head with a pole so that they had to
send two to the hospital and the rest
were in the guard house waiting to be
court marcheld and would hav been severly punished but did not wait for there
trile.

The fourth regt of N. C. cavalry will
start back to N. C. tomorrow morning.
We hav very fine and warm wether at
presant. It makes me think a bout being
at home to go a corting and squeaze
some of the girls for I no that they
would like to be squeazed a little. We
hav plenty to eat such as bread and meat
but would like to hav something better.

I received a letter from J. E. two
weeks ago. He wrote that his health was
very good and has duty but lite which
he had to do. You can tell mother that I
got the pair of socks which she sent
with D. M. Harkey.[3] My hand which I
had burnt is just about well so that I
can write a little a gain.

I would like to no if the girls goes
corting as this is leap year and there year
to go see the boys. I think if I was at
home they would shorely come to see
me but if the girls will go to see the
boys they will hav to go some distance
be fore they will find them. And so I
think if they hav any boys at home they
would be better to hold on to them for
the boys out here are a getting pretty
bad.

I must come to a close for this time
for I do not no if my letter will interest

you a nuf to read all of it or not. I remain your brother as ever,

J. A. Smith to M. C. Smith

*brök: broke.

144. January 26, 1864

Private William P. Cline, "The Catawba Braves," Company K, 46th Regiment N.C. Troops, letter to his wife, Mary C. Cline, Newton, Catawba County, N.C. Source: William P. Cline Papers, Southern Historical Collection, University of North Carolina at Chapel Hill.

This is the last letter from Private William P. Cline of Catawba County. Private Cline gave in to his desire to see his wife again and deserted on August 19, 1863. He returned to duty on September 28, 1863, and was placed under arrest before being returned to his company. William P. Cline was killed in action at the battle of Wilderness, Virginia, on May 5, 1864.[4]

Va Camp near Orgen C. H.*
January the 26 the 1864

Dear Wife

It is with pleshur that I drop you a few lines to let you no that I am well hopen when thes few lines come to your hand may find you all in good helth. I reseved your leter that you rote on the 8 of dis month and I was glad to hear that you was all well. Me and H. H. Caldwell[5] got our box dis morning and we was glad to see it come for we hant drawd any meat in two or three weeks. It come in a mity good time. You sed that they was taxing the cows. I dont no what the poor people will do if dis war dont come to a close but I think that it will come to a close by dis spring or some time before. I think that they are about out of enthing to eat.

We have had some mity purty wether for the last week but we have had some mity hard wether the first of dis month. It will be gone by spring and we are still

here yet I wood like to be at home to be plowing but I dont know when I will git dire but I stil live in hopes that I will git done some time. I no that dis old war will stop some time and will all be free and a gone. I got my pares and apels and they was all good. They was the first that I have eat dis winter for I must come to a close by asken you to rite as sune as dis comes to hand. You must excuse my bad riten. Direct your leters to Richmond 46 Reg Co K in the care of Capt Bost.

W. P. Cline to M. C. Cline

*Orange Court House, Virginia

145. January 28, 1864

Lt. Colonel William G. Morris, 37th N.C. Troops, letter to his wife, Dallas, Gaston County, N.C. Source: Mr. Charles Daniel Wilson, Dallas, N.C., and the letters of William G. Morris, William G. Morris Collection, Southern Historical Collection, University of North Carolina at Chapel Hill.

January 18 marked six months of incarceration for Lt. Col. Morris at Johnson's Island. His letters grew continuously shorter the longer he spent in prison. During his tenure as major in the 37th Regiment, Morris' service was very active and involved. In his previous work, Morris was a carpenter. It is interesting to see how working men deal with boredom. Here Morris talks about a possible transfer to Point Lookout, Maryland, and advises his children to keep up their studies.

Johnsons Island Ohio
January 26th 1864

Dear Companion

I am well & Doing as well as usual at this place, I trust these lines may reach you & find you all well. The last letter I recd from you was dated November 15th 63. I am very anxious to heare from you. I have been writing to you every two weeks. It is reported here that the prisoners are to be moved from this place Soon. Whether for exchange or to another prison I dont know but I think the lattor most likely. The probibility is that we will be Sent to Point Lookout. The friends here are generally well Except Lieut Ramseur has something like Rheumatism. I did not receive your letter in time to say to you to hire Bill. If any friend is passing you had better have my trunks brought home. Wm. Barber can Give an order for the One in Richmond. I think I have clothing Enough till Spring. Keep the children at School if possible. I hope to find them all advanced in there Studys when I arrive home. Eleanora & Mary can lern Charles & Catharine at home a great deal. I hope they will take an interest in so doing. Give my love to all.

Your affectionate, Husband
W. G. Morris

146. January 28, 1864

Private Thomas C. Riddle, Company D, 42nd Regiment N.C. Troops, letter to his wife, Sophia Riddle, Farmington Township, Davie County, N.C. Source: Ann Ellis Sheek and as printed in the Davie Dossier.

This is the second letter from Thomas C. Riddle of Davie County, N.C. Three months have passed since his last featured correspondence (see number 134); notice how things have changed. He was very thankful for the baked goods sent from home and is even complaining about what little food the troops are being issued. Also indicative of a declining situation was the execution of men for desertion as well as the desire for peace among a great many of the troops. Thomas survived the war and returned home to Davie County, where he would live until his death in 1909. He is buried at Macedonia Moravian Church in Farmington, N.C.

Camp 24 miles northeast
Wilmington, N.C.
January 28, 1864

Dear family,

I received your kind letters dated 14. I was very glad to hear from home for I had been looking for a letter for a long time. I did not get Emerson's letter you spoke of. I got all the letters you sent. I want you to give me the date of all my letters you get there after. I was well pleased with the letters the children sent to me. I want them to be good children and be smart for I will come home sometime and I want to find smart children. I am sorry to hear Jonty[6] has got to be lazy for he told me he would be a good boy. I want you to get Wood if possible for it won't do to let the land lay idle. I would like to be there a few days to make some arrangements for you but I can't come before spring. I got the cakes and pies and apples and sausage you sent me. They were all good. I wish I had some more for we are only getting 2 ounces of bacon per day and I pint of meal not sifted. We have to shoot three men tomorrow for desertion. The whole Regiment is in an uproar now about it. I don't have to shoot for I am on guard till tomorrow night. We have all sorts of rumors in camp but no reliable news. We are now 24 miles from Wilmington working on breastworks. I don't know when we will go back to camp. We are in 15 miles of New River, not far from the Yankee line. Great confusion among the soldiers. All want peace not caring how so all can get home. Some think the Army will break to pieces in the spring. All in favor of going back in the Union hoping there will be a convention. The home guard in Hanover County is called into service and about 800 in Wilmington drilling.—My mess crowd is all well and I will tell you who they are William Hood, Nathan W. Smith, W.A. Smith, Giles Etchison, Peter

Cicero Durham, Cleveland County's "Fighting Quartermaster." (Courtesy of the N.C. Division of Archives and History.)

Allen, S.M. Foster, Robert Orrell, Peter Harman, and Hiram Speaks.—We have all been in one mess for a long time. I have given you about all the news I know. I have received two numbers of the press. I send you all my love hoping I will see you all in peace before six months.

I am in fine health. Hoping you are all well. Tell Emerson to write to me again. I want you to tell Copes to write to me and I want you to write every week and tell me who wrote your last letter. I could not make out the handwriting. I could read it very well. Do the best you can till I come. If you don't get a letter from me again soon don't be uneasy, for I shall try to do the best I can for myself. I

still remain your loving husband and son.

> T.C. Riddle to Sophia R. Riddle, Nancy Riddle and my dear little children.

147. February 4, 1864

Duplicate receipt from Colonel Lee Roy M. McAfee, 49th Regiment N.C. Troops, to AQM (Capt) Cicero A. Durham. Source: Cicero A. Durham Papers, Private Manuscripts, North Carolina Division of Archives and History.

Lee Roy Mangum McAfee, a Cleveland County–born attorney and commander of the 49th North Carolina, was still held financially accountable as were other officers for providing their own clothing. Instead of being issued uniforms, shoes, and other accoutrements, officers could provide their own, or purchase those items from the government (a duplicate).

Colonel McAfee to Conf. States

4⅝ yds Grey Cloth at $7.00 $28.00
1 Pr Shoes $6.00

I certify that I have received the above articles from Captain C. A. Durham, A. Q. M. 49th N. C. Troops and paid him Thirty-Four Dollars the amount of the above account. I further certify that the cloth is for my own personal use.

> [signed]
> Lee M. McAfee
> Col. 49th N.C.T.

148. February 6, 1864

Alexander Daniel, Taylorsville, Alexander County, N.C., letter to Col. S. A. Sharpe, 5th Regiment NC Home Guard, Statesville, Iredell County, N.C. Source: John McKee Sharpe Papers, Southern Historical Collection, University of North Carolina at Chapel Hill.

While the Home Guard could impress public property into service, compensation was required for private property and material purchased for Home Guard use. Here, a citizen of Taylorsville, Mr. Daniel, writes politely to Colonel Sharpe, commander of the 5th Home Guard (Iredell & Alexander Counties), asking for his reimbursement.

> Taylorsville, N.C.
> Feb 6th 1864
>
> Col. Sharpe
> Sir, I take this opportunity in writing in regards to the past incident regarding the hens, the corn, and the beef that the Home Guard took from me and I can not get the pay without an order from you. They paid for the Beef but would not pay for anything else. You will please do so and order payment so that they may do so. I am respectfully,
> Daniel[7]

149. March 1, 1864

Dr. John F. Shaffner, Surgeon, 4th N.C. State Troops, diary entry. Source: Shaffner Diary, Shaffner Papers, Private Manuscripts Collection, North Carolina Division of Archives and History.

Though no major action was fought between Mine Run and the Wilderness, the armies did not remain inactive. The following entry from Dr. Shaffner describes a daring raid of two columns of Union cavalry. Dr. Shaffner survived the war and was issued a furlough in February of 1865 to return home and marry Caroline Fries on February 16, 1865. The doctor then returned to service and was present until surrender at Appomattox Court House, Virginia, on April 9, 1865.[8]

> 1 March—Rainy cold morning.—Everything is covered with a sleet.—About 9 o'clock we received orders to move at once.—Raining very hard and we would have preferred remaining in Camp—proceeded on to, and through Orange C. H.—Our Regt. halted at Liberty Mills, on the Gordonsville & New Market Pike—with instructions to guard the ford & bridge across the Rapidan at this point.—The rest of the Brigade moved on to Jack's Shop.—The distance made to-day by our Regt. about 14 miles—the other Regts. moved five miles further.—In the evening commenced snowing rapidly.—It is now understood that the Cavalry of the enemy is on a raiding tour.—One column crossed the river on our right and proceeded to Frederick Hall, by way of Spottsylvania C. House.—At Frederick Hall they destroyed a portion of the Rail Road, and it is said were only 15 minutes behind the Richmond

Salem doctor and brigade surgeon, Dr. John Shaffner, 4th N.C. Troops. (Courtesy of the N.C. Division of Archives and History.)

train upon which Gen'l Lee was a passenger.—This column is commanded by Gen'l Kilpatrick.—The other column attempted to reach Charlottesville, but were repulsed and driven back.—It is hoped that we will be able to capture some at least of these raiders,—but our Cavalry is very much reduced in efficiency because of numbers who are home recruiting.—This evening is most disagreeable.—We are all wet and cold—no wood to make fire with.—I crept into an Ambulance and tried to sleep,—best I could.—The men were quartered in the Bridge where they built large fires of rails.—The bridge caught fire several times during the night.

150. March 4, 1864

Sergeant Robert O. Linster, Company C, 4th Regiment N.C. Troops, letter to mother, Iredell County, N.C. Source: Special Collections, Perkins Library, Duke University, Durham, North Carolina.

Two years after his first letter, Private Linster is alive and well with the 4th N.C. State Troops. Bridges were key to the movements and security of an army. It is rare to see troops building fires on top of rocks on the bridges themselves. In the late winter of 1864, Linster and his messmates are enjoying treats and food from home.

Camp 4 NC, March 4, 1864
Dear Mother

Yours of 15 came to hand a few days ago. I have not had time to write in the last few days. We have been on the march through mud, snow and rain. We started last Tuesday morning from Liberty Mills distance 14 miles. We got here 4 o'clock and commence snowing one of them old big Virginia snows. Our Regiment was left to guard the brige accross the Rapidan River. We threw out sharp shooters—the Yankees 18 hundred strong, caveraly, was in 2

Colorbearer John Strikeleather of Iredell County. "I will send my overcoat by him if he can carry it." (Courtesy of the N.C. Division of Archives and History.)

miles of us trying to get to the bridge. We form in line of battle stack arms. Ordrs came to build fires on rocks in the bridge which we did in double quick time and pass the night in fine spirits in the morning Gen. Lee came along gave us a racking for building fires on the bridge. Orderes came a few minutes ago for me to go on guard so I will finish at the guard house. Liet Thomas Davidson and myself are officer of the guard. We were cald out yesterday in line of battle, at Union Church to intercept Kilpatrick* if he should try to get back to the river up this way. I write you by Bustle one of my mess. We are having fine times in the way of eatings. We got six boxes and three of our men is home on furlough. We have 3 hams about 60 lbs four bushell meal 1 bushel dried fruit, butter, molasses, coffee etc greatest plenty. I have been improving finally since coming back. I go on guard about every 3 weeks which is very light duty. Our army is in fine health and sprits I saw Gen Lee day before yesterday he is the finest looking man I ever saw. John Strikeleather[9] will go home in a few weeks. I will send my over coat home with him if he can carry it. We were mustered in day before yesterday. I reckon we will get paid off next week if I don't go on picket. This is was day in our regiment and a fine day to. The wind is blowing pretty smart but there is a good many fellow drying their shirts by the fire with their coat on. Knapsacks is nearly plaid out in the Army 1 pr pants 2 shirts 2 pr drawers 2 pr socks and 1 blanket and oil cloth is all a solider has any use off here. We have no news here no mail for the last 4 or 5 days. Write about Gov Vances speech. I rec that valent—all right. No more I believe. Write soon. Your Son R.O. Linster[10]

General Judson Kilpatrick, Union Cavalry commander.

151. March 7, 1864

Private Edward L. Sowers, Company H, 48th Regiment N.C. Troops, letter to his wife, Nancy Byerly Sowers, Davidson County. Source: Davidson County Historical Museum.

The stories of the privations and hardships of the Confederate soldier are known to nearly all those who have ever opened to pages of a book. This letter by Private Sowers to his wife speaks of walking barefoot in freezing weather. However, despite his hardship, he is more concerned with the welfare of his wife. Edward died of disease near Spotsylvania Court House, Virginia, on May 17, 1864.[11]

State of VA camp near Oring
March the 7 1864
Dear Wife it is by the blessing of god that I am premited to drop you a few line to let you know that I am not rite welt at thise time and I hope when those few line come to hand they may find you well and the children both well and doing well. Dear Wife I had to march the first day of the month barefoot and I wore the skin off my feet and frose them and my toe nailes will come off and they paine me all most to death you never seen sich feet I got. Dear Wife I received you letter and the thing you sent with Miller and I was glad to git them and I was glad to hear form you one more time but sorrow to hear that you meat was stole from you. Dear Wife I wood be glad to see you and talk with you for I have Shed a tear for you for it greave me all most to death to think of you that you have to stay by you self at home and I have to stay out here for I have to suffer so much here for I have to eat dry come bread hale of my time. Dear Wife I wood like to come home and stay with you and the children for I havt got but two letter from home since I left but the one you sent with Miller and if the money is no count that I sent home you must do the best you can with it I want you to write to me a bout the time at home. So no more at this time but remember your husban untell death
From E.L. Sowers to N.A. Sowers

152. March 10, 1864

Miss Eliza W. Wooley, Edinboro, Montgomery County, N.C., letter to friend, Emily Branson, Randolph County, N.C. Source: Branson Family Papers, Private Manuscripts Collection, North Carolina Division of Archives and History.

According to a note made on the actual letter, Eliza and Emily were very good friends, and Emily even taught school before the war at Mr. Wooley's home in Montgomery County. Here Miss Wooley expresses her sorrow over the condition of Emily's mother and communicates her best sentiments, along with trying to update Emily on the happenings while she has been away.

Edinboro[12], N.C. March 10th 1864
Miss Emily Branson,
Dear friend,

We received your letter of the 15th ult., communicating the sad news of the disease of your amiable and respected mother. We all deeply sympathize with you and the family in this bereavement and hope that the Great Disposer of all earthly events will give you and all grace and fortitude to withstand this, to you, afflicting dispensation of his Providence.

Although comparitively a stranger to your mother, I had from my first acquaintance, learned to revere and to love her for her purity of character, her gentle and amiable disposition and her true Christian piety. I can well imagine that the loss of such a mother would cause the sorest affliction to her relatives, but you will have the consolation that her spirit is sweetly resting in heavenly bliss, freed from the cares, anxieties and sufferings of this life. I shall ever remember your mother with feelings of reverence and admiration.

Our friends and acquaintances, one by one, are, in fact, dropping off. Old aunt Polly DeBerry died last Sunday morning. She has been afflicted for years, but for the last few weeks her disease has seemed to fasten on her with a tighter grasp when death ended the scene.

Ann is gone down to Mr. Ewings to see Fanny. She went last Tuesday and was to have returned today, but there was a heavy rain last night & this morning which has raised the river, and I shall not look for her until tomorrow

or the next day. I showed your letter to Fanny and she said she would write you. Kezia wrote you, I think, last week. I would be very glad to hear from you as often as may be convenient and glader still, if you could pay us a visit and spend some time with us. Write soon—
		I remain
		Your Friend
		E. W. Wooley

153. March 20, 1864

Captain Columbus H. Dixon, "The King's Mountain Tigers," Company G, 49th Regiment N.C. Troops, letter to his wife, L. A. Dixon, Cleveland County, N.C. Source: C. H. Dixon Papers (1517), Special Collections, Perkins Library, Duke University, Durham, N.C. (Excerpted from original due to decay.)

Captain Dixon's last letter refers to his nomination to be sheriff of Cleveland County. It is unknown whether he was defeated for election or chose not to accept the position. Dixon was wounded at the Battle of the Crater on July 30, 1864, but recovered and returned to command shortly thereafter. Columbus H. Dixon was killed in action on December 14, 1864, during a mortar barrage near Petersburg, Virginia.[13]

Camp 49th N C Troops
March 20th 1864
Kind and Affectionate Wife,

I have just eat dinner. We had some good Bread, fryed Bacon and Onions. The Government issues Rations to the officers now but they will not sell us any. I like the law very well except when any of our friends comes to see us they must bring their own rations.

The company declares they can not give me up to be the sheriff. They say they will all vote for me if I only will stay with them. They seem very much disturbed about me leaving than I am expecting to leave. Orderly Sergeant Bridges, G. Russell, and several others say that if I leave the company is gone up the spout. They say that Weaver will not do for Captain and Ben is too young etc.[14]

I understand that General Lee has started granting furloughs. We may luck out and get some furloughs before the summer's campaigns begin. Write to me if your school has commenced and tell me how Johnny is doing and if he is a good boy and Kassey if she gives such sweet little kisses still.

Your true husband
C. H. Dixon

154. March 24, 1864

Rev. Jeffrey H. Robbins, Chaplain, 12th Regiment N.C. Troops, open letter to editor of *The North Carolina Presbyterian*, Fayetteville, Cumberland County. Source: *The North Carolina Presbyterian*, Fayetteville, April 13, 1864.

Rev. J. H. Robbins, a Randolph County Methodist, was appointed chaplain of the 12th Regiment North Carolina Troops. The regiment had two companies from his home county of Randolph. In this letter, he is thanking the NC Presbyterian Paper for its complimentary copies which were distributed among the troops. In addition to the regular services performed by the regimental chaplains, missionaries from various denominations would come and visit the troops. These missionaries would help the chaplains and distribute tracts, printed material, and song sheets. In addition, these missionaries would also bring "care packages" which would raise the spirits of the troops. The best source of information on the chaplain's service is *Christ in the Camps*.

Johnson's Brigade
Camp 12th N. C. T.
Hanover Junction, Mar. 24 1864

Dear Brother,

For some time I intended to drop you a line in acknowledging the receipt of a bundle of your paper, which regularly makes visits to my regiment.

It is a very welcome comer, and I take pleasure in distributing it among the soldiers who are always glad to receive it, especially those of your church. For your paper is the only public representation that your church has in the Brigade. The 5th Regiment has an Episcopalian: 12th Methodist; 20th Lutheran; and the 23 has a Baptist Missionary at this time.

Your missionaries have not paid us a visit; we would be glad if they would call by and give us a lift; and truly we are needing it now, as we have the use of a large church and have been holding meetings for a week, night and day. The Chaplains of the Brigade are jointly working together in the "unity of the spirit and in the bonds of peace," for the salvation of the souls of men, except the Chaplain of the 5th Regiment, who is absent.

There is an interest in the Brigade on the subject of religion; a goodly number have professed conversion and the good work goes on.

We are now having a cold snap of weather, but shall continue our meeting if the Lord blesses us with His Presence still, but there is nothing certain in war. It is wisdom to prepare to stay a lifetime at one place, and be ready to leave it on a minutes notice.

Truly Yours,
J. H. Robbins
Chap, 12th N. C. T.

155. March 30, 1864

John Williams, Catawba County, N.C., letter to Col. S. A. Sharpe, 5th Regiment NC Home Guard Statesville, Iredell County, N.C. Source: John McKee Sharpe

Papers, Southern Historical Collection, University of North Carolina at Chapel Hill.

In 1860, Alexander County reported at least one school in each of the county's townships. John A. Williams, a seventeen-year-old teacher from the Newton area of Catawba County, expressed his desire to teach in Alexander when he wrote Samuel A. Sharpe on March 30. Williams represented the average teacher from outside a community, concerned with lodging, and was eventually boarded in a local home. In fact most teachers in Civil War–era North Carolina began their careers somewhere outside of their home county. Williams was reported as a teacher in Taylorsville, Alexander County, through 1870.*

Catawba Station
March 30th 1864

Col. Sharpe—

I understand you would want to have a school in your neighborhood. If you will give me a price sufficient, I will teach for you. Mr. James Watts informed me that you wanted a school and some of you wanted me to take the school. Please inform what you will give and board me or what I can get board at. Address your reply to Catawba Station. Respectfully,

J. A. Williams

Alexander County Census, 1860, 1870, and Catawba County Census, 1860.

156. April 5, 1864

Private Andrew Rinck, Company I, 11th Regiment N.C. Troops, letter to his wife, Rebecca Rinck, Catawba County, N.C. Source: Members of the Rinck/Rink Family: Sarah R. Wallace, Mary R. Harbinson, Edna R. Shufford, Bettie Mims, Brenda Witherspoon, Sarah M. Rink, and Mary Setzer Rink.

With the Army of Northern Virginia

preparing to break winter quarters, men of McRae's Brigade had no idea of the horrors that awaited them only a month later. Rinck's letter reports on the weather, inquires about his brother who is home on furlough after being exchanged, and reports an incident of dishonesty when his shirt was stolen out of his knapsack. Such incidents were rare, or at least rarely mentioned in letters and diaries.

Camp near Orange Courthouse
April the 5, 1864

Dear wife

I this morning take the present opportunity to drop you a few lines to let you know that I am well and truly hope these few lines may find you all well. Dear wife, I received your letter the other day and was glad to hear from you to hear that you was well. I want you to write and tell me whether Brother Daniel got home safe or not.[15] We had a very deep snow here some time ago, and we have had several little snows since then, and we have a rainy time of it now. We have had very bad weather ever since I came back from the hospital to the company. I am glad to hear that you was a getting along with your work as well as you are. Whenever you get a chance to have the baby's funeral preached, you might better have it soon, for chance of me a getting a furlough now is very dull. I want you to let me know whether you got the plank hauled up from the sawmills yet or not. Brother Noah[16] said that he thought he could work some at the porch for you if he gets home. I want you to let me know whether you heard that he got home safe yet or not.

That box you started to send me, everything that was in it got lost. The regiment that I was in got the box or a part of it, and they eat it up and now denies it that they ever got it. The people are not to be trusted these days for I had a shirt stole out of my knapsack. It was the one that you sent with your Uncle Kenery.

I want Daniel as soon as he can to write to me and tell me how all the folks is getting along. I want you to tell Daniel that he should go and see Brother Ephraim and tell him that I would like for him to do my blacksmithing this summer for me. And tell him to write to me and tell me how he will charge for his work, whether he will charge high or not.

I want you in your next letter to write and tell me whether you will have enough meat to do you or not. I would like to be there at home to get some of your sweet potatoes, and I want you to write and tell me whether you have money or not. I want you to tell me whether you got enough for to do you. Dear wife, I have not much news to write that will interest you much, so I will bring my letter to a close by asking you to write to me as soon as you get this letter, so I will close by asking you to write soon. So, no more, only remain your husband until death.

Andrew Rink To Emeline Rink

157. April 11, 1864

Brigadier General Alfred M. Scales, Wilcox's Division, letter to his wife, Kate, Reidsville, Rockingham County, N.C. Source: A. M. Scales Collection, Box 1 (Correspondence), Private Manuscripts Collection, North Carolina Division of Archives and History.

Colonel Scales' life has changed considerably since the last letter featured in this volume (see number 100). Scales' 13th North Carolina participated in the victory at Chancellorsville, a victory in which Col. Scales sustained a wound to his thigh. Scales was sent home to Rockingham County, and while convalescing at home,

Volunteer Andrew Rinck soldiered alongside two brothers in the Eleventh Regiment. (Courtesy of Mary R. Harbinson and the Rink/Rinck Family.)

he was promoted to brigadier general and was given command of Pender's old brigade on June 15, 1863. Scales returned to his new brigade to participate in the second invasion of the north and was wounded in his brigade's bloody attack northwest of Gettysburg on July 1. After only a short absence, General Scales made a complete recovery and was prepared to lead his command on April 11, 1864. In this letter, Scales seems more interested in attending a ball, which he asks his wife's permission to do.

Orange C. H.
April 11th 1864
My Darling Kate

Your welcome letter of the 6th inst reached me yesterday. I rec'd them now regularly every two days & this makes the fourth. They always welcomed with similar fashion & would be if they came every hour in the day. The evening that

I expected one for hours wait upon the mail to come. I can scarcely think of anything else when it does come it is a source of regret that I must wait two more days for another one. I am sorry that mine do not reach you as promptly this must be attributed to the fact that they are first sent to Raleigh and then sent back. This is 5th I have written since you left and all of the others.

There is so little news here to fill out a letter that necessarily in writing that so often & so long there must be a good deal of repetition. I know that you have a gift of writing long letters, and I am nearly ashamed of the short length of letters which I send you and wish that I can only make news as interesting and as welcome to you as your letters are to me. I am sure you will be satisfied as you see we are yet at Orange Court House.

It rained very hard again yesterday evening though we are drilling as I wrote you last to put ourselves in marching condition. Yet the roads are so deep in mud & the weather so inconsistent that I may yet write several other letters from the same camp.

The ladies did not all go back yesterday. All of them are ordered to the south but some are staying to attend the tournament which comes off today & the Ball which comes off tomorrow. I was invited to be one of the judges at the tournament & to give the pleasure of my company at the Ball tomorrow night. I declined for the torn. saying I was feeling unwell & then I wished to respond to other letters today. It makes me much more satisfied and pleasant to write to you, than the things I could see at a dozen such exhibitions. Shall I go to the Ball? My ticket is costing me nothing & is unsolicited. They have sent to Richmond for all the nice things that the market will offer such as cakes & ice cream came to be in the richest profession. In addition to this I am

promised if I will go that not only shall I feed upon all the things I wish to my hearts content but then I will be introduced to the nicest ladies both single and married. A pleasant time is generally anticipated for all. What does my darling say, shall I go?

Remember the ice cream the cake & the wines & that we do not have them every day. Remember the Ladies I shall meet & such ladies, the finest in the land to magnificently arrayed than circumstances, to lighten up with such smiles of welcome & radiant beauty. As Anne Bullock would say "having all sorts of things, but why would you not pay a visit." My ticket is complimentary but I express the sincere hope that I would attend. Shall I go? Can you trust my health to the night air & to all their delicacies, my soul amid so many tempting wines, my constancy among so many fine women? My best love to Effie, Ma & all. May God bless my darling wife.

Your Devoted Husband
AM Scales

158. April 12, 1864

Sergeant Bartlett Yancey Malone, "The Caswell Boys," Company H, 6th Regiment N.C. State Troops, diary entry. Source: Diary of Bartlett Y. Malone, property of the Wilkinson Family. Microfilm copy available in the Southern Historical Collection, Wilson Library, University of North Carolina at Chapel Hill.

A large number of the Union guards at Point Lookout Prison in Maryland were units of United States Colored Troops. In this case, the 3rd Maryland (African-Descent) was detailed to act as prison guards. It must have been odd for many Tarheel soldiers to be guarded by black troops. While none of the captured men from Company H, 6th N.C. Troops, owned slaves, like many other soldiers they had grown up believing that no matter how poor a white farmer was, at least he was better than a black slave. In the following entry, Malone describes some antics with the guards and an accidental shooting while two guards were "playing bayonets." Later in future entries, in Malone's diary, the black guards become very agitated and hateful to the prisoners. The guards demonstrate such animosity that the Commandant of the Prison refuses to allow them into the stockade on several occasions.

The 12th the 3d Maryland Negro Regiment was plaisd on gard around the Prison Camp. When the Negrows first come on gard they wore thir knapsacks and when they was put on poast they puled them off and laid them down at the end of thir lines And Some of our men stole too of them: And when the Negro found it was gone he sais to the next one on post Efrum-Efrum: tell that other Negrow up dar that the white folks has stold my knapsack a redy: The other one sais they have stold mine too but I want caring for the knapsack all I hate about it is loosing Sophys Garotipe.* One day too of them was on poast in the Streets and met up at the end of thir lines and comenced fooling with thir Guns what they cauld plaing bayonets they had thir guns cocked preseantly one of thir guns went of and shot the other one threw the brest he fell dead: the other one sais: Jim, Jim get up from dar you are not hurt your just trying to fool me.

*daguerreotype

159. April 18, 1864

Sergeant Isaac L. Summit, "Catawba Braves," Company K, 46th Regiment N.C. Troops, letter to his wife, Perlina Summit, Catawba County, North Carolina. Source: Geneva Ennis, Newton, North Carolina.

Isaac Summit was born in 1832 to John and Rebecca Robinson Summit of Linclon County, North Carolina. By 1857, Summit lived in Catawba County where he married Perlive (Perlina) Abernathy on February 1, 1857. The couple lived on a farm, where Isaac worked as a tanner, and had two daughters, Elizabeth (b. 1858) and Margaret Ellen (b. 1860), before Isaac enlisted into Confederate service at Camp Mangum on April 16, 1862. Isaac was a member of the Catawba Braves under Captain Adolphus Propst. He was mustered in as a private and rose to the rank of second corporal before he sat to write these lines.[17]

Camp near orange Court House
April 18th /64
Deare Wife

I Seat my self this morning in order to answer your kind letter which came to hand yesterday that was served the seckeon of this instan. I was glad to hear from you all and to hear that you was all well. I can you that I am tolerable well at this time I think my helth is a getting better than it has been for some time. I hope these few lines may reach you all and find you all well I haven't anything of importence to write to you at this time only we [ill] to know the what minit we may be called on to leave this place.

I can tell you that the sack is yours and the straps is Caldwell I can tell you that A visit to the 32 regiment see J S Crouse and the rest of the Boys that I was acquainted with. I can tell you that he was well and The rest of the boys and he said he was A come up to see us all and I saw Augustus Robinson he is in the 32 regiment in co B. Him and Lawson Witherspoon and Several others that I was Acquainted with.

When you write Again tome I want you to write some more About the farm you never told me how the wheat was A doing nor how Ammon Bumgarner was A getting a in of the Cotton and what part he is to give you out of it or weether he is A picking any of the bottom off or not and I allsow I want you to write oftener than you have ben A doing the last letter was wrote this 2 and maild the 7 seventh of this instant I can tell you that we air A enjoying our Selves with our boxes I can tell you that the boys is all generously well and adoing well So I will bring my letter to A close by asking my too littles gales to be good little girls and abey your mother so nomore at present so I remain your as wever

Isaac L Summit to
Perlina Summit

160. April 19, 1864

Second Lieutenant Leonidas L. Polk, "The Anson Regulators," Company I, 43rd Regiment N.C. Troops, diary entry. Source: L. L. Polk Papers, Southern Historical Collection, University of North Carolina at Chapel Hill.

Polk's regiment, along with Lewis' brigade, is part of Gen. Hoke's forces besieging Plymouth, N.C. This entry refers to the Confederate ironclad ram *Albemarle* and Union General Dan Wessells. The next day, Hoke would launch an attack that recaptured Plymouth, placing an important town back in Confederate hands.

April 19—(Tuesday) Lying near the breastworks. Canister & balls flying rapidly. Our dead lying all about Fort Williams and Fort Magazine. I was detailed to take charge of a cooking detail and I had a good and pleasant time at Wagon yard. "Stripes"* still wave defiantly over Fort Williams. The ram *Albemarle* clears the river of enemy vessels. Start back with rations at night. Hoke demands surrender of Plymouth, Wessells† refuses.

*Union flag

†Union General Dan Wessells commanded the Union forces at Plymouth, N.C.

161. April 20, 1864

"Edward Richards," letter to Rosa, Person County, N.C. Source: Louis P. Sherman Collection, Private Manuscripts Collection, North Carolina Division of Archives and History.

The following is signed "Edward Richards," which match the middle initials in James E. R. Yancey of company B, 12th N.C. Troops (see number 91). Possibly the letter writer was Yancey. This possibility is suggested by the fact that no Edward Richards of Granville or Person counties was found in N.C. Cavalry records or in a preliminary search of Virginia cavalry units. Furthermore, the letter is addressed to Rosa, a correspondent and perhaps a love interest of Private Yancey's. The cavalry to which the writer refers cannot be identified. The battle between the companies with leftover fish is humorous; similar stories exist of snowball fights and even dirt clod throwing by soldiers.

Camp Taylorsville, Va
April 20th 1864

Miss Rosa Dear friend

While I am alone and have nothing to do but think of you I will endevor to converse with you by the way of the pen as I am deprived of conversing with you personally. But I hope that will not be the case all ways. We have been very unfortunat of late we both have met up with disappointments allthough we are not by our selves. Disappointments are very common espechely thes days. I am in hopes that the time is close at hand when all things may yet be well with us. Then and not till then can I sit with you and we can converse with each other and enjoy our selves together as I only wish. I think I know who loves me and I am certain I know who I love. So I shall not be discourage by eny means as long as you keep as high spirits, gay and happy. Cousin Rosa I wish we could of had a good chance of talking this subject over to each others satisfaction. I wanted to see you last but the wether was so disagreeable and cold. There seasons chance with out being satisfide and to tell you the truth. Cousin Rosa I would have to be in your secret company some time before I could unvale my sentiments to you as I only wish to do. You are the only Lucile I have met up with yet but what I could explain my sentiments fully with out losing the least regard ever when I begin to talk to you on a certain subject my mind all most becomes demorilism. This is so but ruly it is so. I can not tell now cousin if I have said eney thing as two much on this subject. I hope you will be generous enough to pardon me. This morning is indeed bright and beautiful and the little Birds are sweetly singing while I am sitting in the dome of my little War. But writing to you and listing to their sweet songs. Oh how merry they seem and how gay they appear. Welcome sweet spring, Welcome. Isnt it the most pleasant season of the year but spring would be but gloomy weather if we had anything else but spring. It is Saturday today and I am so sad and lonely. What would I give to see you now and have the pleasure of kissing those sweet little lips or grasping that sweet little hand. All of my messmates are gone down on South River fishing to day. They sint me word a few minutes ago that they had caught 35 very fine fish and they expected to fish all night so if I would come down tomorrow we will have a big fish fry. Myself and several of the Boys went fishing last Sunday. We had fine luck and a heap of fun. We caught 260 fine ones. We also had a little fun last night by fighting a sham battle. My house is about 20 yards from the rest of the cavalry so they divided the company in two parts and handed one half over to me. We then commenced shelling each other with chunks of fish. The firing continued about two hours then we made a charge on the yankees and we caught them and took them prisoner. There was very little bloodshed on either side. The captain got wounded and one private was two. It was the smelliest sight I ever knew to see the fish flying from one side to the other. Well Cousin Rosa it is now time for drill. I must close by asking you to excuse all mistakes you may see in this letter and believe me to ever to be your best fiend and lover. My best wishes are with you. Farewell Dear Rosa. Farewell until I hear from you again.

> Yours with much love
> Edward Richards

Rosa I believed thee true, And I am blest in this believing, Oh I love thee sincerely And few have ever loved like me.

162. April 28, 1864

Molly Alford, Trinity, Randolph County, N.C., letter to Captain John F. Heitman, Company H, 48th Regiment N.C. Troops. Source: Duke University Archives, Duke University.

Molly Alford kept up a regular correspondence with her friend John F. Heitman (Capt. Co. H, 48th N.C. Troops). John was attending the Methodist Trinity College in order to enter the ministry, and was boarded by Jabez Leach. Jabez's niece, Molly, made friends with John, who was twenty years old at the time.[18] Molly is a very good writer for a young lady of sixteen. She appears to enter an intellectual discussion with John regarding the nature of women. The piece of literature to which they refer is unknown. It does not appear that the two were romantically involved, although Molly does allude to her uncle's desire to have John in the family. This is one of eight letters in the possession of Duke University; however, this is the only one still legible.

Trinity College, Randolph County, N.C., c. 1860-1861. (Duke University Archives.)

Trinity, N.C.
April the 28th, 1864

Capt. Heitman,

On my return from a visit of a week to Lexington I found yours of the 31st awaiting my arrival which from its date should have reached me before I left the home but there is so much irregularity in the mail these days that one never knows what to expect when a letter is lined. I spent the week quite fashionably and was there the one <u>big</u> day in David-son—election day, and told my uncle I was almost temped to go and electioneer for Ramsey. I thought he certainly needed either votes or sympathy for he got so few votes there. We have not heard full returns yet from all the countys but suppose we shall receive them tomorrow as the sheriffs are to meet today to confirm votes. I have

never been more anxious for Uncles election—he has endured much from his enemies that it makes me much more joyous over his victory. I suppose his majority will be about 1500 or 1000.

Bud Hollis was with me in Lexing-ton. He is now home on sick furlough of sixty days. He has been ill almost ever since Christmas but is now recovering fast but his time is half out and I fear that his general health will not be sufficent restored. We are enjoying it hugely that he has been with us.

Spring is with us once more and spring weather at last but do all we can it will bring sad forebiddings instead of the usual gay and happy thoughts—not for country—but for the many friends and loved ones who must stand in this blood-thirsty world against the foe. Many weeks have passed yet I trust in

Providence that god could some-way come to our aid and end this terrible bloodshed. But what I base my hopes upon I cant tell if he favors the Confederacy, but if not it will give up only at the end of bloodshed eventually.

You say you think Irving's description of the character of (illegible) except the LOVE part. I was thinking that the truist of all. I can agree that in such horrible conditions love can become a "cruel awareness" and yet you should know better. I do agree with Irving in his impression of women generally—if a woman seeks for a man's heart it is that she may help him in some way. She teaches him tenderness and cour-tesy and how to open up before his vision nobler aims for his ambition etc., etc. Of course there are some women vain triffling, and ambi-tious of conquests but they are the exception—not the general who are truly hearted and can be found on any hill.

All your friends around Trinity are well. I saw Mrs. Shaw at church Sunday. She was looking very well. Dr. Douke—or uncle Douke preached the funeral of Madeline and Russie Robbins at Hopewell[19] and as a sermon it was splendid. I was quite a priveledge to hear something as that.

Uncle Jabez has just came home he always inquires often with you much intent. He and aunt Nancy seem to consider you as a part of the family and I am sure one of their grandaughters. I am somewhat conscious when she asks often about you as she does sometimes. I imagine you thinking "it is well she is over her sheet she could make it more entertaining." I plead guilty and stop—

Truly always,
Molly

Captain John F. Heitman received this letter while at Petersburg, Virginia. (Duke University Archives.)

163. May 1, 1864

Unidentified female, Person County, letter to her cousin, an unidentified Granville County soldier. Source: Louis P. Sherman Collection, Private Manuscripts Collection, North Carolina Division of Archives and History.

The following letter is written by an unidentified female from Person County, N.C., with the initials "C. F. C." She is writing to a supposed cousin who is in service at the time. The letter is a kind of love letter, filled with playful riddles.

Furthermore, the letter suggests that perhaps a secret love affair is going on between the letter's writer and its recipient. With 1864 being a leap year, it was a custom for the ladies to be the active participants in seeking romance, instead of the men.

May the 1 1864

Dear Sir

As it is leapyear I have concluded to send you a few lines to let you know that I have not forgotten you. You may think this is an April fool but it is too late for them. I do not know whether you have ever seen me or not but I have seen you. You must not think hard of this maybee as it is. The day I saw you you looked like a rosebud in the morning of spring. I must come to a close by saying goodby.

Your cousin until death. Who made Moses? Where was Peter when the candles went out? In what month do ladies talk the least? Why is a lover like a crow? Where did the witch of eden lie? What is that which is always brought to the table to eat but never eaten? Why is a wedding ring like eternity? If you give a kiss and take a kiss what does it make? What burns to keep a secret? The heart. Why is a man in love like a lobster? Why is a handsome woman like candy? Who do you love Willy maybe you do not know.

I will tell you if you do not know. Remember your home my Willy boy and the loved ones left behind. Remember the day you took my hand and freely spoke your mind? Come back with the laurel on your brow, won in a glorious fight and then you will see my Willy boy how soon I will be your Wife. You must sing this for me. As I am alone I must come to a close by saying good by. Your friend until death.

C.F.C. to W. D. Y.[20]

164. May 5, 1864

Private Louis Leon, Company B, 53rd Regiment N.C. Troops, diary entry. Source: Leon, Louis, *Diary of a Tar Heel Confederate Soldier*, 1913.

With Grant taking over command in the East, Lee would now have to deal with a commander who had overwhelming superiority of numbers and who would fight him all day, every day. The first clash of these titans came in the dense forest known as the Wilderness. This was the same forest that concealed the flanking march of Stonewall Jackson during the Battle of Chancellorsville.

May 5 (1864)— Moved this morning, feeling for the enemy, and came up to them at noon, five miles from the Run in the Wilderness. It certainly is a wilderness; it is almost impossible for a man to walk, as the woods are thick with an underbrush growth and all kinds of shrubbery, old logs, grapevines, and goodness knows what. My corps of sharpshooters was ordered to the front. We formed in line and advanced to the enemy. We fought them very hard for three hours, they falling back all the time. Our sharpshooters' line got mixed up with Gordon's Brigade, and fought with them. In one charge we got to the most elevated place in the Wilderness. We looked back for our brigade, but saw it not. Just then a Yankee officer came up and we took him prisoner. Some of Gordon's men took him to the rear. Six of our regiment, sharpshooters, myself included, went to the right to join our regiment, but were picked up by the Yankees and made prisoners. We were run back in their line on the double quick. When we got to their rear we found about 300 of our men were already prisoners. The Yankees lost very heavily in this fight, more than we did. Although we lost heavy enough, but, my Heavens what an army they have got. It seems to me that there are ten of them to one of us, It looked strange that we could deliver such fearful blow, when, in fact, if numbers counted, they should have killed us two years ago. In going to their rear we passed through four lines of battle and reinforcements still coming up, while we were satisfied with, or at least to have no more than one line of battle.[21]

165. May 9, 1864

First Lieutenant James A. Graham, "The Orange Guards," Company G, 27th Regiment N.C. Troops, Gordonsville, Virginia, letter to his mother, Orange County, N.C. Source: The James A. Graham Papers 1861–1864, Southern Historical Collection, University of North Carolina at Chapel Hill.

Wounded in the left knee and tired, First Lieutenant Graham describes the previous battle from his hospital bed. Graham was wounded during the fall of 1863 while fighting at Bristoe Station. Graham was wounded in a preliminary skirmish, described in the following letter. During the major engagement, the 27th Regiment (Cooke's Brigade, III Corps) performed very well under fire; however, their loss, as with nearly all units in the Wilderness Campaign, was severe. The following letter describes preliminary action occurring before the general engagement at the Wilderness.

Gordonsville, Va
May 9th, 1864
MY DEAR MOTHER

We have met the enemy at last and so far we have whipped him completely and I hope will continue to do so until we kill them out or drive them across the Rappahannock.

On last Wednesday (4th inst) we left camp about 12 o'clock and started down the Plank Road towards Fredericksburg.

We reached Mine Run about 15 miles from Orange C. H. that night, The Yankees had thrown their whole force across the River during the day. On Thursday morning about daylight we started again our division being in front, Kirkland's Brigade leading and ours next. About 7 o'clock we came upon the Yankees and Kirklands Brigade was thrown into line of battle across the plank-road, skirmishers thrown forward, and soon we commenced driving the enemy. Kirkland's Brigade drove them till 11 o'clock (about 6 miles). Our Brigade was then thrown to the front and relieved Kirkland. We drove them for about an hour (about 2 miles) when we came upon their tine of Battle. Our skirmishers fought their line of battle for some time, but were at last compelled to fall back to our line of battle which was now formed and ready for the Yanks. We were in the thickest forest of little trees that I ever saw. About four o'clock the enemy advanced upon us three lines deep and soon we were at it hot and heavy. Though greatly out numbered, our Brigade and Davis' which were in line stuck to them. After a short while they flanked our brigade on the right, but still we stood and fought them until Walker's Brigade was thrown in on our right flank and brought us all right again. Kirkland's Brigade was then thrown in to help us. I don't know very much about the movements after this as I was struck about this time and had to get to the rear. I was struck by a minnie ball about two or three inches above the knee. The ball has not been extracted yet, but I am getting along splendidly and will get a first rate 60 days furlough. I expect to go to Richmond today or tomorrow.

Our Co suffered pretty severely. The loss as far as I know is as follows viz killed—R. C. Davis—wounded Sergt T. B. Whitted in head, Serg't O. F. Hatch in leg & taken prisoner, Corp'l

Jas. Miles in shoulder, Private Wm H Crabtree—in hip, G. M. Dorothy in face, M. Delany—arm broken, A. J. Forrest—hand, slight, D. C. Paul—hip, slight, M. Ray hand, slight, E. H. Strayhorn—neck, slight, Wm Thompson—head.

I was not with the Company during the fight, but was with Gen. Cooke, and don't know whether this is a full list or not. Maj. Webb had his arm broken on Friday Morning by a Yankee sharpshooter. He is with me and is getting along splendidly. I don't think our Brigade has been actively engaged since Thursday evening, but can hear very little from the battle field except that we whip them every time and are still driving them.

Capt. Walker Anderson, Ord. Off. of our Brigade was mortally wounded Thursday evening and died about 9 o'clock that night. I must close. Do not be at all uneasy about me as I have only a flesh wound and am doing first-rate. Love to all. I remain

Your affectionate Son
James A. Graham

166. May 17, 1864

Adjutant (First Lieutenant) Henry T. Jordan, 55th N.C. Troops, letter to Mary Satterfield, Roxboro, Person County, N.C. Source: Satterfield-Merritt Family Papers, Southern Historical Collection, University of North Carolina at Chapel Hill.

Adjutant Henry Jordan was captured on the first day's action at Gettysburg, Pennsylvania, and was confined to Johnson's Island Prison in Ohio. Jordan would spend twenty months in Federal custody until being received at Cox's Wharf for exchange on March 22, 1865. In contrast, Jordan had spent only six and a half months as Adjutant of the 55th N.C. Troops.[22] In the following letter, Henry writes to his aunt Mary regarding the loss of relatives.

Johnson's Island May 17 1864
My Dear Aunt Mary,

Your beautiful and touching letter reached me two days ago, returning from preaching in the adjoining block, with a heart softened by the eloquent sermon and fervent prayers of the "man of God," whose voice evoked gratitude to God for all the Goodness, strength in hope and confidence in the Lord of hosts to whom all times are alike and to whom the turmoil and sorrow of years is but a moment.

I found your letter in my bed and read it with fast flowing tears. How tenderly and yet with what lofty triumph, what sublime hope! It told of your precious child's departure from this troubled world to the land of the next. My eyes now are so full at the rememberence of it that I can scarcely see to write. And your soldier boy who "leaving in battle no blot on his name, Looks proudly to heaven from the death-bed of fame."

How touchingly, how proudly, how softly & yet hopefully the mother's heart remembers him, mourns over him, exults in him & looks forward to the day of reunion with both her lost loved ones. I too hope that he and his sister have joined hands in that fair land whither God the merciful and good calleth his own & that together they await our coming & watch to welcome our first footsteps on the flowery shore of paradise. There too, I trust, stand my dear brothers Ed & Will,* the pain of whose loss will never leave my heart & all our loved dead.

Nay! They are not dead, but have awakened out of a heavy and uneasy sleep into life. The life for which this life was made. And when our restless and fitful slumber shall end and our eyes open on the light of another world may they rest first on this our dear ones so earnestly looking & longing for us! The morning will yet dawn; the night is passing, and the clever light of the eternal day will be long forever despite the darkness that now enwraps us! My love to all.

Very affectionately
your nephew
Henry T. Jordan

The identity of "Will" is uncertain, as there is reported a William P. Satterfield and a William Jordan, both of whom were alive as of the date of the letter.

167. May 19, 1864

Private M. A. Barrier, "The Cabarrus Phalynx," Company H, 8th Regiment N.C. State Troops, letter to wife, Polly Ann Barrier, Cabarrus County, N.C. Source: N. A. Barrier Papers (373), Special Collections, Perkins Library, Duke University, Durham, N.C.

Private Barrier lived in the Mt. Pleasant area of Cabarrus County with his wife, Polly Ann, and their children prior to December 17, 1862, when he was conscripted into service.[23] This farm laborer had seen service in eastern North Carolina and around Charleston, South Carolina. By the May 19 the 8th Regiment had been moved up to the Petersburg area and defended the city against the forces of the Army of the James.

Cabarrus County clerk Jonas Cook commanded Company H, 8th N.C. Troops, through the spring campaigns of 1864. Cook was wounded twice in combat before his twenty-second birthday. (Courtesy of the N.C. Division of Archives and History.)

Camp 5 Miles from Petersburg
May the 19th 1864

Dear wife

It is with pleasure to me that I have an opportunity of writing you a few lines again. Dear wife I can say to you that I am well at the presant time and hopeing these few lines will find you all in the Best of helth. Dear wife I can say to you that I saw hard times of late. We had a big battle Last Monday. It lasted from daylight till 11 o'clock though we did not get in to too much we had several wounded in our company. D. L. Bost one young Blackwelder and several others slightly.[24] Our men gave the yankeys a good thrasing. They are done back about 6 miles near city point and they have Fortifyed themselves again and our men are pressing them hard. Our force was skirmishing all day yesterday and some going on this mourning. There was a Negro come to our side from the yankeys last Night. He said that the yankeys were leaving for there boats just as fast as they could. I hope it is so for want them to leave and let us alone. The yankeys have a big force and we have a good force too. There are more men here than I ever saw at once. Our loss I think on our side is some between 3 & 4 hundred killed and wounded. I think the yankeys

Canaan Myers, Company F, 1st CS Engineers, helped to construct the Spotsylvania Defenses, 1864. (Courtesy of Janice Myers.)

loss was about the same as ours. We have taken some 3000 prisoners and 5 of the finest pieces of artilery and some of the finest horses.[25] The yankeys say the war has to stop till the fourth of July. I hope it will for the yankeys are getting repulsed at all points.

I am sorry that I did not write oftener of Late but you must excuse me for we had a bad chance of Late to get letters to the post office and the Railroad is or was tore up that our Male did not go and yours did not come to hand. I hant had a letter from you since Edney Barringer come. Dear love I am anxious to hear from you and the children. Dear wife I can say to you that Aaron Hahn was killed Last week beyond Richmond on the field of battle. J. S. Hinesiman is wounded.[26] He is at Richmond in the hospittle. Our boys that were taken prisoner at citty point are relieved and

they saw J. S. Hinesimon and he told them that Aaron Hahn was killed. Dear wife I should be very glad to send you some money that I have on hand but I don't risk it at the presant.

Dear wife I want you to write soon and tell me how you are all getting on with your work and how the crops are. Dear wife I will close for the presant. Though many a mile apart we be so good by till I hear from you again.

M. A. Barrier to my dear
wife Pollyan Barrier.

168. May 19, 1864

Brigadier General Stephen D. Ramseur, Rodes' Division, letter to sweetheart, Ellen Richmond, Milton, Lincoln County, N.C. Source: Letters courtesy of Mr. Paul W. Schnek, Jr., of Greensboro, who donated the extracts of correspondence, S. D. Ramseur Papers, Southern Historical Collection, University of North Carolina at Chapel Hill.

The charge of Ramseur's Brigade at the "Mule Shoe" on May 12, 1864, is one of the critical moments in the history of the Spotsylvania Campaign. The 2nd, 4th, 14th, and 30th North Carolinas were led by their general in a counter-attack, spurred on by pride and the singing of "The Bonnie Blue Flag," which not only stemmed the advance of the Federal II Corps, but caught the attention of General Ewell as "an act of unsurpassed gallantry." Ramseur was painfully wounded during the attack but refused to be moved from the field.[27] The letter below is extracted from the original.

Battlefield near Spotsylvania
C. H., Va
May 19th 1864
My own Dear wife,

By the mercy of God I am still spared to write you a few, rather hasty lines. On the 12th of this month my

Brigade did some of the best fighting of the war. My loss that day was very heavy, especially in men. The officers were quite well comparatively. I was slightly wounded through my right arm just below the elbow. My Yankee horse was shot severely, but yet he still lives. I also received four holes in my overcoat. Some of the troops which were driven early on in the battle behaved shamefully.

The Yankees have been quiet for nearly two days, with the exception of a feeble assault on our lines yesterday the 18th, which we easily repulsed. I think they are attempting to strike the Railroad in our rear. Their loss has been immense—50,000 is the current estimate. Ours is about 15,000 in killed, wounded, and prisoners, 5,000 of those being prisoners.[28] May God give us a victory which will insure peace and independence to our struggling Confederacy.

The Railroads appear to be and are cut in this part of the country, so I suppose I will not hear from you in quite some time. Your last was received two weeks ago. Pray for me and pray for our noble army and the success of our Cause.

S. D. Ramseur

169. May 29, 1864

Eliza Clodfelter, Davidson County, letter to her cousin, Mary Ann Eddinger, Davidson County. Source: Private Collection, Richard L. Conrad, Thomasville, N.C.

The following is a second letter from Eliza E. Clodfelter to her cousin, Mary Ann Eddinger. At the time of this letter, Mary Ann has been widowed for almost a year and a half. Eliza refers to the "boys of seventeen" being taken from the settlement. This was the creation of a company of Junior Reserves in the county in May of

1864. The unit would later become Company C, 70th Regiment N.C. Troops (1st Junior Reserves). The area in which the action is happening is in the vicinity of Rich Fork Church in Davidson County, which was known as "Sowers's Hole." Eliza also addresses the price of goods in the county after inflation brought on by the war.

Sunday Evening
May 29th 1864
Dear Cousin, I have been waiting for a letter from you so long that I have got out of heart of ever hearing from you all any more. I want to hear from you all very bad. None of us are very well at present but are all up and about. I don't know if I can write any thing new that will be of much interest. There is nothing thought or talked of about here but the war. All of the boys seventeen years of age are gone from this settlement. They went last Thursday week. Dan Eddinger and David and Joe Clodfelter and George Waggoner's son are all gone and a great many more had to go.[29] They took Sam Darr without anything but what he had on. It seems like times get worse all the time. I never expect to see any better times but if I live long I expect to see everything destroyed by the Yankees. You may not think this will not be so but if you live you will find it to be so. Solomon Clodfelter's son is killed. Bryant wrote in his letter that John Mock had one arm off and to day we heard that he is dead. Barna Leonard went off to the army and died in a few weeks. Little Adam Sink died with the Yankees. We understand that Joe Sink is wounded in the wrist. Now I have told you all I know about the war.

The people of this settlement are generally healthy. The small pox is among the negroes below town. Henderson has put up a stand for preaching down here on the road where the road turns off to go to Sowers. Jackson and

Hamner are to preach there this summer. I suppose you have heard that our preacher has left and gone to the yankees. Preacher Seinn got killed by falling from his mule on his way home from church. The mule kicked him in the head and killed him dead. We have had a great deal of rain. It rains here nearly every day. Some people in the settlement are suffering for something to eat now. Phillip is at home yet. I do hope that he is and will stay there some of you must try to come and see us if you can. If Phillip stays at home get him to bring you and the girls down sometime this summer.

Alpheus is gone to see Laura's baby today. It can sit alone. Mary Ann, if I could see you I could tell you several things that I don't want to write. Gust Bryant visited some of the soldiers wives a good many times when he was at home last. He paid his visits to one that lives not far from the creek. I must tell you how cheap spun cotton sells. It is fifty dollars per bunch. Wheat and corn is about eighteen or twenty dollars per bushel and very little to have at that. Iron sells from three to five dollars per pound. I reckon you will all be tired of my letters. I must think of coming to a close.

E. E. Clodfelter

170. June 4, 1864

E. U. Linster, Statesville, Iredell County, N.C., letter to his son, R. O. Linster, Company C, 4th Regiment N.C. State Troops. Source: Special Collections, Perkins Library, Duke University, Durham, North Carolina.

In the following letter Mr. Linster updates his son about all the news that he has heard. Soldiers appreciated news from home and were very interested in how the press and the people viewed the war in which they were fighting. Southern news-

papers, such as Salisbury's *Carolina Watchman*, reported on both major theatres of the war, which allows Mr. Linster to tell his son about the cavalry raids of Nathan B. Forrest.

Statesville June 4, 1864

Dear Son

I expected a Letter from you this morning, but did not get one. I will commence writing today and finish Monday, so I will not forget anything I want to tell you.

Your Uncle Fred wrote to us the other day, he said he and Aunt Martha had received Letters from you, he had answered his immialely, and wanted us to write him, if we had heard from you, that your Uncle Mc was well, and fighting away, when he heard from him, which was a few days before, by a wounded soldier, who had passed. Lieut Carleton came up yesterday, is pretty severly tho not dangerously wounded. I have not seen him. I suppose I am will tell you about him, he was gong to write you yesterday, he said. I presume he will give you a general account of all transpiring at the village; yet I tell you something that he may forget.

I sent you the Express and Watchman this week, since I have read a letter in the Watchman* form Nat. He say Lieut Adams is missing, Lieut McNeely of Co A was brot in wounded on the 15th May, and said he saw Sergt Morrison laying dead on the field, who was thought to be prisoner with Adams, but Adams was all the one of Co C missing, supposed to be captured; Gen Grimes was leading Daniel Brigade who was dead, he did not say who was in command of the 4th Lieut Col Wood tho of course; This morning Watchman contains some more details form the Army; on the 3rd skirmishing in several places on the lines, Ewels Corps engaged again, and repulsed the assault of the Yankees, with ease. Yankees said to be drunk again. Gen Lee at Gains Mill in good health and fine spirits. President Davis and Gen Bragg rode to the front yesterday, Richmond quiet as a Sabbath.

The girles here will catch becuse, when they can. I saw Wm Richardson waiting on Miss Reynolds from church, I think he will catch that Bird yet. I accidently have come to he conclusion that Couson Stinson is Miss Mag Alexander's.

One of Vaughns Cavelry rode thru here the morning after they did with no saddle nothing but a Blanket on his horse, which he had stolen the night before and two men came in directly after in hot persuit to get the stolen horse. I have not heard anything more from them but think Cavalry will out-general them, they will hardly overtake Cavalry soon.

Monday morning June 6th 1864

Frank C was up street Saturday he said at one of the engagements he counted on about an acre of ground seven hundred Yankees, they were well dressed, one of them was an officer; Frank said he thought of looking for any valubles there might be on his person, but, he was laying on his back with his eyes open, and seemed to be looking at him so intently he could not venture to molest him.

Gibson came up Saturday with a soar foot he had taken some horses to Va and one of them had hurt his foot. Mr Anderson told me, he said Jo was look-ing quite well.

Did I send you the Paper with the report of the death of Pink Arthurs, he is also reported killed. I have just rec yours of the 1st June am glad you are getting on well; hope you will get a Fur-lough or Transfer, rather a Furlough son you can stay at home, hope if you do get either it will be a Furlough.

Sergt Morrison came up this morn-ing wounded I suppose, he is the one Nat thought was dead on the Field.

Your Pa saw him, do not know, to be him, only suppose to be him.

A good many wounded came up today. They say we do kill more Yankees than they do of our soldiers. The Watchman* this morning says fighting was going on 10 miles from Richmond last Friday. The lines seven miles long, Brockenridge's horse killed & two hundred of his men captured.

Grant is deranged again; as he, intended to make the White house the base of operations and the results so far all we could wish. In Geo skirmishing going on no general engagement but Forest† coming up in Yankies rear if Yankee don't keep a sharp look out somebody will be hurt when our Cavalry chief gets in sight. I am glad you are in more comfortable quarters. I expect Lynchburg is more healthy than Salisbury and more pleasant too. Son, do please write often, if I can hear from you I am not so uneasy about you. I have wrote all I can think of this time. Write soon to Mother

E.U. Linster

*The Carolina Watchman, a Salisbury newspaper

†Refers to a campaign conducted by Gen. Nathan B. Forrest in Tennessee to attack the supply lines of the Federal western armies.

171. June 17, 1864

George A. Williams, letter to his chil-dren, Chatam County, N.C. Source: Williams-Womble Papers, Private Manu-scripts Collection, North Carolina Divi-sion of Archives and History, Raleigh, N.C.

By the end of July, 1864, the 7th Reg-iment N.C. Troops was posted along with Lane's Brigade southeast of Richmond, northeast of Petersburg, near the old Malvern Hill Battlefield. George writes this letter to his children on June 17. Private George A. Williams was killed in action near Gravel Hill, Virginia, on July 28, 1864.[30]

Line of Battle near Malvern
Hill, Va.
June the 17th 1864

Dear children I am blessed with the
oppirtunity of writing you a few lines
this morning which will inform you that
I am still alive though not very well I
am with the company and I hopes this
will come to hand and will find you all
well. We have had a harde time since
the commensement of this campaign. I
am in the hopes we will get some rest
some time soon. Thear is some talks of
our going into camps an I trust in god
that we will. We are faring well and the
rations we draw plenty.

This will in form you that I have bin
looking for a letter for somtime. Dick*
is well and hearty and tell Mrs. Martha
Trice to write to me and let me know
how the children is getting and give my
love and beste respects to your gran
father and gran mother.

I want you to be smarte and allways
have respect for older people and don't
give them any provocation. I want you
to be Smarte and take good advis from a
friend who is capable of advising you. I
will close I remain as ever your father
until death.

G. A. Williams

*In reference to Richard A. Womble, George's brother-
in-law and comrade in Company G, 7th Regiment
North Carolina State Troops.

172. June 26, 1864

Sergeant Andrew Jackson Price, Company A, 39th Regiment N.C. Troops, letter
to his wife, Union County, N.C. Price
Papers, Private Manuscript Collections,
N.C. Division of Archives and History.

Mr. Price was one of nine men from
Union County to serve in the Army of Tennessee. Private (later Sergeant) Price offers
one of the few accounts of action in the
Western Theater of the war by a Piedmont
soldier. Sergeant Price was reported present

until he was paroled at Meridian, Mississippi, on May 9, 1865. Overall, by June 26,
1864, North Carolina had only four regiments in service with the Army of Tennessee under General Joseph E. Johnston:
29th NCT, 39th NCT, 58th NCT, and
60th NCT. His letter is written prior to the
battle of Kennesaw Mountain, which
occurred on June 27. General Sherman's
troops advanced on Confederate positions
in an attempt to snap the Army of Tennessee's center. The assault failed, giving
the Confederates a small victory. However,
after the battle Sherman continued to
advance beyond Johnston's flank, driving
southeast toward Atlanta, Georgia.

Kennesaw Mountain
near Marietta, Ga.
June the 26th 1864

Dear Wife I take my pen in hand to
drop you a few lines to in form you
that I am well at present hoping these
few lines may find you enjoying the
same good blessing. This is the second
letter that I have wrote you since I have
bin here but I do not know wheather
you got the other letter or not. We
got to our Regment yesterday was a
week ago they were fighting. When we
got there they had been fighting more
or less every day since we fell back to
the mountain. Last night was a week
ago and have helt our position ever
since.

We are at the top of the mountain
and the yankees are at the feet of it. We
can see them every day and here them
talking. We have not had a regulary
engagement in our Brigade since we
have got on this mountain. We have bin
under heavy cannon nading all the time.
Several of the men killed and wounded
by bum shelles. They have bin fighting
hard on our left but I do not know how
the fight went.

We were on picket yesterday. Our
Regment was on picket one day and
night we were in a pretty hard place &

we had four men wounded in our company yesterday while we were on picket. I am sorry to say that two of the men was men who came with us from Camp Holmes. One was that Mr. Thompson that you saw at the hospitle at Raleigh his foot was struck by a shell and tore it to peaces his leg had to be amputated. The other one was A. S. Gaddy from Union County he was struck by the same shell in the foot but I think the foot can be saved.* The balance of the Union boys is very well but Rom & Mars[31] they are sick at the hospitle.— I am very well pleased with our offersers. Our Captain[32] cant be beat in the confederacy. I feel thankful to my God that I have escaped so far. Nothing more at present. Write soon I remain your husband. A. J. Price

Direct to Atlanta, Ga. Ector Brigade 39 Reg N.C. Troops in care of Capt. Dycke.

*Identities of Thompson and Gaddy are unknown. No exact name matches, or reports of injury confirm a solid identity throughout the 39th Regiment.

173. July 1, 1864

Corporal Isaac L. Summit, "Catawba Braves," Company K, 46th Regiment N.C. Troops, letter to his wife, Perlina Summit, Catawba County, North Carolina. Source: Geneva Ennis, Newton, North Carolina.

Grant's campaign drew closer and closer to Richmond and Petersburg. Nearly a month had passed since Private Summit's regiment was part of Grant's repulse at Cold Harbor, Virginia. In another two months, Isaac would find himself carrying the colors of the 46th Regiment during the battle of Ream's Station on August 25, 1864. Isaac led the charge without his brother Henry P. Summit of Company H, who was captured at the Wilderness and was to be confined at Pt. Lookout, Maryland, then Elmira Prison, New York.[33]

Line of battle near
The James River
July the 1 1864

Dear Wife

I seat my self to Write you a few lines to let you know that I am yet amongst the living I can inform you that I am well hopping these few lines may find you all well aand doing well I can inform you that we have got to vary good place on the account of fiting I can inform you that thay have been a fiting vary hard about Petersburg. It is a bad chance to get letters through on the account of the railroads a being cut in too and and it will be some time befour it will be for use the boys is tolerable well at this time the Yankees throught som chearns over at us acasionly but thear is no damage done yet we have plenty and we have got tobacco twiste. Since we been on this march thea is but three days if old grant to come on yet if he don't get to come to Richmon till the 4 of July I think he will leave and go bac though I don't know if he will. I could Write heap but I don't know if I will have time I have writtins too letters to you Since I have got any one I write one to pillip and one to pah but I don't now if you got them or not by the railroad being cut in too this letter I will sende letter by mail so I think it will get home.

I wood like to know if HH Caldwell has got home or not I heard that he got a Sixty days furlow but never got as on the account of the road a being cut but I hope he got home I heard that thay had a hard fight a bout stony creek yesterday and we a whip them and taken a lot of preseners and waggones and artillery So I will come to a close by asking you to write when ever the mail will come throught so no more at present

yours as ever
Isaac L Summit To
Mrs Perlina Summit[34]

174. July 10, 1864

Second Lieutenant Leonidas L. Polk, "The Anson Regulators," Company I, 43rd Regiment N.C. Troops, diary entry. Source: L. L. Polk Papers, Southern Historical Collection, University of North Carolina at Chapel Hill.

Grimes' Brigade continues its campaign into Maryland and with every step moves closer to Washington, DC. The "regiment slept in line" is a reference to "sleeping on arms," a kind of bivouac where soldiers sleep with their arms close by in case of a surprise attack or a need for a quick movement during the night or early morning.

July 10—(Monday) Yesterday we were of course very busy. We started the march on Washington City and passed several small villages and marched 20 miles and took up camp in a corn field. Today we pass through Rockville, full of sympathy for us. I got a good breakfast from Mrs. Harding. From this place to Washington the people are loyal. We pass the Silver Springs and reach Blair P. Spring farm house at 2 pm. Some of our men die from exhaustion. Drive in enemy skirmish line. We then moved around in the orchard to support our forward skirmish line. The regiment slept in line.

175. July 17, 1864

Private Augustus A. Clewell, Company B, 1st Battalion, N.C. Sharpshooters, letter to his sister, Margaret Clewell, Salem, Forsyth County, N.C. Source: Clewell Letters, Private Manuscripts Collection, North Carolina Division of Archives and History.

Despite their adventurous name, the 1st Battalion Sharpshooters often performed very menial and boring duties. As an example, the second stint of Provost Duty for the battalion ran from December

1863 to August of 1864, a duty of nearly nine months. Particularly humorous is the way Clewell, twenty years old, describes the cities of Kinston and Goldsboro.[35]

Kinston, July 17th 1864
Dear Sister,
I have just returned from Goldsboro and eaten a hearty dinner, or perhaps you would call it supper as it is six o'clock and therefore don't feel much like writing. I received your letter written about three or four weeks ago, on the evening before the raid, only a few hours before the alarm was given, and forgetting it at the time, I never thought about it any more until Mother mentioned it in her letter. I don't recollect what was in it, but am almost sure that I read it all, but for fear that I didn't, I'll hunt it up one of these days when I have more time and read it again.

I saw Sue and Mat in Goldsboro a few days ago, but only spoke a few words, by this time probably they have reached Salem. I am getting tired of this portion of the country and wished we could go to Maryland. I should like to be with Early at present. I know. I know his troops will live well. Petersburge has no inducements. I would rather be here than there, but Winchester, Harper's Ferry and that country up there in Paradise compared with this swampy country. Kinston is an <u>awful</u> dull place, and Goldsboro is <u>ten times worse</u>.

Are you going back to Williamsboro or not? I don't know where or when I heard it, but it seems I heard somehow that you were going to teach school in Thomasville. I believe I'll go at that business when the war is over. Anything but work. I want to know what you are going to do, and how you are spending your time.

It is nearly dark and if I don't finish this before dark it will never be finished. Of course. Tell mother and Annette that I'll answer their letters before long if I can think about anything to write. What is the reason Johnny didn't write any more? I haven't heard a word from him since he wrote that Mr. Shaffner[36] "burnt some chimney swallows to smoke some fire out that he was building in the house." Give my love to all, and let me hear from you soon if convenient, and if not, it don't make any difference. I don't care at all. It is dark so I must close.

    I remain your affectionate brother

        Gus

176. July 23, 1864

    "Edward Richards," Staunton Hospital, Virginia, letter to his cousin, Rosa, Person County, N.C. Source: Louis P. Sherman Collection, Private Manuscripts Collection, North Carolina Division of Archives and History.

    The following letter comes from "Edward Richards" to Rosa, a popular recipient in Person County. (See number 161.) The following letter was written on captured Union paper with patriotic images of a flying eagle and a Union solider standing with a flag. The piece also features a patriotic song entitled "Now Let Our Chief Be Alone," a song about the success of General Grant during the battles of Chattanooga, Tennessee. Before he begins his letter this soldier states where he got such goods.

    This is a sheet of Yankee paper that I captured at Frederick City after I was wounded. I think the Yankees might have to change their song.

        Stanton General Hospital[37]

        July the 23th 1864

Cousin Rosa

    After a long march and several hard fought battles I will now endevor to drop you a few lines thinking probably you would like to hear from an absent

friend one whome esteems you so highly and would almost give his life to see you now. Cousin Rosa since I last wrote you which I think was the 23 June. I have ben in two bloody battles and several skirmishes. On the 4th day of July we deprived the yankees of their picknick and fine doings at Harpers ferry tho we had to do some very hard fighting before they would consent for the rebels to picknick by the great river. After we took the plase the Boys eat and drank so much as they wanted of every thing that you could call for. We then filled our haversacks and some filled ther canteens with nice liquor and then crost over in MD and drove the enemy to Frederick City. Then they was reinforst by the 6th Corps unit of 15000 of one hundred day men. On the 9th inst we over took them drawn up in a line of battle waiting for our arrival. We pitched in on them with our little handful of broken down men. We soon had the field blue with ther dead & wounded. We also captured fifteen hundred prisoners. The last I saw of them they was skeddadling in every direction and our cavalry drove them into Baltimore. We then tore up the rail road from there to Washington. [Remainder of letter is illegible.][38]

177. July 30, 1864

    Citizens of Yadkin County, letter to Major J. R. McLean, commandant, Camp Vance, Morganton, N.C. Source: Pearson Collection, Perkins Library, Duke University.

    The following letter contains a request by the leaders of Yadkin County to the commander of Camp Vance, Major McLean, to hold several men in connection with the Bond Schoolhouse Shootout. Union sentiment and animosity over conscription practices of the local authorities culminated in a standoff between several armed men and members of the

Yadkin County Militia. This uprising was put down, but the problems and the tensions of the county were not relieved. If the men returned they would be seen as inspiration to other Unionists and dissenters. For a full, detailed description of the affair, refer to Casstevens, Frances, *The Civil War in Yadkin County, N.C.*

> Yadkinville July 30, 1864
> Maj J. R. McLean
> Camp Vance

Major:

My attention has been called by Mrs. Speer to your letter of the 27th to her husband, the Sheriff. The Sheriff is absent and will be for a day or two and Mrs. Davis leaves here this morning for Camp Vance. I write to give you some information in regard to the 'Yadkin refugees' now in your custody.

Their are bills of indictment and capiases in the hands of the Sheriff against Wm, Lee and Ben Willard for the murder of James West &John Williams in the School House fight. Also against Enoch Brown and Hardee Allgood who are said to have been captured with the Willards. These men are all conscripts and have been ordered into service and one of them, Allgood, is a deserter from the Army. It will not do to send them to the county to be imprisoned, Our jail is entirely unsafe, to say nothing of the danger of their being rescued by their friends as heretofore. Elkanah did assist in forcing the jail a few weeks ago as can be proven. He did not try to disguise himself.

A very important question is, what is to be done with the balance of these men who went off in that company with the Willards. It is worse than idle to send them to the army, better turn them loose here, because if sent to the army they will be certain to desert and will bring arms with them and perhaps induce others to desert. Doubtless, some better meaning men were persuaded off

with them, but very few. If these men are not allowed to get back to this county, we are now in a fair way to clean it out. At least the prospect is better than it ever has been. If they come back we shall have terrible times. As to what should be done with the Willards I can only suggest that they be kept in some *very* safe place until some action is taken in the matter.

> Very Truly
> W. A. Joyce

I concur in the above. The Willards must not come back, and if they are sent to the army they will come.

> Jos. Dobson

I concur fully in this letter

> R. F. Armfield

178. August 1, 1864

Private James W. Gibson, "Catawba Guards," Company F, 23rd Regiment N.C. State Troops, letter to brother, Joseph F. Gibson, Catawba County, North Carolina. Source: Catawba County Historical Association. Transcription courtesy of Mrs. Addie Cloninger.

Since Gibson's last letter (see number 44), a lot has changed for this 30-year-old soldier. His regiment has seen victory around Richmond, the hellish combat of the Wilderness and Spotsylvania, two invasions of the North, and Early's Raid on Washington, of which Private Gibson says, "I do believe they could have taken the place if we got there 2 hours sooner we could have taken the place with all ease in the world."[39] The following two letters were written together.

> Camp Bunkerhill VA
> August 1 1864

Mr. Joseph F. Gibson

Dear Brother I once more seat my self to drop you a few lines to inform you that I received your very kind letter dated June the 9th it was on the road over one month and a half before it came to hand. It reached me in good health but Im in ill health at present a slight attack of fever but I hope it will sweat off. I am very sorry to hear the bad news that you relate to me in you letter, But he that giveth and taketh all things knoweth what is best and my sincere belief is that she is one to rest and better off than either of us. But we should all prepare for a better place than earth.

There has been the greatest change in the army since you left.[40] You could not imagine I do not believe that there could be a half dozen packs of playing cards found in our army at this time and you scarcely ever hear a man curse an oath but everything has been greatly changed since you left. This has been one of the most laborious campaigns since the war so far and a likely hood of a continuance during this summer my division has not had a weeks rest since the 4 day of March when the campaign first opened. Our brigade has been thrown into or transferred from Roades Division to Earlys and now Remsours Division.

Johnstons Brigade and Ramsours Division. We have made one of the grandest rades this summer ever made since the war. Made more captures and saved more stores and stock cattle and horses. I tell you we brought out a many a horse and steer and with the loss of so few men we lost but nine. We fronted Washington they marched into George-town 4 miles from the great yankee capital and I do believe they could have taken the place if we got there 2 hours sooner we could have taken the place with all ease in the world.

Companion letter

Camp Bunker hill VA
August 2nd 1864
Dear Farther, Mother Brothers and sister. I now have the opportunity of writing you a few lines informing you that I am still alive and doing the best I can I have been very unwell for the last four days but am now recuperating and soon will be able for dutie in a day or two our troops are all in good health generally and fine spirits they have been so successful in this summers campaigns that they think the war is all most over and I think the long looked for and soon hoped for will appear next spring and that is peace and freedom indepen-dence once more is all we ask to be a happy people.

Persons before this war didnt know what it was to be happy nor they did not know when they were doing well. But if we have the pleasure of being a free people I think we will all appreciate our happy condition more dearly than we ever have here to fore. But it is impossible for me to try to tell you any thing about the war for you havnt got the slightest idea how people do live in the army. I received one letter from J. F. Gibson that gave sad news that is that Martha was dead. I was shocked when I heard it not hearing of being sick at all. But that is the road we have to travel the rode to death, life is uncertain but death is sure. He that giveth taketh away and we should rejoice in all his doings. At least she is better off than any of us she is at rest I hope out of the troubles of this world. She appeared to be the pet of our family and was the youngest of us all. The almighty knows what is best. Well I will close for the present by asking you to give my very best respects and tell them to all to write to me soon We have had but little time to write since we have been in this campaign. I would not have time now if it was not that I am not able to work. But I am not able to work and I am trying to ancer my letters I want you to write soon and we now how you are getting with these hard times yours most respectfully till death direct as heretofore
J. W. Gibson

179. August 31, 1864

Second Lieutenant Leonidas L. Polk, "The Anson Regulators," Company I, 43rd Regiment N.C. Troops, diary entry. Source: L. L. Polk Papers, Southern Historical Collection, University of North Carolina at Chapel Hill.

This final entry from Polk was submitted just prior to his resignation to return to the North Carolina Legislature. Between the battles of Monocacy (July) and Winchester (September) a series of moves and counter-moves were conducted by both Union and Confederate Armies in the Shenandoah Valley. This entry describes such an attack by Rodes' division on Federal Cavalry.

August 31— (Wednesday) Rodes' Division sent down to drive back Yankee cavalry under Gen. Averill. We found him below Darksville and drove him without difficulty beyond Martinsburg. We captured very large quantities of supplies and forage. The division is ordered to cook rations of meat, crackers, and I receive a box of new clothing. I got a good saddle. Our quick attack caused them to retreat and burn their wagons. Rodes' Division turned back at 2 pm. We arrived in camp fatigued having marched about 22 miles.[41]

180. September 5, 1864

Private Andrew Rinck, Company I, 11th Regiment N.C. Troops, letter to his wife, Rebecca Rinck, Catawba County, N.C. Source: Members of the Rinck/Rink Family: Sarah R. Wallace, Mary R. Harbinson, Edna R. Shufford, Bettie Mims, Brenda Witherspoon, Sarah M. Rink, and Mary Setzer Rink.

After the brutal summer campaigns of 1864, the 11th Regiment was posted in the trenches outside of Petersburg, Virginia. In this letter, Andrew talks about his lack of writing materials due to the destruction of his knapsack by a cannonball. The attack which Rinck mentions in his letter cannot be identified, but the dates of "last week" and the action and location described would put it near the battle of Reams' Station, Virginia, on August 25, 1864. After a trying winter, the Petersburg line collapsed on April 2, 1865. One of the men taken prisoner by the Union 6th Corps was Andrew Rinck, who was already wounded in the throat and right shoulder. Private Rinck died of his wounds at Fort Monroe, Virginia, eleven days later.[42]

Petersburg
September 5th, 1864
My dear and beloved companion
I shall embrace this opportunity of writing to inform you that I am at the hospital. I am not very well, but I hope that I will get better soon. I hope this will find you and family well. I received a letter from you not long ago but have had no chance to write until now. I lost all my paper and envelopes by a cannon ball. It cut off my cartridge box, tore my knapsack all to pieces from off my back, tore my coat on the elbow and on my side. I was not hurt, only bruised a little on my side. Everything in my knapsack was lost. David Glen[43] was kind enough to give me paper and envelope to write this letter. I had no money to buy anything.

This was done in the last charge we made last Thursday. Was a week ago on Sunday before we charged the Yankees from their breastworks. We lost two killed and several wounded. We lay in their breastworks from morning until after dark in water about knee deep. We retreated back that night about one mile and was put on picket that night. The next day the Yankees charged our picket line and drove us back. We formed a line in the woods and kept firing on them until dark. I stood behind a tree and shot until I was about out of ammunition. I then started back when a ball tore my pants about my ankle but did not touch my skin. I feel thankful to God that he has kept me through so many dangers. I don't like to charge the Yankees, but they had taken the railroad between Petersburg and Weldon, and they had to be driven from it between the two places that we charged them. They have a fort built that we cannot charge them out of.

I have nothing more particular about the fight. My legs are swelled and I have a boil on my knee that I can scarcely walk. My hands are also swelled and tender. My appetite is tolerable good. I would be glad to be at home and help you eat something better than bread and meat, I think I would soon get well. I still hope through the blessing of God to get home some time to stay.

I want you to send me a little paper and some envelopes. You can send them in your letters. Write to me how the children are getting along. I would like to know whether my little boy grows much or not and if he thinks much of his cap that I sent him and if my girls think much of their books that I sent them and whether they are learning much or not. I want them to learn all they can. They will find learning worth more to them than thousands of gold and silver as far as that is concerned.

Myself and brother Daniel are at the hospital together. Daniel had been at the hospital and was sent back. We went to the hospital together yesterday morning. Daniel is very poorly with the diarrea.[44] You wrote to me that Daniel Whisenhunt wanted me to write to him but there is no chance of me doing that now as I have lost all my paper and envelopes. I want you to let him read this letter as soon as you have the chance. I want him to send a letter to me.

Nothing more, only remain your affectionate husband until death.

Andrew Rink to
Emeline Rink

181. September 6, 1864

Sergeant Bartlett Yancey Malone, "The Caswell Boys," Company H, 6th Regiment N.C. State Troops, diary entry. Source: Diary of Bartlett Y. Malone, property of the Wilkinson Family. Microfilm copy available in the Southern Historical Collection, Wilson Library, University of North Carolina at Chapel Hill.

Even in the harshest prison conditions, faith played a key role in the soldier's life. A vacant cook-house serves as a Sunday school for Malone and his comrades. The space of this selection covers four days in his diary, and the only significant occurrence is when the prison's surgeon allows them to have potatoes and onions in their bean soup in order to stop scurvy. This demonstrates the lack of events and the immense boredom of prison life.

The 2d day this is And our Rations gets no better we get half a loaf of Bread a day a smal slice of Pork or Beef or Sault Beef for Breakfast for Dinner a cup of Been Soup and Supper we get non Mr. A. Morgan of South Carolina has a vacon Cook House which he has bin teaching School in evry Sience last Spring he is a Christian man he preaches evry Sunday and has prayers evry morning befour School we have a Preacher to evry Division in the Camp Mr. Carrol preaches to our Divi which is the 8th This is the 5th day of the month and we are going to have Been Soup with onions in it to day for dinner we will have Potatoes and Onions boath to morrow the Dr had them sent in here for rebs to se if they would not stop Scirvy My health is very good to day which is the 6th of Sept. 64. But I cannot tell how long it will remain so for it a rainng and very coal to day And I have not got eney Shoes

182. September 30, 1864

Major General Stephen D. Ramseur, Early's II Corps, letter to wife, Ellen Ramseur, Lincolnton, Lincoln County, N.C. Source: Letters courtesy of Mr. Paul W. Schnek, Jr., of Greensboro, who donated the extracts of correspondence, S. D. Ramseur Papers, Southern Historical Collection, University of North Carolina at Chapel Hill.

On May 27, 1864, Ramseur was promoted to command Early's old division, and did so through the drive through the Shennedoah Valley, marching within a few miles of Washington and back through the Valley again. Following the battle of Winchester (September 19, 1864) the weight of Federal infantry and cavalry had begun to drive Early's proud valley force. Despite the reverses, Ramseur still seems confident. The letter below is extracted from the original.

> Camp near Waynesboro,
> Virginia
> Sept. 30th 1864

My own Dear Wife,

I have been too busy and too much mortified to write you for several days. At Winchester, after some very hard fighting, we had prevailed against the largely superior forces in our front and on our right, when the enemy's cavalry in heavy force broke our cavalry on the left and created a terrible disorder throughout our lines. We lost my friend General Rodes. We then fell back to Strasburg, or Fisher's Hill. Here the enemy concentrated heavily on our weak point (guarded by our cavalry) and threw everything before them there and then pounded in on our left and rear. I am sorry to say that our men were very much slaughtered and did not keep order nor fight as well as they have done so far in the Valley. We then retreated to Port Republic and from there to this point 12 miles from Staunton.

I am daily expecting General Early to advance. I believe if we could get enough Cavalry to ever hold the Yankee Cavalry in check that our Infantry can drive back Sheridan's forces. I can not tell you how much I have thought of you during the past trying week. I do hope you have not given up your bright, hopeful spirits. Anybody can be hopeful when everything is prosperous. Adversity calls for the nobler qualities of our nature. Continue my beloved to be brave for nothing but God's mercy has spared our lives. Cease not to pray for us and for our Cause.

I still feel confident of the final triumph of our Cause. It may be long and weary time, but above all things let us never despair over the establishment of our independence. We must steel ourselves for great trials and sacrifice ahead and have brave hearts for any fate. I would give anything to be with you, but the recent battles and defeats will make it almost impossible for me to leave this army now.

> S. D. Ramseur.

183. October 17, 1864

Richard A. Cole, captain and ordnance officer, 59th Battalion Home Guard, petition to Gov. Zebulon B. Vance, Raleigh, N.C. Source: The Richard A. Cole Papers, Private Manuscripts Collection, North Carolina Division of Archives and History.

To be discharged from service in the Home Guard required written approval from the governor. Any petition had to convince Zebulon Vance that the individual was incapable of active service and could provide service for the state in an agricultural or manufactory capacity.

> {State of North Carolina
> Moore County}
> To the Governor of North Carolina:
> The petition of Richard A. Cole of said county would respectfully show that he

is in delicate health and has been for several years; that he is not able to endure hardships of any kind, that he has not done a regular days laboring for a considerable length of time; that exposure to cold affects his lungs and then he is subject to Diarrhea which injures him very much; that although he can not stand cold and endure hardships yet by taking care of himself his is able to attend to business and have work carried on; that he has a good farm for this country and six hands to cultivate his said farm; that he usually makes good crops of grain; that he has no person to attend to his farm but himself; that he has a wife and four children; that in addition to his own farm his mother-in-law has a good farm for this country, and five hands to cultivate it, that she has two sons both in Confederate service, one of them is at home on wounded furlough now but is ordered to report next Saturday; in the absence of her sons your petitioner has to give all his attention to her farm, and should your petitioner be sent to Goldsboro he verily believes that his own farm and his mother-in-law's will be neglected; that his mother-in-law is an aged woman in delicate health and has no white person living with her but a single daughter— That the petitioner's own mother is a widow, aged and in very feeble health and has been for many years. She is living in Carthage, having no farm, and her little son, and a daughter, whose husband is in the war, and has been ever since 1861, are living with her and they are dependant upon your petitioner in a good measure for their support; in consideration of the promises your petitioner verily believes that he will be of much more service at home than he can be in the field, and thereupon prays his Excellency to grant him an exemption from service in the Home Guard

R. A. Cole

Sworn to and subscribed before me this 17th day of Octbr 1864

AH. McNeill

This person A. H. McNeill appeared before me, Col. B. M. Richardson, as gentlemen of veracity and credibility who having sworn say they are acquainted with R. A. Cole and his family, and the facts set forth in this petition they believe to be true

William B. Richardson
Thomas B. Spoon

I cheerfully approve the within petition October 20th 1864, E.T. Williams, Captain

184. October 17, 1864

Brigadier General Stephen D. Ramseur, Rodes' Division, letter to wife, Lincolnton, Lincoln County, N.C. Source:

Major General Stephen D. Ramseur, mortally wounded at Cedar Creek. (Courtesy of the N.C. Division of Archives and History.)

Letters courtesy of Mr. Paul W. Schnek, Jr. of Greensboro, who donated the extracts of correspondence, S. D. Ramseur Papers, Southern Historical Collection, University of North Carolina at Chapel Hill.

Despite reverses in the field for the Ramseur's division, October was the month of his one-year wedding anniversary and the month of the birth of his first child, a daughter named Minnie Ramseur. Two days later, General Ramseur was mortally wounded and captured in action while rallying his division at the battle of Cedar Creek. A friend from West Point, George A. Custer, came to visit Ramseur the next day. Ramseur's last words were: "Bear this message to my precious wife—I die a Christian and hope to meet her in heaven." Ramseur died on October 20, 1864, not knowing whether he had a son or a daughter.[45] This letter is extracted from the original.

> Camp near Strasburg, Va
> October 17th 1864
> My own darling Wife,
> I received late last night through the Signal corps the telegram. It has relieved me of the greatest anxiety of my life. I hope that my darling precious wife and our darling babe too are well.
> I can not express my feelings at this present moment. I don't know how I can bear the separation from you very much longer. I must see you and be with you and our little Darling and the telegram did not state whether we have a son or a daughter!
> Tell sister Mary for pity's sake if not love's sake to write me a long letter about my little wife and baby! May God bless my darlings and me and soon reunite us in happiness and peace as a truly joyful family. Goodbye sweetheart, with love so inexpressable,
> > Your Devoted Husband
> > Dodson

185. October 21, 1864

Private Jesse Hill, Company K, 21st Regiment N.C. Troops, letter to wife, Emeline Chitty Hill, Reedy Creek, Davidson County. Source: Mr. Junius Hill of Lexington, N.C., and Jesse Hill letters, North Carolina Division of Archives and History.

Jesse Hill (1828–1882), a member of company K, 21st Regiment N.C. Troops, worked as a farmer. On August 20, 1850, he married Emeline Charlotte Chitty. Jesse and Charlotte would have only one child, Dock (1857). Jesse was conscripted into service on January 1, 1864. He was reported present until hospitalized in Richmond, Virginia, on March 27, 1865. Jesse recovered from his illness and was reported present until he was captured at Sayler's Creek, Virginia, on April 6, 1865. Jesse was confined at Newport News, Virginia, until June 27, 1865, when he was released after taking the oath of allegiance. After the war, Jesse returned home to his family in northern Davidson County. He lived in the Arcadia area until his death on January 2, 1882. He is buried at Good Hope United Methodist Church. His letters, which belong to Junius L. Hill, were transcribed and edited by Chris Ripple and are now housed in the NC Division of Archives and History.[46] In the following letter, Jesse Hill describes the battle of Cedar Creek, which occurred on October 19, 1864. For Early's Valley Army, it would be a big defeat. The army retreated toward New Market and set up camp there. Jesse talks about the spoils of war he captured from the Federals as well as the condition of his messmates.

> Oct. the 21st 1864
> in camp near New market
> dear companion i sere m self to write you a few lines to let you no that I am tolerble well and I do hope these few lines may find you in dock in good helth and doing well I can tel you that I am broke down my feet is all blisters

and my legs is stiff and I hav suffered more than I ever did in my life I can tel I was in another hard fight the hardiest fight tha we ever had yet I com out safe again me and Franklin Lashmit is together not hurt but both broke down we attacted the yankeys the 19th before day and run them back about 3 or 4 mils kiling and taken lots of them and captareing ever thing tha had and then tha reinforced and giv us the worst whiping we ever had and run us back and we ar running yet we hav run back about 35 miles and hav stop to rest alittle and yet to gether we was scaterd ever wher through the mounttains and tha kild and wonded lots of us and taken lots of prisners I sopose tha is aboout on houndred men in my Redgment and 10 in my company Alexander Waisner Robert fisher Franklin Spauch and 5 or 6 more is all mising you can tel Mr Hedrick* that I think his son was taken prisner the last he was seen the yankeys was all a round him I my self run and keep all my tricks that I had got I run a bout 5 mils and tha run me through the river twise the river was about 50 yards wide and it was waist deep to me but tha never got me and I had to lay down wet and tha was a big frost at morning and I had no fire and but one blanket you may no how I far now I will tel you what I capturd I got a pocket book with 44 dollars of green back and a nap sack and a blanket and a good oil cloth and pare of boots and severl other little tricks and little pocket knife.† I do wish I had my things at home but I glad that I say I com out safe for tha was lots of our men kild I dont see how I ever com out safe for the bullets and grape and shel com so thick and tore up the men the peces of flesh flew all over me and the fel all a round me the dead lay thick for bout 4 miles long and 2 miles wide I tel how meny thousand was kild but tha was a site I wont you to let others see this leter land I want them to write to

me I hant had no letter from home yet but I hope I will son get one this is 4 that I rote so I will close for this time by saying rite soon and give me all the nuse you can so I remain your tru housband until deth Jesse Hill to Emoline Hill direct to Richmond

the 21st Redgment
Co k Hokes old
Brigade

*Reporting local men lost during the battle

†Many poorly equipped Confederates helped themselves to captured goods from Federal soldiers. Among the prizes were greenbacks (paper money) and an oilcloth (a rubberized, water-proof piece of canvas).

186. November 12, 1864

Brigadier General Alfred M. Scales, Wilcox's Division, letter to Kate, Reidsville, Rockingham County, N.C. Source: A. M. Scales Collection, Box 1 (Correspondence), Private Manuscripts Collection, North Carolina Division of Archives and History.

Scales had survived yet another year's campaign and remained at the head of his brigade, achieving consistent service with A. P. Hill's Third Corps at the battles of the Wilderness and Spotsylvania Court House and the defense of Petersburg. This letter finds Scales getting things in order for winter quarters, procuring supplies from his home for his brigade, and wishing to put his affairs in order by settling his debts.

Petersburg Nov. 12th 1864
My Own Darling Wife
I have delayed writing longer than usual in the hope that I would be able to get a short leave to visit you but after waiting a week my application came down disapproved for the present. I only asked for 5 days, but Genl Lee thought it imprudent to allow me that at this time. I was fearful it would be so, yet was much disappointed when I found that I could not go.

We occupy pretty nearly the same position as when you left except our lines are more extended & I shall send for you as soon as I feel that we are permanent. To send before that would or might subject you to a great inconvenience. You must therefore be patient as I shall certainly send the very first moment I deem it safe. The weather is getting quite cold & we get orders today to find winter quarters & I shall start out today to find my winter quarters.

You must make Stephen put up some large boxes or barrels of sweet & Irish potatoes & peas & whatever else he has. We shall need them as I fear provisions will be very scarce here this winter. Make him have those things ready by the time you start. In my next letter I hope to be able to tell you to come on. Dick's will send for his wife & you will be together.

I look for Effie's money today from Richmond and will send it to her the first opportunity. The amount will be about $14.00. She can draw the balance when she needs. I would advise her to do whatever the Dr. thought ought to be done for Benney but I fear it will not be in my favor to go with her to Richmond.

Lincoln is certainly elected and there is no telling when the war will end. We must first determine to fight it out and look for the end when it comes. I saw Genl Lee yesterday and he was in fine spirits and more dispensed to joke than I ever saw him. My good lady friend, God bless her, Mrs. Waddell told me the other day that she prayed that I might not get hurt, but if I did I must not go to a hospital but come to her home.

Tell Pa when he comes down that I have a lot of 30 or 40 logs all piled up out of which he can make himself a nice selection. I didn't go through the trouble of gathering them up but found them placed away in an old camp by

some soldiers. He must bring you down. I am anxious to see you and hope to see them all this winter. Are they fixing up a box for my Brig? They ought to send two or three boxes & no box must weigh over 100 pounds and should be filled with tobacco. They ought to be plainly marked post as this letter is addressed.

It look this morning as if it would snow and I hope roads will still be in a condition to stop all enemy movements here. Give my best love to all & be ready at any time when I shall send for you. Ask Pa if I will have any money left after paying my debts. I shall need some this winter if I can get it in addition to my wages. Farewell my darling wife, hoping that I will see you soon & write my correct prayer that our God will shield and bless you.

> I am as ever your
> devoted husband,
> AM Scales[47]

PS I have first learned that Genl Wilcox will leave the Division this winter & that Genl Custis Lee will probably be our Maj Genl.

187. November 15, 1864

Private Benjamin Franklin Medley, "The Anson Guards," Company C, 14th Regiment N.C. Troops, letter to cousin, Anson County, N.C. Source: Medley Papers, Private Manuscripts Collection, North Carolina Division of Archives and History.

Benjamin Franklin Medley, born in 1834, worked as a farmer prior to volunteering for service in Anson County on April 22, 1861. The company of which he was a part would be known as the "Anson Guards," Company C, 14th Regiment North Carolina Troops (4th N.C. Volunteers). Medley was recorded as present for the duration of the war until he was paroled at Appomattox Court House, Virginia, on

April 9, 1865.[48] Private Medley gives an honest account of what he calls the "stampede" (retreat) of the Second Corps, or Early's Valley Army. Notice the differences and similarities between this letter and the letter of Pvt. John J. Armfield (see number 188), 30th N.C. Troops, dated the same day.

Camp near Staunton, Va,
Nov. 15th 1864

My Dear Cousin

Your very kind and long looked for letter of the 29th Sept. came to hand some time since and I would have answered it sooner but we have been continually travelling. I was very glad to hear from you and to hear that you had not been much disturbed by the Yankee Raiders. I would like very much to pay your house a visit I know how you do things up right.

No news to give you since the 2nd stampede of the 2nd Corps. Though Genl. Early now has the largest army he has ever had & should he get stampeded again, he is gone up. On the 10th inst our army moved up forward & are now in Winchester and Rashins very scarce. We did not loose many men this stampede. My 2nd Maj. Genl. S. D. Ramseur was killed. Genl. Rodes was my first both are good officers as in the Confederate army.

Scarcely do I see the Regts to which your friends belong. Should I come into contact with them I would be very glad to meet them and find out all that has changed the last time they heard from a letter from home. The soldiers say they write a great many letters but few reach home as of late. No news from the election yet. Never again will times be as good as before the war.

After the last stampede the yankeys ruined the Garden Spot of the world. I guess you heard Sheridans report it was very much correct. Sheridan seems invincible down in the valley. It is a perfect devastation of property. But all things are said to be for the best. I have not been to the Bridge yet but I can soon for there are many curiosities up there. You recelect Ralph Waddle[49] from Ansonville he is in the hospital at Staunton wounded in the last stampede. I am bound to go and see you this winter. You will be surprised when I slip in just in time for supper. Excuse Alas for it is a very cold morning. Write again soon.

Truly yours, B. F. Medley
Staunton.

188. November 15, 1864

John J. Armfield, Company C, 30th Regiment N.C. Troops, letter to wife, Lydia B. Armfield, Deep River, Guilford County. Source: Private Manuscripts Collection, North Carolina Division of Archives and History.

Medley's comrade in Cox's Brigade also had time to put pen to paper on November 15. Over a year has passed since John Armfield was conscripted into service and assigned to the 30th Regiment North Carolina Troops under General Ramseur. John J. Armfield (1829–1865) was a Guilford County farmer before joining the 30th NC Regiment. John was married to Lydia B. Hill on November 27, 1854. The couple would have three children. They made their home in the Deep River community of western Guilford County.[50] Deep River is approximately 11 miles from the Greensboro Station along the N. C. Railroad. In the course of the year John has seen a brutal winter, the Battle of the Wilderness, a fierce counter-charge at Spotsylvania, action in the valley, and even the church spires of Washington, D.C. November 15, 1864, finds Armfield and the 30th North Carolina waiting for an attack from Phil Sheridan's Union forces as they continue to throw up screens and pickets north of New Market, Virginia.

Camp near New Market
Valley of Virginia
November 15, 1864

Since I last wrote you we have done some very hard marching. We were ordered out in the morning of the l0th and marched down the pike road 22 miles. The next day we went within 8 miles of Winchester and formed in line of battle; then went into camp; next day we went into line of battle again and remained all day expecting an engagement every hour. The cavalry and sharp shooters skirmished with the Yankees all day. I could hear the gulls distinctly, the wounded were brought by where I was in ambulances also some of the cavalry horses with empty and bloody saddles, but thank God we did not get into a regular engagement. At night we fell back about 12 miles and camped. Yesterday evening we arrived at our old camp near New Market. It is thought that General Early found Sheridan with such strong force that he thought it best to withdraw without giving him battle. At the last fight in the Valley Early lost nearly all his artillery but he still has a large cavalry force. Part of Morgan's command has joined him recently. The soldiers say we will fight little if any this winter but will go into winter quarters probably. We do not know whether we will remain in the Valley this winter or not. This has been a beautiful county before it was ravished by brutal war, and there is enough clover and grass in the fields to keep hogs and cattle fat, but the fences and barns are nearly all burned on each side of the road. The weather is much colder here than at home and I dread the inclemency of the weather this winter more than the fighting. The country around here is full of cavalry scouts, consequently we can't go out foraging and have to live on our rations alone which is rather scanty. But let us be patient and humble and consider that

our fighting is not our doing, Write to "Rhodes'" division instead of Ramseur's division.

J. Armfield to wife

189. November 24, 1864

Captain Lewis Hilliard, AQM, Salisbury, Rowan County, N.C., impressment notice to H. Hege, Lexington, Davidson County, N.C. Source: Davidson County Historical Museum.

The following is an official request for property for use by the Confederate government. The reason for the demand on the property is unknown.

Mr. H. Hege
I propose to use of you for the use of the CS Government your 2 horse wagon team and driver for two days at schedule price payable in delivering of said property on Monday 21st day of November 1864.
Should you refuse to have the said property at the said price, the same will hereby be impressed, and you are hereby notified not to remove the same and compensation will be made to you according to the Act of Congress concerning and regarding impressments. Lewis Hilliard (Signed), Capt, Quartermaster, Salisbury

This was sent by way of Dr. Shelton[51]

190. December 3, 1864

Private James E. R. Yancey, "The Townsville Guard," Company B, 12th Regiment N.C. Troops, letter to brother-in-law, Willy Lapp, Person County, N.C. Source: Louis P. Sherman Collection, Private Manuscripts Collection, North Carolina Division of Archives and History.

The following letter was written on a captured United States military telegraph form, perhaps captured on the drive in

Maryland during last summer's campaign of Early's Corps. In the following, Yancey describes his winter quarters and the luxuries that he possesses at this stage in the war. This is the final letter featured from Private Yancey of Granville County. Yancey would soldier on with the 12th N.C. until he surrendered at Appomattox Court House, Virginia, on April 9, 1865.[52]

> Camp Ramseur
> Valley of Virginia
> December 3rd 1864
> To Mr. William Lapp[53]
>
> Dear Willy, Yours of the 9th November was gladly received some time ago. I would have replyed before this however but various circumstances prevented me from doing so. Willy I hope you will pardon me for my long delay and I will try and do better next time. Willy I have no news at present that will entertain you in the least. We are having a fine time in camp. We are gone in the winter quarters eight miles from Harrisonburge. Our fare is very good. We can go out in the country and get every thing we want to eat and there is plenty to drink. I am at this time living bully. I have some very good old apple brandy and a plenty of nice sider and nice apples. I wish you was hear to help me enjoy them. John C. Ragens and Robert Holly is both members of my old 12 Regt.* Rogers and several of the Person Boys is hear. Rogers took supper with me last night. We had quite a gay time drinking sider and eating apples. I have found Rogers acquanitence very desently. I think he is a very nice fellow in deed. Willy, I received a letter from Rosa this morning. She was very well. All your family was well with the exception of the hooping cough. She stated that Emma had it and 16 or 17 have it yet. Rosa stated that she was expecting you home soon. I hope you may get off and have a gay time while you are there. Willy when you write you will please present my respects to all. I will no close for the want of news and it is time for the mail to leave. Please forgive all imprefections in this short epistle for I wrote it in a great hurry. You will please except my best wishes hoping you may be successful in getting home & in all your undertakings. I remain your friend and Brotherinlaw.
>
> Farewell
>
> Jas. Yancey

*Actually, John C. Reagan was a private in company A, 13th Regiment N.C. Troops. No service records were found for the other soldier in question.

191. December 4, 1864

Sergeant Bartlett Yancey Malone, "The Caswell Boys," Company H, 6th Regiment N.C. State Troops, diary entry. Source: Diary of Bartlett Y. Malone, property of the Wilkinson family. Microfilm copy available in the Southern Historical Collection, Wilson Library, University of North Carolina at Chapel Hill.

Over a year has passed since B. Y. Malone was captured at Rappahannock Station. In this final entry from Private Malone, he discusses some religious activities on Sunday and a situation with punishment by the Negro guards. Bartlett was sent to Virginia for exchange in late February of 1865 and survived the war. He returned to Caswell County, where he married Mary F. Compton on August 3, 1866. The couple would go on to have ten children between the years 1867 and 1887. Bartlett Yancey Malone died in 1890 at his home in Caswell County, N.C.[54]

> The 4th which was the Sabath I went to meating at the School house Mr. Morgan lectured on the Parable of the Sower & in the eavning I was at the Same plase and Mr. Carol preached a good Surmon from the later clause of the 2 virse 7 chapter of Amos: Theas was the words: By whom Shall Jacob

arise: for he is small. After preaching was over the Sunday School classes met and thir teachers taken up the balance of the day in asking them questions and explaining the Scriptures to them We have white gard now for patroles in camp of knights the Neagros got so mean that the General would not alow them in Side of the Prison they got so when they would catch any of the men out Side of thir tents after taps they would make them doubble quick or jump on thir backs and ride them and some times they would make them get down on this knees and prey to God that they might have thir freadom and that his Soul might be sent to hell

192. December 11, 1864

Unknown female, Richmond County, N.C., letter to Governor Zebulon B. Vance, Raleigh, N.C. Source: Governor's Papers (Vance) North Carolina Division of Archives and History. Excerpted in Hutchinson, John, *No Ordinary Lives: A History of Richmond County, N.C. 1750–1900*, Virginia Beach: Dunning Company, 1998.

Any student of North Carolina Civil War history should find the following letter fascinating. The letter refers to a possible slave revolt in Richmond County expected to occcur on Christmas Eve in 1864. Hutchinson in his history of Richmond County records that the "Christmas Eve Rebellion" was to be carried out by two slaves, Jack and Asa, who were apprehended on December 9. The Richmond county officers, including Judge French, J. A. Long, sheriff, and R. P. Buxton, solicitor, put down the uprising before it was supposed to start. However, the following letter, dated December 11, is evidence of panic among the county residents.[55]

Mr. Z. B. Vance

I think it would not be amiss to give you a short history of the condition of the cuntry here. The cuntry is in a greate confusion at this time and not without a cause. The Negroes are making every effort in the power to murder the people & their intention is to carry it out Christmas? Their plans are to kill all of the white men & old white women & Negro women and have all the yung white Ladys for their companions. Some of them has even gone so far as to tell which Lady he is going to take for his Wife.

Some of them say that it has gone so far that they don't think that it can be stopped. They think it is so near at hand that there will not be time to get men from the armie to stop it. There is not half enough of men in the country to protect it from such here on the Pee Dee. 8 or 10 miles is filled up with Negroes quarters & but 4 or 5 white men & they are very old & not one yung white man in 10 miles.[56]

What do you think of this? Do you supose that we Ladys will be willing to submit to Negro husbands after giving up our Brothers that has been slain on the memorable battle field? & see our old gray headed Fathers murdered by the notorious Negroes.

Now cant you suggest some plan by which this can be broken up? I think as all the white men have been taken of it will be well enough to fill the ranks with the africans.

193. December 20, 1864

Major William B. "Dart" Clement, 10th Virginia Cavalry Regiment, letter to Mattie K. Martin, Mocksville, N.C. Source: W. B. Clement Papers, Private Manuscripts Collection, North Carolina Division of Archives and History.

William Clement was promoted to major on August 25, 1863, and then to lt. colonel on the recommendation of Gen. W. H. F. Lee, but the war ended before the second promotion could be acted upon. Happily, the leave that Dart talks about was granted and was scheduled from January 1 to January 31 of 1865. After the war, Dart returned to his life with Mattie, and the two lived in the area south of Mocksville, where William worked as a merchant and a farmer until his death on January 14, 1895. He is buried in the Clement family cemetery, Mocksville, Davie County, North Carolina.[57]

Camp 10th Va Cavalry
Dec 20th 1864

My dear wife

In accordance with my expectations in my letter of the 16th inst, we have moved camp near Bellfield which is five miles of the N. C. Line. Just think of that darling! We arrived here last night and all are going to work building winter quarters. On the morning we left camp near Stoney Creek was subjected to a severe disappointment and you were the cause of it darling. Reville had just sounded (before day) when the mail carrier came and brought a letter to my tent which he said he had overlooked the night before. I called for a candle and seeing it was directed by your hand I opened it up to read filled with pleasing anticipations of what was in store for me, when, disappointment! Upon opening it I found it was a letter from John Foster. You can write a note to John and tell him I will be at home in a short time, but if he is not able to return to duty, he had better go before the nearest examining board, and let them forward certification. If they will not then he must report immediately to his Regt. Where he will be granted a sick furlough. He then can return home until he gets able for duty. Tell him he has been exchanged and the notice of if published several weeks ago.

I was very much pleased last night darling when I received your letter of the 12th inst. You must not "fight or scratch" Miss P. P. M. yet darling because I expect it was not her fault that you did not get a letter, but it was the fault of your humble servant. Although he could not help it as it was the time "Warren and his Corps" was on the warpath" and really darling, I could not write as I was without any materials and upon the march at all times through rain and sleet. I have tried to be as regular since as before, so I hope darling in this you have received several and are satisfied as to the cause of the delay. I would be very glad to hear of Mrs. P marrying even if it was a man "fifty two years old" and as I think it will be safer for her to marry soon for fear of worse accidents.

I have been so much as ever since that "dratted" Conference met. I have not had a very high opinion of Rev. Mr. S since. If he could not recollect from one day to another that you hadn't been to preaching, or if he recollected, could think of anything to talk about, and had to resort to that each time for a subject. I don't think the strength of his mind displayed by him that he is capable of having an "exalted opinion" of "your piety" or anything else. What do you think of that darling & does that sound like Jealousy?

I am not at all astonished to hear about Col. Connelly's promotion, although I think him totally unfitted for the position, but such places are not always given to those best qualified. The assistance of political friends have much to do with such appointments that qualifications. Though he is nothing but a Brig. Genl of Militia after all, and it would not accept that unless I thought my country did not need my services any longer.

Everything is preparing winter quarters to day whilst I am preparing an application for leave. The leave so long talked of, and sought after, but hard to get. I think I will be successful this time darling though I fear it will be granted from "eighteen days." Will you be satisfied with that darling? So if nothing happens you may look for me between the 10th and 18th of Jany, but do not be too certain darling for you know there is many a mile between the camp and the kiss" and I wouldn't have disappointed as you were last August for anything in the world.

Mr. Heinrich[58] hasn't a very high opinion of Willies colloquial powers and said you all imagined you could understand him very distinctly, but he could not see any difference in his language and that of a crow. Now darling don't get too angry with him when you read this, for he may be nearly right. So you had better leave it to me when I come, and if I can understand him I will say you were right.

I saw Lu Mitchell[59] a few days ago. It is reported that he has resigned and is going to join the Cavalry. I have expected it for some time, as he was Court Martialed some time ago. Give my love to all and every. Merry Christmas to you darling. I wish very much I could be there to spend it with you. I must close as the mail man in hurrying me. Good bye with a kiss from

Your Husband

194. December 21, 1864

Private Jacob P. Culp, "The Cabarrus Black Boys," Company B, 20th Regiment N.C. Troops, letter to his mother, Ann Culp, Mt. Pleasant, Cabarrus County, N.C. Source: J. P. Culp Papers (1331), Special Collections, Perkins Library, Duke University, Durham, N.C.

Jacob Culp was fifteen years old when he heard about the fall of Fort Sumter. This young man worked as a laborer on his father's farm in the Mt. Pleasant area of Cabarrus County. Jacob was the son of John and Ann Culp and had two sisters and one brother. Jacob enlisted in Cabarrus County on February 17, 1864, at the age of eighteen. He was wounded in action at Spotsylvania Court House, Virginia, on May 10, 1864, and returned to duty shortly after. Some time following this letter, Jacob was captured and was sent to Point Lookout, Maryland. He remained at Point Lookout until he was released after taking the Oath of Allegiance on June 24, 1865.[60]

Camp 9 mils South
of Petersburg
Dec the 21st 18 64

Dear Mother,

I received you letter having date of the 11th. I was glad to here from you and the family. We have left the valley and are now close to Petersburg. Every thing has been quiet. Since we landed here the wether has been moderate untill now it is raining at this time. We are building winter quarters at this time and I think we will stay here all winter. I was glad to here that you had all your wheet soed.

A. P. Wats[61] is going home on a 8 days furlough and I want you to send me a box. I want you to send me a half a bushel of sweet potatoes, meat chickens, and eggs and more meat. I want a peck of meal (25 or 30 pounds) of flour, molasses and every thing that you can. You must have them ready to send by Wats. He will not stay at home but there is four days. You need not bake mutch but send meal and flour. I can bake it my self. If the weather is cold send me chickens but if the weather is warm they will be spoiled.

Write often as I am always glad to here from you. I must close at this time. Write soon.

Your son,
J. P. Culp

195. December 25, 1864

Captain Lewis H. Webb, Company A, 13th NC Light Artillery Battalion, diary entry. Source: Diary of L. H. Webb, Lewis Webb Collection, Southern Historical Collection, University of North Carolina at Chapel Hill.

On November 4, 1863, Webb's battery, Company D, 12th Virginia Artillery, was transferred to the newly formed 13th North Carolina Light Artillery Battalion. While the battalion functioned as six separate companies, Webb's battery was assigned to a position in northeastern North Carolina in the vicinity of Weldon.[62]

Christmas! What delightful memories of the happy, happy past, are awakened by the return of this day. Oh with what glee in other days was the sacred anniversary welcomed this one present with others we all remember. Now a sad pall like gloom hangs of the people who were wont in the past, more than any others on this continent, on the return of this day to smile & extend to each other friendly & joyful greetings & to make the season one of happy rejoicings.

Will we ever again witness such joyful times? God in whose hands are the issues of life and death only knows. The sun shines cheerfully & with as much brightness as when our hearts as a people were cheerful and gay. This morning brought another alarming rumor of defeat to our arms & success to those of our enemy. Fort Fisher is said to have fallen.[63]

After Inspection I rode to Weldon to Church. The Reverend Mr. Kingsbury of the Methodist Church preached a sermon, which I cannot but characterize it as in very bad taste to say the least of it. It was a doctrinal sermon (upon infant baptism) and both in matter and manner exhibited too little Christian charity, and too much invective & warmth.

Such sermons I always disapprove of and in particular on such an occasion and under such circumstances as now surround the south. I met at the Church & after services spoke to Reverend Ira T. Wyche, once on our Circuit. Soon after preaching was over and just as Lt. Horne[64] and myself were starting to our horses, Capt. Peterson (with whom Gattie & I had staid while she was in Weldon) called to and pressed us to dine with him, which we consented to do and rode to his home. The Capt., his wife & daughter are most estimable and clever people, the latter pretty, amiable, & interesting. We had a splendid dinner and spent an hour or two very pleasantly, returning to Camp about Sundown.

196. December 30, 1864

Captain James A. Graham, "The Orange Guards," Company G, 27th Regiment N.C. Troops, letter to his mother, Orange County, N.C. Source: The James A. Graham Papers 1861–1864, Southern Historical Collection, University of North Carolina at Chapel Hill.

Over six months have passed since James A. Graham's last featured letter (see number 165). Cooke's Brigade was posted in the trenches outside of Petersburg. James Graham had just experienced his fourth Christmas of the war. On November 2, 1864, Graham was officially promoted to captain, a position in which he had actually been serving for almost eight months. In this letter he mentions having Christmas dinner, and he talks about the band of the 27th being sent back to North Carolina to play concerts and raise money to buy schoolbooks for the members of the Brigade.

Camp 27th No. Ca. Inf'y
December 30th 1864

DEAR MOTHER

I wrote to you last Saturday by Alex, but he was in such a hurry to leave that I had time to write only a short note. We had very pleasant time last Monday. Maj. Webb, Capt. Sloan and I had a big Christmas dinner and invited about a dozen friends so that our Christmas passed off very pleasantly. I wanted Johnny. & Robert to come down that day, but they could not get off. Our bill of fare for dinner was bacon & cabbage, turnips, potatoes fried & boiled, ham, chicken, turkeys, geese, beef &c with cake for dessert. It was the best dinner I have ever yet seen in camp and I enjoyed it, especially as I had to go on picket that night in the rain. I received the gloves and gave them to my company. Please return my thanks to the ladies for them. I believe it is customary to return thanks for such things through the paper, but I am no hand for newspaper writing.

I intended sending you a lot of bottles by Alex but I had no way to send a box to town and Alex could not carry it on his shoulder as it is about 8 miles. I will however send them as soon as I can. Our Band starts to North Carolina tomorrow to give concerts to raise money to purchase schoolbooks for this Brigade. We are going to establish a school in each Reg't while we are in Winter Quarters and I hope much good may result from it. The band will be in Hillsboro on Wednesday & Thursday I expect.[65]

We have had no mail for about ten days until today and only a small one then. I dont know what is the matter with the mail but I hope it may come regularly now; for, if we are deprived of the mail, we will fare but poorly in camp as we have very little pleasure now except from the letters & papers we get.

Everything is quiet on our lines and, from the state of the weather I think is likely to remain so for some time.

As the mails are so irregular I will send this by one of the Band who will mail it some where on the road. Write soon

Love to all. As ever
Your Affectionate Son
James A. Graham

1865

"There is time enough yet for this. Our rations have been about the same, a little corn meal and pickled pork, or little flour and bacon. We get this about enough for the day to make one good meal for a hungry man."

> —Private John J. Armfield, Company C, 30th Regiment N.C. Troops, Petersburg, Virginia, February 17, 1865.

"I can't sleep for thinking about you. You say you hope to soon be called out again. You do so for you have not been in the service long enough to know the horror yet and the hardships and sufferings. How greatly our poor soldiers exchange with you if they could."

> —Mrs. Mary A. Satterfield, Roxboro, Person County, North Carolina, to her son in Raleigh, North Carolina, March 4, 1865.

"On the morning of the 12th we heard that Lee had surrendered on the 9th, and about 400, myself with them, took the cursed oath and were given transportation to wherever we wanted to go. I took mine to New York City to my parents whom I have not seen since 1858."

> —Private Louis Leon, Company B, 53rd Regiment N.C. Troops, Point Lookout Prison, Maryland, April 12, 1865.

"But it is all over now. Yet, though the sad, dark veil of defeat, is over us, fear not the future, but meet it with manly hearts. You carry to your homes the heartfelt wishes of your General for your posterity. My comrades, farewell."

> —*Major General Robert F. Hoke, Greensboro, North Carolina, May 5, 1865.*

197. January 28, 1865

Louisa Morris, Dallas, Gaston County, N.C., letter to her brother, Ambrose Costner, Hardin Township, Gaston County Prison, Ohio. Source: Mr. Charles Daniel Wilson, Dallas, N.C., and William G. Morris Collection, Southern Historical Collection, Wilson Library, University of North Carolina at Chapel Hill.

Louisa had been without both her brother and husband for a considerable amount of time. William had been a prisoner since July 3, 1863, and doubtless had had little news regarding her brother-in-law and those outside his immediate family.

Dallas Gaston County NC
Jan the 28th 1865

Dear Brother

This morning finds us all in tolerable health. Mother has been sick but is better. The friends are all well as far as I know. I hope this may reach you & find you in good health. I have not heard from youre family since you was here. We have just received five letters from my Husband after this long and painful anxiety it is a great relief indeed to know that he is still living & well but very distressing to know that he is in such destitute and suffering condition without the power to relieve him. But I hope my box will soone reach him and will be some relief to him. I have nothing of importance to write you. I will send his two latest letters to you but perhaps you have also got one. He says

he has written to you very much. He tries not to complain but I know he is suffering more than he is willing for me to know of as he tries to be cheerfull under the present circumstances. Please write me soone & let me know how you are getting along and if you have heard from Henry & the news if there is any. Oh that this cruel war could end we could all meet in peace. May God guide & protect us all is my constant prayer. Mother and all the children send their love to you.

Your affectonate Sister
Louisa Morris[1]

198. January 31, 1865

Private John J. Armfield, Company C, 30th Regiment N.C. Troops, letter to wife, Lydia B. Armfield, Deep River, Guilford County, N.C. Source: John Armfield Papers, Private Manuscripts Collection, North Carolina Division of Archives and History.

Private Armfield writes this letter in the hopes that his unit will be assigned in North Carolina so that he might get a chance to visit his wife if the column passes through Greensboro. By September of 1864, the Confederate authorities were trying to broker a peaceful settlement. This hope was unrealistic since Lincoln was committed to complete victory. The fall of Atlanta and capture of Savannah by December of 1864 proved to Lincoln that his army could finish the war. In the interest of diplomacy, he and key leaders of Congress carried on negotiations proving that compromise with the South was still on their agenda.

January 31st, 1865

Dear Wife

Things are quite unsettled in this part of the army at this time. There came orders at about 3 o'clock last night to cook one day's rations and pack up our things and be ready for marching by daylight. I was on guard duty and did not have much time to get ready, but when daylight came we did not start, and it is now one o'clock in the day and we haven't started yet. We may go off tonight, no one can tell. I will not mail this till morning, and maybe I can give you more information about where we go if we move; some say to Weldon, and some say to Wilmington. We will not know until we get there, but they better not take us into North Carolina especially by Greensboro for someone might go to see his family.*

There is great talk about peace in the army, and most of the soldiers think the war will end in the spring, but I fear it is deception. Mr. Blair has come to Richmond from Washington twice recently and I understand that there are two commissioners sent to Washington from Richmond, but whether peace comes in the spring I hope and pray to the Almighty that I may see you again before the spring opens in full or before the weather becomes very warm. At least if we march on that side of the James river, I intend to make effort and take the consequences.

J. Armfield

*The Deep River community was located just south-west of Greensboro. Portions of what was Deep River are now within the modern city limits of Greensboro, N.C.

199. February 5, 1865

Private James W. Gibson, "The Catawba Guards," Company F, 23rd Regiment N.C. State Troops, letter to parents, Catawba County, North Carolina. Source: Catawba County Historical Association.

The following is the last letter from James W. Gibson. By February of 1865, the 23rd Regiment was posted outside of Petersburg, Virginia, defending that city from the besieging Union Army. James refers to a peace envoy sent to the North to negotiate a settlement, but has little faith in a peaceful outcome. Gibson has also filed for a furlough, in an attempt to return home.

Camp Johnson Brigade
Near Petersburg VA
February the 5 1865

Dear Farther,

I seat myself to drop you a few lines to inform you that for the last week I have been especting a furlough but have not had the pleasure of see it yet. I look for it monday and that is the day after tomorrow. I hope it may come and I will start as soon as possible after I get and it will be Tuesday morning if it approved alright, and we have considerable excitement in camp today it is reported that the Yankees are advancing, if this be true it will be very uncertain what this may postpone I hope not but I hope this tail is not reliable at all. At the same time it may be true if this nice weather continues thir will be a movement of some sort before many days it appears I have the worst luck in the world when ever I make application for furlow there is something turn up that it either never comes back or comes disapproved that has been my experience in the war so far. This is the third furlow that I have had forwarded for me since I have been in the service and never received a scratch of a pen in the way of a furlow yet. But I am in hopes that this will come alright for me to visit my home and friends once more before the spring campaigns opens for I believe that this summer their will be one of the most active campaigns of the war and one of the most severe campaigns ever witnessed upon earth. We cant say what our diplomats may suffer before they leave Washington, they may do something before they return to dixy I hope they may succeed in this great undertaking for the words of honorable peace is the words we all want to hear worse than any thing else upon the face of the earth. We are all tired of this war the yankees are all tired of the war God bless. Some of the officers may be in favors of carrying on the war but they are the only men that appear to be in favor of war. I dont want to give you to imagine that we are willing to go into the union that is not the case

       Yours respectfully J. W.[2] Probably I may see you when my furlow comes approved I continue to be respectfully.

200. February 16, 1865

John Milton Worth, Asheboro, Randolph County, letter to son, Hon. Jonathan Worth, Raleigh, Wake County. Source: Hamilton, *The Correspondence of Jonathan Worth*, 1909

John Milton Worth, the father of Jonathan Worth, was given a very difficult assignment. As the ranking civil official, Judge J. M. Worth was to utilize the law to stabilize the rebellious situation in Randolph County. Beginning as a Quaker protest, the county's opposition to conscription had transformed the Uwharrie Mountains into a haven for Unionists, deserters, and outlaws. The conduct of the "Outliers" was lawless, and their style of combating the Home Guard and militia units sent into the area resembled the guerrilla combat of the Vietnam War. The

Confederate authorities contributed to the depravity by abusing civilians and contracting independent bounty hunters to round up deserters and outlaws. What began as an idealistic protest evolved into a partisan war that spilled over into the counties of Davidson, Montgomery, and Moore.[3] Apparently the task of stabilizing the situation was so great that Judge Worth proposed working with some of the "Better Class" deserters to apprehend those deserters who were committing crimes. Judge Worth seems pushed into this idea by the inability of the Home Guard to defeat the deserters and the state's inability to supply their only internal defense force. The situation in Randolph County has become so bad that the commander of the Home Guards wants to make a deal with deserters to help stop lawless behavior in Randolph.

Dear Sir.

    There is no spot upon this earth more completely subjugated than Randolph County. There is not a day that passes but what someone is robbed of all the parties can carry away. There are bands in nearly all parts of the county unless it is stopped we will be utterly used up. My object in writing is to suggest whether some arrangement cannot be made with the military authorities to offer the better class of deserters some terms if they will organize and drive the robbers from the country or exterminate them. In a late call for the Home Guards many failed to appear and what did disbanded immediately on finding that Gen. Gatlin declined to furnish rations for them. I am fearful they will not come up for reorganization. Many of them are afraid and many more are in heart with the deserters. I do hope that something may be done, it is a horrible condition.

    I have studied the matter in all its views and I know that nothing but a much larger force than we can get or some terms with the Home Guards and the better class of deserters will save us from utter ruin. I hope you may have time to talk to somebody—the Governor, Gen. Gatlin[4], or perhaps Gen. Holmes.

> J. M. Worth
> Asheboro

201. February 17, 1865

Private John J. Armfield, Company C, 30th Regiment N.C. Troops, letter to his wife, Lydia B. Armfield, Deep River, Guilford County, N.C. Source: Private Manuscripts Collection, North Carolina Division of Archives and History.

The 30th North Carolina was posted along with Cox's Brigade in the trenches defending Petersburg from the armies of General Grant. In this letter, Armfield discusses Confederate currency and silver and describes the outpost system of the United States Army. The system of "picketing" involves providing a protective screen around the various armies. Men are rotated in this system with certain amounts of time spent on the front lines as sentinels, in small groups as pickets, and in the rear as the "grand guard."[5]

> Camp near Petersburg
> February 17, 1865

On account of the swelling of my feet and ankles I am excused from drill and fatigue consequently find time to write a little. Nothing to write about expecially but still here in this miserable loathsome business with no very bright prospect of getting out of it. I have been in the army near 4 months but never in a fight yet for which I feel very thankful that a kind providence has sustained me through all the hardships I have had to suffer. Often when I have been on the march and was on the point of giving out, I would pray as I marched along and it seemed that my strength returned and I would be able to go along and keep up with the others.

I sent you a letter sometime ago with $5.00 bank note in it with instructions to send me the worth in Confederate money and have heard nothing from it since I wrote you. My Confederate money has about played out and I have spent about all the little silver I brought with me. Of the gold I have spent none nor do I intend to do so till I start home or somewhere else. We will have to go on picket on the lines again next Saturday. If my ankles do not get well I will not have to go, but I think they will, and if they do and I am exposed to rough weather they will be as bad as ever. Picket is very hard business. We have to go on front line and remain 24 hours then we are relieved and go back to rear lines (this is where the cabins are) and only get rest of 24 hours. We only have to stand one hour out of every three when we are on the front line, but without any comfortable place to rest or sleep other two hours.

The weather is quite mild and pleasant today, but we had some rain and sleet yesterday. We have not had so much snow and hail here as there has been in North Carolina. We have not had sleet enough to break the timber and neither have we had snow enough to cover the ground more than two inches. There is time enough yet for this. Our rations have been about the same, a little corn meal and pickled pork, or little flour and bacon. We get this about enough for the day to make one good meal for a hungry man.

I drew a soldier's shirt today.

> J. Armfield

202. February 18, 1865

Captain Lewis H. Webb, "The Ellis Artillery," Company A, 13th NC Light Artillery Battalion, diary entry. Source:

Diary of L. H. Webb, Lewis Webb Collection, Southern Historical Collection, University of North Carolina at Chapel Hill.

Saturday the 18th—This morning I essayed the cooking science again, and words are inadequate to express all that befell me. I found some beef and thought to have a steak, but as grease was needing in which to cook it. I made a search for some fat meat & found a little but not enough. In my search I found a cup containing something that looked like lard, or bacon fat, and as it seemed to be clean, I put a goodly quantity in the spider where my meat was & congratulated myself on my good fortune. It soon melted and my steak was soon simmering in it. But as the spider grew hotter I noticed a very remarkable foaming & frothing, which I could not understand, and upon examining closely, the grease I had put in the spider, I found, it was on the shade of Soyer, that I was cooking a beef steak in soap—yes soap.

Imagine reader my trouble, and to add to it Lt. Horne laughed his sides almost sore, while my house & door were crowded with the pitying faces of half a dozen or more of my men. My face burnt with the heat of the fire I was bending over, and elongated by the trouble which so rushed upon me, I must have been indeed a "sight."

But I could not afford to lose the meat, so hastily forking it out of the foaming and frothing compound in the spider I proceeded to wash it and soon after I put it on again & succeeded after a while in burning it to a crisp and then frying a few pancakes, which with some molasses made our breakfast long after everybody else was through eating.

203. March 3, 1865

Private Joseph Huneycutt, Company H, 42nd Regiment N.C. Troops, letter to his wife, Nancy, Stanly County, N.C. Source: *Stanly News and Press*, July 7, 1961.

If you had one last letter to write to your family, what would you say? Below, Private Joseph Honeycutt writes such a letter to his wife and four children on the eve of his execution for desertion.

My dear wife

I have to state to you the sad news that tomorrow at 12 o'clock that I have to die. I have to be shot to death for starting home to see my wife and dear children, and was arrested and brought back and court-martialed and am to be shot at 12 o'clock.

Me and D. M. Furr have to be shot, but thanks be to God I am not afraid to die. I think when I leave this world, I will be where Mary and Martha are. Dear Wife, don't grieve for me. Try and not. I drempt last night of seeing you, but I shall never. You shall see your husband no more. I want you to raise my children in the way they should go. My dear son Julius, this is my last order to you. I want you to be a good boy and try to serve God and be a good man. Farewell, Julius, I must leave this world. And my son Ephraim, try to be a good man and serve God. My daughter, Rebecca, I bid farewell to you. Be a good girl and go to preaching. Farewell, my dear son, Joel. You have no daddy now. Be a smart boy and mind your mother. My dear Wife, Nancy, I have to bid you farewell. I want you to keep what things you have and pay my debts. I want Julius and Ephraim to have my shop tools. I have a looking glass for Rebecca. I want her to remember me. I have a little book for Joel to remember me by. I want you to send the children to school. I must close my letter, I have no chance to write more. I bid farewell to your mother and father and their brothers and sisters. I must leave this world.

With all my love,
Joe

204. March 4, 1865

Mr. J. A. Boyden, letter to unknown cavalry officer. Source: Military Collection, Box 66, Folder 2, North Carolina Division of Archives and History.

March 4 was the approximate date which Sherman's forces, specifically Union cavalry under Gen. Judson Kilpatrick, crossed the Pee Dee river at several points in an attempt to disguise their movements on Goldsboro. The following letter describes events occurring mostly in Anson County in regards to Sherman's advance and Hardee's retreat.

Sherman is crossing the Pee Dee for a distance of 40 miles extending from Cheraw up to Dumas' Ferry in Anson County, 7 miles from Ansonville. Hardee is falling back as rapidly as possible. He was in Rockingham last Saturday & Sherman's forces were on three sides of him saith a captain from his army. It is reported that Wadesboro was burnt, that we captured several hundred prisoners in Anson—175 of which number have reached here—most of them are at White's Store.[6] Hardee sent the Rail Road rolling back from Cheraw to Florence & after evacuating the former place, he burnt the bridge (Pee Dee) behind him.

J. A. Boyden

205. March 4, 1865

Mary Satterfield, Roxboro, Person County, N.C., letter to son, Raleigh, Wake County, N.C. Source: Satterfield-Merritt Family Papers, Southern Historical Collection, University of North Carolina at Chapel Hill.

George and Mary had only two sons of military age: Edward Fletcher, who was killed at Gettysburg, and William P., who enlisted at Camp Holmes on March 18, 1864. Service records indicate that William P. Satterfield (Co. A, 55th N.C. Troops)

was captured at Five Forks, Virginia, on April 1, 1865, and confined at Point Lookout, Maryland, until June 14, 1865.[7] The letter describes an outlaw band similar to those in the Uwharrie Mountains and in Yadkin County that were being pursued by the local Home Guard commander. Visible is the reluctance of the Satterfields to give their son any more money. They give in, however, and send it anyway.

March the 4 1865

My Dear Son,

Pattie received your letter yesterday from Raleigh and one from Hillsboro. I was glad to hear from you and troubled to hear that you were sick and so dissatisfied that your letter was one of complaint. I am convinced that you are not treated as you ought to be and if we could do better you should not stay there.

I can't sleep for thinking about you. You say you hope to soon be called out again. You do so for you have not been in the service long enough to know the horror yet and the hardships and sufferings. How greatly our poor soldiers exchange with you if they could. You said you would rather leave than for it to be said about my son that he deserted. I hope you will let and I ask the Lord to help you pray often and direct you is the prayer of your mother.

Your Papa was so troubled when I read your letter to him. He said he could not please you that you thought more of spending money. You have 45 dollars in pocket money and he says that is more than he can afford and is more than he intends to supply.

Well my son I reckon you think Mother is giving one of her lectures this morning may you profit by it is my sincere prayer. I am glad to tell you that Mat is improving. She seemed at one time near the eternal world, but God in his goodness heard the prayers offered in her behalf and has spared to be a comfort to her parents as I hope you will be to yours. Ida Wilkens is quite sick. I haven't seen her in tens going on to day.

We hear that there is very bad news in the Army as there is from the county. John Whitt, Tom Whitt, Jim Roswell, three Buchanons, and Moses Chambers is the ring leaders of this outlaw party who I expect for he is mean enough to do any thing. Col. Johns has sent out 90 men in search of them with five days rations.* Mrs. Whitt is very much destroyed. She has the sympathy of every one that has seen her. If things continue in such a state long surely we must be a subjugate people. May God deliver us from all our enemies ought to be the prayer of every one.

Well my son, it is time for this letter to go to the office so I must close. Write soon and let me know how you are and if you are sick. I am coming to see you, I expect, very soon. I will send you thirty dollars to buy a cap with, it is the last I have. Be a good boy and hope alls well be well.

Your Mother
M. A. Satterfield

*These men are all from Person County. Colonel Johns was the local home guard commander.

206. March 9, 1865

Private John J. Armfield, Company C, 30th Regiment N.C. Troops, partial letter to his wife, Lydia B. Armfield, Deep River, Guilford County, N.C. Source: Private Manuscripts Collection, North Carolina Division of Archives and History.

John's last letter demonstrates the typical uncertainty regarding troop movements during the Civil War. Often, soldiers would not know their final destination until they reached it. Here a move to strengthen defenses south of the Weldon Railroad against Federal troops was being conducted. This action would result in the battle and Union victory at Five Forks, Virginia.

I write to let you know I am well and alive. Our brigade was brought down here last Friday and relieved one brigade of Pickett's division. Since then the balance of Pickett's division has been released by General Mahone's division and have been sent off somewhere I don't know where. I don't know where the balance of our division is. Some say they have gone to North Carolina and some say to Lynchburg and some that they are still in camp near the south side of the Railroad.* If they do go to North Carolina I hope and pray our brigade will be sent with them but I have not much hope of such move. We are pretty comfortably situated here on the lines. We have much better position than we had on picket before. Our quarters are comfortable and picket is not hard but there is every precaution used against desertion to the enemy. If I have to remain in the army I had rather stay here than any other place in Virginia for I do not believe there will be any fighting done on the lines along here but it will be done on the right and left of the army. But there is no good place in the army and I long very much to be relieved of it but am almost ready to dispair.

J. Armfield[8]

*The balance of Rodes' Division was posted well to the south of Armfield's position at the junction of the Weldon Railroad, Five Forks, Va.

207. March 10, 1865

Captain Lewis H. Webb, "The Ellis Artillery," Company A, 13th NC Light Artillery Battalion, diary entry. Source: Diary of L. H. Webb, Lewis Webb Collection, Southern Historical Collection, University of North Carolina at Chapel Hill.

With the fall of Petersburg nearly approaching, and Sherman's movements on Goldsboro, North Carolina, the war for Captain Webb was drawing to a close. In this last featured diary entry, Webb discusses the national day set aside for fasting and prayer by the Confederate government. The small engagement at Kinston on the 8th was inconsequential to the outcome or even delay of Sherman's advance.

Friday the 10th

Today was set apart by the Congress of the Confederate States, and the President thereof, as a day of Fasting, Humiliation, and prayer, that God may, in his Divine mercy forgive our manifold transgressions and in our humility see fit to grant us, the blessings to our distressed & bleeding land which we so much desire.

O Lord we beseech Thee, to look compassionately upon us, to forgive our sins, to make us a better people, & to bless our efforts for freedom. Have mercy upon us as sinners, Inspire us, we pray Thee, with that contrition and that humility true and sincere repentance. Grant, O father, that our sacrifices this day may meet Thine approval; that they may ascend not as those of "the wicked which are an abomination," but as the prayers or the righteous which are Thy delight. Almighty God, we pray Thee, to be with us continually, to fill our hearts with Thy grace, to cause us to trust in Thee, to make us indeed that "Happy people whose God is Lord." Amen.

Just before starting to Church, Dr. Steele came into Camp. He reached Weldon this morning with a detachment of Senior Reserves in charge of prisoners captured on the 8th at Kinston, where from all accounts we gained a decided advantage over the enemy. God grant this is the forerunner of other and greater victories which may result in our independence.

It rained hard most of the forenoon. When I reached Weldon, I took off my saddle carrying it on inside of the offices at Head Quarters and met Col. Galliard. I was very glad to meet the good old gentleman again. He had come up in the morning with the Yankee prisoners on the way to Richmond.

The Reverend Mr. Burton preached at the Methodist Church who, as he told me after the sermon, "told the people of their sins as well as their hopes." His sermon was well suited to the occasion and forceably delivered.[9]

208. March 17, 1865

Private Jesse Hill, Company K, 21st Regiment N.C. Troops, letter to his wife, Emeline Hill, Reedy Creek, Davidson County, N.C. Source: Private Manuscripts Collection, North Carolina Division of Archives and History.

With the war winding down, Jesse does not have a lot to talk about except the present condition of the unit. When Jesse Hill talks about where the ditches blew up last summer, he is referring to the Battle of the Crater.[10]

March the 17th

dear companion I set my self to writ you a few lines to let you no that I am not well yet but I am som better I think but I am with my company and hav ben all the time tho I hant don any duty in three or four weeks and I hant able for duty yet but I hope these few lines may find you all well and doing well. I will say to you that we have moved in front of Petersburg in the diches close to where tha had that blo up last somer it is a bad plase but I hope I will be shore to get home one time more but it looks like a hard chance but I dont want you to trouble your self about me for it dont do any good. I want you to do the best you can maby I will get home sometime a nother I am going to take cear of my self and try to get home again now I will tel you how near we ar to the yankeys our brest works and the yankey brest works is about 1 houndred yards apart and keep fireing at ech other all the time but tha hant any of our men got hurt yet. We have be here three days I will say to you that you rote the 6th and I was more than glad to here from you and to here that you was well I want you to writ and let me what the nuse is thar about the yankeys a coming thorugh thar. Tell Father I want him to write to me if he pleses and give me the nuse I hant any good nuse to writ at this time we get but miry little to ete but I cant ete what I get for it fit for a well man to ete but let a lone a sick man if I had somthing that was fit to ete I would get better faster if I dont get better in a short time I will go to the hospittle I will hav to close in hoping to here from you soon writ as soon as this comes to hand and direct to Petersburg this from your loving housband

Jesse Hill to Emoline Hill[11]

209. April 12, 1865

Private Louis Leon, Company B, 53rd Regiment N.C. Troops, diary entry. Source: Leon, Louis, *Diary of a Tar Heel Confederate Soldier*, 1913.

For the veterans of the Army of Northern Virginia the war was finally over. News reached the prisons of the North and procedures we put in place to release the men held within its walls. To get out of prison, a soldier must take the "Oath of Allegiance" which was to swear loyalty to the United States, and he must be issued papers from the Prison's commandant to "notarize" this release. After almost a year in prison, Lewis Leon is a free man. The war is over and Leon ends his diary with parting thoughts on his service.

April 12 (1865)—I suppose the end is near for there is no more hope for the South to gain her independence. On the

10th of this month we were told by an officer that all those who wished to get out of prison by taking the oath of allegiance to the United States could do so in a very few days, There was quite a consultation among the prisoners. On the morning of the 12th we heard that Lee had surrendered on the 9th, and about 400, myself with them, took the cursed oath and were given transportation to wherever we wanted to go. I took mine to New York City to my parents whom I have not seen since 1858. Our cause is lost, our comrades who gave their lives for the independence of the South have died in vain; that is, the cause for which they gave their lives is lost, but they positively did not give their lives in vain. They gave it for a most righteous cause, even if the Cause was lost. Those that remain to see the end for which they fought—what have we left? Our sufferings and privations would be nothing had the end been otherwise, for we have suffered hunger, been without sufficient clothing, barefooted, lousy, and have suffered more than any one can believe, except soldiers of the Southern Confederacy. The four years that I have given to my country I do not regret, nor am I sorry for one day that I have given. My only regret is that we have lost for which we fought.

210. May 1, 1865

Circular of Major General Robert F. Hoke's farewell address issued at Greensboro to members of his division. Source: R. F. Hoke Papers, Private Manuscripts Collection, North Carolina Division of Archives and History.

Generals formed indescribable bonds with the men under their command. Lincolnton native Robert F. Hoke was no different. General Hoke had commanded his troops through service under both Generals Lee and Johnston fighting the last

Lincolnton's Robert Hoke, a boyhood friend of Stephen Ramseur, commanded a division at Bentonville. (Courtesy of the N.C. Division of Archives and History.)

action at Bentonville, North Carolina, on March 19–21, 1865. By May 1, 1865, Hoke's Division in the Department of North Carolina contained Bakers's Junior Reserve Brigade, Kirkland's Brigade (17th, 42nd, 50th, 66th North Carolina),and Clingman's Brigade (8th, 31st, 51st, and 61st North Carolina). Hoke returned to his life in Lincolnton and later was a pioneer in the North Carolina insurance industry.

HEADQUARTERS
HOKE'S DIVISION

NEAR GREENSBORO, N. C.,
MAY 1, 1865.[12]

SOLDIERS OF MY DIVISION:

On the eve of a long, perhaps a final separation, I address to you the last sad words of parting. The fortunes of war have turned the scale against us. The proud banners which you have waved so gloriously over many a field are to be furled at last; but they are not disgraced, my comrades. Your indomitable courage, your heroic fortitude, your patience under sufferings, have surrounded them with a halo which future years can never dim. History will bear witness to your valor and succeeding generations will point with admiration to your grand struggle for constitutional freedom.

Soldiers, your past is full of glory! Treasure it in your hearts. Remember each gory battlefield, each day of victory, each bleeding, comrade. Think then of your future.

"Freedom's battle, once begun,
Bequeathed from bleeding sire to son;
Though baffled oft, 'is ever won.'"

You have yielded to overwhelming forces, not to superior valor. You are paroled prisoners, not slaves. The love of liberty, which led you into this contest, burns as brightly in your hearts as ever. Cherish it. Associate it with the history of your past. Transmit it to your children. Teach them the rights of freedom, and teach them to maintain them. Teach them the proudest day in all your proud career was that on which you enlisted as Southern soldiers, entering, that holy brotherhood whose ties are now sealed by the blood of your compatriots who have fallen, and whose history is coeval with the brilliant record of the past four years.

Soldiers, amid the imperishable laurels that surround your brows, no brighter leaf adorns them than your connection with the late Army of Northern Virginia. The star that shone with splendor over its oft-repeated fields of victory, over the two deadly struggles of Manassas Plains, over Richmond, Chancellorsville and Fredericksburg, has sent its rays and been reflected wherever freedom, has a friend. That star has Set in blood, but yet in glory. That army is now of the past. The banners trail, but not with ignominy. No stain blots their escutcheons. No blush can tinge your cheeks as you proudly announce that you have a part in the history of the Army of Northern Virginia.

My Comrades, we have borne together the same hardships; we have shared the same dangers; we have rejoiced over the same victories. Your trials and Your patience, have excited sympathy and admiration, and I have borne willing witness to your bravery. It is with a heart, full of grateful emotions for your services and ready obedience that I take leave of you. May the future of each one be as happy as your past career has been brilliant, and may no cloud ever dim the brightness of your fame! The past rises before me in its illimitable grandeur. Its memories are part of the life of each one of us. But it is all over now. Yet, though the sad, dark veil of defeat, is over us, fear not the future, but meet it with manly hearts. You carry to your homes the heartfelt wishes of your General for your posterity. My comrades, farewell.

R. F. Hoke
Major-General

211. June 10, 1865

Gen. Rufus Barringer, Fort Delaware Prison, Delaware, letter to his children, Concord, N.C. Source: The Rufus Barringer Papers, Manuscripts Department, Southern Historical Collection, University of North Carolina at Chapel Hill.

A Cabarrus County soldier, Rufus Barringer volunteered for service at age 41 on May 16, 1861, and was appointed a captain of Company F (Cabarrus Rangers), 1st NC Cavalry. Captain Barringer commaded his company through the Brandy Station fight (where he was wounded) and through the Gettysburg Campaign. He was promoted to major on August 16, 1863, then to Lt. Colonel on October 17, 1863. Afterwards he was assigned to temporary command of the 4th NC Cavalry and was com-

missioned as a brigader general of a brigade of NC cavalry under W. H. F. Lee's Division. Barringer was captured on April 2, 1865, when his brigade was nearly destroyed.[13] In the following passage he describes what a daily routine is like as a member of the incarcerated population at Fort Delaware National Prison. Overall, his outlook on prison life is fairly good. He addresses the physical surroundings, daily happenings, recreation, and a booming craft industry among the prisoners. Especially touching are the loving words of advice to his children from behind the stockade walls.

Fort Delaware, Del.
June 10, 1865

My dear children

I was happy to receive your sweet little letters again. It has been a long time since I had the pleasure. Oh! How many sad scenes I have gone through since I last wrote you. But, while I have seen and heard of suffering so much, our heavenly Father has been good to me. I have been fairly treated by the Yankees and have found many friends and had good health and have had plenty of food to eat. For all these blessings I feel very thankful. I doubt not you have been good children. That you have studied your cypher* and been good to uncle Victor[14] and aunt Ria and assisted them to keep the house and said your prayers every night and I hope that they have been answered in the blessings shown to you and me in sparing our lives and preserving our health and giving us so many comforts.

I will tell you now what it is to be a Prisoner of War. They dont place you in a prison like a jail. The put you in a large lot with a great high fence all around it and one high gate. The have cheap frame houses built and all rooms inside are called "Barracks." In the barracks they put up shelters called bunks or she-bangs. In there the men sit, sleep, and all the time except when they walk about and take their meals.

In the center there is a wide open space and they can walk about and take exercise. Sometimes they run, jump, pitch quorts, they roll each other up in blankets, play marbles, etc. In the corner of the lot is a square building called the dining room. When breakfast is served the men march out of the barracks in long lines to their tables and give them their bread, meat, and soup and then they march back to each of his bunks and eats his "grub." They have no knives or forks. They have a tin cup or a little tin bucket for soup. But if they have money they can buy from the sutlers store. Many make things to eat and to fix up with. They do all sorts of work. Some make and mend clothes. Some make all sorts of nice & curious rings, heart pins, necklaces, wooden

chains, shirt buttons and sell them to Yankee soldiers. Some wash clothes.

We all have to clean our own bunk and sweep and clean our Barracks. The barracks are laid off in Divisions—each Division has a chief and all have to attend roll call once a day. A yankee sergeant calls the roll. Some officers have been in here and have never been out. Some are so ragged, so am I (it is hard to keep clean) and some look pale and weak. Such is prison life. My advice to you is to live honestly, do your duty, be good and God will protect and sustain you. I hope and pray that we may all live to meet—enjoy many years of peace and happiness and part only to meet in Heaven. Give much love to Uncle Victor and Aunt Ria and accept a Fathers blessing from your affectionate
Papa

*Multiplication tables

Appendix 1: Statistics on the Distribution of Documents

DISTRIBUTION OF DOCUMENTS BY COUNTY

County	Number of Documents	Author(s)
Alamance	6	John A. Long, J. F. S., T. M. Shoffner, Letitia Long, John W. Jones
Alexander	3	Jonas A. Bradshaw, A. Daniel
Anson	9	Robert T. Wall, Leonidas L. Polk, J. A. Boyden
Cabarrus	7	M. Melchor, Edmund Shoe, J. Barnhart, John A. Smith, M. A. Barrier, Jacob Culp, Rufus A. Barringer
Caswell	9	Bartlett Y. Malone
Catawba	13	James W. Gibson, William Cline, Andrew Rinck, J. Williams, Isaac Summit
Chatham	3	George Williams, Richard Womble
Cleveland	3	Columbus H. Dixon, L. M. McAfee
Davidson	14	Julius Loftin, James W. Cameron, George Eddinger, John Leonard, D. W. Badgett, Berry Kinney, Hughey Clodfelter, Eliza Clodlelter, Felix Miller, John F. Sink, Jesse Hill
Davie	10	Harrison Hanes, William B. Clement, Jacob Hanes, Thomas C. Riddle
Forsyth	12	Alfred Belo, Caroline Fries, Augustus Clewell, Dr. John F. Shaffner, J. P. Nissen, F. Fries, Henry W. Ayer
Gaston	7	William G. Morris, Eliza W. Nims, Louisa Morris
Granville	8	Charles C. Blacknall, N. A. Waller, James R. Yancey, John F. Coghill
Guilford	7	Jonathan Worth, Calvin Wiley, John J. Armfield
Iredell	8	J. C. Turner, William M. Adams, Robert Linster, John F. Gibson, Jamina Thomas, E. U. Linster
Lincoln	8	Stephen D. Ramseur, Amanda Murph, Robert F. Hoke

205

County	Number of Documents	Author(s)
Mecklenburg	10	Louis Leon
Montgomery	2	Hartwell S. Pool, Eliza Wooley
Moore	5	John A. Jackson, Richard A. Cole
Orange	8	James A. Graham
Person	6	E. Fletcher Satterfield, E. Richards, Henry T. Jordan, Mary Satterfield
Randolph	8	Jonathan Worth, Julius Robbins, Thomas Branson, Benson Lassiter, Molly Alford
Richmond	8	Lewis H. Webb, Anonymous female
Rockingham	6	Alfred M. Scales, J. Thompson
Rowan	13	W. Lillycross, Thomas Gillespie, Ashbel S. Fraley, Soldiers' Wives, H. Hilliard
Stanly	2	John C. Pickler, Joseph Huneycutt, Huneycutt
Stokes	6	Laura C. Myers, Mary C. Moore, Elizabeth Waggoner, John W. Hundely, Mary C. Farris
Union	3	Archibald Curlee, George Richards, Andrew J. Price
Yadkin	7	John W. Armsworthy, Citizens of Yadkin County

DISTRIBUTION OF LETTERS AND DIARIES BY RANK, SEX, LOCATION, AND LETTER RECIPIENT'S LOCATION

Rank of Author[1]

Privates	Non-Comm.[2] Officers	Company Officers	Staff & Field Officers	Civilian
86	24	41	25	33

By Location

Location Written				Location Addressed		
War Front	Domestic (NC)	Other		War Front	Domestic (NC)	Other
175	33	0		1	205	2

Letters only: By Sex

Authors		Recipients				
Male Authors	Female Authors		Male Male	Male Female	Female Female	Female Male
186	19		43	96	5	14

Relationship of Female Recipient to Letter Writer		
Wife	51	(an additional 5 are addressed to wife and famly)
Sweetheart	9	
Sister	17	
Mother	9	
Unknown relation	5	

Notes

1. The rank for each author is counted for each letter featured in this work.
2. Bandsmen, Ordinance Officers, and Chaplains included

Appendix 2:
Lt. Ashbel Fraley's
"Purposes for Brigade Drill"
and "Maxims of War"

PURPOSES FOR BRIGADE DRILL

1. To keep the men from enjoying a little rest, which they so much need.

2. To take out the sick men that the Surgeon always refuses to excuse from duty (though they are scarcely able to walk) that our Colonels and Generals may have the gratification of seeing them faint & fall in the broiling sun.

3. To make the men careless in drill that the officers may have the pleasure of speaking to them as slaves.

4. To exasperate the men beyond the endurance of paitience, that they may curse & swear so the devil will reap the greater harvest in eternity.

5. That the General and his aides may show their uniform suits; and (though they do not know it) their ignorance.

MAXIMS OF WAR

Maxim the 1st: When you take a strong position from the enemy, leave it, and let them have it again, that you may have the fun of taking it a second time.

Maxim the 2nd: When you are going to attack the enemy be certain to march your army 25 or 30 miles immediately preceeding, so as to have your men well fatigued. Backward movements must be resorted to when you are nearer the enemy than the above named distance.

Maxim the 3rd: In the winter season, when the weather is severely cold & rainy; roads muddy & nights dark and cloudy, be certain to always march after night. In the summer when it is hot and sultry; especially in the month of August "when the dog star rages" commence your march at 9 o'clock and push on without stopping till night.

Maxim the 4th: When you have an important order to communicate to the men "immediately" it should be sent to the commanders of the Regiments so that they are enabled to deliver it to the company commanders at midnight or other such time of night when the men are most certain to be asleep.

Maxim the 5th: In marching an army it is never necessary to stop to rest until the Major General's 4 horses are broken down. This is the criterion in all cases. Fully equipped men can certainly march as long as 4 horses carrying alternately the vast mental weight of a responsible & humane Major General.

Maxim the 6th: Always on a march draw the men's rations so that they will have to cook them at night. In this way they can march all next day. They never need sleep. However they must keep quiet when cooking so that the Brigadiers and Major Generals can sleep.

Appendix 3: The Anatomy of a Typical Soldier's Letter

Being free of military censorship, some Civil War letters feature a good deal of detail, honest evaluations of the army and the conduct of its commanders. Others offer a "typical" report. These latter essentially feature the same general componets. Listed below are these components and some elaboration. Following the list is a letter from Private John W. Armsworthy, marked to show how the components were used in this particular letter.

1. Date & Location

This usually contains the location of the writer's unit. Nearly ninety percent of the time, the location is first listed either above or to the left of the date. The date is secondary and is often abbreviated by month and by year (Dec the 4th /62). Both seemed to be nearly always aligned along the top or right margin of the paper.

2. Greeting

Greetings come in many different forms, some of the more popular ones being "Dear Wife, I Seat myself to drop you a few lines," "I take the present opportunity to write to you," and "I hope that you are enjoying the same blessings."

3. Current Situation

Many things are covered in "current situation," that generally followed the greeting. A soldier's health, appreciation for a previous letter, the weather, whereabouts and health of local men, or a description of location, among various other things. In more detailed letters, this includes information on battles, skirmishes and special happenings in the army.

4. Items from Home

While the majority of soldiers were issued clothing from the state, items from home were used to supplement those issues. Items of a non-military nature such as vests, shirts, scarfs, socks, gloves were in great demand, especially during colder weather.

5. Bill of Fare

This is a report on the soldier's diet and what types of rations consist of an issue. Of course, the evaluation of rations fluctuates according to their quantity. In more lean times, a popular expression is "our fare is meager and we have had hard times."

6. Advice/Requests for Those at Home

Finally, coming at the close of the letter, is the advice and requests from home. This is a closing effort to ask any questions about relatives, ask them to write, or to advise on farm and family matters. These are often rushed as they are written when the letter's author knows he is running out of paper.

7. Closing

The closing of a letter was almost as individual as the greeting. Some of the more popular ways to close a letter included: "Your husband until death," Your brother until death," "Your friend," "I remain," "Your obedient servant," and "Write soon and often." Following the signature of the author would come a way to direct the letter. This was a nineteenth century return address. Letters were always directed to a soldier's company in care of the Company commander.

> [1]Camp near Fredricksburg December 4th 1862
>
> [2]Dear wife I seat myself to drop you a few lines to let you know that I am well at present & hope these few lines will find you all enjoying the same blessing. [3]I received your kind letter Dated the 23rd of November & I was glad to here that you was all well I am sorry to state that I have not got the box that you started to me. I would be glad to here whether you have heard from them or not. Lovel seams to hate it mity bad that he could not bring them. He said he had some boxes for himself and had to leave them. [4]I dont want you to send me any clothing if you have the chance except a par of pants & one vest. I have got a par of gloves. I want some new suspenders that is all the clothing I want at present for I cant carry them for we may have to march for several days at a time. I would be glad if I could get something good to eat from home. If I could only be there. I would be glad if I could get a furlow to come home at Christmas but I fear there is no chance for there is lots of Yankees not far from us but it all quiet that is there is no fiting & I dont think there will be here. Jackson's Army is here. Capt Spear is now Major of the 28th Regment. I would be glad to see the 28th Reg. but the guard wont let anybody pass, they are only about two miles from us. [5]I am faring very well, we have a plenty to eat yet but it is not very good, it is Beef & crackers it is dry eating. I am still cooking for the capt. [6]I get plenty to eat & that is good. I want you to write soon & give me all the news. You must excuse my short letter, I will do better next time. Tell father to write, this will do for you & him, as I thought very strange of his not helping bawl your corn. I send my best respects to Aunt Edney & Uncle Mathew and all the rest of mine & your folks, [7]write soon.
>
> J. W. Armsworthy

Appendix 4:
"A Prayer for Those in Distress"

A PRAYER FOR THOSE IN DISTRESS

O God, whose mercy is everlasting, and whose compassions fail not; look down with pity, I humbly beseech Thee upon the sufferings of the sick, wounded, in prison, or in any other distress, in the service of our country. Give them the spirit of patience and fortitude in every trial, with a right understanding of themselves and of Thee; impute not unto them their former sins, but strengthen them with They blessed spirit. Look, O Lord, upon their infirmities; hear the voice of their complaints; and give them in Thy good time, peace and deliverance, through Christ our Savior. And comfort all those, who, in this time of trouble and strife, are in suspense and anxiety, or bowed down with grief. Raise up friends, I pray Thee, to help and protect the fatherless and widow, and families left in need; give to all who fly to Thee for succor, the continued comfort of Thy countenance here, and so sanctify their afflictions that they may work for them an eternal weight of glory hereafter; through the merits and mediation of Jesus Christ, Thy Son, our Lord. Amen.

From the Confederate Soldiers Prayer Book, *written by the Chaplain of the 32nd Regiment N.C. Troops and published in Petersburg, Virginia, 1863.*

Notes

1861

1. William Graham, James' younger brother, probably considering enlisting into service. From family listing, *Orange County Census*, 1860.

2. This source will be hereafter cited as "Hamilton, *Correspondence of Jonathan Worth*, np."

3. The Anson Guards were formed in Wadesboro, Anson County, N.C., on April 22, 1861, electing Robert T. Wall, a clerk of superior court, as their commanding officer. The company and its ninety-one men arrived in Raleigh on May 2, 1861. Manarin and Jordan, *N.C. Troops 1861–1865: A Roster*, 14 Volumes, North Carolina Division of Archives and History: Raleigh, N.C., 1976–1998, 5:413. Hereafter cited as "Manarin and Jordan, *N.C. Troops*."

4. Manarin and Jordan, *N.C. Troops*, 3:17.

5. During the battle of Bethel, Major Theodore Winthrop of Connecticut, a gifted novelist and one of Butler's staff officers, led an unsuccessful attempt to flank the North Carolinians on the left. The attack was easily repulsed and as a result, Major Winthrop was killed in front of the Companies B & G, 1st Regiment NC Volunteers, the "Hornet's Nest Rifles" and the "Burke Rifles" respectively. Hill, Daniel H. Jr., "Volume Five: North Carolina," in Evans, Clement G., ed., Confederate Military History. Broadfoot: Wilmington, N.C., 1899, 1989. 5:18–19. Hereafter cited as "Hill, in *Confederate Military History*, 5."

6. Private Henry Lawson Wyatt, Company A, 1st Regiment NC Volunteers (six months) was born in Richmond, Virginia in 1842, but resided in Edgecombe County, North Carolina when he volunteered for service in the "Edgecombe Guards" on April 18, 1861. He volunteered and was killed in an attempt to burn an abandoned house in between the lines used to shelter Federal sharpshooters and troops. Manarin and Jordan, *N.C. Troops*, 3:8.

7. In reference to Colonel Daniel Harvey Hill and the 1st North Carolina Volunteers' victory at the Battle of Big Bethel, Virginia, on June 10, 1861. After the end of the engagement, Confederate losses totaled 1 killed and 11 wounded, while Federal casualties were 18 killed and 53 wounded. Hill, in *Confederate Military History*, 5: 19–20. For additional information refer to Private Louis Leon's entry of June 10, 1861.

8. Employment and preliminary military service information from *Davie County Census 1860*, and Manarin and Jordan, *N.C. Troops*, 4:86.

9. Union losses totaled 71 men killed and wounded, nearly six times the Confederate loss, but did not exceed that. Refer to the information in footnote seven.

10. William Frohock Kelly: Captain, "The Davie Sweepstakes," Company G, 4th N.C. Troops. One of Davie County's wealthiest sons, Frohock Kelly was appointed Captain on May 15, 1861, and resigned after "being passed over"

on February 5, 1863. Manarin and Jordan, *N.C. Troops*, 4:75.

11. Personal information for Belo comes from the town of Salem in *Forsyth County Census 1860* and also Manarin and Jordan, *N.C. Troops* 6:564.

12. Captain Rufus K. Wharton, commander of another company, "The Forsyth Greys" from Forsyth County. Jordan, *N.C. Troops*, 6:574.

13. Belo would lose a bid for re-election as company commander on April 26, 1862, but later served as a Major in the 55th North Carolina (Davis' Brigade), being wounded twice and fighting a famous duel with an officer from Alabama. Mast, Greg, *State Troops and Volunteers*, N.C., Division of Archives and History: Raleigh, N.C., 1996, 90. Hereafter cited as "Mast, *State Troops and Volunteers*."

14. Service record for Captain Lewis Henry Webb from Manarin and Jordan, *N.C. Troops*, 7:174.

15. Manarin and Jordan, *N.C. Troops*, 4:36.

16. Private Turner would eventually rise to the rank of Lieutenant, faithfully serving through the ranks, being captured once, and wounded twice in combat. Lieutenant Turner commanded his company at the surrender at Appomattox Court House, Virginia on April 9, 1865. Manarin and Jordan, *N.C. Troops*, 4:36.

17. Military and Biographical information from the *Alamance County Census: 1860*, and Manarin and Jordan, *N.C. Troops*, 5:332.

18. Senior Captain James H. Wood of Rowan County's Company "B" who commented on the companies military conduct. Captain Wood rose to the rank of Lieutenant Colonel in the 4th Regiment. Manarin and Jordan, *N.C. Troops*, 4:9.

19. Private Adams was promoted to corporal in December of 1862 and then to sergeant on March 3, 1863. Sergeant Adams was wounded at Chancellorsville, Virginia on May 3, 1863, and was captured at the Wilderness. After being confined at Elmira Prison, NY, William was released after taking the oath of allegiance on June 21, 1865. Manarin and Jordan, *N.C. Troops*, 4:36.

20. According to the Minutes of the Court of Pleas and Quarter Sessions, David Loftin is listed as the county's sheriff, with J. A. Park, John Michael, E. S. Harris, and Sidney Watford listed as constables. In addition, the same document lists fourteen magistrates in the county who had sworn loyalty to the Confederate States. *Davidson County Court of Pleas and Quarter Sessions, 1861.*

21. Biographical and military information from Cloninger, Addie, *Notes on James W. Gibson*, in the author's possession and from Manarin and Jordan, *N.C. Troops*, 7:198

22. Joseph F. Gibson, brother of James W. Gibson, was a resident of Iredell County, North Carolina. Joseph served as a Private in Company C, 4th Regiment N.C. State Troops. Manarin and Jordan, *N.C. Troops*, 4:40.

23. Manarin and Jordan, *N.C. Troops*, 5:332

24. Many soldiers from Company B were detailed to function as musicians after January of 1862. Manarin and Jordan, *N.C. Troops*, 5:286–287, 287.

25. *Ibid*, 7:566.

26. McKinon and Dowd: Both members of the "Moore Independents," Company H, 26th Regiment N.C. Troops, Jordan, *N.C. Troops* 7:801–807.

27. From *Forsyth County Census: 1860*.

28. Doctor Isaac H. Tanner, Surgeon, 11th NC Volunteers. Manarin and Jordan, *N.C. Troops*, 6:539.

29. Charlie Bahnson: son of respected Moravian minister and native of Switzerland George Bahnson. Charlie would later enlist in the First Battalion, North Carolina Sharpshooters. *Forsyth County Census: 1850 & 1860*, and Bahnson, Dr. Charles, *Recollections of the Civil War*, Edwards & Broughton, Raleigh, N.C., 1903.

30. Prominent carriage and coachmaker of Salem, Henry W. Meinung. *Forsyth County Census: 1860*.

31. The exact wording of the incident according to Webb is found in Manarin and Jordan, *N.C. Troops*, 7:174, and is as follows: The disaffection came out of an incident at Manassas when he disciplined several members of his company for raiding a peach orchard. The Punishment, in Webbs words was to "march them along the guard path in front of a bayonet which happened to have a sentinel behind it.

32. Thomas Refers to Private Henry T. Thomas, who died of typhoid fever on September 23, 1861. *Ibid*, 7:184

33. Third Lieutenant Ben Covington a 23 year old, whose rebellion against Webb eventually lost its momentum. Covington would loose his post when defeated for re-election on May 31, 1862. Other Lieutenants opposed to Webb included John W. Cole and William Wall. *Ibid,* 7:175

34. Service record for deceased solider, John R. Hagler in Manarin and Jordan, *N.C. Troops,* 6:451

35. *Cabarrus County Census: 1860.*

36. The reference "G. P. Johnson" refers to Peter Johnson (1846–1914), Private, Co. F, 53rd N.C. Troops. Peter was born in 1846 to Clinton and Sarah Johnson. He worked as a carpenter prior to volunteering for service in Randolph County on April 2, 1862. He deserted and was reported absent without leave from September 1, 1862 through February 28, 1863. Peter returned to service and later deserted to the enemy at Gettysburg, PA on July 3, 1863. He was confined at Ft. Delaware National Prison until released after taking the Oath of Allegiance. Manarin and Jordan, *N.C. Troops,* 13:126

37. Private Shoe was captured at Roanoke Island on February 8, 1862 and was paroled at Elizabeth City on February 21, 1862. Shoe rejoined the regiment in August of 1862 and was reported present until wounded in the neck at Fort Harrison, Virginia on September 30, 1864. Edmund was reported absent wounded through October 1864. Manarin and Jordan, *N.C. Troops,* 4:62.

38. Service record from roster appendix in Driver, Robert E., *History of the 10th Virginia Cavalry Regiment,* H. E. Howard: Lynchburg, VA, 1992, 102. Hereafter cited as "Driver, *10th Virginia Cavalry.*"

39. The unit in question was the "Rowan Artillery," company D, 1st NC Artillery. Private Lillycross, a miner and native of England did not receive his transfer, but went on to soldier with the 4th Regiment and was wounded in action twice during the war. Manarin and Jordan, *N.C. Troops* 4:109.

40. Manarin and Jordan, *N.C. Troops,* 4: 29.

41. According to a company commander in the Sixth N.C. Troops the action at Manassas was as follows: "We were led on, avoiding exposed places so as to keep out of the sight of the enemy, until we were brought up in front of what is known as the "Henry House," near which a battery of artillery was posted and throwing its deadly missiles into the Confederate lines. It was a short time before [the 6th Regiment's charge] these guns were silenced and captured. But in those few minutes Colonel Fisher and many others had been killed. It was a critical time. On this ridge or plateau, on which the Henry House stood, was the hardest fighting of the day. Here it was that General Bee, a short while before he was killed, bravely calling on his men to stand firm against the heavy columns that were coming against them, pointed down the line to General Jackson, saying: "Look at Jackson, he stands like a stone wall!" Quoted in Ray, Neill, "Sixth Regiment," in Clark, Walter, ed., Histories of the Several Regiments and Battalions from North Carolina During the Great War 1861–1865, 1:298–299. Hereafter cited as "Clark, N.C. Regiments."

42. "Alfred M. Scales" in Powell, William S., ed., *The Biographical Dictionary of North Carolina,* Five Volumes, University of North Carolina Press: Chapel Hill, 1994. 4:291. Hereafter cited as "Powell, *Biographical Dictionary.*"

43. Cousin Kate: Refers to Kate B. Henderson whose father was Colonel Archiblad Henderson. No relation between the two has been established. Powell, Biographical Dictionary 4:291.

1862

1. Information on C. C. Blacknall found in Blacknall, Oscar, *Biographical Sketch of my Father,* No Date, Oscar Blacknall Papers, N.C. Division of Archives and History, and additional information on Blacknall and family was taken from *Granville County Census: 1860,* and Manarin and Jordan, *N.C. Troops,* 7:26, 143.

2. Colonel William J. Hoke, of Lincolnton, served as the commander of the 23rd Regiment N.C. Troops from July 12, 1861, to May 10, 1862. Manarin and Jordan, *N.C. Troops,* 7:143.

3. Captain Josiah Pender, a 40 year old Carteret County Merchant before being commissioned as a captain in the artillery on May 21, 1861. He resigned his commission on December 19, 1861, after going before a court-martial

on charges of desertion. Jordan, N.C. Troops, 1:114.

4. Information from Jordan, *N.C. Troops*, 4:86, and *Davie County Census: 1880*.

5. Robert Osborne Linster volunteered in Iredell County at the age of 18 on September 21, 1861. He was promoted to sergeant in November of 1862. Jordan, *N.C. Troops*, 4:43.

6. Information on the battle of New Bern, N.C., from Mast, *State Troops and Volunteers*, 224–225. Along with one of the most complete photographic collections every assembled, the author, Mr. Mast, provides a great description of the battle and the course of the war from the perspective of North Carolina units who participated in the conflict.

7. On March 8, 1862, the C.S.S. *Virginia* steamed down the Elizabeth River into Hampton Roads. After ramming and sinking the wooden steam sloop Cumberland, the *Virginia* attacked the fifty-gun frigate the U.S.S. *Congress*. The next day saw the dawn of a new age of naval warfare when the CSS *Virginia* (*Merrimac*) battled with the Union Ironclad USS *Monitor*. The two fought to a standoff on March 9, 1862. Information in Catton, Bruce, *American Heritage New History of the Civil War*. Viking Press: New York, 1996, 154.

8. Biographical information on Augustus S. Clewell was taken from the Town of Salem, Forsyth County Census: 1860, and from Manarin and Jordan, *N.C. Troops*, 3:28, 6:574.

9. Captain Rufus K. Wharton, of Forsyth County and commander of Company E, 21st North Carolina, Manarin and Jordan, *N.C. Troops*, 6:574.

10. Colonel Robert M. McKinney, elected colonel of the 15th N.C. Troops (5th Volunteers) on June 24, 1861, led his troops until he was killed in action at the battle of Lee's Mill, Virginia, on April 16, 1862. Service Record in Manarin and Jordan, *N.C. Troops* 5:502.

11. Hugh, Joseph F., Adolphus, and William Gibson, all brothers of James W. and children of John A. and Mary Leazer Gibson of the Shiloh township of Iredell County. By 1860, however, James was already a resident of Catawba County. *Iredell County Census 1850*, *Catawba County Census: 1860*, and Cloninger, *Notes*.

12. In addition, this letter is valuable for its use of phonetic spelling. Cline, a modest farmer, used this form of spelling by sounds in all of his featured correspondence. Personal History in "Cline Family," *Catawba County Heritage*, Winston-Salem: Hunter Publishing, 1986, 102, and military information from Manarin and Jordan, *N.C. Troops*, 11:230.

13. After being loaned to the University of North Carolina for transcription and preservation, the diary of Bartlett Yancey Malone was returned to the family in 1960. The transcription of the diary was first published in the James Sprunt Historical Series, a publication of the University of North Carolina at Chapel Hill in 1919, and was later made into a book entitled *Whipt'em Everytime*, and was again reprinted by Broadfoot & Company of Wendell, N.C.

14. Refers to Thomas J. "Stonewall" Jackson, Confederate general. Actually, Jackson never had more than eighteen thousand, which is cited as a liberal estimate of the Confederate strength in the valley compared to Banks's force of thirty-eight thousand Union troops. Catton, Bruce, *American Heritage New History of the Civil War*, Viking Press: New York, 1996, 136.

15. Manarin and Jordan, *N.C. Troops*, 4:14.

16. *Ibid.*, 4:463.

17. Lieutenant Colonel Edward Graham Haywood. Colonel Haywood was a Wake County attorney before being appointed to serve as Lieutenant Colonel of the 7th Regiment. On June 27, 1862, Haywood was promoted to Colonel, and led the regiment through the Seven Days campaign and was wounded at Second Manassas and Chancellorsville. Haywood resigned due to blindness caused by his wounds on July 22, 1864. Manarin and Jordan, *N.C. Troops*, 4:405.

18. Gibson would survive the campaign and was sent to the hospital and home as a result of his illness on November 3, 1862. He was reported on leave, absent sick, and on detached service for the remainder of his service. Military information from Manarin and Jordan, *N.C. Troops*, 4:40. Information on inadequate supply of 4th N.C. State Troops from a conversation with historian Eric Hall, interview, 12 October 2001.

19. Stephen Webb, a distant cousin of Lewis' who served as a private in the 23rd N.C. Troops and was wounded in the thigh at Seven Pines. *Richmond County Census 1860*, Manarin and Jordan, *N.C. Troops*, 7:184.

20. Thomas Benson Ledbetter, a private in Co. D, 23rd N.C. Troops, wounded in action at Seven Pines, Va on May 31, 1862. Manarin and Jordan, *N.C. Troops*, 7:180. Ledbetter would later return to duty and was reported present through December of 1864.

21. Organizational information on the First NC Sharpshooter Battalion, or the 9th NC Battalion found in Manarin and Jordan, *N.C. Troops* 6:375, 3:75.

22. Rufus K. Pepper, Lieutenant Colonel of the 21st North Carolina Troops, would die of his wounds sustained at Winchester, Virginia on June 10, 1862. Manarin and Jordan, *N.C. Troops*, 6:539.

23. The Fourth Regiment went into action with 545 men under Lt. Colonel Byan Grimes. In the end, only fifty-four soldiers answered the roll. The Regiment lost 160 killed and mortally wounded in addition to at least 250 more men wounded. This estimation of 410 casualties is approximately 75 percent casualties, or three out of every four. Figures found in Mast, *State Troops and Volunteers*, 289, and also in Osborne, E. A., "Forth Regiment" in Clark, Walter, ed., *North Carolina Regiments*, 1:237–240.

24. Information from Chatham County Census: 1860 and from Manarin and Jordan, *N.C. Troops*, 4:482.

25. For a description of election day activities in Davidson County, refer to Molly Alford, letter to John F. Heitman, 48th N.C. Troops, 28 April 1864.

26. Information from Manarin and Jordan, *N.C. Troops*, 12:508.

27. McCorcle refers to Captain John T. McCorckle, Assistant Quartermaster for the 52nd Regiment. McCorckle, a 37-year-old attorney from Stanly County, served on the regimental staff until he resigned while under charges of "drunken conduct and failure to return to camp" on October 29, 1862. Manarin and Jordan, *N.C. Troops*, 12:507–509.

28. Military service for Hartwell Pool from Manarin and Jordan, *N.C. Troops*, 5:71. Background information from Lassiter, *Pattern of Timeless Moments*, 310–311.

29. Biographical information from Richard L. Conrad notes on the Eddinger Family and interview 26 April 1998. Service records from Manarin and Jordan, *N.C. Troops*, 11:386.

30. This reference is in regard to a question Mary Ann Eddinger had asked her husband George in a letter dated August 11, 1862. It refers to Private Jesse H. Osborne, a hireling in Davidson County who was reported present through December of 1864 with the 48th Regiment. Manarin and Jordan, *N.C. Troops*, 11:390.

31. Of the six Eddinger men—father John and his five sons: Daniel, George, John R., Phillip, and William Mack—Phillip, George, and John Sr. died within three months of each other. Phillip and George died of disease within miles of home, and John Sr. was killed in his home by a Negro while attempting to stop a robbery. By the end of the war, only two Eddingers, Daniel and William, survived. Watford, *Civil War Roster of Davidson County*, 68–69, and Richard A. Conrad, interview, 25 October 2001.

32. After the letter, Sergeant Myers was wounded in the left arm and captured at Gettysburg. He was confined at a military hospital in Baltimore, Maryland until November 17, 1863, when he arrived at City Point, Virginia, for exchange. Myers was reported absent wounded on furlough until August 18, 1864, when he was retired to the Invalid Corps. Manarin and Jordan, *N.C. Troops*, 12:452.

33. Living with Myers in 1860. *Stokes County Census: 1860.*

34. Refers to Dr. A. S. Bitting, a wealthy Stokes County physician with over twelve thousand dollars in personal property. According to the letter, he is suffering from dropsy and perhaps mental illness. *Stokes County Census: 1860.*

35. Manarin and Jordan, *N.C. Troops*, 13:319.

36. General John Pope, commander of the Union Army of Virginia. Defeated at the Battle of Second Manassas. The credit for the theft of Pope's coat and the Union payroll over $350,000 should be attributed to cavalry commander Fitzhugh Lee. The capture of the Union commander's coat and personal baggage delighted Stuart, and gave him something to trade for the return of his hat which was lost earlier in the fall. Davis, Burke, *Jeb Stuart: The Last Cavalier*, New York: Rhinehart & Co., 1957, 171–172.

37. Captain Speer of Yadkin County, N.C.,

and commander of Company I, 28th Regiment N.C. Troops. Speer was appointed to command the company on August 13, 1861. Manarin and Jordan, *N.C. Troops*, 8: 207.

38. Manarin and Jordan, *N.C. Troops*, 9:120.

39. Biographical and military information from *Gaston County Census: 1860*, and Manarin and Jordan, *N.C. Troops*, 9:576.

40. All members of Morris' former company, the "Gaston Blues" company H, 37th North Carolina Troops. Jordan, *N.C. Troops*, 9:566–578.

41. All transcripts of featured Vance correspondence came from Johnston, Frontis, ed., *Zebulon Vance Letters*, Raleigh, Division of Archives and History, 1963. However, the proper first citation relating to the A. L. S. Governor's Papers is given in the source line to provide the reader with a location to view the original document.

42. Giles Mebane was a key Alamance County political figure, was serving as a North Carolina Senator for Alamance and Randolph Counties in 1862. Ashe, *Biographical History of North Carolina*, 7: 335–338.

43. G. M. G. Albright refers to Captain Albright, Company F, 53rd N.C. Troops, was wounded in the right knee at Gettysburg, Pennsylvania on July 1, 1863, so severely that his leg had to be amputated. Albright was captured on the retreat from Gettysburg and died of his wounds in Federal hands at Frederick, Maryland on July 16, 1863. For more information see July 1, 1863, entry for Leon, Louis. Manarin and Jordan, *N.C. Troops*, 13:119.

44. The firm of Cyrus Mendenhall, E. P. Jones, and Grafton Gardner began production of a Missssppi pattern rifle in Jamestown, Guilford County on November 1, 1862. Their contract with the state called for 5,000 guns at $21 each. Typical progress produced between forty and eighty rifles per month. NC Quartermaster Contracts, Quartermaster Papers, Box 107.

45. Under the leadership of Calvin H. Wiley, the state's public school system was kept open throughout the war. While the system suffered from the loss of many conscription-aged teachers, it was able to function and stressed the basic elements of learning. Private colleges did not fare so well, especially those all-male institutions. Salem Academy for Girls actually grew. Trotter, William R., *Silk Flags and Cold Steel*, Winston-Salem: Blair, 1988, 135. Hereafter cited as "Trotter, Silk Flags." Biographical Information on Calvin H. Wiley from Powell, *Biographical Dictionary of North Carolina*, 2:427–440.

46. Vance affirmed his commitment to education in an address given before the Legislature on November 17, 1862, when he asked that the Legislature defeat any bill which would take away educational funding and transfer it to the war effort. Quoted from Johnston, Frontis W., ed., *The Papers of Zebulon B. Vance*, Raleigh: North Carolina Division of Archives and History, 1963, 231. Hereafter cited as Johnston, "Papers of Z. B. Vance."

47. Unfortunately this is the last entry for Lt. Fraley. Fraley's illness was something he tried to hide from his men and he did not mention it in his diary, fearing he would be thought less of as a soldier for missing the Maryland campaign due to disease.

48. The 27th North Carolina attacked through the West Woods and advanced into Mumma's Swale, inflicting heavy losses on Knapp's Pennsylvania Battery. The success of the attack of the 27th North Carolina and 3rd Arkansas, took even Graham by surprise as he later admitted in a post-war article. Priest, John M., *Antietam: The Soldier's Battle*, New York: 1989. 156–158.

49. Lt. James Y. Whitted, an Orange County tobacco manufacturer was wounded in the knee and captured during this attack. He returned briefly to this command, before resigning due to his disability. Manarin and Jordan, *N.C. Troops*, 8:62.

50. Out of 325 present for duty, the 27th Regiment sustained 199 casualties (31 killed in action, 168 wounded) at the battle of Sharpsburg. Losses were second in the Brigade to the 48th Regiment which suffered 217 casualties. Priest, *Antietam: The Solider's Battle*, Appendix, 322.

51. Francis Levin Fries (1812–1863) and Henry William Fries (1825–1902). Francis was born in Salem of a leading Moravian family, educated at Nazareth Hall in Pennsylvania, studied law under Emanuel Shober and practiced only briefly. His interest in business made

him give up the law and join the Salem Manufacturing Company (cotton), and in 1846 to establish the F. & H. Fries Company (wool) with his brother Henry. Henry was also born in Salem, studied at John Beck Institute at Lititz, Pennsylvania, and joined his brother as a full partner in F. & H. Fries Company on his twenty-first birthday. After the death of Francis Fries in 1863 his brother operated the business. Francis Fries was a member of the House of Commons in 1858 and a director of the North Carolina Railroad. He was a Democrat. Powell, *Biographical Dictionary of North Carolina*, 2:159 Also quoted in Johnston, *Papers of Z. B. Vance*, 255.

52. Private Mason Tarpley, enlisted in Alamance County on July 7, 1862, at age 32. Private Tarpley would die of "variola confluent" in a Richmond Hospital on December 17, 1862. Manarin and Jordan, *N.C. Troops*, 14:201.

53. Private Archibald Curlee was 18 years old when he volunteered for service in Monroe, N.C. on March 20, 1862. Curlee was reported absent because of sickness from September through December 1862. For the remainder of the war, Curlee was reported at various hospitals and was detailed as a shoemaker. Manarin and Jordan, *N.C. Troops*, 13:151.

54. For more information on the Confederate monetary crisis see: Schwab, John C., *The Confederate States of America: A Financial and Industrial History of the South During the War*, New York, 1901.

55. Pender's Brigade (Sept. 1862) consisted of the 13th, 16th, 22nd, 34th, and 38th North Carolina Troops. Watford, Chris, N.C. *Infantry Regiments, Battalions, & Companies*, 1996, Appendix 3.

56. Refers to Private Isaac H. Thomas, Company H, 4th N.C. State Troops, a volunteer soldier who enlisted at Statesville on June 13, 1861. At the time this letter was written to Vance, Isaac was serving as a Sergeant in company "H" of the 4th N.C. State Troops. Manarin and Jordan, *N.C. Troops*, 4:94.

57. Manarin and Jordan, *N.C. Troops*, 10:69, and biographical information from the Taylorsville PO, *Alexander County Census: 1860*.

58. Manarin and Jordan, *N.C. Troops*, 14:197.

59. In reference to Private William James McCray, Manarin and Jordan, *N.C. Troops*, 14:197.

60. *Gaston County Census: 1860*.

61. George Richards was born in Cornwall, England, and was employed along with his brother, Thomas, to "explore for copper and gold." George volunteered for service at age 26, on June 5, 1861, and was reported present through July 3, 1863, when he "gave up" at Gettysburg, Pennsylvania. Richards was confined at Fort Delaware, Delaware until September 4, 1863, when both he and his brother took the oath of allegiance and joined the US Army, being assigned to Company D, 3rd Regiment Maryland Cavalry. Note that there is no mention of Richards' wounds suffered at Malvern Hill which sent him home to recover. Manarin and Jordan, *N.C. Troops*, 7:490.

62. Captain Robert G. Stanly Austin, 82nd Regiment NC Militia, Monore District. Bradley, Stephen, *North Carolina Confederate Militia Officers Roster*, Wilmington: Broadfoot, 1992.

63. Manarin and Jordan, *N.C. Troops*, 7:206.

64. Federal losses at Fredericksburg, December 13, 1862: 1,284 KIA, 9,600 WD, 1,769 CAP & MIA, total=12, 658, Johnson, Robert and Clarence Beull, eds., *Battles and Leaders of the Civil War*, 4 Volumes, New York: The Century Company, 3:180. Hereafter cited as "Beull, *Battles and Leaders*."

1863

1. Service records from Manarin and Jordan, *N.C. Troops*, 4: 86, also *Davie County Census: 1860*.

2. Manarin and Jordan, *N.C. Troops*, 9:523–524.

3. Colonel William M. Barbour, appointed Colonel on June 30, 1862, and Lieutenant Colonel John B. Ashcraft, promoted to Lt. Colonel upon the resignation of Charles N. Hickerson. Manarin and Jordan, *N.C. Troops*, 9:522.

4. Recorded as Jewish soldiers by Manarin and Jordan, N.C. Troops, 13:81–87. All except Corporal Wertheim survived the war.

5. Private Leonard wants out of the service. He cites his weight loss of nearly 70 pounds in six months. This kind of loss was severe, but not

uncommon among Confederate soldiers who were hospitalized. He even suggests that his mother Polly could convince the surgeons to grant him a furlough to come home.

6. Lieutenant Branson was promoted to captain on March 26, 1863, and led his company faithfully through the battles of Bristoe Station and Petersburg until he was killed in action near Globe Tavern, Virginia, on August 21 or 22, 1864. Manarin and Jordan, *N.C. Troops*, 10:188.

7. Charles C. Blacknall would rise to the rank of colonel on August 15, 1863, after being wounded twice and incarcerated in Johnson's Island Prison. Blacknall returned to his command on May 1, 1864, and led the 23rd North Carolina as its commanding officer until he died as a result of wounds received at the battle of Winchester (September 19, 1864) in a local hospital on November 6, 1864. He was placed beside his former commander and great friend, Colonel Chrisite. Manarin and Jordan, *N.C. Troops* 7:143.

8. All members of Morris' former company, the "Gaston Blues" Company H, 37th North Carolina Troops, Jordan, *N.C. Troops*, 9:566–578.

9. Aaron Katz, first mentioned here. Refers to Private Aaron Katz, company B, 53rd N.C. Troops, who served as a private until being appointed to serve as Sergeant Major of the Regiment prior to July 1, 1863. Manarin and Jordan, *N.C. Troops*, 13: 65, 83.

10. "Scales Family," *Rockingham County Heritage*, Hunter Publishing: Winston-Salem, N.C., 1983, 566.

11. *Person County Census: 1850*, Manarin and Jordan, *N.C. Troops*, 7:253 & 12: 506.

12. Henry T. Jordan, Regimental Adjutant of the 55th N.C. Troops, Manarin and Jordan, *N.C. Troops*, 12:430.

13. Satterfield survived the Suffolk campaign, and was even involved (not personally) with Major Alfred Belo's duel with an Alabama officer over the blame of the loss of a battery during the campaign. Satterfield led his company into Pennsylvania and in the Pickett-Pettigrew attack. Satterfield was one of three men given the honor of advancing the farthest at Gettysburg. Fletcher Satterfield was killed in action on July 3, 1863. Manarin and Jordan, *N.C. Troops*, 12:506.

14. Notes on the Cameron-Badgett-Redwine Families, copy in the author's possession.

15. The 62nd Ga Cavalry was a crucial part of the defense of eastern North Carolina. Here, Daniel is talking about actions taken under Gen. Daniel Harvey Hill, a North Carolinian who was in charge of preventing any further Union advance and defending the Weldon Railroad in the spring of 1863.

16. Manarin and Jordan, *N.C. Troops*, 12:90 and *Cleveland County Census: 1850, 1860*.

17. Actual losses from battle of Chancellorsville are as follows: Union losses 1606 (KIA), 9762 (WIA), 5919 (Capt or Missing) 17287 (Total US Loss); Confederate: 1649 (KIA), 9106 (WIA), 1708 (CAP) 12463 (Total) Figure as reported in Buell, *Battles and Leaders*, 3:237.

18. B. Stutts: Private in Company H, deserted prior to Chancellorsville Manarin and Jordan, *N.C. Troops*, 7: 571.

19. Private Jackson went on to serve with the 26th North Carolina in every campaign in which the unit participated. He was reported present throughout the war until he was surrendered at Appomattox Court House, Virginia on April 9, 1865. Manarin and Jordan, *N.C. Troops*, 7: 806.

20. Clodfelter's service is reported in Driver, Robert, *10th Virginia Cavalry*, 104.

21. William A. Hedrick and Hamilton McGuire were both classmates of Hugh Clodfelter at Yadkin and both joined their friend in service. Driver, *10th Virginia Cavalry*, 108–115.

22. All members of Company C, 21st North Carolina, all Stokes County men conscripted the same time as Hundley. Manarin and Jordan, *N.C. Troops*, 6:557.

23. Evans, *Confederate Military History*, 5: 341–343.

24. In folk legend in Davidson County, "Wagner's Woods" were notorious as a place where those who wished to avoid conscription or deserters dodging the Home Guard hid out. Apparently, as the situation worsened, Wagner's Woods became a crowded place. "Notes on Davidson County Civil War Stories," copy in author's possession.

25. Sergeant Bradshaw was captured at Gettysburg, Pennsylvania July 1–5, 1863. He was confined at Point Lookout, Maryland, via Fort Delaware, Delaware, until he died at Point Look-

out on August 11, 1864. Manarin and Jordan, *N.C. Troops*, 10:69, and biographical information from the *Alexander County Census: 1860*.

26. Columbus F. Bradshaw was still at home by this time, though he would join his brother Jonas in service with the 38th N.C. Troops and John A. Query who was at home after being discharged due to the provisions of the Conscript Act on November 5, 1862. Manarin and Jordan, *N.C. Troops*, 10: 68, 71.

27. Manarin and Jordan, *N.C. Troops*, 4:269.

28. Noblin, Stewart, "Leonidas L. Polk," in Powell, *Biographical Dictionary of North Carolina*, 4:110–111.

29. Leonidas and Pamela would have two daughters by 1860. The couple would go on to have six daugthers, and a son who died in infancy. Noblin in Powell, *Biographical Dictionary of North Carolina*, 4:111.

30. McMatthews: Second Lieutenant William McGill Matthews. Born in Mecklenburg County in 1841 and resided there as a farmer prior to volunteering for service on March 10, 1862, and was mustered in as a 1st Sergeant. Afterwards he was elected to the post of Second Lieutenant on June 12, 1862, and was reported present until wounded in the right side of the face at Gettysburg, Pennsylvania on July 1, 1863. Manarin and Jordan, *N.C. Troops*, 13: 78. Alexander: Third Lieutenant Marshall E. Alexander previously served in Company B, 1st Regiment NC Infantry (6 months) and re-enlisted in this company on March 11, 1862, with the rank of sergeant. Alexander was elected third lieutenant on June 12, 1862. He was reported present until wounded in the left arm and captured at Gettysburg, Pennsylvania on July 1, 1863. *Ibid.*, 13: 78.

31. Information from Manarin and Jordan, *N.C. Troops*, 1:186, and *Catawba County Census: 1860*.

32. Murph was reported present at his post in the Artillery until September 9, 1864, when he received a furlough from a hospital in Charlotte, N.C. Private Murph returned to service shortly thereafter and was reported present when his battery was transferred to Fort Fisher. Daniel Washington Murph was killed in action during the first attack on Fort Fisher on December 25, 1864. Manarin and Jordan, *N.C. Troops*, 1:186.

33. After being wounded at Gettysburg, Hundley died on or about July 28, 1863, of unreported causes. Manarin and Jordan, *N.C. Troops*, 7:559.

34. Margaret Dalton, born in 1832, married D. N. Dalton, a tobacco planter prior to 1860. The Dalton real estate holdings in 1860 were well over $36,000. *Stokes County Census: 1860*.

35. Louisa Farris, the oldest child of Mary and Charles Farris, b. 1857. *Stokes County Census: 1860*.

36. Members of 43rd North Carolina Troops, Manarin and Jordan, *N.C. Troops*, 11:130–150.

37. Si Wolf: Private Cyrus H. Wolfe, born in Mecklenburg County in 1842 and enlisted on April 15, 1862. Wolfe would soldier in company B, until being transferred to the regimental band in 1864. Manarin and Jordan, *N.C. Troops* 13: 88.

38. The soldiers in question from the 3rd NC were responsible for the murder of Adjutant Richardson Mallet at Scottsville, Virginia on August 28, 1863. Manarin and Jordan, *N.C. Troops*, 11:134.

39. The raid on Holden's office was conducted by the 2nd and 20th Georgia Infantry regiments. Editorial letter in *Raleigh Standard*, September 14, 1863, regarding an incident at his office. Three days prior, Holden received a letter from Colonel E. M. Sargo, 20th Georgia, stating that any attempts to sell the Standard would not be tolerated due to Holden's anti-confederate position. Within days, two regiments, reported by Holden as the 2nd and the 20th Georgia raided the office and destroyed what they could before stopped by officers. Despite being a huge critic of the Governor, Holden was supported in his complaint against the rioters by Governor Vance. Raper, Horace W. and Thornton W. Mitchell, eds., *The Papers of William Woods Holden*, Raleigh: NC Division of Archives and History, 2000, 141–143.

40. Manarin and Jordan, N.C. Troops, 7:209.

41. A fellow soldier, Francis M. Medlin wrote this letter for the illiterate Womble. However, according to Manarin and Jordan, *N.C. Troops*, 4:480, the only Medlin in the company was Private George Medlin.

42. Identity of soldier "Dean" was actually Private John A. Deal, Company G, or Rowan

County. John Deal volunteered for service at age 18 in Rowan County on December 17, 1862. He was killed in an accident on the Wilmington & Weldon Railroad on October 9, 1863. Manarin and Jordan, *N.C. Troops*, 10:260. The railroad accident described is not at all uncommon. In fact L.L. Conrad of Davidson County lost a leg in an accident on the Raleigh and Gaston Railroad, while at least two soldiers from the 58th N.C. Troops were killed accidentally while guarding a train of Federal prisoners being transported to Mississippi.

43. Manarin and Jordan, *N.C. Troops*, 4: 86.

44. Private Lassiter would return to regular duty in February of 1864. He was reported present until captured at the battle of the Wilderness, May 6, 1864. Lassiter was confined at Elmira Prison, Elmira, New York until June 16, 1865, when he was released after taking the oath of allegiance. All biographical and military information from introduction and note taken from Manarin and Jordan, *N.C. Troops*, 10:81–82.

45. From Watford, Christopher, *The Civil War Roster of Davidson County, North Carolina*, Jefferson, N.C.: McFarland, 2001, 162. Hereafter cited as "Watford, *Civil War Roster*."

46. Sink was born on August 18, 1842, to Michael and Lucy Tussey Sink. John lived in the Tyro area prior to volunteering for service on November 26, 1861. He was mustered in as a sergeant and was promoted to first sergeant on July 1, 1862. John would be appointed to serve as third lieutenant on November 20, 1862. He was reported present until wounded in the right elbow and right forearm near Petersburg, VA on June 18, 1864. John was reported absent wounded until discharged from service on February 6, 1865, by reason of disabling wounds received. After his discharge, John returned home, where, on December 16, 1866, he married Callie Smith. John and Callie would have six children: Mary Elizabeth (1868), William (1872), Lee David (1873), George (1874), Walter (1879), and Ora Lucy (1881). John moved to the city of Lexington in the 1870s where he became a respected citizen and a master carpenter. John died on April 14, 1885. He is buried in the Lexington City Cemetery. In his letter, John describes the military force in eastern North Carolina, and talks about some of the more pleasant moments afforded during service. Watford, *Civil War Roster*, 214–215.

1864

1. Manarin and Jordan, *N.C. Troops*, 5:95.

2. John Allen Smith would be promoted to Corporal on July 1, 1864, and was reported present with his new duty through December of 1864. Manarin and Jordan, *N.C. Troops*, 2:60.

3. David M. Harkey, Private in Company G, was wounded in action at Upperville, Virginia on June 21, 1863, and was wounded again on May 5, 1864, in the right shoulder by shrapnel. Private Harkey was retired to the Invalid Corps on August 11, 1864. Manarin and Jordan, *N.C. Troops*, 2:57.

4. Manarin and Jordan, *N.C. Troops*, 11:238.

5. H. H. Caldwell: Private in Company K, 46th North Carolina Manarin and Jordan, *N.C. Troops*, 11:238.

6. Johnty refers to Thomas's boarder and day laborer, Jonathan Burton. *Davie County Census: 1860*.

7. Taylorsville P. O., *Alexander County Census: 1860*.

8. After the war, John and Caroline would have five children. John served as a physician and as a leader in medical associations in the 1860s and 1870s. Shaffner entered political life in 1878, being a commissioner and later a mayor of Salem, N.C., through 1884. Shaffner served as president of the Salem Water Company, Winston-Salem Building and Loan Association, and served as a board member on the Western North Carolina Railroad and the Salem Boy's School. John died on September 18, 1908, and is buried in the Salem Cemetery, Winston-Salem, North Carolina. Powell, William S., *Biographical Dictionary of North Carolina*, 5:319–320.

9. Sergeant John Strikeleather, colorbearer of the 4th North Carolina who volunteered to carry the colors after the entire color guard was killed or wounded at Seven Pines, Virginia. Strikeleather carried the colors of the 4th Regiment until the surrender at Appomattox Court House, Virginia, on April 9, 1865. Manarin and Jordan, *N.C. Troops*, 4:24.

10. Linster would soldier on with the 4th N.C. State Troops until paroled at Appomattox Court House, Virginia on April 9, 1865. His rank on parole was given as "ordinance sergeant." Manarin and Jordan, *N.C. Troops*, 4:43.

11. Manarin and Jordan, *N.C. Troops*, 11:59, and Watford, *Civil War Roster*, 224.

12. Edinboro: A town in Montgomery County, originally named by Scottish settlers after Edinburgh, eventually abandoned. Powell, *N.C. Gazetter*, UNC Press: Chapel Hill, 1968, 158. Hereafter cited as "Powell, N.C. Gazetter."

13. Manarin and Jordan, *N.C. Troops*, 12:90.

14. Men identified in company: Acting First Sergeant John L. Bridges, Lieutenant Sylvester Weaver, and Benjamin Dixon who would later be promoted to Captain on January 1, 1865. Manarin and Jordan, *N.C. Troops*, 12:90–92.

15. Daniel Rinck was captured at the battle of Falling Waters, Maryland on July 14, 1863. This battle was the last major rear-guard action of Lee's retreat from Gettysburg. Daniel was confined at Point Lookout, Maryland until paroled and transferred for exchange on March 16, 1864. It is believed that he was granted a furlough to come home as he is not listed as absent without leave upon his return to the company in May of 1864. Manarin and Jordan, *N.C. Troops*, 5:93.

16. Noah Rinck, formerly a Private in the same company. Brother Noah was the oldest of the brothers in Company I and served nearly two full years prior to being discharged from service due to "paraplegia." Manarin and Jordan, *N.C. Troops*, 5:93.

17. Summit, Glen, "Issac L. Summit and the Battle of Ream's Station" with citation to Notes by Daniel Summit of Lexington, N.C. Glen Summit's Notes in possession of the author 11 October, 2001.

18. Notes on John Franklin Heitman and Molly Alford, August 1999, in the author's possession.

19. Hopewell United Methodist Church, in Northwestern Randolph County.

20. Believed to be William Daniel Yancey (Co. B, 12th N.C. Troops), born in 1843. He worked as a Granville County farmer prior to volunteering for service on April 26, 1861. He was wounded in action at Malvern Hill, Virginia, on July 1, 1862. He returned to service sometime in early 1864 and was assigned to light duty until he was retired to the Invalid Corps on October 24, 1864. Manarin and Jordan, *N.C. Troops*, 5:140.

21. The 53rd North Carolina was with Daniel's Brigade on the extreme right of the Second Corps, driving one body of Federal troops, before coming into a clearing an encountering a Union line supported by artillery. Leon was captured here, but not before the following story is recorded. "On May 5 or 6, 1864, the sharpshooters of this regiment were annoyed by one of the Federal sharpshooters who had a long rifle and had climbed up in a tall tree where he could pick off our men. Private Leon, of company B (Mecklenburg), concluded that 'This thing had to be stopped,' and taking advantage of every knoll, hollow, and stump, he crawled near enough for his rifle to reach, took a 'pop' at this disturber of the peace and he came tumbling down. Upon running up to his victim, Leon discovered him to be a Canadian Indian, and clutching his scalp-lock, dragged him into our line of sharpshooters." Morehead, "53rd Regiment," Clark, *N.C. Regiments*, 3:258.

22. Manrin and Jordan, *N.C. Troops*, 12:430.

23. Some controversy exists about the final disposition of Private Barrier. NC Service records state that he was captured in 1864, while a pension filed by his wife states that he was killed in action at Plymouth, N.C. As the battle of Plymouth was on April 20, 1864, that option is illogical due to the date of the letter. Manarin and Jordan, *N.C. Troops*, 4:592, *Cabarrus County Census: 1860*, and personal notes.

24. May 16, 1864, saw the battle of Drewery's Bluff, Virginia. In the action Private Daniel L. Bost was wounded in the face and L. H. Blackwelder was killed in action. Manarin and Jordan, *N.C. Troops*, 4:594.

25. The admitted Federal loss by both corps involved in the battle was 4500 and of that number 1478 were reported missing. Buell, *Battles and Leaders*, 4:212.

26. Private Aaron Hahn and J. S. Hineseaman, Manarin and Jordan, *N.C. Troops*, 4:596.

27. Evans, *Confederate Military History*, 5:342.

28. Reported Casualties from May 12 action at Spotsylvania Court House: US 18,399, CS

3100 (II corps), Beull, *Battles and Leaders*, 4:182–184.

29. Members of company C, 1st Battalion Junior Reserves on May 24, 1864. The company was later known as company C, 70th Regiment North Carolina Troops (1st Regiment North Carolina Junior Reserves). "70th Regiment," Moore, Walter C., ed., *Roster of North Carolina Troops*, 3:112.

30. Manarin and Jordan, *N.C. Troops*, 4:482.

31. Rom refers to Private S. M. Rone, a soldier with the 39th NC until he was captured at Spanish Fort, Alabama on April 8, 1865. Mars: Private G. L. Mars, was also captured at Spanish Fort on the same day, but was transferred to Vicksburg, Mississippi on May 6, 1865. No further records. Manarin and Jordan, *N.C. Troops*, 10:116–119.

32. Captain Arthur Dyche, was transferred from the 19th North Carolina Troops (2nd Cavalry) as a private on October 31, 1861. He was elected to the rank of 2nd Lieutenant on February 14, 1862, and was promoted to 1st Lieutenant on December 24, 1862. On June 30, 1863, Arthur Dyche was promoted to Captain and led company "A" until August 15, 1864, when he resigned due to unspecified reasons. Manarin and Jordan, *N.C. Troops*, 10:112.

33. Hahn, *The Catawba Soldier of the Civil War*, Hickory, North Carolina, 1911, and Summit, Glen, Isaac L. Summit, Notes.

34. Summit was mortally wounded in action while advancing the colors of his regiment as part of Cooke's attack on Ream's Station. Isaac was removed from the field and taken to Richmond's Winder Hospital where he died on September 9, 1864. His wife, Perlina would be widowed. After the war, she suffered through several problems and even had two boys out of wedlock. Eventually, the stress of life was too much for her to take as she was admitted to the State Hospital in Morganton where she died on August 11, 1917. Summit, Glen, Isaac L. Summit, Notes, and Hahn, "The Catawba Soldier of the Civil War," Hickory, North Carolina, 1911.

35. Clewell survived the war, but moved out of Forsyth County prior to the 1870 Census. *Forsyth County Census: 1870, 1880*.

36. Henry Shaffner, neighbor of the Clewell's in Salem, *Forsyth County Census: 1860*.

37. To support the belief that "Edward Richards" is James E. R. Yancey his service record states that he was "wounded by a shell fragment during Early's Valley Campaign July 9 to August 11, 1864." Manarin and Jordan, *N.C. Troops*, 5:140.

38. The description of the battle is consistent with the action taken by Early's Valley Army. On July 9, 1864, the Confederates seized Frederick and advanced on Washington, D.C. The column passed through Rockville, and by 2 p.m. Federal defenders began to shell Confederates resting in a grove. Betts, William, D.D., *Experiences of a Confederate Chaplain 1861–1864*, Greenville, SC, 1900, 43.

39. In addition to all that had happened, Gibson was captured at South Mountain, MD on September 14, 1862, and was confined at Ft. Delaware, Delaware, until he was paroled and transferred to Aiken's Landing, Virginia, on October 2, 1862. Gibson was declared exchanged on November 10, 1862, and returned to his life as a solider. Manarin and Jordan, *N.C. Troops*, 7:198.

40. Joseph F. Gibson, (4th N.C. State Troops) after recovering from an illness was sent home to Statesville on detached service from February 1864 to September 1864. No further records. Manarin and Jordan, *N.C. Troops*, 4:40.

41. After the war, Polk became one of North Carolina's central political figures. Polk was a member of the NC Constitutional Convention, and helped to restore his family and his county after the war. In 1874 he emerged as a leader in the "Grange," a political alliance of farmers, and with the help of Zebulon Vance, created the State Department of Agriculture, which he presided over until 1880. In 1886, he began the magazine *Progressive Farmer*, which still runs today, and pushed for two educational projects; The N.C. College of Agriculture and Mechanic Arts (N.C. State University) and the Baptist College for Girls (Meredith College) in Raleigh. Polk became a fast-rising star in the N.C. Farmer's Alliance, which held two million members when Polk was elected President in 1889. Polk was very active in the political campaigns of the early 1890s and was a leader in a move to build "Alliance Democrats" as a state and national party instead of a third party

which could be overshadowed by the growing Populist party of the Midwest. Polk worked in politics until his death on June 11, 1892. "Polk," in Powell, *Biographical Dictionary of North Carolina*, 4:110–111.

42. Apparently the 11th N.C. Troops were the victim of a flanking or enfilade attack from the regiment's left as Federal troops swept through the trenches. Rinck died in Federal custody on April 13, 1865, at the age of forty-two. Manarin and Jordan, *N.C. Troops*, 5:6, 93–94.

43. Private David Glenn, Co. I, 11th Regiment N.C. Troops, Manarin and Jordan, *N.C. Troops*, 5:91.

44. Service records for Daniel Rinck do not mention this stay in the hospital. Daniel was reported present through February of 1865. Manarin and Jordan, *N.C. Troops*, 5:93.

45. Evans, *Confederate Military History*, 5:343.

46. Watford, Civil War Roster, 111–112.

47. Scales survived the war, but was sent home on sick leave when the Petersburg line was broken and the Army retreated to Appomattox Court House. After the war, Scales resumed practicing law in Greensboro and served as a State Legislator from 1866–1869. In 1874, he was elected to Congress from the Sixth District. Scales served as a Representative on Capitol Hill until 1884. In 1884, Scales, a Democrat ran against an anti-prohibitionist Republican, Tyre York, of Wilkes County. Scales won by a majority of twenty thousand votes. His term as Governor (1885–1889) was rather uneventful, but Scales used his position to draw attention to transportation shortfalls and suggested that the Federal government use surplus funds to aid State education. Alfred Scales lived the remainder of his life in Guilford County until his death on February 9, 1892. Surviving the former State Legislator, US Congressman, Confederate General, and North Carolina Governor was his wife Kate Henderson Scales, and their adopted daughter, Kate Lewis Scales. Downs, Alan C., "Alfred Scales," Powell, *Biographical Dictionary of North Carolina*, 4:291.

48. Manarin and Jordan, *N.C. Troops*, 5:421.

49. Identity of Ralph Waddle is unknown; however, there was an Archibald Waddell serving in the same company as Private Medley. Manarin and Jordan, *N.C. Troops*, 5: 423.

50. Notes on Armfield from Guilford County genealogist newsletter, copy in author's possession.

51. Refers to Dr. John H. Shelton, a native of Davie County, and employed as a physician in Davidson County before the war. Dr. Shelton received his medical training at the University of North Carolina and was commissioned to serve as a surgeon with the 66th Regiment NC Militia (Davidson County), but at this time he was reported on the "examining board" for the North Carolina Home Guard out of Salisbury, Rowan County, N.C. Watford, *Civil War Roster*, 206–207.

52. Manarin and Jordan, *N.C. Troops*, 5:140.

53. Believed to be Rosa's oldest brother, a resident of Granville County before the war. *Granville County Census: 1860.*

54. Postwar biographical information found in "Malone Family," *Caswell County Heritage*, Hunter Publishing: Winston-Salem, N.C., 1985, 367.

55. The rebellion was to take place on Christmas Eve and was to take the county by surprise. County officials learned of the plot nearly a week before this letter and arrested the ringleaders on December 9, 1864. As a result, additional slave conspirators were arrested and placed in jail. The civil officials wrote to Vance and assured him everything was normal in Richmond County on the 9th. In addition, three units of Richmond County home guard were called out and equipped to fight off such an uprising if it would still be able to be carried out. Though the situation was under control, rumor escaped, and even Captain L. H. Webb received rumor of this rebellion while posted in Weldon, N.C. For further reading: "The Christmas Eve Rebellion" in Hutchinson, John, *No Ordinary Lives: A History of Richmond County, N.C. 1750-1900.*

56. The largest portions of Richmond County which had slaves were the townships of Steele's, Mineral Springs, and Black Jack, Hutchinson. *Richmond County Census, Slave Schedule: 1860.*

57. Driver, *10th Virginia Cavalry*, 102.

58. Heinrich: 1st Sergeant, Company B, 10th Virginia Cavalry, Driver, *10th Virginia Cavalry*, 118.

59. Mitchell: Refers to Lucio Mitchell, 2nd

Lt. Company D, 10th N.C. State Troops (1st Artillery) who was appointed adjutant (1st Lieutenant) of the 46th North Carolina on October 13, 1862. He resigned his commission after being court-martialed on December 8, 1864. Manarin and Jordan, *N.C. Troops*, 11:134.

60. Military service information from Manarin and Jordan, *N.C. Troops*, 6:451, biographical information from *Cabarrus County Census: 1860*.

61. Allen P. Watts a private from Culp's Company who volunteered on the same day in Stanly County, North Carolina. Private Watts was reported present through December of 1864. Manarin and Jordan, *N.C. Troops*, 6:455–456.

62. Manarin and Jordan, *N.C. Troops*, 1:552.

63. Fort Fisher was attacked on December 24, 1864, but held against the Union flotilla. However, a portion of fortifications known as "Battery Anderson," defended by a company of the 42nd North Carolina, was captured in detail.

64. Henry R. Horne, 1st Lieutenant formerly with the 12th Virginia, transferred over with Webb. Manarin and Jordan, *N.C. Troops*, 1:552.

65. The 27th Regiment Band consisted of fourteen musicians and was led by a Lenoir County man by the name of John Spence. Manarin and Jordan, *N.C. Troops*, 8:9–10.

1865

1. William Groves Morris survived his term in prison, being released at Johnson's Island, Ohio. Morris did not return to service and with the end of the war he returned to his Dallas home. In the years following the war Morris continued his trade, and was known for the construction of some of the most durable homes in the county. He was also a local architect and respected member of the community who served one term in the North Carolina State legislature. Interview with Mr. Daniel Wilson, 24 November 2001.

2. James survived the war and returned home to Catawba County where he married Malinda Rebecca "Linnie" Wike on March 28, 1866. The two were married despite an eighteen-year age difference and became the parents

of eight known children. James continued his life as a farmer and a blacksmith until his death on November 2, 1898. He is buried at Immanuel Lutheran Church in Catawba County, North Carolina. Cloninger, *Notes on James W. Gibson*, 11 October 2001.

3. The full story of the "Outlier Campaign" resembles closely the conflict in the mountains. While Home Guard authorities there faced organized units of Union forces and a hostile civilian population. The Randolph County insurrection was fueled by individual partisan bands who were loosely led by "Colonel" William Owens, a native of Davidson County. Eventually, the 7th Regiment N.C. Troops would be dispatched to the region to deal with the problem. However, in all terms of practicality, not even Confederate regulars were able to fully contain the situation. This was a major concern of Governor Vance; beyond operating through the Home Guard and Militia, however, little could be done in this ever-deepening hole of dissent. The most thorough work on the "Outlier Campaign" was done as a dissertation by William T. Auman entitled "Neighbor Against Neighbor: The Inner Civil War in the Randolph County Area of Confederate North Carolina." This was also featured as an article in the *North Carolina Historical Review* for January 1984. Quoted in Trotter, *Silk Flags*, 145–162.

4. Gen Richard C. Gatlin: State Inspector and Adjutant General, succeeding Gen. James G. Martin at that post. Clark, *N.C. Regiments*, 1:5–8.

5. The finer aspects of the "outpost" were written in Mahan's New York Milita Manual of 1849.

6. "White's Store: A Community in Southwest Anson County." Powell, *N.C. Gazetteer*, 532.

7. Manarin and Jordan, *N.C. Troops*, 12:264.

8. This is the last letter from Pvt. Armfield. John was captured at Five Forks, Virginia, and was sent to Point Lookout National Prison in Maryland. John was confined at Point Lookout until he died as a prisoner of war on June 8, 1865, nearly two months after the surrender of Lee. He is buried in the Confederate cemetery at Point Lookout, Md. Manarin and Jordan, *N.C. Troops*, 8:343.

9. Captain Webb survived the war and was

paroled in Nash County, North Carolina, on April 20, 1865. After his parole, Webb returned home to Richmond County, North Carolina. Manarin and Jordan, *N.C. Troops* 1:522.

10. Here Jesse is referring to the spot in the Petersburg lines which was the site of the Battle of the Crater during the Petersburg Campaign. Grant's plan was to mine underneath the Confederate lines and place explosives in the shaft. When the explosives detonated, a huge hole would be ripped into the Rebel lines causing massive confusion and allowing his troops to take advantage of the situation and exploit the breakthrough. This plan was successful, at least in its first stages. The mine exploded underneath Confederate troops sending massive panic through the lines. The error was made by Black troops of the 9th Army Corps. Instead of striking the disoriented lines around the breach they decided to charge into the crater left by the explosion. This fateful mistake left the black troops trapped and unable to escape the large pit. Confederate troops, after regaining their organization, had an easy time picking the colored troops off one by one from the rim of the crater.

11. This is the last letter from Jesse. Jesse sol-diered with his regiment until he was captured at the battle of Sayler's Creek on April 6, 1865. Jesse was confined at Newport News, Va until June 27, 1865, when he was released after taking the oath of allegiance. Mr. Hill returned to his wife and son where he lived out the rest of his life as a farmer. Jesse died on January 2, 1882, and is buried at Good Hope Methodist Church in Davidson County, N.C. Watford, *Civil War Roster*, 111–112.

12. The actual surrender of Johnston's Army of Tennesee and all forces in the Department of North Carolina occurred in present day Durham County, N.C., at the Bennett Farm on April 26, 1865. With that the official "mustering out" of Johnston's scattered army took place at Greensboro in early May, where the troops received paroles and were paid a Mexican silver piece for their service. Trotter, *Silk Flags*, 321–326.

13. "Barringer, Rufus." Warner, Ezra, *Generals in Gray*, Baton Rouge: LSU Press, 1957, 1987, 1994, 17.

14. Refers to Rufus's brother, Victor Barringer, who also served as an officer in the 1st NC Cavalry before resigning on September 30, 1861. Manarin and Jordan, *N.C. Troops*, 2:11.

Bibliography

Primary Sources

William M. Adams Papers, Special Collections, Perkins Library, Duke University, Durham, N.C.

John J. Armfield Papers, Private Manuscripts Collection, North Carolina Division of Archives and History, Raleigh, N.C.

John Wesley Armsworthy Letters, Private Collection, Mr. Bob Furches, Clemmons, N.C.

William H. Badgett Collection, Davidson County Historical Museum, Lexington, N.C.

Rufus Barringer Papers (1028z), Southern Historical Collection, Wilson Library, University of North Carolina at Chapel Hill, N.C.

Oscar Blacknall Papers, Private Manuscripts Collection, North Carolina Division of Archives and History, Raleigh, N.C.

Branson Family Papers, Private Manuscripts Collection, North Carolina Division of Archives and History, Raleigh, N.C.

M. J. Boyden to unknown recipient, Box 66, Folder 2, Military Collection, North Carolina Division of Archives and History, Raleigh, N.C.

Augustus Clewell Papers, Private Manuscripts Collection, North Carolina Division of Archives and History, Raleigh, N.C.

William Pinkney Cline Papers (5019z), South- ern Historical Collection, Wilson Library, University of North Carolina at Chapel Hill, N.C.

John Fuller Coghill Letters (1724), Southern Historical Collection, Wilson Library, University of North Carolina at Chapel Hill, N.C.

Richard A. Cole Papers, Private Manuscripts Collection, North Carolina Division of Archives and History, Raleigh, N.C.

Davidson County Court of Pleas and Quarter Sessions, 1861.

Columbus H. Dixon Papers, Special Collections, Perkins Library, Duke University

Cicero A. Durham Papers, Private Manuscripts Collection, North Carolina Division of Archives and History, Raleigh, N.C.

The Letters of George W. Eddinger, Mr. Richard L. Conrad, Thomasville, N.C.

Federal Census of North Carolina Counties: Alexander (1860), Cabarrus (1860), Catawba (1860), Chatam (1860), Cleveland (1850, 1860), Davie (1850–1860), Forsyth (1850–1880), Gaston (1860), Granville (1860), Guilford (1860), Iredell (1850), Orange (1850, 1860), Richmond (1860), Stokes (1850–1860).

The Diary of Ashbel Fraley, Typescript, nd., np. Rowan County Public Library

James and Joseph Gibson Letters, Catawba Historical Association, Newton, N.C.

Thomas Pinkney Gillespie Letter, Miscellaneous Civil War Collection, United States Army Military History Institute, Carlisle Barracks, Carlisle, PA

James Augustus Graham Papers (0283), Southern Historical Collection, Wilson Library, University of North Carolina at Chapel Hill, N.C.

Catharine E. Hanes Papers (4045), Southern Historical Collection, Wilson Library, University of North Carolina at Chapel Hill, N.C.

Harrison H. Hanes Papers, Special Collections, Perkins Library, Duke University

John Franklin Heitman Collection, Duke University Archives

Jesse Hill Papers, Private Manuscripts Collection, North Carolina Division of Archives and History, Raleigh, N.C.

Robert Frederick Hoke Papers, Private Manuscripts Collection, North Carolina Division of Archives and History, Raleigh, N.C.

Hundely Family Papers (4971), Southern Historical Collection, Wilson Library, University of North Carolina at Chapel Hill, N.C.

Leon, Louis, *Dairy of a Tarheel Confederate Soldier*, 1913.

Long Family Papers (3269), Southern Historical Collection, Wilson Library, University of North Carolina at Chapel Hill, N.C.

McClelland Family Papers (3869), Southern Historical Collection, Wilson Library, University of North Carolina at Chapel Hill, N.C.

F. M. Y. McNeely Papers, Private Manuscripts Collection, North Carolina Division of Archives and History, Raleigh, N.C.

The Diary of Bartlett Yancey Malone (3455), Southern Historical Collection, Wilson Library, University of North Carolina at Chapel Hill, N.C.

Benjamin F. Medley Papers, Private Manuscripts Collection, North Carolina Division of Archives and History, Raleigh, N.C.

William Groves Morris Papers, Mr. Charles Daniel Wilson, Dallas, N.C.

A. C. Myers Papers, Special Collections, Perkins Library, Duke University

Miscellaneous Collections, Davidson County Historical Museum, Lexington, N.C.

Nims and Rankin Family Papers (4255), Southern Historical Collection, Wilson Library, University of North Carolina at Chapel Hill, N.C.

John Dalton Phillips Papers, Private Manuscripts Collection, North Carolina Division of Archives and History, Raleigh, N.C.

John Calhoun Pickler Letters, Mr. Joseph Pickler, New London, N.C. and Stanly County Genealogical Society

Leonidas Lafayette Polk Papers (3708), Southern Historical Collection, Wilson Library, University of North Carolina at Chapel Hill, N.C.

Andrew J. Price Papers, Private Manuscripts Collection, North Carolina Division of Archives and History, Raleigh, N.C.

Stephen Dodson Ramseur Papers (1567), Southern Historical Collection, Wilson Library, University of North Carolina at Chapel Hill, N.C.

The Thomas C. Riddle Letters, Mrs. Ann Ellis Sheek, Clemmons, N.C. and the Davie Dossier.

The Andrew Rinck (Rink) Letters, The Rink Family, Mary R. Harbinson

Julius Alexander Robbins Letter (2424), Southern Historical Collection, Wilson Library, University of North Carolina at Chapel Hill, N.C.

Satterfield and Merritt Family Papers (4361), Southern Historical Collection, Wilson Library, University of North Carolina at Chapel Hill, N.C.

Alfred M. Scales Papers, Private Manuscripts Collection, North Carolina Division of Archives and History, Raleigh, N.C.

Shaffner Family Papers, Private Manuscripts Collection, North Carolina Division of Archives and History, Raleigh, N.C.

John McKee Sharpe Papers (3592), Southern Historical Collection, Wilson Library, University of North Carolina at Chapel Hill, N.C.

Louis B. Sheman Papers, Private Manuscripts Collection, North Carolina Division of Archives and History, Raleigh, N.C.

Dr. J. E. Smoot Collection, Private Manuscripts Collection, North Carolina Division of Archives and History, Raleigh, N.C.

John Franklin Sink Letter, Davidson County Historical Museum, Lexington, N.C.

The Isaac L. Summit Letters, Mrs. Geneva Ennis, Newton, N.C.

R. T. Wall to NC Adjutant General's Office, Box 36, Folder 2, Military Collection, North Carolina Division of Archives and History, Raleigh, N.C.

Lewis Henry Webb Papers (1767), Southern Historical Collection, Wilson Library, University of North Carolina at Chapel Hill, N.C.

Williams-Womble Family Papers, Private Manuscripts Collection, North Carolina Division of Archives and History, Raleigh, N.C.

SECONDARY SOURCES

Bahnson, Dr. Charles, Recollections of the Civil War 1861–1865, Raleigh: Edwards & Broughton, 1903.

Barrett, John G., The Civil War in North Carolina, Chapel Hill: UNC Press, 1963.

Betts, Alfred, ed., Experiences of a Confederate Chaplain by W. D. Betts, D.D., Greenville, SC, 1900.

Blacknall, Oscar, Biographical Sketch of My Father, unpublished manuscript. Np, nd.

Bradley, Stephen, North Carolina Confederate Militia Officers Roster, Wilmington: Broadfoot, 1992.

Caswell County Heritage, Winston-Salem: Hunter Publishing, 1985.

Catawba County Heritage, Winston-Salem: Hunter Publishing, 1986.

Catton, Bruce and James McPherson, eds., American Heritage New History of the Civil War, New York: Viking Press, 1996.

Clark, Walter, ed., Histories of the Several Regiments and Battalions from North Carolina in the Great War 1861–1865, Goldsboro and Raleigh: State of North Carolina, 1901.

Cloninger, Agnes, Notes on James W. Gibson, np, 2001.

Davis, Burke, J.E.B. Stuart: The Last Cavalier, New York: Rhinehardt & Company, 1957.

Driver, Robert E., History of the 10th Virginia Cavalry Regiment, Lynchburg, VA: H. E. Howard, 1992.

Evans, Clement A., ed., Confederate Military History, 17 volumes, np: Confederate Publishing Company: 1899, Wilmington: Broadfoot Publishing Company, 1987.

Hahn, George W., The Catawba Soldier of the Civil War, Hickory, N.C.: Clay Printing Company, 1911.

Hamilton, Dr. J. G., ed., The Correspondence of Jonathan Worth, Volume 1, Raleigh: Edwards & Broughton, 1909.

Hutchinson, John, No Ordinary Lives: A History of Richmond County, N.C. 1750–1900, Virginia Beach, VA: Dunning Publishing Company, 1998.

Johnson, Robert and Clarence Beull, eds., Battles and Leaders of the Civil War, 4 Volumes, New York: The Century Company, 1888.

Johnston, Frontis W., The Papers of Zebulon B. Vance, Raleigh: North Carolina Division of Archives and History, 1963.

Lassiter, Mabel, Pattern of Timeless Moments: A History of Montgomery County, N.C., 1976.

Manarin, Louis H. and Weymouth T. Jordan, Jr., comps, North Carolina Troops 1861–1865: A Roster, 14 volumes to date, Raleigh: North Carolina Division of Archives and History, 1966–.

Mast, Greg, State Troops and Volunteers: A Photographic Record of North Carolina's Civil War Soldiers, Raleigh: North Carolina Division of Archives and History, 1995, second printing, 1995.

Philpott, Racheal, The Letters of Felix Miller to his Wife, np, nd. Copy available in Davidson County Public Library, Lexington, N.C.

Powell, William S., ed, The North Carolina Gazetter, Chapel Hill: UNC Press, 1963.

Powell, William S., ed., Biographical Dictionary

of North Carolina, 4 volumes, Chapel Hill: UNC Press, 1994.

Priest, John M., *Antietam: The Soldier's Battle*, New York: Oxford University Press: 1989.

Raper, Horace W. and Thornton W. Mitchell, eds., *The Papers of William Woods Holden: Volume 1: 1841–1868*, Raleigh: North Carolina Division of Archives and History, 2000.

Rockingham County Heritage, Winston-Salem: Hunter Publishing, 1983.

Schwab, John C., *The Confederate States of America: A Financial and Industrial History of the South During the War*, New York: Schwab, 1901.

Trotter, William R., *Silk Flags and Cold Steel: The Civil War in North Carolina: The Piedmont*, Winston-Salem: John F. Blair, Publisher, 1988.

Warner, Ezra J., *Generals in Gray: Lives of the Confederate Commanders*, Baton Rouge, LA: LSU Press, 1959.

Watford, Christopher M., *The Civil War Roster of Davidson County, North Carolina: Biographies of 1,996 Men Before, During and After the Conflict*, Jefferson, N.C.: McFarland & Company, 2001.

Watford, Christopher M., *North Carolina Regiments, Battalions, and Companies: An Order of Battle*, unpublished manuscript, 1997.

Index

Adams, William M. 17, 102–103
Alamance County, NC 16–17, 19–20, 69–70, 77–78, 86
"Alamance Regulators" 19
Alexander County, NC 85–86, 117–118, 148–149, 154
Alford, Molly 159–160
Anson County, NC 7–8, 119–121, 128–129, 158, 172, 176, 182–183, 197
"Anson Guards" 7–8, 182–183
Appomattox Court House, Virginia 182
Arkansas Troops, 3rd Regiment 86
Armfield, James 183–184, 191–193, 195, 198
Armsworthy, John W. 63–64, 68, 84–85, 91, 99–100, 114–115, 140–141
Asheboro, NC 7, 34, 42, 195
Ayer, Henry W. 79–80

Badgett, Daniel W. 107–108
Barnhardt, Jacob C. 95
Barrier, M. A. 143, 165–166
Barringer, Rufus 202–203
Belo, Alfred Horatio 11–12, 21
Bennett, Lorenzo 124
Bennett, Risdon T. 132
Bentonvile, NC 201
Bermuda Hundred, Virginia 165–166, 171
Berrier, Esther 25
Bethel, Virginia 9,11, 41
Blacknall, Charles C. 33–36, 44–45, 88–90, 98–99
Bradshaw, Jonas N. 85–86, 117–118

Brandy Station, Virginia 118–119, 125
Branson, Thomas B. 97–98
Breedlove, James A. 34
Butler, Benjamin F. 9

Cabarras County, NC 23–24, 95, 143, 145–146, 165–166, 188, 202–203
"Cabarras Phalynx" 24
Cameron, James W. R., 49–50
Camp Life 9–10, 14, 17–19, 26, 37–38, 42, 46, 73, 82, 96, 99–100, 102, 105, 121, 128, 139, 144–145, 175, 185, 188, 202
Carolina City, NC 23, 36
"Carolina Rangers" 25
"Caswell Boys" 47–48, 90, 118, 144, 156–157, 185–186
Caswell County, NC 47–48, 90, 108, 118–119, 137, 144, 156–157, 177–178, 185–186
"Catawba Braves" 46–47, 56–57, 146, 157, 171
Catawba County, NC 18–19, 45–46, 56–57, 106, 143–146, 153–155, 157–158, 171, 174–177, 193–194
"Catawba Guards" 18, 45–46, 174–175, 193–194
Cedar Creek, Virginia 179–181, 183
Chancellorsville, Virginia 109–114, 130, 155
Charleston, SC 98
"Charlotte Greys" 8
Charlotte, NC 8, 127
Chatam County, NC 55–56, 135, 169–170

Civilians 11–13, 21, 23, 34, 62, 67–68, 79, 83–84, 93, 98, 103–104, 112, 116, 118, 120–121, 124–125, 127, 128,149, 152, 154, 156, 159–162, 167–169, 172, 179, 184, 186, 189, 197, 199
Clement, William B. 25–26, 113, 125–126, 186–187
Cleveland County, NC 108–109, 148, 152–153
Clewell, Augustus A. 43–44, 53–54, 91–92, 172–173
Cline, William P. 46–47, 56–57, 146
Clodfelter, Eliza 116–117, 167–168
Clodfelter, Hugh 112–113
Clothing 6, 20, 28, 39–41, 44, 47, 56, 64, 76, 79, 85, 102, 119, 147, 151, 154, 203
Coghill, John F. 134
Cole, Richard A. 20, 178–179
Conscription 36, 39, 42, 46, 54, 69–70,73, 74, 78, 80, 87–88, 98, 100, 116, 139–141, 167–168, 194–195
Cook, Jonas 165
Covington, Benjamin 23
C. S. S. *Albemarle* 158
Culp, Jacob P. 188
Curlee, Archibald 78

Danville, Virginia 11
Davidson College 119
Davidson County, NC 17, 23, 33, 48–49,60, 96, 107, 111–113, 116–117, 138–139, 141–142, 151, 167, 180–181
Davie County, NC 10–11, 25,

233

37, 92–93, 125–126, 132–133,
  135–137, 147–148, 186–187
"Davie Sweepstakes" 10–11, 37,
  92, 132, 136
Davis, Jefferson 50
Deep Gully 101–102
Democratic Party 29
Desertion 23–24, 36, 78,
  94–95, 101, 116, 131, 145, 147,
  167–168, 194–196, 198
Dickson, Sam 10
Dickson, Stephen 10
Discipline 22–23, 38, 70,
  132–133, 136, 147, 188, 196
Disease 19–20, 22–24, 36, 49,
  72, 78, 96, 109, 117, 127, 132,
  138, 167–168, 177, 200
Dixon, Columbus H. 108–109,
  152–153
Drill 6,9,10, 17, 19, 22, 39, 46,
  50–51, 102, 112, 130, 156
Durham, Cicero 148

Early's Washington Raid 172–
  173
Eastern North Carolina Cam-
  paigns 101–102, 107–109, 145,
  158, 172–173
Economy 71, 73, 77, 80–81, 84,
  96, 100, 103–104, 112, 116, 124,
  144, 168, 179, 182, 195
Eddinger, George W. 33, 60
Eddinger, William M. 60
Education 70–72, 153–154
Elections 57, 152–153, 160, 182
Elmira, New York 171
Equipment 7–8, 39–40, 44, 52,
  77, 110, 119, 121, 126, 148, 151,
  176, 181

Farris, Mary Jane 126–127
Finances 69, 81, 100–101,
  103–104, 106, 121, 124, 131,
  148, 151, 179, 182, 195, 197
Fisher, Charles C. 28
Food rations 8, 17, 19, 28,
  37–38, 44, 72–78, 86, 99,
  103–104, 110–111, 117, 136, 147,
  151, 158, 177, 202–203
Foraging and Food Gifts 8, 20,
  49, 56, 84, 96, 99, 111, 120,
  121, 125–126, 141, 146, 154,
  185, 188
Forsyth County, NC 11, 21–22,
  43–44, 53, 64–65, 74, 76–77,
  79, 91–92, 131–132, 149–150,
  172–173
"Forsyth Rifles" 11–12, 13
Fort Delaware, Delaware 57,
  114, 202–203
Fort Fisher, NC 189
Fort Macon, NC 6,9, 21

Fraley, Ashbel 48–51, 54, 57,
  58, 60, 62–63, 68, 72–73
Fredericksburg, Virginia 84, 86,
  88–90, 93, 97, 99, 114
Fries, Caroline 11, 21–22
Fries Mill Company 76–77, 80
Furloughs 9, 10, 35, 94, 98, 100,
  125, 129, 153–154, 171, 181,
  193

Garysburg, NC 10, 14, 17
Gaston County, NC 33, 66–68,
  86–87, 93–95, 100–101, 130–
  131, 146–147, 192
Georgia Troops, 62nd Cavalry
  Battalion 107–108
Germanton, NC 61–62
Gettysburg, Pennsylvania 57,
  107, 121–122,125–126, 155
Gibson, James W. 18–19, 45–46,
  51, 174–175, 193–194
Gordonsville, Virginia 43, 48,
  49, 93, 163
Graham, James Augustus 6,
  9–10, 39–41, 74–76, 122–124,
  163–164, 189–190
Graham, NC 77
Granville County, NC 34, 44–45,
  81, 88–90, 98–99, 134, 158
Greensboro, NC 70–72, 76, 80,
  192–193, 200–201
Guilford County, NC 43,69–72,
  183–184, 191–193, 195, 198

Hagler, John R. 23
Hanes, Harrison H. 10–11,
  37–38, 92–93
Hanes, Jacob H 132–133
Haywood, E. G. 18, 50
Heitman, John F 159, 161
Henderson, Kate 29–30, 81, 104
Hill, Daniel H. 8,9, 12, 44, 63,
  107
Hill, Jesse 143, 180–181, 199–200
Hilliard, Lews 184
Hillsboro, NC 6, 106, 190, 197
Hoke, Robert F. 192, 200–201
Home Guards 147–149, 153, 178–
  179, 194–195
Hospitals 53, 96, 138, 140–141,
  173, 197
Hundley, John C. 91, 113–114, 126
Hundley, Sallie 104
Huneycutt, Joseph 196

"Iredell Blues" 15
Iredell County, NC 14, 16, 18,
  38–39, 48, 51, 83–84, 102–
  103, 148, 153, 168–169

Jackson, James A. 20–21, 36–37,
  109–111

Jackson, Thomas "Stonewall"
  48–50, 63,66, 110, 115
James, Enos 10
Jamestown, NC 69–70
Jewish soldiers 8–9, 95–96, 102,
  118, 120–122
Johnson's Island, Ohio 130–131,
  146–147, 164, 192
Johnston, Joseph E. 44–45
Jones, James W. 86
Jordan, Henry T. 164–165

Kelly, William F. 11, 37
Kennesaw Mountain, Georgia
  170–171
Kernersville, NC 11, 80
Kilpatrick, Judson 197
Kinney, Berry 111–112
Kinston, NC 40, 95, 102, 109,
  172, 199

Lane, James H 94
Lassiter, M. Benson 137–138
Lee, Robert E. 58, 66, 109, 116,
  120, 129, 138, 140, 150, 181
Leon, Louis 8, 9, 12–13, 95–96,
  101–102, 118, 120–122, 131,
  162–163, 191, 200
Leonard, John H. 96
Lillycross, William 26
Lincoln, Abraham 19, 129
Lincoln County, NC 115–116,
  124–125, 129–130, 140, 166–
  167, 178, 179–180, 192, 200–
  201
Linster, E. U 168–169
Linster, Robert O. 38, 150–151,
  168
Loftin, Juilus J. C. 23–24, 48,
  108
Long, John A. 16, 19–20, 86
Long, Letitia 77–78
Lynch, George 10

Magruder, John B. 9, 44
Malone, Bartlett Y. 47–48, 90,
  92, 108, 137, 156–157, 177–
  178, 185–186
Manassas, Virginia 18–19, 28–29,
  37,62–65, 67
Maryland Campaign 65–68, 72–
  73
McAfee, Lee R. M. 148
Mecklenburg County, NC 8–9,
  11–12, 95–96, 101–102, 118,
  120–122, 131, 162–163, 191,
  200
Medley, Benjamin F. 182–183
Melchor, M. 23
Mendenhall, Jones and Gardner
  Co. 69
Miller, Felix H. 138–139

Mocksville, NC 25, 186–187
Montgomery County, NC 59, 151–152
Moore, M. B. 79
Moore County, NC 20–21, 36, 109–111, 178–179
"Moore Independents" 20, 36, 109–111
Morehead City, NC 6, 20
Morris, Louisa C. 192
Morris, William G. 33, 66–68, 93–95, 100–101, 146–147
Movements of the Army 149–150, 162, 163, 172, 176, 193
Mull, Peter 106
Music 20, 28, 118, 133, 189–190
Myers, Canaan 166
Myers, Laura E. 61

Naval battles 41, 107, 129
New Bern, NC 36, 40–41
Nims, Elizabeth 86–87
Nissen, John P. 74, 80
North Carolina Troops: 1st NC Volunteers 8, 9; 1st Battalion Sharpshooters 53, 91–92, 172–173; 4th Regiment 10, 14, 16–17, 26–29, 37–38, 48, 50–52, 54, 57, 58, 61, 68, 72–73, 93, 102–103, 131, 136, 150; 6th Regiment 47–48, 90, 92, 108, 118–119, 137, 156–157, 177, 185; 7th Regiment 23–24, 48–50, 55–56, 134–135, 169–170; 8th Regiment 24, 143, 165–166; 9th Regiment (1st Cavalry) 145–146; 10th Regiment (1st Artillery) 27, 11th Infantry 143–145, 154–155, 176–177; 12th Regiment (2nd Volunteers) 96–97, 153, 158, 184–185; 13th Battalion (Light Artillery) 189, 195–196, 198–199; 13th Regiment (3rd Volunteers) 16;19–20, 29, 81–83, 104–105; 14th Regiment (4th Volunteers) 7–8; 59, 111–112, 182–183; 15th Regiment (5th Volunteers) 41–42, 45, 20th Regiment, 23, 188; 21st Regiment (11th Volunteers) 11–12, 43–44, 62, 66, 91, 113–114, 126, 143, 180–181, 199–200; 23rd Regiment 12–14, 19, 22, 33–36, 44–46, 88–90, 98–99, 134, 174–175, 193–194; 24th North Carolina 105–106; 26th Regiment 20, 36, 109–111, 119; 27th Regiment 39–41, 74–76, 122–124, 163–164, 189–190; 30th Regi-

ment 183–184, 192–193, 195, 198; 32nd Regiment 157; 33rd Regiment 64–65, 37th Regiment 33, 66–68, 93–95, 100–101, 130–131, 146–147; 38th Regiment 85–86, 117–118, 137–138; 39th Regiment 170–171; 42nd Regiment 135–136, 141–142, 147, 196; 43rd Regiment 119–121, 128–129, 158, 172, 176; 46th Regiment 46–47, 97–98, 146, 157–158, 171; 48th Regiment 33, 60–61, 96, 99–100, 138–139, 151, 159; 49th Regiment 108–109, 148, 152–153; 52nd Regiment 57–58, 62; 53rd Regiment 78, 95–96, 101–102, 118, 120–122, 131, 162–163, 200; 54th Regiment 63–64, 68–69, 84–85, 91, 99–100, 114, 140–141; 55th Regiment 105–106, 164–165; 57th Regiment 77–78, 86; 84th Militia 95

Opposition to war 7, 18, 42–43, 74, 79–81, 129–130, 133, 173–174, 194–195
Orange County, NC 6–7,10, 38–41, 74–76, 122–124, 189–190
"Orange Guards" 6,9, 39, 40, 124, 189–190

Parks, Charley 10
Pearson, Richard M. 80
"Pee Dee Guards" 12–13, 22
Pender, William D. 47–48, 82
Person County, NC 96–97, 105–106, 158–159, 161–162, 164–165, 173, 184–185, 191, 197–198
Petersburg, Virginia 60, 85, 119, 129, 152, 165–166, 171, 176–177, 181, 188, 191, 193, 195, 198–200
Pfohl, William 65
Picket Duty 43–44, 52, 90, 93–94, 98, 101, 107, 133–134, 170–171, 176–177, 195, 198
Pickler, John C. 57–58
Pine Hall, NC 78–79
Pioneer Mills, NC 23, 95
Plymouth, NC 158
Point Lookout, Maryland 137, 146, 155, 156–157, 171, 177–178, 185–186, 188, 191, 197, 200
Polk, Leonidas 119–121, 128–129, 153, 172
Pool, Hartwell S. 59
Price, Andrew J. 170–171

Prisoners of War 28, 35, 109–111, 114, 122, 126, 140–141, 147, 156–157, 162–163, 171, 176–178, 185–186, 188, 202–203

Quakers (Friends Meeting) 42, 79, 80, 194

Raleigh, NC 47, 131, 133, 191
Ramseur, Stephen D. 102, 112, 115–116, 129–130, 140, 166–167, 178, 179–180, 183
Randolph County, NC 7, 34, 41, 97–98, 137–138, 152, 153, 159–160, 194–195
Rappahannock Station, Virginia 137, 140
Reidsville, NC 11, 81, 104–105
Religion 9–10, 12, 17, 24, 59, 67, 86, 108, 152–153, 177–178, 185, 189, 199
Richardson, George 87–88
Richmond County, NC 12, 22, 52–53, 128, 186, 189, 195–196, 198–199
Richmond, Virginia 51–52, 55, 59, 77, 122–124, 138, 171, 199
Riddle, Thomas 142–143, 147–148
Rinck, Andrew 143–145, 154–155
Roanoke Island, NC 24
Robbins, Rev. Jeffrey H. 153
Robbins, Julius A. 41–42
Rockingham, NC 12, 186, 197
Rockingham County, NC 29–31, 73–74, 81–83, 104–105, 113, 155–156, 181–182
Romance 24–25, 30, 82, 97, 105, 117, 126, 130, 159, 162
Rowan County, NC 26–29,48, 50–51, 57, 59, 60, 62, 68, 72–73, 103–104, 184
"Rowan Rifle Guards" 26

Salem, NC 11, 21–22, 43, 64–65, 76, 80, 92, 172
Salem Female Academy 21
Salisbury, NC 103–104, 127, 168, 184
Salisbury Bread Riots 103–104
Satterfield, E. Fletcher 105–107
Satterfield, Mary 191, 197–198
Scales, Alfred M. 29–31,81–83, 104–105, 155–156, 181–182
Scott, Sarah 7
Seven Days Campaign 19, 49, 54–55, 57
Seven Pines, Virginia 37, 52, 54–55
Shaffner, Dr. John F. 21, 131–132, 149–150
Sharpe, S. A. 148–149, 153

Sharpsburg, Maryland 73, 75–76, 97
Sheperdstown, West Virginia 72
Sherman, William T. 197–198
Shoe, Edmund M. 24–25
Sink, John F. 141–142
Slavery and Slaves 7, 41, 71, 101, 119, 165, 167–168, 186
Smith, John A. 145–146
Smithfield, Virginia 19
South Mountain, Maryland 19, 68
Speer, William A. 63, 85
Spotsylvania Court House, Virginia 136, 151, 166–169, 188
Spurgeon's Sermons 10
Stanly County, NC 57–58, 196
Statesville, NC 14
Staunton, Virginia 73
Steele, William 64
Stephenson, Laura 18
Stokes County, NC 61–62, 78–79, 104, 113–114, 126–127
Strikeleather, John 150–151
Suffolk, Virginia 16
Summit, Isaac L. 157–158, 171

Temperence Hall 13
Thomas, Jemina 83–84
Thomasville, NC 127–128
Thompson, John 73–74
Tomlinson, Allen 42

Trinity College 160
Turner, John C. 14–16

Union County, NC 78, 87–88, 170–171
United States Colored Troops 156–157
United States Congress 29
University of North Carolina 6, 70

Vance, Zebulon B. 68, 70, 73, 76, 78–79, 84, 87, 104, 129, 178
Vicksburg, Mississippi 116
Virginia Troops: 10th Cavalry Regiment 25–26, 112–113, 125–126, 186–188; 12th Artillery Battalion 52–53, 126

Waggoner, Elizabeth 104
Wall, Robert T. 7–8
Waller, N. A. 81
Waters, Calvin H. 43
Waughtown, NC 74, 80
Webb, Lewis H. 12–14, 22–23, 128, 189, 195–196, 198–199
Weldon, NC 8, 189
Whig Party 7
Whitted, Tom 10
Wilderness, Virginia 146, 162–163, 175

Wiley, Calvin H. 70–72
Williams, George A. 55, 135, 169–170
Williams, John 153–154
Williams, Nancy 10, 38
Williamsburg, Virginia 47
Wilmington, NC 7, 42, 136, 141–142, 147
Wilson, Hubbard 113
Winchester, Virginia 53–54, 82–83, 174–175, 178, 183–184
Womble, Richard A. 134–135
Women 6, 12–15, 17, 21–22, 25, 30–31, 37, 62, 97, 104, 112, 116–117, 119, 124–127, 130, 136–137, 145, 151–152, 159–162, 186
Wood, John 16
Wooley, Eliza 151–152
Worth, Daniel G. 7
Worth, John M. 195
Worth, Jonathan 7, 34, 42–43, 79, 194–195
Wyatt, Henry 9

Yadkin County, NC 63–64, 68–69, 80–81, 85, 99–100, 114, 141, 173–174
Yancey, James E. R. 96–97, 184–185
Yorktown, Virginia 9, 44